D1569697

CHE WANTS TO SEE YOU

CHE WANTS TO SEE YOU

THE UNTOLD STORY OF CHE IN BOLIVIA

CIRO BUSTOS

Translated by Ann Wright

With an Introduction by Jon Lee Anderson

VERSO

London • New York

This English-language edition published by Verso 2013
Translation © Ann Wright 2013
First published as *El Che Quiere Verte*
© Javier Vergara 2007

1 3 5 7 9 10 8 6 4 2

Verso
UK: 6 Meard Street, London W1F 0EG
US: 20 Jay Street, Suite 1010, Brooklyn, NY 11201
www.versobooks.com

Verso is the imprint of New Left Books

ISBN-13: 978-1-78168-096-4

British Library Cataloguing in Publication Data
A catalogue record for this book is available from the British Library

Library of Congress Cataloging-in-Publication Data

Bustos, Ciro Roberto.

[Che quiere verte. English]

Che wants to see you : the untold story of Che in Bolivia / Ciro Bustos ; Translated
by Ann Wright ; With an Introduction by Jon Lee Anderson.

pages cm

"This English-language edition published by Verso 2013. First published as El Che
Quiere Verte."

Includes index.

ISBN 978-1-78168-096-4 (alk. paper)

1. Guevara, Che, 1928-1967. 2. Guerrillas–Bolivia–History–20th century.
3. Bolivia–History–1938-1982. I. Title.

F2849.22.G85B8713 2013

980.03'5092–dc23

2013005819

Typeset in Fournier by Hewer UK Ltd, Edinburgh
Printed in the US by Maple Vail

To Ana María

To Paula and Andrea

To the memory of Avelino

Many people survived that combat, and they are all invited to write their memoirs, and add their experiences to our knowledge of those events. We ask only that, when telling their story, they do not deviate from the truth, or say something incorrect just to clarify or magnify a personal position or pretend they had been in some particular place.

Ernesto Che Guevara,
Prologue to the *Diary of a Revolutionary War*

Then, in Bolivia, there were some Argentines, like Tania – who was actually German although she had been born in Argentina – and Ciro Roberto Bustos whom Che had known for a long time. Che always talked a lot about 'El Pelao'. I met Bustos in Bolivia.
Che's Teachings, interview with Harry Villegas Tamayo ('Pombo'),
by Nestor Kohan, 11 October 2003

When a man is born, he can choose one of three different paths. If he chooses the one on the right, the wolves devour him; if he chooses the one on the left, he will devour the wolves; if he continues straight on, he will devour himself.

Anton Chekhov

Moreover, we do not know if the universe belongs to the real world or fantasy.

Jorge Luis Borges

'I want you to tell me what Tania said when she met you in Córdoba.'
'That you wanted to see me, I replied.'
'No, no. I want you to tell me exactly what she said. In her own words.'
'Ah, well. She said, "Che wants to see you."'

Contents

Introduction

By Jon Lee Anderson

It has been nearly five decades since the epic life-and-death story of the Argentine-born revolutionary Ernesto 'Che' Guevara entered into the modern literary canon. The posthumously published diary of the literate, handsome young man who sought to bring socialism to the world through armed revolution and died doing so in Bolivia in 1967 rapidly became an international cult classic, a tragic new bible for a rebellious generation. The unavoidable parallels between the end of Che's life and the mythologized passion of Christ made his story all the more potent, helping to ensure his legacy as the ultimate symbol of sixties idealism. Today, Che Guevara's face is one of the most widely reproduced images in the world, universally recognized as an icon of youthful defiance against orthodoxy. In his adoptive homeland of Cuba, where the Castro revolution has endured for over fifty years, Che has become the emblematic patron saint of its officially cherished socialist principles. To millions of youngsters everywhere, meanwhile, 'Che lives', as the old slogan goes, if only on their T-shirts, while others seek even now to emulate his example on new battlefields. Not surprisingly, for the few surviving men and women who fought under Che's orders, life has never been the same.

Of the fifty-one guerrillas of various nationalities who joined Che in Bolivia, most were either killed in action or, like himself, executed after being captured. Only three out of the original eighteen Cubans made their way home again. The two Peruvians died. Out of twenty-seven Bolivian fighters, only seven survived. Most of them were captured and imprisoned; several switched sides and worked to apprehend their former comrades. Every war has its contingent of traitors.

There were three Argentine guerrillas including Che, but only one survived. He was Ciro Roberto Bustos, a young artist-turned-revolutionary, and the author of this memoir. Bustos was already a key operative in Che's fledgling guerrilla network in Argentina, when, in early 1967, Che summoned him to Ñancahuazú, his new, secret guerrilla base camp in south-eastern Bolivia. Che himself had only been there a few months. Ñancahuazú was supposed to be the training ground and staging post for a future Latin American guerrilla army that would spearhead a 'continental revolution' against US-backed imperialism in the hemisphere. Once a Bolivian foco was established, the cadres from Peru, Argentina, and neighbouring countries would 'irradiate outwards', taking their revolutions to their homelands. Che's idea was to spark off 'two, three many Vietnams' simultaneously, overwhelming the Americans' capability to suppress them. In trying to do so, their imperial system would be weakened and destroyed once and for all. Che intended to lead the future Argentine foco himself.

Unfortunately for Che, the existence of Ñancahuazú was discovered by the Bolivian army prematurely, while it was still in the embryonic stage, and while he was away, on a gruelling, six-week training march through the wilderness with his small group of volunteers. This setback coincided with Bustos's arrival in Ñancahuazú. He was accompanied by a young Frenchman, Régis Debray, a Marxist theoretician who had just published *Revolution in the Revolution?* a theoretical treatise on the very guerrilla strategy that Che was putting into practice in Bolivia. Debray had come to meet Che and to receive his instructions on creating an international solidarity campaign on behalf of the Bolivian revolutionary cause. Bustos was there to confer with Che on how best to proceed with the Argentine armed underground. A previous attempt at starting a guerrilla foco, in which Bustos had participated, had failed catastrophically three years earlier. Bustos had been a lucky survivor.

Now, the authorities' discovery of the guerrilla presence at Ñancahuazú had triggered an early initiation of hostilities. As Bolivia's army sent in troops, and also warplanes, to attack them, Che and his men were forced to go on the run. It was an abrupt end to Che's hopes for a stealthy, well-organized beginning to his ambitious new revolutionary project. When the enormity of the fiasco dawned on him, Che remarked with characteristic fatalism: 'So, the war has begun.'

As Che broke up his fighters into two smaller groups in order to escape the army dragnet, Bustos and Debray hiked out of the battle zone in the hopes of slipping away undetected and carrying on with their respective missions. They were immediately arrested by soldiers in Muyupampa, the first community they came to. It was April 1967.

For Bustos and Debray, days of terror followed as they were interrogated by their army captors in Camiri, the garrison town where they were taken after their arrest. An early sighting of them in captivity by a local reporter who took their photograph and published it may well have helped save their lives. Debray's high-level political affiliations in France (his mother was an official of the ruling Gaullist party) soon brought international visibility to their case, and with it a certain guarantee of protection. A pair of CIA agents, Cuban–American exiles who had been brought in to assist the Bolivian army's anti-guerrilla operation, showed up, and began to question them more deeply. In the beginning, Bustos used a false name. He was Frutos, a travelling salesman – but soon, his true identity was revealed. He was forced to admit his links with Che's guerrilla band in Bolivia, but managed to keep secret his role as Che's operative in the Argentine underground.

Under pressure from the CIA agents, Bustos drew pictures of the guerrillas he had spent time with and of the Ñancahuazú camp. He did so knowing that the identities of many of the guerrillas were already known thanks to photographs discovered at the base camp. According to one of the CIA agents, who spoke about it years later, Debray 'sang like a canary'.

It is a fact of life that most people who fall into the hands of their enemies in wartime break under the pressure, and talk. They may try to mitigate or otherwise colour their information, as Bustos did, but they provide it because they have no choice and are usually threatened with death, sometimes having been tortured first. Bustos and Debray were right to feel afraid of their captors; most of the guerrillas who subsequently fell into the Bolivian army's hands were shot dead.

In the coming months, as their guerrilla comrades were hunted down, Bustos and Debray were brought to trial. For Che himself, the end came on October 9, 1967. He had been wounded and captured in battle, held overnight in a dirt-floored schoolhouse in a tiny mountain hamlet, questioned repeatedly by various officers. He was then executed, shot to death by a Bolivian army sergeant on the orders of Felix Rodríguez, one of the same CIA men who had interrogated Bustos and Debray.

A few weeks later, Bustos and Debray were sentenced to thirty years in prison. Three tedious years of detention in Camiri dragged by, with no end in sight. Then something unexpected, but very fortunate, happened. In December 1970, after a failed military coup, a left-leaning general, Juan José Torres came to power. As Bolivia's president Torres moved quickly. Bustos and Debray were amnestied, put on a plane and flown to neighbouring Chile. There, the socialist politician Salvador Allende had become president just three months earlier, gave them a warm welcome. (They were very lucky indeed; Juan José Torres lasted only ten months in power before a right-wing officers' faction overthrew him. He fled into exile in Argentina, where he was murdered by the military junta's death squads in 1976.)

After a time in Allende's Chile, Debray returned to Paris, where he resumed his professional life as a professor, thinker and writer. He served as a special adviser on foreign affairs to the socialist Mitterrand government in the 1980s, and eventually broke with his old mentor Fidel Castro, excoriating the Cuban leader publicly for his traits of stubbornness and arrogance; he accused Che of possessing similar character defects.

Reunited with his wife, Ana María, and their two young daughters, Paula and Andrea, Bustos remained in Chile, where he was given work in a publishing house. Shortly before Pinochet's violent coup against Allende on September 11, 1973, he decided to return to Argentina, and thus narrowly escaped being caught up in the murderous military crackdown that followed. But in Argentina the dirty war against the Left had already begun as well, and Bustos soon found himself at risk. Some of his friends were killed; others disappeared. In January 1976, Bustos requested political asylum in Sweden for himself, Ana María, Paula and Andrea. It was immediately granted. Once in Sweden, the family was relocated to Malmo, the southwestern port town, and there they stayed.

When I met Bustos in Malmo in 1995, I found a man who was in a deeper, lonelier exile than I could ever have imagined. He seemed to be still living in a state of limbo, as if he had left Argentina, but never really arrived in Sweden. After nearly two decades there, he still did not speak Swedish. He was alone, divorced from Ana María, although he saw her and their daughters regularly. He had a few friends – exiles from Latin America like himself – with whom he met up in bars or restaurants. Bustos's most constant companion, however, was Gema. She was a young, playful German Shepherd, with whom he went everywhere, and who shared his spacious second-floor flat on a residential street.

The nature of Bustos's exile also showed up in his relationship to his art, for he was a painter who, to all intents and purposes, no longer painted and never exhibited. He explained that it was because of the Swedish fashion for postmodern conceptual art, which he took me to see in a series of galleries around Malmo: I recall a toilet decoratively enamelled with the Swedish royal crest; a photographed dog turd set into a ceramic tile and placed at the centre of the floor of a large room – and so forth. Bustos's art was painterly and figurative; his canvases hung around his flat and were, to my eye, both beautiful and sad; all of them were large oil paintings of nudes, men and women embracing, reclining, rendered in gorgeous ochre hues, like the hulks of rusting ships. None of them had faces. This disquieting omission struck me as a testament to Bustos's cauterized existence, symbolic of an extreme and long-lasting pain.

Bustos had not spoken about his revolutionary past to anyone for many years. We began talking, and we didn't stop. I stayed for a week. What I learned from him during those days dramatically enhanced my knowledge of Che Guevara, of the Cuban Revolution, and of the heyday of revolutionary ferment in Latin America.

At the time, I had been researching Che Guevara's life for several years, and had learned that there was a consistent pattern of behaviour amongst those people who had been close to the late revolutionary. Most remained clubbishly loyal to Che's spirit and legacy, as well as to the espoused socialist ideals of Cuba's revolution, and were generally self-effacing about their own past roles. There were several good reasons for this, other than revolutionary modesty. Many of them had suffered greatly for their allegiances. In the wave of anti-communist repression that had swept Latin America in the intervening years, most had lost close and dear friends, and sometimes relatives, too. Silence was the best way to survive, and then it had become habitual. In the early nineties, however, following the collapse of the Soviet Union, there was a shift in the atmosphere, and some guerrilla veterans began to open up about their past activities, often for the first time.

In Cuba, where I had gone to live so as to better research Che Guevara's life, an officially sanctioned Che historiography prevailed for years. In the months and years following Che's death, a narrative of events had been set out and, over time, the script had become unbudging. In this narrative, Che had gone off to Bolivia by his own choice, and in the field, he had bravely fought and died. Che's ordeal had become the Cuban Revolution's ultimate passion play, an account of revolutionary sacrifice that helped validate Cuba's place in the firmament. There were no Cuban failings in this narrative, no deceits nor betrayals other than those committed by 'others', a grab-bag of mostly Bolivian characters who, it was implied, were unreliable and had dragged the whole enterprise down. Che's own published diary suggested there was more to the story, but few were able to question the official interpretation. There were holes in other parts of the chronology of Che's life, such as the mysterious two-and-a-half-year gap between the time he vanished from Cuba and reappeared in Bolivia. About all of this, however, silence reigned.

With the help of Che's widow, Aleida March, and a handful of other people who had known him well, I overcame some of the obstacles in Cuba, eventually gaining access to Che's personal archives, containing several of his unpublished diaries. This gave me a much greater insight into Che's thinking at crucial points in his life. As I travelled beyond Cuba to conduct interviews and research in Argentina, Bolivia, Mexico, Russia, and other countries, I realized that I could take very little of the received wisdom about Che's life for granted. Mythology, urban legend, and, in some cases, intentional obfuscation clouded the real narrative, and it took both detective work and luck to separate fact from fiction.

One of the least satisfactory chapters in the official narrative of Che's life was the so-called Salta episode, a guerrilla expedition to northern Argentina that he had organized and entrusted to an Argentine protégé, journalist Jorge Ricardo Masetti. In April 1964, after less than a year in the field, 'la guerrilla de Salta' had ended in disaster, with most of the fighters involved either killed or captured. In the debacle, Masetti, leader of the self-described EGP, or Ejercito Guerrillero del Pueblo, had vanished, never to be seen again. Afterwards, it was rumoured that Masetti, who had named himself Comandante Segundo, had actually been Che's advance man for the Argentine revolution he'd supposedly hoped to lead, but the Cubans denied this. They dismissed the Salta fiasco as a minor event, just one out of a long list of unsuccessful guerrilla focos that Che had organized. Neither was there any indication that the failure of Salta had anything to do with Che's final, fatal mission to Bolivia a few years later. But it did, of course, and Ciro Roberto Bustos, who had been written out of the history books as a marginal character, had played a crucial role in both.

It was Che's widow, Aleida, who helped set things in motion. She arranged for me to interview Alberto Castellanos, a Cuban who had been one of Che's bodyguards and was a survivor of Salta. From the amiable Castellanos, I learned that Che had personally planned the Salta expedition and held high hopes for its success. He confirmed that Che had intended to come and lead the guerrillas himself once the foco was up and running. He had been captured and had spent three years in prison in Argentina, but had fortunately managed to keep his Cuban identity secret. Castellanos didn't go too deeply into the causes of the debacle, but urged me to talk to several of the Argentine survivors, and he contacted some of them on my behalf.

I travelled to Argentina, where I met with Héctor Jouvé, who had been Masetti's deputy. Like Castellanos, Jouve had been captured. He had spent ten long years in prison, however. For the first time ever, he spoke about what happened in Salta. As he did, a picture of horror began to emerge. It became clear that one of the main reasons the foco had failed was because Masetti had effectively gone crazy soon after he and his men had entered the jungle. He had become doctrinaire and bullying, and at the first signs of weakness amongst his untrained followers, mostly young volunteers from Argentina's cities, Masetti saw crimes punishable by death. After impromptu trials in the jungle, he had two of them executed. While Masetti was busy terrorizing his followers, a local contingent of carabineros, Argentina's rural paramilitary police force, was dispatched to the area where the guerrillas had installed themselves after reports of armed strangers had raised suspicions. As would occur a couple of years later in Bolivia, the guerrillas engaged the intruders in a firefight, prematurely alerting the authorities to their presence. Reinforcements were sent in to hunt down the guerrillas, and Masetti's foco was quickly routed. Jouvé was the last man to see Masetti alive. He said that he suspected that Masetti had either starved to death where he had left him stranded or become lost, in the cloud forest, or else had committed suicide.

Jouvé spoke fondly of Bustos, whom he called 'el Pelao' – Baldy – and described him as Che's point-man in Salta, someone who could shed a great deal of light on its long-buried history. He suggested I talk first to Henry Lerner, another Salta survivor, who was living in Spain.

In Madrid, I learned that Lerner had also been marked for execution by Masetti. Lerner had been spared at the last minute. It seemed less than coincidental, however, that Lerner, as well as the two other men Masetti had executed, Pupi and Nardo, were Jewish. Lerner was keenly aware of this fact but said he had always resisted the notion that Masetti's enmity might have been motivated by anti-Semitism. But as we dug up the past, old suspicions returned. Like many of Argentina's radicals of Lerner's time, Masetti had come out of the Peronist movement, which had bewilderingly managed to straddle the political spectrum from the ultraright to the ultraleft. As a younger man, Masetti had belonged to the Tacuara, a virulently anti-Semitic Catholic group modelled on Spain's Francoist Falange. Although he had since become a man of the Left, it seemed possible Masetti never reconciled his two extremes, and once in the jungle, the power he had acquired that brought out the worst in him.

After my meeting with Henry Lerner, Bustos told me to come see him in Sweden.

In Malmo, Bustos confirmed what Jouvé, Castellanos and Lerner had told me and added a great deal of important additional detail. He confirmed the connection between Salta and Che's subsequent expedition to Bolivia, and revealed that Che had been planning an armed revolution in Argentina as early as 1962. Bustos, who had arrived in Cuba as an enthusiastic revolutionary volunteer in 1961, had been quickly recruited for Che's Argentine project by Alberto Granados, Che's old *Motorcyle Diaries* buddy. Granados had moved to Cuba after the revolution and had lived there ever since.

Bustos disclosed that he and the other members of the Che's Argentina team had received their initial training in spycraft and the use of weapons in Cuba and then, following the Missile Crisis, had gone to Czechoslovakia and onto Algeria for more training. He acknowledged Masetti's harshness and confirmed the brutal executions Massetti had ordered, as well as his own part in one of them. In the case of Pupi, the first victim, the execution was botched, he explained, and he had been forced to fire the coup de grace, shooting a bullet into the mortally wounded man's head.

Bustos had survived the Salta catastrophe otherwise unscathed and made his way back to Cuba. There, Che had asked him to return to Argentina as his liasion with the leftist underground there, and had eventually summoned him to Bolivia, where fate awaited them both.

In the end, history is complicated. In the story of Che Guevara's bloody demise in Bolivia, there has long been a tendency by survivors, as well as historians and analysts, to seek out culprits for what happened. The Bolivian army and the CIA agents, who secretly executed Che and many of his comrades, didn't expound a great deal about what they had done after the fact. They didn't need to, because they had won a battlefield victory, but they also had their war crimes to keep quiet about. For the Cubans, meanwhile, Che's defeat was casually attributed to the faults of 'others', a potage that included the betrayals of some of the captured

Bolivian deserters, as well as Bustos, for the drawings he had made in captivity. Others blamed the Bolivian Communist Party leadership, which had withdrawn its support for Che once he was in Bolivia, leaving him exposed and vulnerable. The area chosen for Che's base camp at Ñancahuazú had been selected by the Party leadership and clearly had been highly unsuitable; many believed this was no accident. Any mistakes that had been made by members of Cuba's secret services, meanwhile, not to mention the decisive role played by Fidel Castro himself, who had chosen Bolivia as the theatre for Che's foco, were swept aside. The story that Ciro Bustos tells here is a candid one in which we can see that the final chapter in Che's life was the result of a complicated alchemy that included all of the above, not to mention luck, or the lack of it, and, not least, Che's own decisions. In the end, we are reminded, the outcomes of the mightiest of human enterprises are dependent on human nature.

Che Wants to See You is also the account of an extraordinary period in contemporary history in which thousands of young men and women around the world, inspired by Che Guevara and his Cuban comrades, believed they could change the world through armed revolution. They mostly failed, but left behind a remarkable legacy of shared idealism and sacrifice.

This book is ultimately part of that legacy, the journal of a life lived to the limit in pursuit of an ideal, with all of its consequences. There are many memories here, some of which are bittersweet jewels. Here is Bustos recalling how horseflesh, which he was forced to eat in order to survive in Bolivia, reminded him of the smell of Pupi at the moment he shot him dead. And there is the time when he overheard Che recite aloud verses from the Spanish poet León Felipe as they marched together through the Bolivian bush. It was one of the worst of times, but for Bustos, it is a most cherished memory of Che Guevara and of their shared revolutionary life.

Preface

This is a book about remembering, in two senses of the word. It is a memoir, not a biography, nor a book of history, political theory, or essays. It is the story of a stage in my life that goes off at tangents, into the future and into the past, when need be. The important thing is not my life, but what happened around it and what I witnessed. So writing in the first person singular is inevitable, because I am only recounting what I saw, heard, felt, listened to and read, as well as what I did, thought, and occasionally said. Nothing is presumed, added or invented. It is not a fictional account, these are real events, some of them small, and others transcendental, and they have all come together one by one to form my identity. There was no other way to tell this story than by looking frankly and openly inside myself; it is personal and unique. I am present throughout the book not for self-glorification, but to testify through all my senses to what was happening around me.

It is also a book written from memory. The avalanche of information I collected over the years overwhelmed my lack of writing experience, and I found that although I had such and such a detail to hand somewhere, I couldn't get at it without wasting days and weeks in a fruitless search. I eventually reached such a state of uncertainty, each doubt multiplied by hundreds of versions, that I chose to abandon all the material I had accumulated — cuttings, photocopies of articles and other kinds of documentation — and rely solely on my memory. A quote from García Márquez, which

I read opportunely, supported me in my decision: 'Truth is only what memory remembers.'

For dates and names, I have used about six books on the subject. The rest of the information was there, more or less organized for reference purposes, but always wrong, like coins hidden under tumblers in a magician's trick. Memory, in any case, is like a coiled spring, waiting to be released. Sometimes fascinating things occur, comparable to the fishing technique of Laplanders who spend hours sitting beside a hole in the ice, with a fishing line rolled round their finger disappearing into the invisible waters, tugging on it gently from time to time, unperturbed, nothing happening, until, suddenly, a magnificent specimen emerges from the ice. I spent days and weeks with my mind blank, tugging the line a little and letting it go, until the whole spool unravelled unexpectedly. Sometimes it seemed as if someone was sitting inside my head dictating to me or, rather, that they were manipulating my fingers. Images appeared that I had not thought of since those days: meals, places, vehicles, situations, even music and smells. Naturally, not all the millions of moments that form a life are there. I read somewhere that the psyche filters bad memories that could harm the spirit, just as the body heals wounds.

It might seem as though some things are missing from the historical context, such as, for example, the nature of revolutions, and not just the Cuban. But to me this is a different topic, one that merits special analysis or scientific examination from defined political and ideological stances, and that is not the aim of this book, nor is it within my capabilities.

A large part of the book takes place at a time when almost everybody, including 90 per cent of its current detractors, loved the Cuban Revolution, even if the majority of them used it shamefully. There is no way anyone can accuse me of that. Nor can anyone surmise any financial interest on my part. For almost forty years I have refused any offer that would have meant an inappropriate use of the events and, particularly, any use of them for personal gain.

Comments about the form and style of the text are inevitable because I am not a professional writer. But some clarification is not only possible but necessary. For example, something that friendly pre-publication readers pointed out: Che's Cubanized Spanish. While it is true he spoke with a pronounced provincial Argentine accent – that's unquestionable – he always used Cuban vocabulary. Not even in nostalgic asides to friends did he indulge in Argentine vernacular. Also, some of the information revealed might make people uneasy, since it has been secret for decades. But it is no longer secret. Some of it has been disclosed by the Cubans themselves, in biographies or enemy documents, not forgetting the international actions of the Revolution's troops.

There were names I could not find, lost in the whirlwind of time. Others, which no doubt exist in my books and documents, were simply left out. But, in any case, it was never my intention to produce a catalogue of events or a telephone directory. I would rather admit I don't remember, as has often happened, than pretend or invent. Of course, there will be unintentional errors in names, dates, chronology, etc. Transferring memory to paper presupposes some poetic licence despite one's best intentions, because images cannot be copied and pasted like new technology. They have to be turned into words and phrases with a certain harmony, and, if possible, elegance. And, yes, as happens when we recount our dreams, we can't capture them accurately before they fade and become slightly deformed. I don't think the errors are serious enough to distort the story, because I would have noticed, but in any case they would not be intentional or in bad faith.

Undertaking this task so long after the events, despite the insistent voices of friends urging me to do so earlier, has created a double slippage. First, potential readers – except for a few survivors – will be of a new generation, unfamiliar with the pre-globalization era, when more defined ideological camps implied a greater commitment to political struggles, even if only in writing, and therefore a greater recognition for the characters behind these words. These days, if it were not for the T-shirt industry, no one would even know what they looked like. Second, this book was written far from the natural environment in which the events took place, at the opposite geographical pole, and this has influenced my writing. Alone with my ghosts, without clear reference points, their lights and shadows are reflected on my keyboard.

Ciro Bustos
Malmö, April 2005

Part One

Cuba

1

Mendoza: Where It All Started

Mendoza is a unique city. The streets, all of them, are lined with trees. This is not a quirk of nature. It demonstrates the perseverance of its population and their creativity, traits nurtured in a culture inherited from the original inhabitants, the Huarpes, a peaceful tribe who loved trees and sat in their shade watching their crops, chewing on carob pods as sweet as their dreams. But dreams are closer to real life than fantasy, and real life depends on water. So they put their imagination and efforts into taming the water that gushed turbulently down from the snow-capped mountains some sixty kilometres away. The question was how to coax a modest tributary of brown water stemming from the mountain torrents into changing course. Tailoring the mountain slopes into channels meant not only hard work, but also rare engineering skills. And then, once down on the plains, what better way to distribute the water efficiently than by inventing the system of culverts which characterize the city of Mendoza to this day? It is the only city in the world to have irrigation ducts down both sides of every street, running parallel to the rows of trees spaced five or six metres apart that need watering once a week if they are to be kept fresh and healthy – a task undertaken by the people of Mendoza themselves, because without that there would be no plants, no vegetation, no fruit, and no trees beyond the native *jarrillas*, *chañars* and carobs, in whose shade the Huarpes rested.

The horses that the conquistadors brought, along with their primitive muskets and own natural brutality, played a defining role in the conquest of Indian land. But the gentle Huarpes, once their blood was up, and with early notions of guerrilla warfare, understood they had to learn from the invading enemy, and systematically stole the horses they saw frolicking happily in the grasslands. The horses, knowing on which side their bread was buttered, switched enthusiastically to the side of the indigenous people and, within a few years, breeding freely and increasing rapidly in number, had moved seamlessly into a privileged place in the tribal hierarchy: the chief or warrior, his horse, his wife. Over time, this combination produced a truly fearsome enemy for the invaders, and the Indian raid, the *malón* (a word with cynical implications: the mob, the baddies, the Indians, versus the victims, the goodies, the Whites), was their strategy for recovering stolen property. The horse, now naturalized, and running free in the wild, became a major factor in the 'savages', early success.

The Spaniards arrived with a considerable thirst on them, after a long journey exacerbated by thoughts of wineskins oozing good Spanish wine, trickling down their throats and over beards dry with heat and dust. So the sight of suspicious fields of neatly planted maize brought on a desire to replace them with vineyards stocked from their native Navarre, Catalonia, Andalucia or that magical sap from the banks of the Duero. Whatever the story, the contribution of these thirsty pioneers laid the foundation of Mendoza's subsequent wealth. The settler population developed an unhurried pastoral existence, despite periodic attacks from other plains tribes who, I suggest, were after the casks of red wine, the remarkable product the barbarians brought, almost better than their own drink brewed from carob. The town grew into a beautiful city soothed by two musical murmurs: the leaves of the trees in the mountain breeze, and the waters tinkling down the irrigation ducts along the streets.

I have enjoyed roaming these streets since as a child I first accompanied my father on his walks. And later, with my select gang of hooligan friends, I escaped from home at the sacred hour of the siesta, when the heat is overwhelming and, as the saying goes, only tarantulas and snakes dare cross the pavements. Jumping from one mountain of weeds to another, our expeditions took us through adjacent neighbourhoods, from the railway yards to the Cacique Guaymallén Canal (this good *cacique*'s invention before Mendoza was founded), round the outskirts of the city, through the large park and beyond to the foothills of the Andes. Our explorations were benign, never destructive or harmful. At most we stole fruit from homes where pear, medlar or plum trees lined the fences. We were real creatures of the city, exercising the freedom to enjoy it, learn its secrets, carve out an identity, and become citizens. As the writer Naguib Mahfouz said, 'Our homeland is our childhood.'

Mendoza is the capital of the province of the same name, and its urban norms have been stamped on all the towns, villages and smallest of hamlets inside these vast 148,928 square kilometres – larger than Switzerland, the Netherlands, Belgium and Denmark put together. Over time, the basic features of trees and irrigation channels have come to characterize the whole region. So has prosperity, a prosperity built on the intensive cultivation of vines and the growth of the wine industry, now the fifth largest producer in the world, and also on the subdivision of land, helped by natural fertility and the dividends from its produce. Anyone who owns twenty-five acres of vineyard is a millionaire. While he enjoys his summer holidays in Viña del Mar (Chile), his land is overseen by a manager and his family, and worked by the humble descendents of the indigenous peoples mixed first with poor Spaniards and Italians, and later with immigrants from all over the world, attracted by the dream of conquering paradise by the sweat of their brow. But not everyone's dream came true. After independence, the lands seized from the original inhabitants were distributed by the incipient local oligarchy exclusively among their peers, leaving the masses still in poverty. What's more, the latter – artisans and soldiers, tradesmen and smallholders, agricultural labourers and *gauchos* – were dependent on the vagaries of the Buenos Aires Customs House, the first established centre of power, now representing the export interests of the British.

It is at this point that there begins a dual history, or a dual telling of Argentine history that pits historians against one another. On the one hand, the history of rich Argentines and their wealth, and on the other, the history of poor Argentines. History does not develop linearly in an unstoppable succession of ultimately constructive events, but is twisted and forced to benefit a class that presupposes and assumes the primacy of its rights, inalienable under their law, and divine according to their bishops.

The whole structure of the nascent state, with all the weaponry at its disposal, was built to serve the landed oligarchy. If the national heroes of Argentina were filtered through a sieve, only glittering gold nuggets like Moreno, Castelli, Belgrano and San Martín would be left at the bottom. The rest would be washed away in a purifying flood.

Take Rivadavia, the first constitutional president of the Republic. The first thing he did was legalize dispossession, by granting property rights over vast expanses of farmland and urban areas to the national bourgeoisie, his friends. Argentina, ruled by an increasingly rich minority, enjoyed a high rate of economic growth thanks to two insuperable gifts from heaven: the best prairies in the world, with fertile topsoil providing pasture for herds of cattle that increased in size at the same pace as the demand for hide and beef from the metropolis; and almost free labour provided by a seemingly endless influx of European immigration, and completely free in the case of the subjugated indigenous people. The latter were eventually wiped out rather than willingly give up their land, thus making way for the colonization of the furthest reaches of the country by the starving masses of Europeans arriving by boat every day.

On 4 June 1943, at a turning point in the Second World War, the armed forces staged a coup against their own civilian government. The ideologue behind the coup, Juan Domingo Perón, was to become a key figure in the political landscape for the remainder of the century. No ordinary soldier, no dull lover of barracks life, no servant of the oligarchy, he had concrete plans and had made good use of his previous post as military attaché at the Argentine Embassy in Rome. As he would later explain to the Army chiefs of staff: 'Gentlemen, the Russians will win the war. Social reform is on its way. Either we make our own revolution and lead it, or we will be swept away by history.' But he needed charisma to win over the people. A stroke of luck came his way in the shape of a national catastrophe, an earthquake in the province of San Juan. At a gathering for the 10,000 victims, he had the good fortune, superlative good fortune as it turned out, to meet the person who would become the bond of steel between him and the proletariat, and bind herself to him in marriage: Eva Duarte – Evita.

Peronism brought the biggest change in social structures, and ways of thinking, in Argentine history. The working class ceased to be a faceless mass and took power. Above all, they were no longer a tool to be used, abused and discarded. They became human beings, protagonists central to the life of the nation. For the first time in history, the poor downtrodden masses arrived in Buenos Aires as its masters, not its street cleaners.

A passion for travel rather than sport, made me, in the words of Bernard Shaw, 'leave school in order to get an education'. I set off for Salta, in the north of Argentina. I did not know then that whenever you leave a place, you are reborn, over and over again. But it really was like that. The journey opened up a whole new world, another country, much more Argentine, less Spanish, less Gringo than the Mendoza I lived in, a world of amazing natural beauty.

Northern Argentina showed me a reality the Left refused to see, and influenced my nascent political consciousness. The country was Peronist. As a lesson in practical politics, it was a defining experience. Since vagrancy was not subsidized, I had to find work from time to time, and this took me to one of Argentina's largest sugar mills, El Tabacal in Orán, Salta, where the sugar cane harvest was about to begin. I was given the job of overseeing the

Indians who fed the sugar cane into the crushers on the platform beside the mill where the trains loaded with cane arrived. El Tabacal was a huge mill, self-sufficient in both cane and food from its vast plantation. It was closed to public traffic, guarded by its own police and run by a staff of technicians, some from overseas, skilled workers and ordinary personnel. The majority of cane cutters were Chahuanco and Toba Indians. The mill would collect them from the forests of Salta each year in cattle trucks, give them space on the river banks to build straw huts, provide them with a minimum amount of food, and after the harvest was over, take them back home, with no further costs.

To a mind like mine filled with utopian socialist ideas, and despite my encounter with a real country in a process of change, Peronism seemed more like a stumbling block than a road to revolution. It did not stand up to scientific Marxist analysis. Its heterogeneous, something-for-everyone character – a mix of bible and boiler-room as the tango goes, of cops and robbers – hindered any effective manifesto.

And then, Eva Perón died. She was the person who might have radicalized the movement. In fact, she had embodied the rage, the class ingredient, the banner of the poor. Her passing left millions orphaned, and uncoupled the train from the engine. On the day of her funeral, it drizzled on Buenos Aires and on the soul of half the country. For the poor, it was as if the light illuminating their hopes had gone out.

The Argentine Communist Party was a typical petty-bourgeois party, divided into an arcane leadership, in the style of the Soviet Communist Party, and a militant rank and file. The few roots it had in the masses were swept away by Peronism, leaving space only for the middle class, professionals and students. There was, however, a larger sector on the Left that had been there almost from the birth of the nation, influenced by Rousseau's 'Social Contract' and inspired by Argentina's most brilliant independence heroes. This Left later absorbed the ideas of Marx's First Socialist International, but did not join the party and became what were known as 'fellow travellers'. In any case, the drama of continental realities south of the Río Grande stemmed not from the indigenous nature of a population that had been exploited since the Spanish Conquest, but from the exploitation itself, now firmly in the hands of the empire to the north.

The Catholic Church, which had used Peronist power to impose religious education in schools and colleges, now began to oppose him, supported by its historical strongholds: the army and the oligarchy. Perón abolished religious education, passed the divorce law, made illegitimate children equal before the law, withdrew subsidies to Catholic schools – and thereby precipitated the end of his own term in office.

On the morning of 16 June 1955, I was staying with Pepe Varona, a friend who subsequently became the official set designer of the New York Opera. I was preparing a set of proposals for advertising posters for an American travel agency when, around noon, we heard warplanes overhead. Without a second thought, we dashed up to the roof of Pepe's hostel, on the corner of Montevideo and Rivadavia streets, and from there, with heavy hearts, we watched the criminal attack on government house in the Plaza de Mayo, no more than ten blocks away. The first wave of planes turned right over us, and continued on between Rivadavia and Avenida de Mayo, their guns firing on the Casa Rosada. We could see other planes coming in over the River Plate, nose-diving on the plaza and unloading their bombs and shrapnel. It was a murderous attack over streets crowded with cars and pedestrians, pensioners feeding the pigeons in the square, and children playing on the grass. Men and women fled in terror, dragging their kids, fanning out from the epicentre of the crime. We were just going back into the hostel, to listen to the radio, when a second, smaller squadron appeared and resumed the attack.

Back on the roof, we watched the battle in full swing. By now the army loyal to the president had deployed anti-aircraft guns and was returning fire, filling the sky with black puffs and the air with a pungent odour and a terrible sound of thunder. The

aircraft, extending their radius, flew in just behind us, before
going towards the Casa Rosada and on to the War Ministry building on Paseo Colón. At the end of the park, they headed towards
Uruguay and disappeared into impunity. Ambulance and fire-
engine sirens ripped through the silence settling over the city,
normally so noisy at that hour, just past 1 p.m. A couple of hours
later, a third group of stragglers, three fighter planes coming in
from the West, strafed the three targets again, before flying off
over the river, bound for Montevideo. Privileged Argentina,
tired of wrinkling its nose and containing its hatred of the plebs,
had gone to confession, genuflected, crossed itself, and sought
the blessing of their chaplains and bishops, before finally attacking the fallen angel, Perón, and his demonic *descamisados*.

The dead quickly lose their identity and become difficult to
count. The actual number of casualties in a massacre is rarely
known. Similar world events have suffered from the same lack of
mathematical precision. The numbers are minimised 'to avoid
panic', and forgotten for political expediency. We never knew
how many people died in that attack, although they were in the
hundreds. 'Five for each one!' bellowed Perón in his speech that
afternoon. The streets began filling up in the opposite direction to
the previous stampede. Angry, threatening groups marched in
from the outskirts of the city, home to the manufacturing industries and Peronists (the city itself was never Peronist), and as
night fell columns of thick smoke rose from several parts of the
city. A Dantesque glow turned some buildings red.

2

News of Castro's Revolution
Reaches Argentina: 1958

By 1958, homemade pipe-bombs were going off all over Argentina's industrial cities. Made from bits of iron piping stuffed with dynamite, with a fuse sticking out of a hole in a screw top, they caused a pretty convincing explosion. A new slogan, 'Perón Vuelve' (Perón is coming home), began appearing on walls.

Meanwhile, union leaders determined to cling on to power by any means morphed into the 'union bureaucracy' and ousted the masses as the natural leaders of the workers' movement. The Peronist Party was proscribed, its leaders exiled or jailed. The 'new leadership' – the unions' secretaries and treasurers – fell in behind the country's most reactionary right-wing forces. Union headquarters became bunkers from whence bodyguards accompanied their bosses to night clubs or the races. Economists of the cattle and grain oligarchy ran the economy on behalf of the military regime and, at the behest of US imperialism, joined the network of international organizations like the IMF, IDB and GATT with its Latin American adviser ECLAC, and drowned in acronyms any possibility of domestic industrial development. On the contrary, they adopted an economic policy which condemned Argentina to a secondary role as producer and exporter of primary products.

Arturo Frondizi, a lawyer and dissident member of the Radical Party, emerged as a possible candidate in the forthcoming elections. His friend Ricardo Rojo, also a lawyer, journeyed to

Caracas with other emissaries to seek the good graces of '*El Viejo*' Perón, who was there in exile playing with his dogs. A subtle web was being woven with threads from Perón's own skein; like a puppet-master, he tugged a little here, pulled a little there, and conspired daily with the many different pilgrims visiting the Peronist Mecca. Frondizi's negotiations prospered and he went on to sign a pact with Perón that would ensure electoral victory for Frondizi's party through the majority vote of the Peronist masses. In return, he would restore the social, economic and political gains Perón had made, and revoke laws restricting Peronism. In February 1958, Frondizi was elected president.

Frondizi's economic policy was probably the most sensible the Argentine industrial bourgeoisie had ever come up with. The idea was very clear and seductive. We lived in one of the continent's richest countries, but were like poor people content just thinking we are rich. Resources do not exist unless we extract them. What use are oil reserves if we don't exploit them, turn them into foreign currency to develop the country, import technology, industrialize? Frondizi's thesis passed from hand to hand in the form of a book, *Petrol and Politics*, which denounced the power of the multinational oil companies, who exercised global control through corruption and blackmail, backed by force. But like Perón, Frondizi did not hold all the cards. At the transactions, agreements and concessions stage that every electoral policy has to undergo, it was undermined by 'enemy' strategists – the powers that be, the cattle and grain barons allied to US imperialist multinationals.

When the new administration came to power, a total of twenty-eight oil contracts were signed with foreign companies, twenty of them from the US. Other contracts setting up industrial plants, especially in the car industry, put most of Argentine industry in foreign hands, an insuperable barrier to the implementation of the Radical Party's policy. In fact, the exact opposite policy was implemented. Not only was oil not used to fuel the national industrialization programme, but after Frondizi was defeated four years later, it transpired that US and British companies had been paid more to drill for oil than if we had bought it directly from them on the world market and kept our crude deposits intact. The systematic surrender of our natural resources was shameless and absolute. Foreign companies earned enormous sums. The race to denationalize was unstoppable: shipping, distilleries, naval ship-yards, radio stations, furnaces and farmland passed to the Argentine private sector, and in the case of oil to Standard Oil, Texaco or Shell. The de-capitalization of the country forced us to take 'loans' from those same countries that had thoroughly plundered our national patrimony. US and European banks, the IDB, the Eximbank and the World Bank, together with the IMF, made the loans conditional on a series of restrictive measures that saw thousands of workers lose their jobs. 'Frondizman', as the cartoonist Landrú's magazine *Tía Vicenta* called him, was not made of national steel or oil. He was made of Coca Cola.

My wife Claudia's parents had a holiday home in Potrerillos, a valley in the foothills of the Andes on the road to Chile. One Sunday in the spring of 1958, *Radio El Mundo*'s midday international news programme announced it would be broadcasting an interview with Cuban guerrillas in the Sierra Maestra led by Fidel Castro, an already mythical figure even before he was famous for his beard, his outsize cigars (described by US journalist Herbert Matthews) and his audacity. Some years earlier, he had attacked the Moncada military barracks with about a hundred men, most of whom were killed, but he still went on to invade the island by motor launch with another hundred suicidal maniacs, again most of whom were killed, and then marched into the mountains with a handful of survivors. Among them was a doctor from Argentina.

With the whole South American continent between us, my image of the guerrillas was not so much political as romantic and adventurous. But it fired my imagination and awoke expectations. Insanity is generally closer to reality than cold reason. Argentine political journals were full of rigorous analyses of 'important' regional events, in which the World Bank or IMF, the State Department or CIA, carried more weight than some fantasy character no matter how bearded. But I was an avid reader of *Primera Plana*, a magazine that had already published an article on Cuba (its editor Jacobo Timerman had a nose for a story), and its accounts of the Bolivian revolution and the disaster in Guatemala had set my pulse racing.

I was determined to listen to the programme. So, leaving the family barbecue, I sat in the shade glued to the radio. The interview had been recorded by *Radio El Mundo*'s international news editor, Jorge Ricardo Masetti. If Fidel's followers on the motor launch were suicidal maniacs, Masetti was cloned from them. From a Catholic Nationalist background, he nonetheless admired men of action, *caudillos*, leaders: not men who turned the other cheek but those who fought for their ideas and inspired others to follow. He was the kind of journalist who took risks, was attracted by the scent of danger, lured by it. The story behind the interview from the Sierra Maestra is an adventure in itself; full of instinctive actions, risks and gambles. Masetti recounted his amazing experiences, and his conversion from investigative foreign journalist to rebel with his own revolutionary cause, in his book *Those Who Fight and Those Who Mourn*.

Financed by *Radio El Mundo*, Masetti went to Cuba in March 1958 armed with a cryptic note from Ricardo Rojo for his friend the Argentine, and a contact in Havana who could put him in touch with the revolutionaries. The Havana contact sent him to Santiago de Cuba, into the lion's den. After interminable waiting and changes of safe houses, he met the people who could get him into the Sierra Maestra to search for the guerrillas. A host of hazardous exploits later, he reached the advance guard of the Argentine whom the Batista regime had dubbed a dangerous Communist agent. On his last legs, Masetti was finally taken to Che's camp. For both of them, it was a relief to be able to talk on the same wavelength, use the same slang, and discover the same rather acerbic and ironic sense of humour. This affinity immediately became attraction and friendship. They worked on the interview, sometimes under enemy fire. Che then had him taken to the Commander in Chief.

Despite the new assault on his emotions caused by meeting Fidel Castro, Masetti got through his long dreamed of interview. He asked Fidel about the genesis of the 26th of July Movement, his ideas for transforming a society of exploiters and exploited, his political convictions, revolutionary aspirations, etc. The interview was broadcast from the primitive Rebel Army radio transmitter and was heard all over Cuba. For the first time, the leader of the *barbudos* was talking directly to his people.

Back in Havana, living clandestinely, Masetti learned that the interview's re-transmission by Venezuelan and Colombian radio stations had not been picked up in Buenos Aires. As far as his journey's funders were concerned, the work had not been done. So, he performed what Rodolfo Walsh called a 'heroic feat of Latin American journalism'. He went back to the Sierra Maestra and did the interviews all over again.

What impressed me most listening to Che was not his public discourse, nor his revolutionary message (actually there wasn't one, since the Buenos Aires radio station concentrated on his role as an Argentine mixed up in almost Bolivarian wars of independence). No, what drew me to him was first and foremost his voice. It wasn't the arrogant pompous voice of a politician or professional demagogue. It was a voice that could have belonged to a brother, or friend, nothing strident, like having a quiet conversation in a café. He spoke almost apologetically about getting himself noticed for something he considered self-evident: acting in accordance with his commitment to a cause, a reality that needed no explanation. If he did not take sides, did not get involved, he would be betraying himself. But taking sides meant fighting, because to defend ideas of social justice you have to take up arms. Che also took the opportunity, as if he were a contestant in a tango show, to say hello to his mother and other members of his family to whom he owed an explanation for his enforced two-year silence.

In a few words, he had demolished the doubt over whether he was an adventurer in search of glory and profit, or a mercenary in the service of foreign causes. The suspicion of imperial penetration of some description or other vanished. Masetti brought this up. 'What about Fidel's communism?' he asked. 'Fidel isn't a communist. Politically you could call him a revolutionary nationalist', answered Che.

The programme continued with Fidel Castro, who was the main dish. But I only had ears for Che, that resonant voice I was hearing for the first time, the voice of truth. Fidel was more grandiloquent, added to which his Cuban accent had something unreal, distant, about it. He was the leader and therefore somehow out of reach. Fidel was dignity standing tall, talking to a dormant America. But the other voice spoke to me personally, from conscience to conscience.

The Cuban Revolution became the focal point of my politics. I began copying articles and sought out Masetti's recently published book. The interviews inspired me to go to Cuba the following year and find the truth for myself. But meanwhile, there were new developments. Encircled by Che's troops, the city of Santa Clara fell on the last day of December, 1958. The dictator Batista boarded a plane at dead of night and flew off into the arms of Uncle Sam. The Cuban Revolution exploded with a force that eradicated any ambiguous or reactionary doubts about the need to bring about social change and replace the power structures underpinned by imperialism. It exploded like a depth charge and, at the same time, a forbidden fruit. Both those defending multinational interests and the man on the street pricked up their ears at this unique event, so different from the pacific, fraudulent, controlled elections by pact, which history had accustomed us to. The lines of dominance and dependence had always been passed from hand to anxious hand between the political agents of local aristocracies. These usual gentlemen's agreements, between demons and bandits, seemed about to be torn up. The Latin American Communist Parties initially criticized the 'militarist', 'putschist' experiment in Cuba as petty bourgeois deviation. But when faced with the spontaneous support of the people and the growing prestige of the Revolution's young leaders, they finally realized it was a gift from heaven come to rejuvenate their tired discourses, and decided to appropriate it. The cultural establishment, as we have seen, burst out in praises, odes, hymns, and even adulatory red masses, beginning with the canonization of the Communist Party, and the control and administration of revolutionary fervour by the Central Committee.

Meanwhile, democratic channels were closing again in Argentina. The union bureaucracy lurched between manipulating the masses and flirting with the army, capitalism and the brutal Peronist right-wing. Factory occupations, strikes in packing plants, sackings and bankruptcies all made the political air unbreathable, accompanied by deafening background music courtesy of the pipe-bombs. The government took control of the CGT (the principal trade union movement), handing it over to select members of the Peronist bureaucracy and pro-imperialist unions, with the State Internal Disorder Plan (CONINTES) already in place. The most combative unions were now in open confrontation with three groups: the government, the army and the union bureaucracy. The army patrolled the streets of Mendoza, pointing machine guns at passers-by, while I put the finishing touches to my plans to go to Cuba.

3

My Journey to the Island: April 1961

Feverish, almost conspiratorial, activity possessed us. Claudia and I had to get money together and find a way of travelling that fitted our limited means. An English passenger shipping line sailed from the port of Valparaiso in Chile to Southampton, England, and after navigating the Panama Canal, stopped at Havana. The Pacific Line's *Queen of the Sea* was making its last voyage before being withdrawn from service. A travel agency in Mendoza made the arrangements to buy the tickets.

Diplomatic relations between Cuba and the US had been broken off, and the latter was putting pressure on the rest of Latin America to follow suit. The 'concerto' of nations opposed to Cuba had begun under the US baton. *La Coubre*, a French ship carrying the first shipment of arms bought in Belgium by Cuba, exploded at Havana docks killing a hundred and leaving several hundred wounded. In this uncertain climate, we packed our belongings and confirmed our reservations. We wanted to get there as soon as possible. If we had to fight to defend the Cuban Revolution, we were ready. Cuba was so fashionable that news of it was more up to date than Stock Exchange information. We knew that visas for Cuba were controlled by the good will of the Latin American Communist Parties who, in a rush of inter-party ardour for the Cuban Communist Party (PSP), had taken the task upon themselves. In other words, the more recommended by the Communist International you were, the better. The idea, which went against the spirit of the Revolution, was justified by the fact that the communists were the only organized political force able to guarantee the level of revolutionary purity or sympathy, or at least that was the idea. So I resorted to an old school friend, Petiso García, who happened to be the son of the secretary of the local Communist Party, no less. I went to see him but came away empty-handed. In what appeared to be social-bureaucratic practice, he greeted me at the door but did not invite me in. I asked him to explain to his father that I needed a certificate of good moral standing to present if need be. Petiso duly went in only to come out with a recommendation from his father not to go to Cuba: 'it is a uniquely Cuban experience that has nothing to do with us. We have our own reality; we need to put our own house in order first.' That was a no, then. This negative from the party supremo stymied any other possibility. We left with no recommendation whatsoever.

The departure date was 15 April 1961, the same day as the air attack on Havana, a taste of the invasion to come two days later. The ship's radio had a worrying tendency to interrupt the anodine musak with hysterical communiqués in English on the situation in Cuba. But at one stage during the afternoon, there was a news flash in Spanish which reported the bombing, though with no details as to the consequences. That is why my memory of the first days on board was zero, a black hole, no images. Docking at Callao, passengers were told they had half a day to see the city of Lima, to which we would be taken by a shipping company bus. In Lima I searched for a newspaper to dispel my anxieties, only to find one that talked of an invasion of Cuba by the Yankee navy from Nicaragua. Back on board, there was an atmosphere of euphoria among the passengers and crew. The latter thought the stopover in Cuba would be apocalyptic – all fiery *mulattas* and rum. The passengers were sorry they would miss the chance to see the *barbudos* in the flesh, but thanked heaven the communist threat would be over. There was nothing for me to do but watch the coast rising and falling over the bows. The next morning, news flashes came thick and fast then became increasingly sparse as the day went on. The dining room looked like the Titanic as we crossed the Equator. Who knows if the popping champagne corks and bubbling laughter at dinner were celebrating the crossing or a victory for debauchery. Judging by the bulletins, the war in Cuba was still going on. But the paucity and ambiguity of the news, plus the faces of the ship's officers, revived my hopes. A few days later, we reached Balboa, port of entry to the Panama Canal.

Again they announced that passengers interested in seeing Panama City would be taken by bus to the city's main street in the morning, and returned in time for dinner. Crossing the city by bus, I noticed a modern building with a sign saying 'Anthropological and Archeological Museum' and right beside it a kiosk selling cigarettes and newspapers. We made a bee-line for it. The kiosk, I mean. There was no dark tobacco on board, and the Negros we had brought with us had gone up in smoke amid the bombing and disembarking. I couldn't smoke American cigarettes, so our first task was to replenish our stock. The kiosk attendant was a garrulous fellow with a Caribbean accent. While showing me his range of dark tobacco, he asked the fatal question. 'Where are you from, *chico*?' 'Argentina', I replied with quiet pride. '*Coño*, you're Argentine!' he shrieked and proceeded to slag off Argentines and their mothers. He ended up throwing a handful of what looked like dollars onto his magazine counter. 'Look at that, look what he's done to our dignity, to our money, *coño*, your compatriot, that bloody Argentine, that butcher Che.' And he showed us the new Cuban peso note, on which the president of the Cuban National Bank had merely signed 'Che.' He was a Cuban who had fled the Revolution, with a furious hatred for those he blamed for his exile. I paid for the cigarettes to avoid getting involved, and went to the museum next door. In tropical countries, fossils are more trustworthy than lippy street vendors. The newspaper I had bought before the incident carried a complete if somewhat venomous version of the defeat inflicted on the invading forces. It had all ended with the surrender of 300 Cuban mercenaries on a military operation directed and financed by the CIA and the Pentagon, but which had served to strengthen the ties between the Revolution's leaders and the Cuban masses.

The ship's captain received orders to cancel the stop-over in Cuba. Instead, he stopped in Curaçao, then doubled back to Maracaibo, in Venezuela. We anchored there the following morning but the passengers were not allowed off, as it was to be only a short stay. By noon the passengers were getting restless, wondering what was going on. Around three in the afternoon, the captain summoned me to his cabin, as if I were an aristocrat travelling below the decks. To put it bluntly, there was an insoluble problem. The ship had to sail straight for England now that the stop in Cuba had been cancelled. He could not alter his orders for the sake of two passengers. However, the situation was complicated because the Venezuelan immigration authorities refused to allow passengers without Venezuelan visas to disembark, least of all those bound for Cuba. I argued that our contract said we had to be taken to Cuba, not Venezuela, and that getting us there was his responsibility, not ours. He said his company would pay the cost of whatever means of transport we used. He thought by air would be most suitable, if we agreed. In that case, I insisted, he could use his authority to get us a visa. He mumbled a form of acquiescence. I couldn't help but imagine Captain Cook boiling with rage in his place. British phlegm had increased proportionately with the loss of empire. He added that he was waiting for one last demarche in Caracas which, he assumed, would solve the problem. The ship had to leave no later than five. 'And what happens if it isn't solved?' I asked. 'You can visit Sussex', he answered. A couple of hours later, the delegated official arrived with two military looking characters. The solution, conjured up between the British authorities and Venezuelan immigration, was to allow us to disembark but be kept under house arrest until the next flight to Cuba. Naturally, flights had been suspended for the foreseeable future.

Nevertheless, we disembarked with all our luggage. The Venezuelans broke the agreement and two days later we had to leave our hotel in Maracaibo, not with any great regret I might add, since sharks patrolled the other side of the metallic mesh protecting the hotel's little bay. We were taken to Caracas over a mountain range in a police van and dumped in a far from exclusive hotel. The next day, we were taken to Maquetía airport and put on a plane to Mexico, via Guatemala. The reason for deportation was our visa for Cuba, the bad boy island with which Venezuela had just broken off diplomatic relations.

Cuba's international airport is called Rancho Boyeros. I got a stiff neck straining to look out of the plane's window to see the island through the cumulus and nimbus clouds that moved like a flock of sheep under the fuselage. We dipped through the white wool and lost sight of it until the clouds suddenly parted and we saw the sea of palm trees waving in the breeze to welcome us. We were in Cuba. The flight had been a fiesta; the handful of euphoric passengers sang and danced in the aisles, shouting revolutionary slogans and 'Viva Fidel!' They were people on official business abroad, trapped by the suspension of flights after the Bay of Pigs invasion and now returning to their posts. Flying over the Gulf of Mexico and the Caribbean, they gave us a crash course in revolutionary fervour, anticipating what proved to be the norm on *terra firma*.

When we finally got permission to disembark, the humidity embraced us like the Revolution itself, enveloping our bodies, sticking to our skin, dripping down our necks – an all-embracing way of life, breathing, sweating, tongues dry, hearts beating, yet exultant, exuberant, enthusiastic. Huge drops of rain fell here and there, raising clouds of vapour as if on a hot tin roof. And the voices! Cubans talk at the tops of their lungs. Incongruously, in the midst of the din, a quartet struck up with Cuban folk music, *guajiras* and *sones*, to welcome the new arrivals. What with the Tannoy and the cries of the porters and umbrella sellers, it was like running the gauntlet to get to a safe haven, but with no escape. The journey down the motorway to Havana was the visual equivalent of the airport racket. Multicoloured posters shouted victory slogans about the aborted invasion, imperialism, Cuban exiles, and the departed bourgeoisie. Rifles held aloft by olive green arms, above beards like continental forests, caricatures of guerrilla fighters giving the Miami mercenaries a kick up the bum, with Uncle Sam cowering, green with fear. Nothing solemn, nothing tragic.

Havana was a splendid city, a mixture of colonial style and modern architecture, built against a natural background of palm trees and bourgainvilleas, with narrow multi-coloured streets, crossed by wide avenues, surfed by huge luxury cars speeding and hooting, controlled by coordinated traffic lights, with planned agility. Convincing the taxi driver we did not want a plush hotel, but a family pension, took the whole journey and proved fruitless; nothing would convince him we belonged in the Old City. He dropped us at the Hotel Colina on 23rd Street, just by the University in the modern suburb of Vedado.

When you get to a new country, first impressions are often best. Waking up the following morning, at almost noon due to the musical cacophony in the lobby that went on till two, I began a relationship with a people who have the gift of seducing you for life. The city was a fiesta of *joie de vivre*, with music everywhere, and multifarious smells: from luxury aromas like cigars and coffee, to the whiff of the port in the background, and the pervasive odour of fried fat from carts selling pork crackling. A cart of oysters with hot sauce, another with oranges peeled round in strips (a local invention), coffee stalls on every corner, making endless cups, a stand with breaded fish fillets here, another with avocadoes and limes there. Flowers, fruit, freshly baked bread, strong cigarettes and cigars, *very* strong women's perfumes, and so on. The city is full of aromas, each more tempting than the last.

Nobody dresses formally, Argentine-style, in a suit and tie. It would be crazy here, as well as looking ridiculous. The men wear white *guayaberas* or unbuttoned shirts outside their trousers. The trousers look like tents, enormously wide but tighter at the ankle. The women, their sinuous carnality exposed to furtive pursuers, painted like Japanese opera stars, part the crowd before them with their very presence. Everyone is armed, at least verbally. Buses, called *guaguas*, force their way through by blowing horns and screeching breaks. Lottery touts add their voices to vendors of other wares under arches, in galleries, on corners, and in squares. Two types of uniform stand out: olive green with a peaked cap could be either the rebel army or the police; blue grey with a beret is the newly created military police, which had made its debut at the Bay of Pigs. Beards are no longer in evidence since the new shaving law was introduced, with exceptions made for the historic *barbudos* of the 'Granma'.

The general climate of enthusiasm was heightened by the May 1st celebrations the following day. Expectations were higher than usual because Fidel was giving his first speech since the Bay of Pigs. On the day itself, you only had to follow the sea of people with placards and kids on their shoulders, straw hats and uniforms, maracas and drums, a huge wave of people headed for the Plaza de la Revolución. The guerrilla leaders led the parade, arms linked at the head of a multitude of happy faces illuminated by patriotic fervour. 'Cuba sí! Yanqui no!' The red and black of the 26th of July Movement dominated the sea of banners, challenged only by the Cuban flag. The river of people was unstoppable, moving to the rhythms of guerrilla anthems, rousing songs, and voices shouting 'Viva . . .' and 'Muerte . . .'. Reaching the square and getting near the platform seemed impossible. A mass of people converged in front of the (horrendous) statue to the apostle José Martí.

The May 1st celebration was the first mass demonstration I attended in Cuba. A million people, the papers said. In some ways it was like the Peronist demonstrations in the Plaza de Mayo, where I had never felt comfortable. Yet here the atmosphere was visually and psychologically different. Missing was that sense of menace that emanated from Perón's *descamisados*, the lepers of Argentine politics as John William Cooke called them, who jumped and waved their headbands and ragged shirts, furiously banging their drums, as if to the scare the wits out of the Argentine bourgeoisie. In the Plaza de la Revolución there were no threatening dispossessed people fresh out of the shadows, smelling power. These were happy musicians, in a joyful parade.

The difference, of course, lay in the struggle to take power, in which the Cuban people had participated (although they didn't all fight) while the Argentine masses had received it vicariously. The Argentines' anger was still contained, their class-based rage unexpressed, compared to this pure joy of power achieved by passion and the sacrifice of lives. The only thing I remember of Fidel's speech, which brought the event to a close, was the formal declaration of the socialist nature of the Revolution. It was, however, the most important bit. It opened a new and decisive phase in the struggle of the American people. A struggle I dreamed of joining.

But first I had to legalize my situation in Cuba. Picking one's way through the mire of bureaucracy is always a prickly task, difficult anywhere. But in Cuba the bureaucratic machinery had been destroyed: no one knew anything; no one followed any logic or tradition; everything was new and pretty well improvised. Most positions of responsibility had been abandoned by people fleeing the revolutionary tide in panic, and taken over by youngsters with absolutely no experience. Administrators, company directors, heads of state enterprises and bodies vital to a functioning society were replaced by almost illiterate peasants and workers whose willingness and apparent honesty was their only skill. In some cases, they had absolutely no knowledge of the matters they were supposed to be dealing with. In others, one ideology was substituted with another – one caste destroyed and replaced by another diametrically opposed, implying a rapid and experimental reconstruction of a new order. Things now depended more on good will, luck and the energy that new decision makers brought to the job of deciding between the opportune and the opportunist, between the interests of the Revolution and urgent necessities. The chaotic situation was being run via 'purity of origin', that is, by ideological red corpuscles. The People's Socialist Party, i.e. the Cuban communists, only recently incorporated into the triumphant ranks of the Revolution, now occupied the key posts. It filtered and selected personnel, including whole branches of the civil service, and had its eyes firmly set on the mechanisms of power. The rationale was that the PSP had to protect and strengthen the ranks of the Revolution, which had not only been openly attacked at the Bay of Pigs but was also being sabotaged daily both by Miami exiles and directly by the US government, which was diverting its efforts from military action to permanent terrorism.

The word *gusano*, meaning worm, became part of everyday parlance in describing counter-revolutionaries. In one of his speeches, Fidel talked of exiles being like *gusanos* in an apple, destroying the fruit of the people's efforts and sacrifice. Miami was the dung heap where *gusanos*, who abandoned their country in its hour of need, ended up. *Gusano* attitudes, behaviour and even thoughts began to be detected, and dealt with like a pest, with ideological, verbal, written and armed pesticides. One method adopted for foreigners was to make them prove their political credentials, not freely and democratically, but in a sectarian and rigorously pro-communist way. Another more general measure was the creation of the Committees for Defence of the Revolution (CDRs), neighbourhood-watch organizations controlling the activities and lifestyles of the inhabitants of an area, block, or even street depending on the density of the population. They started life as a passive vigilante system, with no right to intervene, but morphed into a Hydra's head, or Big Brother. Nothing escaped the gaze of the CDR. Depending on its make-up, it could help a neighbour with problems, or send him to prison.

Anyway, I needed to legalize my situation, and find a job. I began the exhausting task of running round offices and official bodies. I had no friends or contacts. We ended up in ICAP (the Cuban Institute for Friendship with the Peoples of the World). I met the director, my first senior official in the state apparatus, Ramón Calcines, a communist. He was quite young, and very handsome, like the star of a gangster film. He sent me on my way cordially, assuring me they would find something, we would be useful somewhere, all hands were welcome, etc. In these grave times for Cuba, he said, they were grateful to foreign volunteers. 'But who are you, *chico*? See that little *compañera*, she'll take your details, then we'll see. *Patria o muerte!*' The little *compañera*, a *mulatta* poured into clinging olive green, explained that I had to bring credentials from 'my' party, to add to my CV. Meanwhile she would find me something. I left wondering how I would get round my lack of credentials. The job the little *compañera* found me was temporary, but I had to start somewhere. The Cubans were hosting the first industrial exhibition from the Socialist Republic of Czechoslovakia and they needed designers, decorators, painters, etc. – a field where we could be useful. 'And your credentials, *mi amor*?' I explained that I had sent off for them – which was not exactly true – and that it would take time to get a reply. 'But *chico*, without credentials, the Turquino looks tiny next to our problems!' Turquino is the highest peak in the Sierra Maestra.

On the road to Rancho Boyeros there is an industrial zone with huge exhibition halls where the Czech exhibition was to be held. A Czech interior designer was charged with installing it. He was a tall, blond man who looked and behaved like a librarian, and spoke very basic guttural Spanish in a low voice while he polished his specs. Strictly professional, he indicated what he wanted and didn't appear again until the work was finished. He soon showed signs he was satisfied, and even appreciative. He arrived at seven to find the place empty except for his foreign technical staff, and went round picking up scattered tools, waiting for the Cubans to turn up after eight, or even nine. When he got to our design table, he let off steam about the workers' lack of punctuality. 'They'll never build socialism like this', he said. The Cubans always had an excuse: they'd been on guard duty, in a political meeting, training with the militia, in a literacy class. And they really did seem very tired. They took on too many things and did none properly.

One morning, the Czech appeared with someone who was for me a transcendental figure: the Dutch documentary filmmaker Joris Ivens. I had admired him since I saw two of his most important films, *Power and the Land* (1934) and *Spanish Earth* (1937), at the Cine Club in Mendoza run by my Jewish friend David.

The 'Flying Dutchman', as this incomparable man was known, had studied optics before he became a filmmaker and was a specialist lens maker. He chose not to stay at home quietly in his prosperous family business, however, preferring to get involved in the century's major social and political upheavals. A tall man of about sixty, with unruly greying hair, he was filming the installation of the exhibition. He said hello as the Czech introduced us.

4

Starting Work in Cuba

The Habana Libre hotel in Vedado, on 23rd Street and L, was the heart of extra-revolutionary activities. Fidel, a leader without a home, could be seen in the early hours going up to the top floors where he spent the night. The guests, foreigners for the most part, wandered about till late in the large carpeted salons, interconnected by Hollywoodesque staircases. Bellboys in red jackets with gold braid could be seen attending to awestruck *campesinos* on delegations from the interior to an assembly on the agrarian reform, or children from Oriente province on a visit to the capital, or giggling schoolgirls with starched cuffs on a nursing crash course, or youth brigades holding meetings by the lifts. An atmosphere of supercharged subversion filled the lounges and corridors, dislodging the privileged decadence of the local elites and the omnipresent pre-packaged taste of the *gringos*.

Joris Ivens was staying at the Habana Libre. He asked me to help with the captions on his documentary, and we formed a bond. It was a reverential relationship on my part, and on his, I think, due to a need to keep the all-consuming Cuban reality at arm's length, and talk to someone neutral yet just as amazed by the tropical exuberance. He spoke Spanish like an American but we understood each other perfectly. Interested in what had brought us to Cuba, he suggested we go to his hotel 'where anybody who is anybody goes'. So, that same afternoon I walked the couple of blocks from the Colina and disappeared into the carpeted bowels of the Habana Libre. Whenever I met him after that, he was always with someone important. One night he introduced me to a woman in militia fatigues. She was Argentine, not Cuban. Her name was Alicia Eguren, the wife of the Peronist leader, John William Cooke. Alicia was cordial though quite curt and very inquisitive, as if she needed to ascertain which camp you were in. Not long afterwards she invited us to meet her husband up on the fifteenth floor, where they had a suite with large windows overlooking 23rd Street. Gordo Cooke, also in militia uniform, with a long beard that lay on his chest when he bent his head, had an unlit cigarette butt between his lips and ash splattered over his stomach. He was very nice and friendly. We were quickly on first-name terms like old friends, although I found it a bit disrespectful. To avoid misunderstandings, I made it clear I was not a Peronist but he was not interested in past affiliations; what mattered was the future. We talked until midnight. After that, whenever we met Alicia, we went up to see Gordo. Alicia was a kind of advance guard fishing for Argentines, who were then sucked up into the necromancer's cave. Our friendship with her developed on the ground floor, in the hotel's lounges and cafés, and with Cooke on the top floor, among Argentine newspapers, magazines, books and his own writings, scattered all over the floor. The soles of his campaign boots were as shiny as sugar cane, or even shinier thanks to the plush carpets covering his habitat. When I asked about Che, Cooke said Che was why they were there. Alicia was more emphatic. 'Che is mine!' she said. For an Argentine, she boasted, all roads to Che passed through her.

One evening the hotel hosted an exhibition of blindfold chess, organized by Miguel Najdorf, an Argentine grandmaster and world champion in the field. Originally from Poland, he was in Buenos Aires at a chess tournament when the Second World War broke out and was the only member of his family to survive the Nazi death camps. I recognized him from a fleeting encounter with him and his wife on a Number 60 bus in Buenos Aires.

A section of a large salon on the ground floor had been cordoned off. Inside were several widely spaced rows of tables.

The challengers were seated on one side. On the other, blind-folded, was Najdorf accompanied by an assistant who brought him a chair if he wanted to sit down. The assistant called out the number of a table, the room fell silent; the challenger called out his latest move. Najdorf, deep in concentration, repeated the sequence of moves already played then made his move, which his assistant executed. The audience sighed with relief while the maestro moved on to the next of the thirty or forty challengers (his record was fifty-four) and repeated the miracle. At the end of the second row of tables, immersed in his game, was Che. It was only the second time I had seen him.

A couple of weeks earlier, I had read about an event commemorating the Spanish Civil War to be held in the Galician Centre, a baroque building on the corner of the Parque Central. Che would be there with General Enrique Lister, one of the great symbolic figures of the Spanish Republic. There was a huge crowd at the entrance. The room was long and narrow, crammed with rows of seats already occupied, and people standing against the walls, in the corridors, and sitting on the window sills. The ceiling fans were working overtime trying to recycle the air, but it was like stirring soup in which the audience were cooking.

Lister recalled the Civil War: the people's militias, the role of the Communist Party, the International Brigades, and the support given by the USSR. Then Che spoke about the atmosphere in his family when he was a child, sitting round the wireless listening to news from Spain, as if the tragedy was affecting them personally, like all Argentines and other Latin Americans whether they were descendents of Spaniards or not. It informed his belief in the invincibility of the people's struggle if its leaders have the same level of commitment, sacrifice and unity, over and above ideological schisms. He ended by paraphrasing an Antonio Machado poem and offering Lister his pistol if that same will to defeat Francoism would lead him to take up the armed struggle again. Che's speech was not demagogic. His aim was not to persuade anyone or to milk applause. He spoke to say things he believed in or, at least, dreamed of.

Now here he was in the hotel, in front of his chess board, deep in thought, jotting things in his notebook after every move. In his well-worn fatigues, shirt outside his trousers, caught at the waist by his cartridge belt with his pistol on the right, the pockets of his shirt stuffed with papers, cigarettes and pens, his dusty unpolished boots, and his beret on the floor, between the legs of the chair. A woman who, like the crowd of us crammed together in front of him was not watching the game but Che himself, slipped under the cordon in a gesture of daring – or lack of vigilance by his body-guard who was nowhere to be seen – knelt beside him, picked up the beret and handed it to him politely. Che, surprised but courteous, thanked her, but a few minutes later, with a sideways glance at his audience, put the beret back on the floor. The match ended with the hopes of most challengers dashed, Che's included. In this particular battle, the strategist in chief was Najdorf.

One day Joris Ivens introduced me to a Mexican anthropologist, who was to be instrumental in finding me work. The National Institute for Tourist Industries (INIT) – one of the bodies created by the Revolution – wanted to build a country-wide tourist infrastructure and invest in new areas. It decided to revive traditional handicrafts that were of little practical use but had anthropological value and would generate jobs for local people. Ornaments made of hemp, shells and precious wood were common in Cuba, but in Oriente province there was also an original pottery-making tradition. It no longer made everyday utensils but the INIT wanted to revive it to make ceramic handicrafts. The Mexican girl knew the head of the project. He had asked her to study the possibility of setting up a workshop in Holguín, a town on the north coast of Oriente. The problem was that her already limited anthropological knowledge was theoretical, and she knew nothing at all about making clay pots.

Coincidentally, I had worked with ceramics on two occasions and had gleaned a basic knowledge. A fellow student at Mendoza

Art School also attended the university's School of Ceramics and he used to bring his creations round to my house. I got interested in the technique and ended up going to the workshops with him. I watched him prepare and apply varnish, glaze and various other combinations, depending on the desired degree of plasticity and hardness. Later, in Buenos Aires, I helped a colleague of my wife's build an elaborate circular pottery kiln, with saggars (refractory containers) and moulds for liquid clay and clay paste, so we could produce whole series of pots by casting.

The Mexican girl thought she had won the lottery. She told me her boss was interested in my know-how. We went to see the project director, a sweaty Swiss weighing 120 kilos, in black suit, shirt and tie, wiping his brow with a handkerchief. I explained I was not a professional technician, that my knowledge was purely empirical. He seemed to have sussed the calibre of the staff he already had, and after a good chat decided that, compared to them, I was a genius. He offered me the job of running the handicrafts workshop in Holguín. This meant leaving Havana and potential contacts, but it also meant getting to know the interior of the island and the real Cuban people: the *campesinos*, the *guajiros*. What's more, Oriente was the cradle of the Revolution. I took the job.

There was a diesel train that took ten hours to do the 700 kilometres between Havana and Holguín, but it was worth it. Going out into the countryside is to begin to know Cuba. The modern world of Havana, luxurious and fickle, disappears as you leave the city limits. The towns and cities of the interior are decidedly colonial, with a marked African influence, not only in the people, as in Havana, but in the streets, the houses, the balconies with washing hanging, the galleries, verandahs, raised pavements, signs, shops, curiosity and noisy brouhaha.

Holguín province seemed a little different, and I soon realized why. It is an agricultural region like most of Cuba, but the land is richer, with meadows, woods, beaches, large sugar mills and a semi-feudal society based on sugar cane. It also has the island's

most important nickel reserves. The city of Holguín is orderly
and quiet. The poor – cane cutters and seasonal labourers in the
sugar mills, and a whole range of unemployed, underemployed
and destitute – have been pushed to the southern outskirts of the
city, to a huge shanty town made of yaguas, palm branches and
bark precariously tied to poles for the hut roofs and walls, and
stones to hold the thatches down.

The first thing I did after arriving at my Holguín hotel was to
go out and get my bearings. The city was built round a central
tree-filled square, with paved roads stretching for two or three
blocks, more built up to the north away from the highway. It
seemed very pleasant, but there was not much to see. I went into
a café for a coffee, my breakfast in those days. The people who
ran the café were my first friends. The second thing I had to do
was sort out the so-called infrastructure of my new life.

The solution to everything depended on slotting into the
bureaucratic organogram, acquiring full rights and obligations.
Apart from the traditional official bodies like the municipality,
public works, electricity and water, etc., there were the new ones
which called all the shots. Urban reform, agrarian reform, confiscated assets, CDRs (the committees for the defence of the
Revolution), militias, literacy brigades, were all part of an entity
called Integrated Revolutionary Organizations (ORI) that
wielded absolute power. It had been created by merging the
organizations that had fought (the guerrillas' 26th of July Movement and the Student Directory) with those that had dithered
(the communists of the PSP). The latter, however, got their
cadres in place first.

In Oriente, the ORI-northern region was run by a communist,
Rita Díaz, the power behind the throne, and a redhead to boot.
She was not very tall, chubby but shapely, and mysteriously fitted
into tight olive green fatigues and blue militia shirt. With her hair
caught in a sort of loose bun under a green beret, she looked more
like a French resistance fighter than a tropical *miliciana*. She was
very temperamental but had a good sense of humour, was both

friendly and energetic, and highly expeditious. She put her weight behind the handicrafts workshop from the start and promised to help us find staff among people she trusted. Meanwhile, Claudia and I had to find a house, furnish it, join the militia and, of course, do political work. We would stay in touch with her. 'That's great, *chico*! An Argentine like Che . . . the most beautiful man in the Revolution!' she said as she waved goodbye with a 'come and eat at my house', but no firm date.

A young lawyer, Evelio Rodríguez, was in charge of Urban Reform in Holguín. For our workshop, he suggested a former fruit farm: an enormous old house with two interior patios and a large piece of land behind. It would be fine. Repairs to the floors and roof were needed, but it was do-able. For Claudia and me, Evelio picked an apartment half a block from the main square, and no more than three blocks from the workshop. It was on the first floor, with stairs straight down to the street where, as if to mitigate our nostalgia, there was a tree, the only one on the block. It was not very big but satisfied our somewhat bourgeois need for comfort, and its excellent bathroom met with immediate approval. Large transparent lizards wandered over the frosted glass, but Evelio said they were the best line of defence against mosquitoes. We went to choose some furniture and the following day the house was just about habitable.

Within a week there was a rhythm to my work. It was hard – seven in the morning to twelve at night on normal days – but absorbing. I was the boss, but also the bricklayer, carpenter and designer: removing roofs to replace woodwork and broken tiles, knocking down walls, making a bathroom, connecting the plumbing, installing electricity (under electric company supervision) or painting white walls. Cuba was almost totally dependent on imported materials and our work showed how far its commercial sector had deteriorated. As stocks ran out there was no way of replenishing them. There was a shortage of nails, screws, wire, plaster, fuses, files, etc., so finding materials was the first battle.

I joined the militia, training a couple of days a week and doing night guard duty in official buildings or important work places. This general level of vigilance was not only necessary, it was also a way of mobilizing people on a political level. It played havoc with productivity at work, however. I could see how elastic time-tables were, and although I used firm rational arguments, it had no effect. To make things worse, after the Bay of Pigs the army produced an emergency plan for defending Holguín in case of attack, not an entirely crazy idea given the city's strategic position on the north coast. It comprised encircling the town with three or four lines of trenches to be dug by voluntary *milicianos*, better at digging holes than being soldiers. This pick and spade job was done on (Red) Sundays until five in the afternoon. It flayed your hands but included a free lunch.

All problems to do with the workshop went straight to Rita, that is, to the ORI, the powerhouse of the Revolution. No cement in the building material yards? Go and find Rita. No rivets? Rita will phone someone; 'What the hell's happened to those rivets, *chico*?' That's how we did the impossible for the first few months.

The Swiss director, who seemed to live in his huge Lincoln Continental, appeared at least once a month, surrounded by economists and planners from JUCEPLAN, the Central Planning Board, an entity in charge of reorganizing the economy and educating cadres. It meant a wasted day. And not only for us, because these crazy economists applied undigested Soviet models, from an economic system of which they knew neither the internal workings nor the results, as we eventually saw when the practices of the 'political cadres' whose inflated aims and results were made public. The Swiss, still sweating, was creating the inevitable national bureaucratic apparatus to fit the tangle of budget proposals, inputs, expenses, investment and production, while we were still building our basic infrastructure, because we had no precedents, no ideas and no pots. Luckily, the Mexican girl's folkloric ideas of going back to the primitive ceramics of the indigenous Taíno and Siboney peoples – hand-moulded clay pieces baked on a tribal fire – were discarded. The argument against, which I subscribed to, was that you could not devote an entire wages, equipment and administration budget to an experiment only useful in an Anthropology Department science lab.

She was transferred back to Havana, and was replaced by a young administrator, Melchor Casals, who was not even twenty. He took over the planning days, and every now and again came with us to Havana for administrative training. The permanent staff comprised an improvised technical director (me); a very capable designer (Claudia); a teenage administrator (Melchor); a communist delegate-cum-worker (Cucho); an actual carpenter (Argeo Pérez), and three trainees. The responsibility kept me awake at night. But in the nick of time I managed to get the latest books on ceramic techniques: pottery, clay, varnish, kilns and temperatures. I got some locally, sent for more from Havana, and built up quite a good theoretical base on the subject.

When work on the building was finished, Argeo made me a draughtsman's table and the second stage began. Using millimetre graph paper, I designed every piece of equipment, shelving, work tables, sinks with covers, sinks without covers, sinks with drains, etc., and arranged them according to their place in an eventual production line. Various types of potter's wheels; tables for casting, moulding, kneading, filing, varnishing; rooms with warm air circulating through the floor-to-ceiling shelving, for drying the varnish.

Then came the period of experimenting with the equipment and materials. We needed prototypes already finished and fired. I designed a circular kiln with a one-cubic-metre capacity, with saggars arranged in the shape of an orange cut in half, with flames circulating upwards in a spiral, impelled by pressure from a ventilator. To build the ventilator, and especially the burners, I needed the help of specialized technology. The ventilator was built in a local workshop, but for the burner I searched the length and breadth of Cuba before Rita found me a group of Soviet engineers in the nickel processing plant at Nicaro. They designed and built an initial burner for the circular kiln and, later, a second one with more capacity and precision.

Halfway along the road from Holguín to Havana I had spotted an area of red clay. We took a sample and it proved to have excellent drying and plastic qualities. We went personally and chose a truckload of the best clay and began the process of washing, grinding and kneading large quantities of this formidable red paste. It gave us a beautiful range of plates, cups and vases, with a single colour varnish inside and the natural red clay on the outside. Don't forget that this was the mid-sixties, and Cuba was running out of practically everything, a critical situation in which the first things to break are plates. Hence, we channelled production into crockery.

But work wasn't my only worry. Political control had degenerated into Stalinist sectarianism, spreading through Cuban society like a virus. A person's political past counted for more than his skills when it came to evaluating who would get positions of responsibility. The majority of the population were stuck because very few had a communist past. In the case of foreign workers, supervision was by representatives of the Communist Parties back home. The job of vetting the Argentine contingent fell to an engineer from Buenos Aires, a certain Fontana. He worked and lived in Holguín, and it wasn't long before he turned up at the workshop. Dressed in militia fatigues, with his beret under his epaulette, like a US Green Beret, he introduced himself as the 'president' of the colony of Argentine volunteers sent by the Communist Party to support the Revolution. After running a critical eye over our facilities, which seemed to interest him, he said I had to come to his office to register my details and be briefed on the colony's obligations. The unresolved question of credentials that would make me legitimately useful (which I thought I had left behind in Havana) raised its ugly head again. The engineer, his son and daughter-in-law, both architects, worked in the Oriente department of the Ministry of Public Works. Most of the Argentines sent by the party were professionals, since the majority of the Cubans in the mass exodus to Miami had been professionals, stripping the state of technocrats, top civil servants, doctors, economists, etc. Cuba needed to plug the hole. The Argentines – over 400 of them – were not there entirely out of altruism and international solidarity. They earned excellent salaries, of which they sent up to 50 per cent into succulent bank balances at home. With the rest, they maintained a standard of living that was higher than most in the government, ministers included. My salary was much, much more modest.

I went to Fontana's house in the hope of forestalling a collision with the hierarchy, at least until I had enough support to disguise my being a political orphan and to regularize my status. Fontana felt empowered by his role of watchdog and put me through a sort of spy novel interrogation, examining my entire life back to my childhood. He quickly established that I would have my work evaluated periodically, and would have to report any failings to him. 'We must perform to the best of our abilities, as human beings and as party activists', he said. He insisted on having all my details, so I had to send to Mendoza for the required references after all. After thousands of miles, trials and tribulations, it turned out my bosses were not Cuban but Argentines with whom I had absolutely nothing in common.

5

'Compañero, *Che Is Expecting You*'

Cucho lived in the yaguas shanty town, on the outskirts of Holguín. He was an old communist, though his militancy went no further than reading the weekly *Hoja Semanal* after passing it round among his friends. Rita told him to introduce me to his neighbours and support my activities, although there was still no organized political work there. My first thought on seeing the place was that nothing could be done until these people were removed from this putrefaction and given a decent place to live. But things don't work like that, not even in Cuba. There was no decent place, and the inhabitants weren't cattle that you could just herd back and forth.

There is no formula for starting socio-political work in these circumstances, even with a revolutionary government aiming to outlaw demagoguery and replace it with action. Anthropologists, who don't pretend to change things, try to blend in with the locals, adopt their customs, live like them, eat like them, begin to dream like them, and by so doing get to understand them. The literacy brigades do this, but in situ. Teaching people to read and write is a huge step forward, although to be fair, in Cuba illiteracy was no more than 25 per cent nationally, and only above that in rural areas. Shanty towns are spectres of misery everywhere. The usual description of their inhabitants as coming to the city peripheries from some distant nowhere in search of opportunities is far from true. They are neither *campesinos* nor city dwellers. They have left their huts, but have no houses. No countryside, no future. And in the main, no water.

I got to know Cucho's family, his neighbours and his fellow communists – no more than a handful of them in a densely populated area. There was a 'social centre', that is, a fenced-off dance floor of flattened earth and a stage at the end for musicians. The audience brought their own chairs, if they had them. A small curious crowd was gathering, mostly women, under the faint light from a bulb hooked up by extension cable to an empty police checkpoint. Cucho's image of himself as a rabble-rouser went into overdrive with a fanciful introduction of me, as a hero from generous foreign lands come ready to give his all for Cuba. After a difficult moment breaking the ice with muttered introductions, the meeting opened up to questions and in no time we established a whole programme of activities based on looking at the Americas, past and present. We would meet on the dance floor for an open debate twice a week after the evening meal. For me this meant an urgent visit to the National Publishing House's library and bookshop to get books on Cuban, Caribbean and US history, to fill the serious gaps in my knowledge.

Cubans had mixed feelings about Americans, or *Yanquis* as they called them. On the one hand, the present situation, with invasions, sabotage, blockade, and other acts of aggression, made them hate the Gringos and support the Revolution. On the other hand, they secretly admired them. All their most popular images, from movies, to Cadillacs, gangsters, cowboys, skyscrapers, millionaires and chewing gum, were American, creating a subliminal belief that the Americans were superior beings. Added to which, even deeper down, a real fear of the Russians kept raising its head, much to the despair of Cucho who had to dispel the myth that communists stole children. Apparently the story of the Spanish 'war children' taken to the Soviet Union under an agreement with the Republic, with the idea of saving them from Fascism, was ingrained in the minds of the world's Catholics. Not only were children stolen, they were pickled and eaten.

No matter what historical event came up, we spent the allotted time discussing it. The meetings were lively, full of avid participants who came religiously on the appointed days, and even started coming prepared with questions, and contradictions. Looking back, I can see I had become a kind of Pope without a script, acting outside the rigorous restrictive canons of a party organization. We had said there would be open debate, and there was. The point was to extract, from the clash of history and reality, a positive take on the Revolution, of the tasks it proposed, of the sacrifices being demanded of them, yes, even of them, the poorest class of all. The revolutionary leadership was setting the example. There was no abuse, no rank, no privilege. The leaders worked day and night, with practically no sleep. The age of miracles had descended on the island, and the miracle was honesty. The weekly discussions – jokingly called 'the yaguas Forum' – were noticed, and my political stock shot up in Rita's eyes. Not as far as 'President' Fontana was concerned, however. He gave me a deadline to fix my residence in Cuba (as he had some significant control over me).

The workshop meanwhile, with its spanking new roof and two working kilns, was ready to start production. We had already made crockery prototypes, and were experimenting with moulds for the liquid clay. The burners had already arrived. On my first free Saturday I had been to Moa, a village on the north coast, to talk to the Soviet engineers at the nearby nickel plant. They kept themselves to themselves, wrapped in nostalgia, well provided with musical instruments, books and records, in a nice, although isolated, house on the beach. They had a smattering of Spanish so between them they had managed my questions and answers, greeting my appeal for technical help with the burners enthusiastically. It had taken a whole afternoon to explain exactly what I wanted.

They did not mix much with the other foreign professionals living there, but they did mention an Argentine couple who were doctors. On my second visit, I had been to see this couple who invited me to dinner. We talked into the night, our good spirits fuelled by a few beers. While her husband was making coffee, the young female doctor said something that struck a chord with my latent feeling of unease. 'I see you're very excited about the Revolution, Ciro. Your disillusionment will be very painful, I'm afraid. Communists are coming out of the woodwork like mice, taking over everything, to get at the cheese.' The phrase remained engraved in my memory like a hieroglyphic chiselled in granite. It was only her opinion, of course, but they had been sent by the Argentine Communist Party so this inside-take on things surprised me. Their being suspicious about why I was in Cuba was perhaps part of a general continental-wide policy, to impose ideological control and situate the Cuban Revolution within the Cold War: a policy of the Communist International.

Melchor, our administrator, talked to me about his future during our long nights on guard duty. He wasn't happy doing office work and, like all those in the shadow of the generation that won the war in the mountains (and the city), he felt none of the jobs available brought him closer to Mount Olympus. He and Xiomara, his skeletal girlfriend, believed, like the youngsters in Russia in 1917, that the Revolution was a time for creativity and giving art free rein. They dreamed that once the state had solved production problems by recuperating their legitimate means, and faced the basic challenges of the new society, like education (which it was doing), housing and health, etc., it would prioritize culture, and this would be a springboard for launching Cuba into the first world, not in the banal GDP sense, but in terms of Art, Cinema and Literature. Melchor wanted to study theatre and had heard that the university in Santiago, on the other side of the Sierra Maestra, was going to open a theatre school at the start of the 1962 school year. He wanted me to help him leave the workshop and register for the preparatory course. But it was nearly the end of the year, and the kilns were working. Not an easy moment.

The first time the big kiln reached 1,100 degrees and was working to capacity, I was overjoyed. I cooled it down slowly overnight and went to bed in the morning, leaving Cucho on guard. I wanted to be there with the whole staff when the oven was finally opened. One refractory box had broken along with some pieces in other boxes, but in the main everything was intact. The colour of the clay was beautiful, albeit a slightly paler red, and the black, blue and grey were very successful despite being imperfectly applied. I tapped the pots with the tips of my fingers, the sound was perfect. We all played tunes on the cups, plates and jars, in a concert of joy and pride. And confidence. What I had promised had come to pass, warts and all.

Rita finally gave Melchor permission to leave for Santiago on condition he returned for a few days each month to do the workshop's books. We celebrated New Year with our new friends, poor but with the warmest of hearts. For the first few months of the New Year the tension between Fontana and me was mitigated because the workshop was running well. All the same, his deadline was approaching. Then Fidel appeared on TV and made a furious attack on Aníbal Escalante, the most hard-line Stalinist in the old Communist Party, a member of the ORI's national leadership and the visible face of the sectarianism sweeping through the political and administrative bodies. I felt a great relief at this dismantling, albeit temporarily, of Stalinism.

When the workshop was running smoothly, Melchor introduced a discordant note. The rector of his art school in Santiago wanted me to come and teach art, or art appreciation to be more precise. The students needed to learn about art, its history, its significance and transcendence. I appreciated the offer, but I declined. I barely had time to sleep. I couldn't even leave the workshop to teach in Holguín, let alone on the other side of the Sierra Maestra. Melchor came back with another proposal. If classes were on Saturday and Sunday, I could travel on Friday night, teach on Saturday and Sunday morning, and return late on Sunday night. I don't know what possessed me to try it. Perhaps the example set by Melchor's determination. After all, I had not come to Cuba to be a potter.

The road to Santiago wound through hills and cane fields. The last fifty kilometres were breathtaking. The Sierra Maestra was like a botanical garden, totally green, with palm trees leaning at a variety of angles, elegant dancers in a choreography created by the cyclones that pound the mountains and flatten the forest. The River Cauto crossed the road a couple of times. The city of Santiago appeared below the road and extended out round the bay, following the contours of the mountains. Looking for my hotel, I felt as if I were in New Orleans, seeing the same type of buildings, broad-walks with railings, and wrought-iron balconies, and because most of the lively crowd were black and it was hard to tell if they were walking or dancing. The next morning Melchor took me to the university campus.

The Faculty of Medicine had lent the Theatre School some of its classrooms. The students were different from my political audience in Holguín: they were more interested and dynamic, and focused on the context and tasks of the Revolution seen through the prism of art. But like the workshop, it was my responsibility to mould this pure young clay, not knowing either if I was up to the job or what the results would be. Again I felt as if everything I said was received like desert rain, and it was my duty to make it drinkable, not ideologically or aesthetically contaminated. By general consent, the classes were organized around slides and art books, arranged in periods, schools, countries and cultures. We would have our work cut out. There was also a bit of colour theory, drawing, perspective, volume and some practical exercises.

On my second week in Santiago, I heard there was an Argentine looking for me. He was waiting by my truck in the car park when I came out of class. He was a short, jovial-looking man, slightly provincial, and good natured. He could easily have been the gardener, but he turned out to be a doctor, a professor of pathology in the Faculty of Medicine. This was Dr Alberto Granado, friend of Che and companion on his motorcycle journey round South America. After the Revolution, Che had invited him to work on the island. Alberto invited me to his house to meet his wife and children since, he said, Saturdays and

Argentines were synonymous with barbecues. Preparing the barbecue broke the ice and by the time we started to talk seriously we were already friends. I glimpsed that my coming to Cuba was starting to make sense.

I stayed until late and when I came to leave, Alberto said that his house would now be my home in Santiago. We would be saving the Revolution money to boot. They made room for me in his study, a narrow room filled with books and toys. In the months that followed, until July 1962, we talked endlessly about recurring themes: Cuba, the Revolution, Latin America, Argentina, Che . . . Che, Argentina, Latin America, the Revolution, Cuba.

On Saturdays, when I came out of class, I would go to Petiso Granado's hideaway, the pathology lab. I would cross a huge hall with rows of stainless steel tables, some with corpses or bits of corpses, then climb some stairs to a mezzanine where I would find Alberto Granado, calmly eating a cheese sandwich as if he were at a picnic in a flowery meadow smelling of lavender, instead of formaldehyde and disinfectant. Then we would go home to resume our discussions; an obsessive mutual, collective, national and international examination of conscience. We discarded all the Argentine political history that had shaped us.

I told him of my travels around the north of Argentina, and the re-emergence of an underclass, descended from the poverty-stricken *gaucho* militias and survivors of the colonialism of yesteryear, who were forging a political presence behind Perón's deceptive populism and, thanks to him, could no longer be ignored. He told me about his own recent journey through the Chaco, the region where I had been. I must surely have asked the reason for that journey, since he was already living in Cuba, but I don't remember an answer that might have made me put two and two together. We talked about the workshop, political control, sectarianism, the militias, the yaguas shanty town. He was always interested in how my political work was going. The weeks passed amid corpses, barbecues and discussions. Then in July, he told me Che was coming to Santiago on the 26th for the anniversary of the attack on the Moncada barracks. The weekend before the visit, Alberto said Che wanted to meet me. He planned a barbecue in his house.

However, two days before the celebrations, I was laid up in bed in Holguín with a stonking cold. The most important day of my life, and I was in no state to drive to Santiago, or even get out of bed. I got someone to call and explain the problem, and say how sorry I was. When I got to Santiago the following week, Alberto said Che had left a ticket to Havana in my name with Cubana airlines, and was expecting me as soon as possible.

On my second visit to Havana's Rancho Boyeros airport, my expectations were different. I still did not know what lay ahead, but I felt that the old me, the spectator, was now sitting firmly in the front row. Sure enough, as Granado had said, a Rebel Army soldier in brand new olive green was waiting for me. He introduced himself as the *Comandante*'s bodyguard, and he was to take me to my hotel. It was none other than the Habana Libre. He filled in forms at reception with surprising agility and accompanied me to my room. He asked if I knew anyone in the hotel and when I said yes, he said I had to pretend to be here for work and not mention the real reason. And finally, he said that I had to be on call; whenever I went out, I had to leave word at the reception. 'You never know when "the man" will be able to talk to you.' I visited Gordo Cooke in his bunker and satisfied Alicia's curiosity about the workshop, Argentines, communists and countryside.

Between two and three in the morning of the second day, the phone rang and a voice said: '*Compañero*, Che is expecting you.' I went down. The bodyguard was there. He took me to the underground car park where a car was waiting. We swiftly crossed Vedado and headed for the Plaza de la Revolución where, after a few security checks, we ended up in the bowels of the Ministry of Industry. We took the lift to Che's office and there, in a sort of kitchen which looked like the bodyguards' bivouac, very young soldiers were drinking coffee or reading. I was to wait here. The opportunity to talk freely at Alberto's barbecue had passed. Che was buried in his usual workload.

Then, a side door opened and Che appeared. He looked very tired – it was by now about four in the morning – and was wearing the same rumpled fatigues I had seen him play chess in. He ordered coffee to be brought to his office and turning to me, said simply 'You're here?' and held out his hand. He said he was in a meeting with a delegation from I don't know where, that unfortunately this time it was he who couldn't talk, that he hadn't time for the conversation he wanted to have with me, but someone would do it for him. I was to wait at the hotel until they came for me. He turned and went back through the door he had come out of. I don't remember uttering a single word.

A couple of days later, some men in civilian clothes (from the intelligence services) came for me. The car drove along the Malécon to Miramar, a smart suburb of villas with gardens, and stopped in front of one. We went into a living room with comfy armchairs, an elegant dining table, and many books. I was left alone, to wait. It was not long before an army officer came in. He did not look like the typical Cuban. He had a short military-style crew cut, large frank eyes, wide cheek bones and jaw, and a playful smile. As soon as he opened his mouth, I knew he was Argentine and that it was Jorge Masetti.

After all, it was logical. He, his interview in the Sierra Maestra, his book, had brought me here. I knew nothing of his life in Cuba. Only that he no longer ran the Cuban news agency *Prensa Latina*, but that Fidel had brought him back to front it temporarily during the Bay of Pigs invasion. I had glimpsed him twice on TV during the public interrogations of the prisoners. We sat down to talk just like two Argentines in a café. It wasn't an exam, just a long exchange of opinions, ideas in common, work experience, mutual friends in Buenos Aires, illusions, disappointments, etc. I could see he knew exactly what I had been doing in Cuba and about my discussions with Granado, because he asked direct questions, like: 'How long were you in Salta?' 'Are there mountains near the Tabacal sugar mill?' Details I had given Granado.

We agreed there had to be revolution in Argentina. And, according to the theory of objective and subjective conditions, the time was ripe. The people were under attack, cheated, trapped, proscribed. The economy was growing, with a large productive capacity in food and consumer goods, but it was being usurped by foreign interests. The industrial infrastructure was developing, with large autonomous sectors, but the multinationals were taking over key areas that would be difficult to recuperate. A strong working class was ready to fight. There was a cultured and well-informed middle class. And an unequalled geographic position: all types of climate from the Andes to the Atlantic, and from the Tropic of Capricorn to the Antarctic. Argentina was the ideal country for a process of revolutionary change that would regain for its people the use of its immense natural resources, its own creativity and will to work, without being strangled by imperialist siege and blackmail.

Masetti said that the armed struggle was a real option. He had already done advanced military training at the new military academy which the Soviets had helped set up for the Cuban Rebel Army. After eight months of intense theoretical and practical training – having to put up with being a foreigner and being called Che's 'poodle' – he had graduated top of his class. This type of training was essential. Unlike Batista's, the Argentine army was extremely professional. Students from all over the continent came to study at our military academies. The project would not be like Cuba, first because of the size of the territory, and second because the population was mainly urban. Also, we had to take into account the level of politicization of the masses affiliated to traditional or populist parties, and with hegemonic influences that were difficult to combat. According to Masetti, the Cuban Revolution had shown that the foco theory would dismantle apparent hegemonies and focus popular support on an unexpected action, i.e. concrete activity instead

of mere promises. The conversation took us into a realm of infinite possibilities, but Masetti was keen to establish the points we
could agree on. He was not acting for himself, but on behalf of
Che, his boss. In other words, if I thought the armed struggle
could succeed in Argentina, Che had an offer to make me.

The project was to give serious military training to a small
group who would set up a guerrilla base in Argentina, to be
commanded by Masetti until after this vanguard group had
consolidated its position and Che himself arrived. There were
too many question marks for my liking, but the bottom line
was, if it was Che's plan and he was involved, I wanted to be in
on it. So we got down to details: how the group would be
formed, when and where the training would begin, the time it
would take, and what we would study. Che would be sole overall leader, totally independent of the Cuban Revolution,
although the Cubans would provide necessary help with infrastructure and equipment. Masetti was happy to discuss any
queries I had about how the plan slotted into the Argentine
political context, but this would obviously need a lengthy
collective analysis and that, he said, would be one of our tasks
during training. Naturally, a commitment to secrecy and the
strictest cell structure was not only a matter of honour, but also
of life and death. By accepting the offer, I took on board this
commitment. In my second meeting with Che, he would define
it more as a commitment to death than to life.

It was getting dark. We had been talking for six hours and my
throat was dry. A very pretty Cuban girl came in to remind
Masetti the children were waiting for him. Masetti apologized for
various shortcomings while he introduced me. Conchita, his new
wife, was pregnant. He fetched the children, who were too shy to
come in, two of them between eight and ten, by his first Argentine wife. He was supposed to take them to their mother's house,
but we still had a few loose ends to tie up; so we continued, aided
by some lemonade. I had to get back to Holguín and confront the
problem of abandoning the workshop at such a critical stage of

production. I had no idea how I was going to do it, without getting myself a bad name and into a political mess. Masetti would talk to Che about it. Then there was my wife Claudia. Although we had already planned to separate, and she would not mind my leaving, she would have to be sworn to the secrecy. She could not be left completely in the dark and be expected to be supportive. Masetti would bring that up with Che, too.

We left it that I would wait at the hotel for another couple of days at least, while he told Che the result of our conversation and my willingness to take part in the project. He made a call, and the security car came back for me. It left me at the hotel in a state of exaltation. I lay on my bed and thought over the events of the past few days, the people I had met, and 'the project', which was no more and no less than what I had come to Cuba for, although I never really thought it possible. And it had happened through a series of coincidences, connected by a mysterious force of destiny. It was after midnight when hunger (I hadn't eaten all day) forced me out of bed, and I went out in search of some food and a large glass of rum.

Masetti came to get me the next day. We met on the corner of 23rd Street and the Malécon, and drove west out of Havana until we found somewhere for a drink and chat. Che would take care of the workshop, and also of Claudia's residency in Cuba until we were in Argentina, or indefinitely if she wanted to stay. I had to get back as soon as possible, because classes would be starting in mid-August. I would find a ticket for tomorrow's flight at the hotel reception.

I arrived in Holguín feeling really strange. Something was tearing at my insides. It was if my body was being emptied of ordinary organs and banal feelings, and replaced by more ascetic, rigorous ones. I was acting from my own free will, nobody was forcing me to do anything, although the idea of a small group, divorced from any political context, seemed like an irrational adventure. And yet, being a small group was what made the plan so rational: more than epic, it was logical. Everything would

eventually revolve round Che being there, but he was not able to
move the project forward as yet, nor come without a minimum of
preparation. It was all about smuggling out the seed, planting it in
land where it could germinate, and cultivating it.

A memorandum from the Ministry of Industry signed by
Che, and addressed to the INIT, was copied to our workshop.
It said I was to be included in a group of scholarship students on
a course in specialized ceramic techniques in Czechoslovakia. I
had to be in Havana by 15 August. The news hit the workshop
like a bombshell. They didn't see getting a scholarship as a
success, rather as abandoning a scheme that represented a steady
job. We had worked in consensus, like a family, without hierarchy or exclusion, each one bringing his skill and enthusiasm. I
tried to convince them that I had contributed all I could, and
that they now knew more about the equipment, kilns and clay
than I did. Rita saw it as almost a personal triumph, at least of
her support for the workshop project. I insisted on giving the
carpenter, Argeo Pérez, the oak table he had made for me. He
had asked for permission to work on it after hours and I had
seen the love with which he polished the wood, made the chairs
and put the finishing touches to the varnish. I saw Melchor and
Alberto Granado for the last time in Santiago when I took the
plane for Havana. Melchor was moved. Granado's eyes were
shining with personal triumph, like Rita's, except that he understood what it all meant.

For the second time in less than fifteen days, I landed in Havana.
The intelligence services were there to meet Claudia and I. While
we waited for the key to her house, we repeated our vow of
friendship and wished each other good luck. Suddenly, the army
appeared in the shape of Olo Pantoja, a captain in Che's column
that had won the great victory in Santa Clara. A bit chubby with
curly brown hair, he told Claudia her house was ready and introduced her to the people who would be looking after her. I was to
go with him. Claudia and I said our last goodbyes, not knowing
if we would ever see each other again. Pantoja took the bag with

my few clothes and books and we got into an army jeep. There was barely enough room because the floor was littered with guns. 'They're for you, to practise with', he said. The time had come. I had to learn to kill. That is, I had to learn to die.

Part Two

Argentina

6

A Project for Utopia

The Cuban saga in the Sierra Maestra had diverse and contradictory consequences. For the Cubans themselves, there was an impact on national politics and economic strategies, and it also affected ordinary people, both socially and psychologically. Abroad, there was an irreversible impact on international relations, with regard to the north–south confrontation. The economic dependence of the south was structurally linked to its military subjugation, and the empire's repression of any sign of national or regional independence was justified by the pretext of fighting communism.

The individual Cubans who had taken part in the epic saga were affected in many different ways. The majority went on to occupy positions in Cuba to which they would never have had access before, since the new society was based not on class but on their own sense of responsibility. Some discovered late in the day that the struggle had not been fought for personal gain, that the bearded fighters had opened the door to social change. Others, like Che, realised that they had to go on through that door and turn military victory into Revolution – that if Revolution does not change society, it is nothing.

Needless to say, Revolution led to confrontation with the continent's dominant power. Moreover, the Revolution's ability to confront the imperial power successfully depended on its capacity to resist the inevitable reactionary attacks. The basic argument was that no small country would have the capacity to resist by itself, and especially not Cuba, an island in the '*mare nostrum*' of the empire, a few kilometres off its coast. It would be naïve and foolish to ignore this obvious fact. It was clearly unavoidable and imperative to create this capacity to resist, not just inside Cuba but outside as well.

Yet this was not just a question of will. The means also have to exist. Without economic autonomy, there can be no political or ideological autonomy. A revolution needs to be independent in all aspects: ties of dependency block the machinery of government and prevent progress. Economic independence is the key. In the twenty-first century, this idea seems redundant because the economy is everything. But in the 1960s, notions of national identity, Western civilization, self-determination, cultural, ethical and even aesthetic patrimony were still considered important. To maintain independence, to have the freedom to negotiate, to accept or reject policies at the international level, was of paramount importance. Especially, to be able to *negotiate*. In this sense, it was clear that Argentina had better prospects than other Latin American countries.

A revolution will never succeed in a poor backward country. Revolutionaries can take power, but nothing else. They will never be allowed to remain in power without surrendering their ideals and corrupting their principles. They will not be allowed to succeed. A victorious revolution is like a cancer spreading through the continent, erupting here and there. Then, if the empire is caught off guard, it will devote all its surgical skills to cutting the cancer out, above all other political considerations. The strength of the Cuban Revolution was to take power by its own means, by the will of its people, in defiance of doctrinal wisdom. Its subsequent unfolding drama was that of a lonely shipwrecked sailor besieged by dangerous sharks.

For Che, the commander of the guerrilla forces in Santa Clara in 1958 that had defeated the Batista regime and brought Castro to power, the danger was only just beginning. The Revolution was prey to all kinds of aggression – political, military, diplomatic and economic – that aimed to force it to abandon its independence and capitulate, or simply be invaded and obliterated. The only way to avoid this fate was to get support from outside Cuba, from a similar kind of independent revolution in an economically important country in Latin America, a revolution capable of consolidating the task of constructing a just society for all its peoples and resisting the pressures and conditions imposed by the existing world order.

This ambitious and adventurous idea became possible only through the single golden thread that sought to marry the power of subjective action with the harsh reality of objective facts: the introduction of myth into politics and war. That is, a physical presence that would lead the struggle, a hero with no national allegiance but who had not forgotten his ties to his homeland – the presence of Che, the Argentine, who believed it was legitimate to fight for a better society, no matter the country, but all the better if it was his own.

This idea embraces everything that Che had learned both from his guerrilla experience and the exercise of power. Two things were fundamental and complementary: the theory of the foco and the theory of the 'new man'. According to the foco theory, a small nucleus of fighters can successfully confront a regular army in a country where there are huge inequalities, because the people will support and strengthen a determined struggle for power. Armed action, directed against the forces of repression and backed up by the guerrillas' impeccable behaviour towards its local *campesino* base and captured soldiers, would also constitute a lesson in how to become a new kind of human being. Personal vices and egoism would be abandoned and replaced by a process of transformation. Through sacrifice, self-control, dedication and suffering, this would eventually lead to an understanding of the importance of solidarity and justice. Were the process to be sustained and developed, an organizational or party leadership would emerge that would draw on cadres influenced by an unwavering revolutionary ethic. When the resulting revolutionary forces came to power, they would create a society without injustice or discrimination. The basis for building this new society would be the 'new man', someone without defects or aberrant inclinations.

Looked at so schematically, the idea is to politics what a simple sum is to mathematics. It lacks any analysis of the situation in Argentina, of the international context, or of history, let alone of the law of probabilities – not to mention common sense and folly. From the point of view of the scientific analysis of human problems, rational intellectuals of the past 150 years had studied, measured, compared and scrutinized every political and social event on the five continents. Yet the most serious and prestigious left-wing intellectuals, cocooned in the most rarefied strands of thinking, were blind to the obvious signs appearing in the edifice of world revolution like cracks in a dam. They deceived themselves and others about the 'new socialist society' that was itself being built, as a matter of fact, on injustice, bloodshed and suffering. Some got a whiff of the smell of death, from tales of famine and repression, but they disguised it – like the bourgeoisie of centuries past – with the perfume of their own intellect and their own theories, and encouraged others to engage in collective deception. Others, like George Orwell, through his professionalism, honesty and humanity, ended up in the 'dustbin of history'.

As for the foolishness of our particular adventure, it is impossible to negate the absolute purity of its intentions. It might be considered irresponsible or just plain risky, but the price was paid by the individual participants. It would be idiotic and criminal to drive down a motorway the wrong way, because the eventual victims would be innocent. Yet accepting danger in order to fight for a better world is an act of sacrifice, involving a renunciation of material wealth and the sublimation of personality. It is not to be confused with terrorist martyrdom, which carries out someone else's designs in return for a place in paradise. No, it is to assume a lifetime of risk, of fighting out of love for the right to a shared future.

Che's project had this transcendental simplicity: forget any idea of glory, confront earthly perils without fear, stand up in this particular tropical region and say 'here we are, here we want to build a new society, in which the fruits of our labours will not be taken away, where our rights will not be violated, where joy is not privatized, where culture is within everybody's reach, where the smell of bread fills our homes, and dreams come with the sunrise to dislodge the terrors of the night. If you want to stop us, you will have to come and find us, and understand that we will fight.'

Security was always our major weakness, both in Cuba (the threat of infiltration of any kind), and also during the time needed for Che to transfer to the guerrilla base that would be set up in Argentina. Responsibility for this first phase of the operation fell to Masetti's small and inexperienced group. Any disaster, at either end of the project, would effectively put an end to it. Che could not come if we failed; the plan could not succeed without Che.

7

An Army of Five Madmen

Captain Olo Pantoja drove from the Malécon to the elegant suburb of Marianao around the Country Club, through streets of luxury mansions abandoned by the bourgeoisie when they fled to Miami. You could tell how exclusive it was by the air. It seemed purer and more transparent than what we were used to in Havana. The mansions, which you could hardly see for leafy trees, were enormous and surrounded by long grass. There was an overall sense of neglect in the contrast between the splendour and silence of the empty streets and the gardens abandoned to weeds and the sigh of the sea breeze. Each house occupied a block or more of luxurious vegetation.

The jeep stopped on a stony verge in front of large gates. At the discreet hoot of the horn, a young militiawoman appeared and opened them wide. The vehicle crunched down the gravel drive, coming to a halt in front of a neoclassical limestone building, slimy with damp and moss, its walls half covered by creepers reaching to the roof, its windows barred and shuttered. The front doors, standing proudly between columns of white marble, were solid wood with extraordinary pointed stained glass insets. They opened to reveal the black and white mosaic floor of an anteroom to a glass-domed indoor garden (like an Andalucian patio) with a fountain in the middle, encircled by wide galleries leading to a succession of doors. There was something modern about the style, a Byzantine-Roman-Californian mishmash that looked as if it was from a Hollywood set.

The Captain, who had jumped out of the jeep and rushed inside the house while I stared incredulously at my magnificent surroundings, reappeared with a couple of individuals, joined by a third from another door at the back. With typical Cuban irony, Pantoja alluded to 'the entire army' as he briefly introduced 'another Argentine' to 'three compatriots'. A cursory handshake left us standing looking at each other. The quartet we formed left a great deal to be desired. Nobody looked like a hero: more like villains in a police line-up. In a comic strip, there would have been a bubble saying, 'I'm not going anywhere with these guys.'

The tension ebbed after Pantoja gave us a quick run-down of our programme: first, unload the weapons from the jeep and put them in a store-room; then a tour of the house and grounds before eating; then wait for Segundo who would come that night, with someone else. We would receive provisions twice a week, as well as being given breakfast and dinner. Our only other visitors would be army personnel involved in the training, accompanied either by himself or his assistant Manolito. Obviously, we would not be allowed out. Olo Pantoja took his leave.

My three compatriots forgot their momentary doubts, and proved very friendly, even happy. An exchange of ambiguous personal questions, and tacitly secretive replies, placed us generally from the Argentine provinces – myself and two others – and the fourth from Buenos Aires. The latter, naturally the most cool, was also the tallest, had the best build, was self-assured but nice and polite with it. He took charge and suggested we continue exploring the house, as they had been doing when I arrived. The other two were from the Chaco. The thin bony one, hatchet-faced, pock-marked, and with a stiff crew cut, seemed a no-nonsense tough guy of few words. The other looked like a meticulous Italian immigrant from deepest Umbria who had swapped his mountain farmer's clothes for a shirt and trousers with an impeccable crease he ironed himself. His attention to detail was obsessive: his shirt sleeves folded only twice, his two top shirt buttons undone to show the hairs on his chest, etc., and very well mannered. None of us seemed to have a name, so the Argentine expression '*che*' filled the gap.

Our food, brought in an army jeep, was barracks food. In Cuba now there was no separate food for officers, as is usual in Latin American armies. Conversation was dominated by the endless twitter of Pepín, our militiaman who we insisted ate with us. He was from a group attached to the Ministry of the Interior (MININT). Sworn to secrecy, he was dazzled by the mission he had been given: to help relax and entertain a group of Argentines led by the legendary Che. He showed a real passion for guns, and knew all the models and their features. Swearing he had used all of them in a variety of circumstances, he imitated the sound they made with a special onomatopoeia: 'Piripitipam!' There was nothing for it but to call him that, *Piripitipam*, from then on.

Cubans ate early, like the Swedes. So it was not even dusk when, having coffee, we awaited the arrival of Segundo, as Pantoja called him. A jeep finally turned up. Several men got out, among them Masetti. His greeting indicated he knew everybody, but did not show how well. He said he was pleased the whole group was here, including a young lieutenant he introduced as Che's bodyguard, name of Hermes, who would be joining the group and living with us 'until death do us part,' as they say. We set up a table under the dome on the patio and began our first meeting as the 'army general staff'.

Masetti had experience of organizing a work schedule with disparate people, so he knew we had to start by getting to know each other. He did a quick profile of everyone present, starting with himself. We all knew who he was, but it was useful to see how he fitted into the picture. He said that, like the rest of us, he was joining something he believed in because the idea came from someone he respected: Che. No one doubted Che's commitment to building the Revolution in Cuba, least of all him. But it had always been clear that Che wanted to take the struggle to Argentina, and Fidel Castro had supported him in this from the early days in the Sierra Maestra. Yet such a transcendental decision could not be left to chance. Che could not just get up and leave tomorrow; he could not neglect one revolutionary duty to take on another. Until such time as he could leave his Cuban responsibilities, he wanted the ground prepared for when – to call a spade a spade – he would be free to lead the armed struggle in Argentina, his homeland. So, time was of the essence.

We needed to set up a base as quickly as possible, explore the terrain, get to know local people, and set up channels of communications. We also needed to establish contacts in the cities, and create a countrywide support network so we could train anyone willing to run the same risks and fight for the same dreams. Such a huge project needed a minimum of people, but a maximum of qualities: sacrifice, stoicism, military skill, humanity. We did not need supermen, only men with moral integrity, human dignity, and a sense of shame at belonging to a society that does not value a man's freedom.

Masetti had already been able to do military training, since the encroaching Stalinism had decreed he was out of political favour for other work. Sponsored by his mentor Che, he was one of the first batch of officers to pass out of the Rebel Army's new military academy. Now a captain, Che had formally appointed him his second in command. The next to be introduced, the guy from Buenos Aires, was a doctor who had arrived in Cuba just before me, motivated by the same instincts and passion. A similar fortuitous chain of events had brought him here. A specialist in preventive medicine, he had worked in the countryside on the chronic diseases endemic to the island and got friendly with several Rebel Army doctors. They noted his enthusiasm for the Revolution and put him in touch with Masetti. From his name, Leonardo Werthein, I guessed he was Jewish.

The lads from the Chaco were the result of the trip my own guardian angel, Alberto Granado, had made there at Che's behest the previous winter, a couple of months before our meeting in his macabre pathology lab. Alberto had contacted left-wing groups in the city of Resistencia, had done a quick evaluation (although way below the required minimum checks), and deemed them potential candidates. He invited them to Havana to discuss the possibility of taking the armed struggle to Argentina. Back in Cuba, Granado organized their trip and they had arrived a few days before the training started.

Of the two, hatchet face was the most able. He was a mechanic, a weapons expert, and had hunted by himself in the '*impenetrable*', the desolate wastes of the Gran Chaco where even the indigenous people don't like going. He knew the history of devastation in Argentina's two northernmost provinces, the Chaco and Formosa, was used to the rigours of the mountainous forests, and familiar with new technology. Rather unsociable and shy, he seemed committed, no holds barred. His name was Federico Méndez.

His friend from the Chaco lost his name in subsequent events, and became Miguel, a pseudonym he chose himself. Of all of us, he looked the healthiest and most sporty, a classic candidate for the Argentine military academy. Then there was me, who coughed the whole time from the aftermath of my recent bout of flu. It eventually turned into a chronic bronchial condition.

Masetti did not want to be involved in those parts of the project Che would deal with personally. His job was to oversee the training and to get the group to bond. We would be taught by a large number of specialist instructors, although numbers were to be kept to a minimum. None of them, no matter how important, must know our real identities. The only exceptions were those responsible for the support operation, like Olo Pantoja, and a team led by Comandante Barbaroja (Red Beard) Piñeiro from the intelligence services. The rest would know only our pseudonyms, and we would get used to calling each other by these names. For example, from now on, Masetti was Segundo. The doctor opted for Fabián, although he would have liked Alejandro, Fidel's name in the Sierra. Federico chose Basilio after a much-loved uncle, his Chaco friend was Miguel, and I became Laureano. Our original documents – passports, Argentine identity papers, driving licences, etc. – went via Segundo to the intelligence services. We were like newborn babies.

The only non-Argentine was Hermes, native of the Sierra Maestra. He had joined the Rebel Army just as Che was made a comandante (Fidel's first appointment) and was forming his own column. He was a young *mestizo*, just a boy then, whom Che taught to read in the few calm moments of the fiercest battles in the Sierra. He had been with Che ever since: during the long march, at the Battle of Santa Clara, and the triumphant entry into Havana. After an army training course, which he finished with the rank of lieutenant, he became one of Che's official body-guards. He had now temporarily left this post so that he could be *in situ* when his comandante returned to his native land. Hermes, a farm boy in a uniform too big for him, was like a typical Argen-tine *cabecita negra*. He would look a lot less conspicuous than us 'posh city boys' lost in the jungle. His immediate task was to inculcate military discipline into the group, establishing a logic that said, for example, whoever was on guard duty from two to four should make breakfast at five, or the person who was best at something should do that the most. As Segundo's expert in guer-rilla matters, he would teach us about exploring, choosing camp sites, and organizing camp life. He was allowed to keep his name given that in Argentina it would mean nothing.

The next step was to turn one of the bedrooms into a dormi-tory. Making us all sleep together would force us to accept that, come what may, we were a group, sharing things, even our personal irritations, dislikes or phobias. The life we had chosen required us to learn to respect each other, our need for sleep, our moods, sense of humour, silences and even our defects and obsessions, as long as they did not disturb the rhythm of the work or were not a deliberate provocation. The desired effect was a kind of symbiosis that would be our insurance policy in time of need. Our common weaknesses and strengths, shared needs and dangers, and joy at successes for the common cause had to become second nature. We had to learn to act as one, never doubting each other, instantaneously, like a gestalt, guided by all-encompassing force.

With this pretty feeble group of men, plus one more who would be appearing any time, the army of Che's dreams came into being: an army of five crazy guys, like Sandino's 'crazy little army' in Nicaragua, although Sandino had five hundred men, not five. In this initial phase, the operation of getting into the country meant it would be risky to be more numerous. It was on this point that we had different opinions, material for discussion and timid analysis. The subject came up repeatedly, but there was nothing for it but to accept the general plan. Being an armed group from the start meant we would have no recourse to the legal system. The idea (an ethical one) was not to operate clandestinely then resort to habeas corpus, but to dispense altogether with the law that only protects the rich and powerful against whom we were fighting. Added to which, we had to bring in weapons, and you can't put those in your luggage. We had to start by breaking civil laws pertaining to immigration and contraband, illicit association and forming an armed group, and military laws of insurrection and conspiracy to bring down the government. These laws were used exclusively against poor people, never against big-time smugglers, corrupt governments and military coup-makers. If we failed, we would be accused of trying to show that justice is not divine, but man-made and the product of a pre-mercantile human condition. Did we think we could do it? We thought we could.

For me, all great social transformations – historical and political contexts notwithstanding – have been led by the genius, will and charisma of a great man: leader and soul, brain and emotion, catharsis of the hidden, even ignored, desires and needs of a people at a given time. No mass movement can get off the ground without the emergence of such a figure, either out of the whirlwind of action, or from serenity and reflection, no matter how much praise populists heap on the masses. They can generate spontaneous social movements, but without the figurehead they are nothing but a boil erupting on the skin. From Spartacus to

Mandela, Alexander the Great to Mao, Jesus Christ to Gandhi, the existence of the leader justifies the moment.

However, there are intellectuals who not only reject the notion of the great leader but actually demonize him and strip him of importance; intellectuals who watch the century go by from their armchairs, building castles in the air — like the socialist camp — without lifting a stone, until the castle collapses and they move seamlessly on to something else. But to lift the stone, you have to roll up your sleeves and run risks, and face the possibility, inherent in history, that your goals be misappropriated, and your dreams turned to dust.

For me, Che embodied honesty and ethical behaviour in the smallest details of every one of his actions. The masses, who will follow a man because of his ideas, even after he is dead, hate intellectual arrogance which, they sense, is expressed in books they will never read, and symbolizes a superior class that despises them.

The crazy side of our project, the feeling that we were insanely on our own, did not intimidate me. It excited me. My only doubt was existential. Do I do it, or do I watch others do it?

8

Training and the Missile Crisis: October 1962

It was daybreak. 'Get up . . . !' barked Hermes. Nobody seemed to have heard him, so he repeated in Cuban: 'Get up, *coño*!' We looked at him as if he were mad. His work schedule had begun with breakfast at six, followed by a series of exercises that from now on would be our introduction to the day. By nine o'clock, we had run, jumped, crawled, and flexed our muscles. Surely there must be some mistake? Then Olo Pantojo appeared with our first 'instructor', an armaments specialist the Castroist rebels had inherited from Batista's army. Another new arrival was Ariel, from the Cuban intelligence services, who would be supervising the team of instructors on behalf of the Interior Ministry. His real name was Juan Carretero. He gave a speech to the effect that his team would do their job to the best of their ability, and try to do justice to the request for assistance from someone whom it was an honour to serve: Comandante Che Guevara. He was sure we would respond with the same effort and dedication. The course would be intensive but he expected that in three months we would have reached a level of preparation on a par with that of a specialist army officer. 'Good luck. *Patria o muerte!*'

The instructor began his class by demonstrating how to use an old German Mauser, model 1894, from the Spanish-American war, and then went on, symbolically, to a US Springfield of the same period, both with a hand-ridden bolt. It was a very powerful gun with a hefty recoil if the poor idiot firing it did not hug it to his body. We had to take it apart and put it together time and time again, piece by piece, until we did it perfectly, and in record time. We had to clean the guns, oil them, polish them, caress them, as if they were erotic objects, until we got used to their roundness, their weight, their smell and their rigid and implacable presence.

We spent a week digging through the entrails of rifles, machine guns, pistols and carbines of all nationalities, ranging from the Winchester used in the genocide of the indigenous peoples of the US, to the modern Belgian FAL rifle used in the more recent dark history of the Congo. The latter was an automatic rifle we would presumably have to face one day, since it was used in Argentina by both the regular army and the Gendarmerie, the special anti-smuggling border police. After weapons dismantling, came shooting practice. We were taken to the Ministry of the Interior shooting ranges in the countryside. By mid-morning, Hermes had destroyed any concept of normality by making us crawl through the undergrowth with our noses to the ground, swing like monkeys through trees, flay our bodies by trying to run through bushes as prickly as barbed wire, and lie immobile on piles of enormous red ants that appeared out of the sand in their thousands. They infiltrated our uniforms and the damp and delicate parts of our skin, covering us from neck to groin with little bags of formic acid that burned like hell.

The cavalry of Olo Pantoja, Manolito, Iván and Ariel, appeared in the nick of time to rescue us from the clutches of that obsessive *guajiro*, who was convinced that to train was to demolish. After a brief snack, we went exhausted, scratched, bruised and swollen, to get beaten with rifle butts and have our ear drums burst by various thunderous explosions until we learned to distinguish between them. They fired over our backs when we tried to wriggle free of the barbed wire we were crawling under, until we thought our arses and souls were indelibly tattooed by gunshot. We also practised with live hand grenades after minimal instruction: 'Wrap your hand tightly around the grenade, undo the safety catch, make sure your angle of flight allows you to throw with an outstretched arm, throw it forcefully and accurately towards the target, drop face down on the ground and count to ten, by which time the grenade should have exploded.' At my first attempt – after Pantoja demonstrated by running zigzag towards some trenches, throwing first the grenade, and then himself head-long behind some rubble – I followed his instructions and we both lay with our hands over our ears waiting for the explosion. Ten seconds, ten minutes, went by but nothing happened. Pantoja went to investigate and came back with the grenade intact. I had forgotten to undo the safety catch.

The explosives instructor was like a fugitive from a Kubrick film. He piled up an arsenal of howitzers, mortars, shells, guns, anti-personnel mines, anti-tank mines, dynamite, bottles of nitro-glycerine, packets of C4 (explosive), potassium chlorate, gunpowder, fuses, every type of detonator, all live and ready to explode at the slightest gaff. Not all at the same time, of course. His attention to safety was absolute, but it was not contagious. 'Do exactly as I do and nothing will happen, *chico*!' But if some-thing did happen, we would all go up in smoke. His appearance did not inspire confidence. He was missing an eye, fingers of one hand or perhaps the whole hand, I don't remember, and he had deep scars on his forehead, irrefutable evidence of previous 'acci-dents'. He insisted safety precautions had to be observed. 'With the safety catch in this position, it can't go off', he said as he banged a mortar ferociously against the table, while we ran for cover petrified. 'The plastic explosive that wreaked havoc in the war in Algeria is like putty, you can drop it, no problem', he said, throwing it on the floor; 'you can chew it and swallow it like marzipan', he added, and ate a mouthful; 'you can burn it,' and he set fire to it.

At the shooting range, his classes verged on collective suicide. The idea was to teach us to make explosives with household materials. We mixed carbons, sugars, sulphurs, chlorates (with wooden tools, of course), put them in a tin, attached a detonator and a timed fuse, or a capsule of sulphuric acid, and buried it. The explosion made a crater one metre in diameter. Our brains started receiving warning signals, and enhanced reactions to the least sign of danger but, above all, a heightened awareness of everything around us.

We got back from the practice range only to fall yet again into the clutches of Hermes who, in the meantime, had planned a complicated commando operation to attack the house. Some members of the team had to defend it and the rest of us had to drag ourselves round the outside trying to get in without being seen. Each day ended with a meal, followed by obligatory reading material before bed, and even the night could be interrupted without warning to send us in pursuit of some fictitious nocturnal objective that the malicious *guajiro* dreamed up for us.

On one of those nights, the sixth (later to be the fifth) member of our group made his entrance. At midnight we had to dress in full kit, carry a backpack with twenty-five kilos of random objects, a rifle with full quota of ammunition, a pistol, provisions and a canteen of water, and set off on a twenty kilometre march, 'the mother of all tests', with ten minutes rest every forty-five minutes, behind our new *compañero*, chief of the Havana Revolutionary Police, Comandante Abelardo Colomé Ibarra. His boyhood nickname, and now his nom de guerre, was Furry. Standing in an official jeep with a radiotelephone, he set the pace through the deserted unfamiliar streets on the outskirts of Havana, respecting the designated rests which coincided with our being about to pass out. In those days in Cuba, a group of men marching round at night armed to the teeth was either part of a counter-revolutionary invasion, or barking mad. That was us.

Furry was very young, barely twenty, another of those boy commanders to emerge from Che's column. He was seriously wounded at the battle of Santa Clara when an anti-tank grenade exploded. It went off a metre from his head, a metal shard piercing his forehead and lodging itself there. His guerrilla war was over, but he went on to have a brilliant military career. He became Cuba's most decorated combat soldier and its highest ranking general. He commanded 15,000 Cuban troops in Angola in 1976, a war that changed the course of the region's history and brought to power Angola's first national people's government under President Agostinho Neto. Furry was recalled to Havana, wreathed in laurels, and replaced by Arnaldo Ochoa, another much-decorated and famous general before he was executed in 1989. Furry was made minister of the interior that year. His slim distinguished face, of white Spanish stock, was turned dark, almost blue/black, by a five-o'clock shadow shaved down to his collar, from whence sprouted a mass of black hair that carpeted his body to his extremities. Hence his nickname.

The march passed off uneventfully. For the record, it was more of a speed trial than anything else, since we were on asphalt roads, doing an impossible-to-fathom circuit, with only the lights of the jeep to guide us. We didn't sleep, even when we got back, because we had to clean and cure our blisters. But we all passed 'the mother of all tests' without asking for clemency. Furry gave us the nod, commenting in passing to Masetti that with us he was ready to go anywhere. Masetti explained it was no idle compliment. Furry would, in fact, be coming with us, to help set up a rearguard base somewhere on the Bolivian-Argentine border.

My relationship with Masetti, begun in his house in Havana, developed on two dissimilar but not mutually exclusive levels. First because I was the only one in the group familiar with our eventual zone of operations, that area of Salta separated from Bolivia by the Bermejo and Pilcomayo rivers, a region covered with tropical forest and inhabited by indigenous cannon fodder for the agricultural, timber and cattle enterprises, and by the poverty-stricken descendents of the ancient Inca Collasuyo, now sharecroppers for the landowning oligarchy. And second because we had become good friends: we had the same sense of humour, we had lived in Buenos Aires at the same time, had mutual friends, shared tastes, a passion for politics, a desire to be involved, but most of all because we liked talking. Masetti did not live in the house but came every day for strategy classes and sometimes shooting practice. The rest of the time he was mired in the quicksands of bureaucracy, setting up the part of the operation Che did not have time for.

As soon as he arrived at the house, he would come and chat with me. I always played devil's advocate. My role apparently was to say 'yes, but . . .', although all I wanted to do, in fact, was to dispel my doubts. The resulting discussions increased our knowledge and confidence in the project. Masetti and I communicated on the same wavelength. We liked fooling about but, as Masetti himself said, we were also down to earth.

For different reasons, but mostly because we saw each other every day and both liked talking, I also became friends with Fabián, the doctor. (Basilio, who had many more technical skills than I, was anti-social, and Miguel did not talk at all). Fabián was, on the other hand, a Che fanatic and a bit of a fundamentalist. He was obsessed with something that was on TV a lot at the time: discovering hidey-holes in abandoned mansions – 'a cache or stash' – where people who had 'temporarily' emigrated to Miami had hidden fortunes in jewellery, art, antiques, etc. We inspected every wall, every nook and cranny, of the house. We even sussed the different widths of certain walls. Using Fabián's stethoscope and our knuckles to knock on particular spots, we eventually discovered two hidey-holes, although the so-called treasure wasn't worth having. One contained a big-game hunting rifle and a double-barrelled shot-gun, quite special. Another had papers and ornaments, sentimental stuff that was difficult to carry. It was all handed over to security.

One afternoon before he left, Masetti announced that Che would be coming that night. Or rather, it would be almost daybreak given Che's duties at the Ministry. We would no longer be a bunch of loose ends who didn't know if they fitted together until an important milestone would give them coherence. With our chief before us, we would be a cohesive unit welding hopes, passions, fears and joys into the metal needed to sustain the heart and soul of such an endeavour. We downed endless cups of coffee in silence. Then Hermes saw an escort jeep, followed by a car.

Che and Masetti got out and came straight to our table under the dome. For some, it was their first meeting. But for all of us, including Masetti and Hermes, it was very special.

The scene is still vivid in my mind. I remember the exact position of the table on the patio, at the end of the gallery, on the left, under the glass dome open to a clammy night sky. I remember how we were seated around it, and I associate it with old Argentine engravings of *cabildos*, council meetings and patriotic gatherings. Except that in the old lithographs, the founding fathers, in velvet jackets with big lapels, are all sitting on one side of a table, facing a throng of citizens. Here, we were all on one side of the table facing a solitary hero sprawled in a chair, letting bureaucracy seep from his exhausted body, as he asked for a glass of water and a coffee.

From his long exposition (the political framework and military plans later merged in my mind with other conversations and analysis), I have retained his sense of solidarity, philosophy, utopia. He said he understood that our presence there, around the table, meant we shared an ethical view of the world, and implied total commitment to our joint project. It had to be made absolutely clear that there would be no benefits in the future, only sacrifices in the here and now. Although the revolutionary objective might be to take power, we would not get the reward, even if the aim were achieved. Most probably none of us would live to see it. 'Remember, as from now, you are dead men. From now on, you're living on borrowed time.'

He said the situation we were witnessing in Latin America was atypical: a new reality, distorted, anti-historical, unacceptable to an empire accustomed to the servile docility of the oligarchies. The Cuban Revolution was a sickness the US system could not tolerate in its dominions. Plans were being hatched daily to destroy it and, in his opinion, they would end up harming it. But Cuba was more than a successful experiment looking for its own way forward, it was the last card for the peoples of America, and they had to play it. The US could destroy Cuba if they chose to wipe out the island, though the price would be very high. But they could not destroy its example, and if it spread throughout the continent, it would be imperialism that would be destroyed. In any case, the task we were setting ourselves was not the utopian dream of defeating the most powerful army in the Americas, but of making our presence felt, so that our people knew the armed struggle was an alternative, and not be afraid of it. Traditional politicians kept vain hopes alive. We would show that the people's dignity and future had to be fought for.

Che added that he could not go much further in the Cuban process. He had given his life to the Revolution but a revolutionary life was not to be wasted behind a desk. He sincerely believed, without false modesty, that he still had a role to play, and by playing it in Argentina he would serve the Revolution in South America as a whole. For this initial stage, he needed our help. We had to learn as much as we could in these classes, and remember how much they were costing the Revolution in increasingly difficult times. It was a bitter pill to swallow, knowing the resources being put at his disposal when every single man, every single dollar, taken from the Cuban budget was a sacrifice. We could not prolong the training more than strictly necessary. We needed to take responsibility for the project – under his leadership – as soon as possible, but Cuba would cover a minimum of the essential organizational support. Our task, as a group, was to keep ourselves safe, establish the camp in Argentina, familiarize ourselves with the region, increase our numbers, and avoid combat until he arrived.

He would visit us as often as he could while we were in Cuba, hopefully once a week, but he could not be sure. The climate of aggression against Cuba was a sign that new attacks were on the way, and we had to be ready by then. But we shouldn't feel we had to sit there in silence: that is, if we had any doubts or things we did not agree with, we should say so, not keep it to ourselves, because soon it would be impossible to withdraw.

He gave us the floor, but as often happens at conferences with a non-professional audience, no one had anything to say. Masetti, on the extreme right of the table, looked at us as if he had asked a question. Fabián played with a pencil, as if he was taking the minutes. Me, in the centre, looked at the others, while Basilio and Miguel, to my left, looked at the floor. Overcome by embarrassment and a sense of the ridiculous, but mostly because I thought saying nothing showed a lack of respect, I spoke. It is impossible to reconstruct my 'discourse', more or less a series of wobbly questions. The overpowering impact of Che's presence drowned out every sound that did not come from him.

I think I asked if we would be supported by any kind of organization once we got there. The reply: none at all, creating them is part of the task. I think I showed a certain incredulity at the disproportionate odds – half a dozen men versus millions. I remember his reply: in Cuba they were only a handful and they won. I think I insisted that, in Cuba, they had been a handful – many more when they had disembarked – but that the 26th of July Movement had been waiting in the wings. It was not the same, he retorted, to go in on a war footing after an event like the Moncada, as it was to go in clandestinely with an exploratory project: the 26th of July Movement came out of a previous isolated experience. I think I evoked the somewhat indigestible image of an ant on the edge of a three million square kilometre cake, and behind the ant image I suggested that our cause would have to prosper from the periphery towards the interior, not the other way round. I also brought up Argentina's unresolved internal political conflict, Peronism. His reply was that Argentina's problem is the dependence and poverty of its people while its wealth is in foreign hands. Peronism is only a symptom; for the struggle, the sickness is what counts.

I think that was how I explained my most immediate doubts, and they were not dismissed. On the contrary, they were adopted as subjects for further discussion. The meeting ended at dawn. Hermes mobilized the bodyguards and Che said goodbye with a mixture of exhaustion and satisfaction.

Classes resumed with renewed gusto. The team of instructors was joined by experts in radio-communications, telegraphy, self-defence, use of telescopic sights for light artillery, bazookas, mortars and recoil-less rifles – all weapons which can be easily captured from the enemy but are no use at all if you don't know how they work. Our instructors put a huge effort into teaching us the most exquisite details of warfare technology. Weapons exert a fascination, they mean danger. Despite their amazing technology, all weapons are horrible. Yet some have the fascination of horror.

We were choosing the best automatic weapons, weighing up size, weight and the most universal calibres. We left out some supposedly superior Soviet ones for the obvious reason that there were none in Argentina. The US infantry had developed a practically indestructible machine gun, the M3: a .45 calibre made completely of steel, with an enormous covered bolt the size of a piston – like a ghetto blaster. It had a hugely destructive capacity, but was very heavy. My preference for it was unfortunate, because I had trouble carrying it later on. The arms manufacturer, *Fabricaciones Militares*, had acquired the rights to make it in Argentina, although it was reproduced in .22 calibre, much lighter but just as effective.

Our apprenticeship continued, both theoretical and practical, and a constant stream of experts fought for the best and largest number of class hours. Well into the course, a special guest appeared, his visit cloaked in secrecy. He was a general and hero twice over, Spanish and Soviet. Masetti introduced him as Angelito. Over sixty, in a uniform without insignia, he was certainly angelic looking, not very tall, a bit chubby and balding, but a picture of health. He was quietly mannered and spoke excellent Spanish. Angelito said he would be lending a critical eye to some of our training sessions. He began there and then. During our stops for rest and food, he talked animatedly, picking our brains no doubt to see if we had any residue of intelligence.

Angelito was an admirer of Che's guerrilla tactics in the Sierra Maestra, and especially in the Escambray, a combination of guerrilla warfare and permanent German *blitzkrieg* which was now studied in Soviet military academies. Angelito had known defeat as well as victory, bitterness and glory. After the final Republican defeat in the Spanish Civil War, he had gone into exile in the Soviet Union with the Communist Party's combat contingent. There he had joined the Red Army and taken part in the victorious offensive right up to the fall of Berlin. Now also a Soviet general, the Soviet Communist Party's central committee had sent him to Cuba to advise on the creation of a new-style professional army. Despite his age, he proved he was in magnificent physical shape by doing back flips from a standing position, like a gymnast. He considered fitness of paramount importance. His name was Francisco Ciutat, a Catalan.

'Russian' weapons had begun appearing in Cuba. First to arrive were rifles (Czech actually) and the cylindrical barrelled 'Pepechá' machine gun, famed for its role in the fall of Berlin. Next to come were the 'four mouth' anti-aircraft guns which fired from four barrels simultaneously. They were being placed in strategic positions round the city, and were also seen being driven round on the backs of new Soviet lorries. The comandantes were now sporting the Macarov, a .45 calibre pistol with a quick-fire burst option that left any target like a colander. And finally, the 'best rifle in the world', the AK47, plus heavy artillery, tanks, etc. But they were just small beer. The big fish did not get much press, although rumours reached even our chaste ears.

The Soviets were building sites for intercontinental missiles. Nuclear perhaps? Between his first visit to our bunker and his second, Che had been to the USSR, talked to Khrushchev and signed military cooperation agreements that included bases and installations on Cuban soil for defensive purposes: radar, ground to ground missiles, ground to air missiles, etc. And why not strategic? Che did not talk to us about this level of military secrets, naturally, but after his trip he appeared less pessimistic. He seemed to be expecting large-scale confrontations and seemed almost to be welcoming them. He urged us to finish our training as soon as possible.

Meanwhile, each member of our group began to specialize, almost by natural selection, following an army unit's classic division of labour into operations, logistics, intelligence and communications. Masetti decided Basilio would be best at operations, Fabián at communications (as well as health), Miguel at logistics, and me at security and intelligence. We began having our classes separately, except for shooting practice and fitness. We also had medical and dental check-ups and I asked them to take an urgent look at my bronchitis, already turning to asthma. I wanted to follow Che's example, but not to that extent!

The training took a new turn, more romantic and scientific. I got very attracted to secrecy. Everything I was taught was secret, for my exclusive use. My self-defence instructor argued, realistically, that learning enough karate to fight even a beginner would take me a couple of years, so he concentrated on techniques to help me escape attacks from behind, or the pincer movements police used, adding a couple of 'lethal' blows for when I needed them. Fortunately, I never had occasion to use them.

October 1962 was a war of nerves, and of words. Accusations flew back and forth between the US administration and the Cuban Revolution. No one appeared to want to give way or try to relax the tension. On the contrary, diplomatic events added fuel to the fire. Ben Bella, having recently taken power in Algeria, arrived in Cuba in the middle of September, evidence of previous anti-imperialist collaboration. Anatole Gromyko, the Soviet foreign minister on a visit to the US, said the weapons delivered to Cuba were purely defensive. But on 22 October, Kennedy appeared on television, the U2 photos in his hand, to denounce the USSR for installing long-range strategic missiles in Cuba. In retaliation, he announced a naval blockade. Cuba declared a state of emergency, put its combat troops on the alert, and called for general mobilization. Che was made Commander of Western Forces — from Havana to the western tip of the island — presumably the first combat zone in the case of an invasion. If the Americans landed, they would not repeat the mistakes they made at the Bay of Pigs. They would try to secure one end of the island, with easy air and sea access, and a single military front.

9

Prague, Paris and Algiers: November–December 1962

The streets of Havana had lost their usual ebullience. Military trucks went by loaded with troops and militias. Sand bags were piled up at the entrances to buildings, and anti-aircraft guns set up in the city's squares. The people, usually so laid-back, became hurried and frantic. An electrifying collective anxiety seemed to have possessed those still trying to get onto overcrowded buses and trucks. Manolito dropped me off at the Revolutionary Armed Forces' hospital in the centre of Havana. It was assumed I would be treated for my bronchial infection and taken straight back to the house; Che wanted our group transferred to Pinar del Río, where his Western Command headquarters was. But the doctor who saw me was a comandante as well as head of the Pulmonary Infections Department and, although he understood the urgency, he was the one setting the timetable. After a series of tests, including a basal metabolism, he ordered a massive attack of antibiotics and ten injections of ten cubic centimetres of aminophylline to be applied twice a day. Five days of jabs, all told. 'You'll leave here good as new, *chico*, straight to the front', he said, as if stopping the Yankee marine corps single-handed depended on me. So I was hospitalized, and the support team came to tell me my *compañeros* had left for Pinar del Río.

The hospital was a modern, well-equipped building several storeys high. I was put in a three- or four-bed room on the tenth floor with a panoramic view. Being a military hospital, it was like a first-rate barracks. The leisure room TV worked but only on one channel: the missile crisis. The chairs were occupied by patients with differing degrees of illness but all predicted certain defeat for the imperialist invaders. Recently operated-upon patients and even those on their death beds demanded their clothes and weapons so they could join up again. Only notices on the walls and a finger on the lips of a beautiful nurse reminded us there should be silence. Doctors appeared, dripping scalpels in hands, at the slightest sign of news or a speech by Fidel. It was war-time euphoria given the military nature of the place, but was nonetheless typical of what the country was going through. The Cubans were ready to be incinerated rather than let arrogant imperialists ride roughshod over them.

The climate of confrontation got worse by the day. The island was blockaded to prevent the passage of Soviet cargo ships, their decks lined with more missiles, as the U2 photographs on US television showed. Looking out to sea, you could see US gunboats anchored at the limits of international waters. US planes violated Cuban airspace every day. On 25 October, a missile from one of the Soviet launch pads brought down one of the notorious spy planes. A rumour went round, Masetti told us later, that Fidel was visiting a Soviet missile site, and Russian officers were showing him the sophisticated control panels, with radar monitors giving precise positions. At that very moment, a high altitude U2 entered Cuban airspace. Putting theory and practice together, the Russian officer demonstrated step by step the sequence of maximum combat alert (deactivation of the security shield, activation of firing mechanisms) as the screen showed the U2 reaching the centre of the island.

'And now what?' asked the Commander in Chief. 'If we get an order to attack, we press this button, the radar guides the missiles, and the plane is destroyed', the Russian officer replied. To everyone's amazement, Fidel stretched out his long arm and pressed the button, murmuring 'Let's see if it's true, *coño!*' That the U2 was destroyed was certainly true. Two hundred thousand marines hurriedly boarded their transport planes, the Flying Fortresses filled their holds with bombs, Cuban soldiers said goodbye to their families, and whoever could do so downed a large shot of rum, in case it was his last.

With bruised arms, perforated by needles, I went off to join my comrades at the front. My journey was in vain, however, because a few hours after rejoining my group, Khrushchev agreed unilaterally to withdraw the missiles from Cuba in exchange for the US taking their missiles out of Turkey, and a commitment of non-aggression towards the island.

Che ordered our immediate return to training, intensified to cut short the timetable. On his second visit after we returned to the house in Havana, despite his exhaustion and sombre mood, he told us of the tension surrounding the crisis. The group had not seen him in Pinar del Río despite being near his headquarters in a cave in Los Portales, so we were all waiting expectantly. I remember him saying how he had been in a meeting with Fidel when there was a phone call from Carlos Franqui, editor of the newspaper *Revolución*. Fidel had thrown the phone onto the map table and, swivelling on his heels, had aimed a violent kick at a wall mirror, shattering it. No one had expected the Russians to take that decision.

Che was very pessimistic about the way the crisis had ended. He was sure that, left to its own devices, the US wanted to attack the Revolution and destroy it. Any other result would not be consistent with imperial intentions. They will never forgive Cuba for existing, and providing an example of a sovereign nation living in dignity and freedom. 'You', he said, 'must pull out all the stops and finish the most important parts of your preparation. The mountains will take care of the physical stuff, but other parts you can't do alone. I want you out of Cuba before November 15th.'

The classes increased and changed, especially mine. A jeep collected me every morning and brought me back at night. I spent hours working on keys and codes, encrypted and unencrypted, counter-intelligence techniques, methods of disinformation, interrogation and counter-interrogation, which in the end, was the only knowledge I ever used in critical situations. A lot of emphasis was put on the moral cost of such activities. Of what you must be prepared to sacrifice in order to be effective: family, pride, reputation, privileges, and life itself as a last resort. My instructors, who had been trained by the Soviets, probably the best espionage school in the world, had a lot of practical experience. I heard detailed accounts of unsung heroes who had given up everything, left their loved ones in that moral maze of ignorance, assumed another respectable (at the same time horrendous) identity, gone undercover to infiltrate Cuban counter-revolutionary groups in Miami, and stayed there indefinitely working for Cuban intelligence. As I learned all this, I felt as though it was a living death.

Yet intelligence did actually work in Cuba. The long lists of thwarted attempts by the US intelligence services to kill Prime Minister Castro and other leaders make the counter-intelligence team justifiably proud. But in the end, it is down to the undercover agents who pay with their honour. They will never be vindicated. We had to wait for the writer Norberto Fuentes to leave the country to discover that one of the 'President's men in the notorious Watergate case was a Cuban agent. The aim of the training was an almost perfect apprenticeship, but "if you screw up, *chico*, you screw up, we don't know you".'

At the same time, we worked on the details for our departure. In those days, Cuba had two ways out to the West for its 'commercial' flights (a euphemism because, one way or another, all the passengers were government officials): through Mexico or Prague. Our group would leave via Czechoslovakia, where we would wait for the infrastructure on the ground near the Bolivian–Argentine border to be put in place. The training programme had originally included a month's combat experience of the 'anti-bandit struggle' in the Escambray mountains, but this was not going to be possible. Otherwise, our general preparation was good.

There would be seven of us, travelling together but separately so to speak, on the first Cubana plane to leave the island for Prague since the October missile crisis: Masetti, Furry, Hermes, Federico, Leonardo, Miguel and myself. There would also be broad intelligence support from the embassy in Prague and from another comandante, Papito Serguera, who would act as the link between us, the Cubans and the Czechs; he would be the only person to see our faces. Specialists in secret operations, under orders from Olo Pantoja, Iván and Ariel, and from time to time, Ulises, another intelligence operative, came every day to bring us reasonably smart city clothes, take passport photos, and work on the invention of our personal profiles, appropriately equipped with family details, occupation and reasons for our journey.

Leaving Cuba, nobody escaped the meticulous eye of the CIA cameras either in Mexico, Gander (Canada), or Shannon (Ireland). When you got off the plane to refuel in Gander, you had to walk to the airport departure lounge in single file down a narrow stairway against a wall at the end of a huge hall. The cameras did not miss a single passenger detail, not only their faces, but also their walk, physique, tics and even socks. Neither could you avoid the KGB's cameras in Prague, Berlin or Moscow. Anything suspicious would lead to a tap on the back from some agent of control. This being so, our first problem arose even before we left Cuba.

One day in the second week of November, we began ridding the house of any trace of Argentine presence. Ariel's people picked up our belongings and Ulises took away the weapons and equipment in a van. He had unloaded a couple of new tyres from the back of the van, his own personal vehicle perhaps, and while arranging rifles, bazookas and machine guns on the floor, kept up a constant enthusiastic chatter. He was sorry he could not come with us because of his skin colour (dark mulatto) but assured us he would be 'in the thick of it' before us because he was going 'just over there, to the other coast', meaning Venezuela, where there were blacks, although not as cute as him. He put the tyres back on top of the pile of weapons and left.

Masetti decided Leonardo-Fabián could visit his family in Vedado while we were both going to get some X-rays. Leonardo had fifteen minutes to go into his apartment, kiss his wife and children and come back out. To me, it seemed more of a torture than a favour. Half an hour later, I sent him a Morse code signal on the horn of our van parked in front of the building. Leonardo came running out, his heart in his boots.

Masetti and I had a conversation about this little episode. Leonardo seemed to get more lenient treatment because he was the first of the group to be chosen and seemed to have some unspecified backing. He had come to Masetti via Che who had heard about an Argentine doctor who was prepared to sacrifice everything. This backing was doubtless in Leonardo's imagination since none of us had any privileges. But if anyone tended to idealize our roles, it was Leonardo. During our chats, illusions of glory could be glimpsed engulfing his dreams. But I reminded Leonardo that the clearest long-term offer we had received was to end up as corpses.

Masetti had insisted from the start that we constantly improve our personal skills because we would each eventually be responsible for a specific area. I had been put in charge of group security both during our journey and afterwards; this implied psychological rather than physical vigilance. I also had to make sure no one put his foot in it and that we programmed into our psyches plausible explanations for the group's every move, so that we would come out of any awkward situation smelling of roses. It would mean implementing what I had learned, without favouritism or pulling rank. It was my job and everybody had to comply. To boost my self-esteem (to make me more ruthless), Masetti told me that Angelito, the Soviet-Spanish general who was evaluating us, had made a very positive assessment of the group as a whole. He had said that individually I was the best (I suppose he meant on a political level) but that he did not recommend taking someone Jewish. Masetti had not told Angelito that it was Leonardo who was Jewish, not me, because he did not want to spark a last-minute argument that went further than personal opinion, since it was clear the Russian general had been given improper access to inaccurate information.

On our last night in Havana, Masetti suggested we put on the smart clothes we had been given to travel in. He himself arrived unrecognisable in a dark suit and tie. Che had suggested he take us for a slap-up meal. We went in one of those impressive American convertibles to the only decent restaurant in those days, the famous Tropicana nightclub, where we ate like shipwrecked sailors, watching the hypnotic and sensual spectacle of the revolution-fired *mulattas*.

At Rancho Boyeros, now José Martí International Airport, Barbaroja Piñeiro, Ariel and some of our instructors, came to say their formal goodbyes in a VIP lounge away from curious eyes. They handed us our passports, prepared by the intelligence services' forgery section. I felt as if a bucket of cold water had been tipped over me. It was farcical. The Cubana plane was leaving in half an hour. Wanting, and needing, to know who I was, I opened my new (Uruguayan) passport only to find that the photograph was of a tall man of about twenty, with blond hair and blue eyes. Although I was bald on top, I actually had a mass of black hair encircling my bald pate, and dark brown eyes. I would also be thirty one in four months. Only a joke (a last-minute test of my role as group security chief), or premeditated sabotage, could explain this stupidity.

'With this document', I protested flippantly, 'I might as well travel with the handcuffs already on.' Masetti grabbed the passport and took Piñeiro aside. Apparently, they had had no choice, it was the only Uruguayan one to hand, and we had built a profile around my being a Uruguayan citizen. Besides, they argued, we were landing in Czechoslovakia, a friendly country. They would send another one through the embassy. This was not exactly true.

We had to run the camera gauntlet at Gander and Shannon. An intelligence service used to fooling the CIA could not use such a feeble excuse, not after three months work. And in any case my final destination was La Paz, not Prague. Again, Masetti said nothing.

Leaving tropical Cuba and landing in the frozen wastes of Prague airport was like waking up as a dung beetle. Papito Serguera was aware of this and was waiting for us with a van full of winter clothes and boots. He drove us for an hour out of the beautiful city to a summer tourist hotel, for government or party members no doubt, beside Lake Slapy, buried under half a metre of snow. The hotel was closed, as was to be expected, but was looked after by a family of caretakers. While a young Czech who worked at the Cuban Embassy filled in all the forms, a beautiful twenty-year-old pushing a cart loaded with bedclothes, signalled to us to follow her. She showed us to our rooms. Doubles for Hermes and Leonardo, Federico and Miguel, and as luck would have it, singles for Masetti and myself. Furry was staying in Prague with the Havana sugar mission, so he left with Serguera. We had a planning meeting and got quickly acquainted with the Czech national miracle: beer. Masetti decreed permanent activity to stop us getting soft through lack of exercise, and this meant an extra job for me: interpreting without language.

I went to ask the girl about meal times and maps of the region. She was called Zlata. Our only common language was drawing. There was paper and pencil on the reception counter and we invented an extraordinary language. I drew a clock and a plate of food, separated by a question mark. She wrote the hour. I drew a rising sun and a steaming cup of coffee. She counted the time on my fingers. This became our means of communication: it was foolproof. Zlata lent us a scale map of paths and villages round the frozen lake. We would choose a house a few kilometres away and set off after breakfast. In this way, we kept much fitter than in Cuba even. The winter kit we had been lent was good and we could walk through deep snow. By adding a few kilometres every day, we were soon reaching the furthest villages. They were small, never more than a dozen houses and barns, but always with a good tavern where, by drawing a picture of steaks, chicken legs, cauldrons hanging over fires and spoons filling soup plates, we created a good atmosphere and, between toasts and hugs, ate some wonderful stews washed down with the best beer in the world. We would return to our hotel sated, and exhausted.

These daily manoeuvres aroused official suspicion and soon reached embassy ears. Perhaps we had unwittingly set off local intelligence's nervous system. We had come across an area of woodland fenced off by metallic sheeting and barbed wire, in the middle of which stood a solid wooden tower with a metal thing on top pointing at the sky. Federico examined it and declared it to be a 'trig point', of geographical and military interest. The last thing we wanted was to upset the Warsaw Pact. Back at the hotel (this strange exclusive complex at our disposal), we dined like red princes, waited on particularly solicitously.

Papito Serguera appeared like a wet blanket with the news that we had to restrict our walks. We could have argued that our 'innocent holiday' was a reward, or even R&R, but Masetti chose to take us back to Prague. He was impatient with Havana's silence, and wanted them to know. The tough marches through the snow were over. Our group split up, with Masetti and Furry going to a hotel in the centre, and the rest of us to the Hotel Intercontinental out near the airport. Every morning a tram from in front of the hotel left us in Wenceslas Square, in the heart of the old city.

We began to feel trapped. Time passed with no news of further plans. Masetti's temperament could not stand anything under-hand, any whiff of a set-up, and he unloaded his frustration by harassing his Cuban contacts. He didn't like grumbling alone, and since he had got used to discussing things with me – or rather talking *at* me – I had many sleepless nights. But I was an obliging witness to his decisions.

After the group left on the morning tram, Masetti asked me to go to his hotel to help decode the messages he had been sending and receiving from Havana. He appeared to have done nothing else since we had arrived. Masetti's antennae, sharpened by being manoeuvred out of *Prensa Latina* by the old guard Cuban communists, suspected a deliberate about-turn in Havana, or even a desire to abandon the plans altogether, over and above the agreement made with Che, now his sole point of contact. However, he had to acknowledge that Che's huge workload might cause him to lose sight of how the project was doing. And don't forget this was not a government plan but Che's personal request for collaboration from a state facing immense difficulties. For practical reasons, both we and Che were reliant on the Cuban intelligence services, and communications were in the hands of a circle of operators with no political autonomy, or perhaps too much: time would tell. The return messages always recommended patience, but gave no timetable. Masetti wanted to take a step sideways and break our dependence on Cuba, at least while we were waiting. This was not easy in a 'socialist camp' country. We needed a more revolutionary base.

One night in his hotel, in the early hours, after a long diatribe questioning the role of Barbaroja Piñeira as a presumed saboteur serving Fidel's prudence (which I found logical, even probable), Masetti decided to stop messing about and get alternative help from his Algerian friends. I slept in an armchair. By morning he was ready to leave and we sorted out his ticket and visa. By midday, he was on the flight to Algiers. He had sent a cable prior to departure and, when the plane stopped in Rome, his Algerian visa was waiting for him. Running *Prensa Latina*, he had got used to moving between countries on the spur of the moment. The technique, he told me, was to not get stuck anywhere. Just take the first flight in the right, or approximately right, direction, and keep sending telegrams. Every country had a telegraph office. Three days later, he was back in Prague with an open and unconditional offer of help for our group, a personal offer from the triumphant leaders of the Algerian Revolution.

In a significant and appreciative gesture, Ahmed Ben Bella, the Algerian president, and Houari Boumedienne, his defence minister, had met Masetti at the airport in Algiers. It was Masetti who had originally broken the barrier of ignorance separating the Cuban Revolution from a people facing Europe's largest army in a cruel struggle for their freedom. He had penetrated the French defences on the Tunisian border with members of the National Liberation Front (FLN) whom he had contacted in Tunis, and reached the mountain headquarters of the leader of the rebel forces, just as he had done all those years before in the Sierra Maestra with Fidel. He had asked Boumedienne how Cuba could help them. 'With weapons', the Algerian had replied. Masetti retraced his steps to Havana, talked to Che and Fidel, and on the basis of his detailed report, Fidel had said: 'There's a Cubana flight to Europe this morning, be on it. Ask Boumedienne where he wants the weapons sent.' Without sleeping, and almost without breathing, Masetti flew back. A ship loaded with enough weapons for a battalion left Havana for Algeria. The ship's captain received a telegram giving its destination while at sea. Masetti was one of that special breed of men, as Che had once said of Frank País. Not for nothing were they friends.

We made hasty preparations to leave Prague for Algiers, with a stop in Paris on the way. We still had our same documents. I bought a bottle of bleach and some cotton wool. I tested various strengths and applied it to my hair. Nothing happened. Then, suddenly, my hair lit up like a light bulb and turned an angry yellow. My face looked like a mask beneath it, and I had to dye my eyebrows to compensate. Masetti, whose humour was pretty dark, said we looked like a cabaret troupe, complete with transvestite. Passport controls were not as rigorous in those days as they are now, so visual details were very important. At the best of times, a flight from Prague to Paris would be expected to be carrying a cargo of potential spies coming to infiltrate the 'free' world. Getting through immigration was where the thin bit of our thread could snap. I let the group pass before I stood in line. The *gendarme* looked at my ridiculous dyed hair, stamped my passport and handed it back to me, saying '*Allez, allez . . .*'.

It was 30th December 1962. We arrived in the country I had dreamed of when I was an adolescent. In my eyes, it was not a new city. I had just been slow to open them. The bus from Orly dropped us at Les Invalides, and a huge taxi took us to a hotel a few blocks away along the Seine: the Palais d'Orsay, at the station of the same name. On the other side of the river were the Tuileries Gardens, with the Louvre to the right. When I opened the blind in my room, the Eiffel Tower was to the left.

The first thing we needed to do was to organize our onward journey. We eventually got reservations for 2 January and Masetti sent a telegram requesting Algerian visas. After that, he gave me a free hand to take the group wherever I wanted. Guidebook in hand, I organized a cultural tour.

The following day was New Year's Eve and Paris 'was a moveable feast'. People greeted each other in the street, and kisses from both sexes were planted on our deprived cheeks. We went to the Louvre, up the Eiffel Tower, to Montmartre where we ate with artists, and along the wide boulevards to the Bastille, where sitting in a corner brasserie reminded me more of Maigret than Robespierre. We got to the Latin Quarter more dead than alive but soon recovered, drinking wine until dawn. Was there another socialist paradise? Do police inspectors blow kisses? Can you sing the Marseillaise? Or the Internationale? Did you know both anthems are French? Not since then, not even at the double goodbye to the century and the millennium, have I experienced such general popular euphoria, so joyous and free from racism and discrimination. We embraced bankers and tramps alike, the difference no more than a work uniform. With champagne, fine cabernet, or fiery grappa in their hands, they offered it to us in glasses, or straight out of the bottle – unpardonable.

The 1st of January 1963 dawned late and bleak, our farewell to our bourgeois life. We devoted the day to museums, combing the boulevards of Saint Germain and Saint Michel for existentialism, looking for the hunchback in Notre Dame, or the phantom at the Opéra, reading newspapers, sipping espressos and Pernods in local bistros. Masetti knew more French than he let on, but he had decided our newspaper reader would be me, who barely remembered any school French, although I did manage to half-decipher the international news.

Leonardo insisted on going to Maxim's, the capital of the culinary arts' most favourite restaurant. 'Just to see the birds that go there', he said. We had to walk there, and we took it slowly. I noticed that every time we passed a post box, Miguel seemed to have a stone in his shoe, and slowed down. I waited for him, and we carried on to the next one, where again he needed to take off his shoe. Nearby was a *pissoir*, one of those numerous Paris locations with practical uses apart from simply peeing. I went in so I could observe him. Sure enough, he went up to the red box. I was behind him in a flash. 'What are you doing?' I asked, as if I had caught him red-handed buying an ice-cream in this wintry cold. I kept the postcard to his mother in Argentina, after assuring him I would consider it a simple error on his part as long as he didn't try it again or move a finger without my permission.

Federico knew Miguel from the Chaco so I asked him to help me monitor the situation. Federico asked for time to discover Miguel's true intentions before I told Masetti. My view, knowing Masetti, was that we had to jolly Miguel along at least until we had got on the plane for Algiers. If we did not, we would be up the Seine without a paddle. My relationship with Federico took a qualitative leap forward. I had instinctively turned to him, not to anyone else, and from then on we trusted each other unreservedly. He became the *compañero* I could trust with my life, and it was mutual. That night, Federico and Miguel came to my room to talk things over. It had been a slip-up, a desire to show off to his family that he was in Paris, deduced Federico, nothing more. We decided to keep the matter to ourselves for now. Once I was alone, I destroyed the card.

10

Death Takes Centre Stage: Algiers, January–May 1963

Algiers is built on the hillsides surrounding a bay. Stairways, like viaducts, straddle the Arab quarter (the Casbah), and divide it clearly from the French area. We were driven along the seafront to the very west of the bay, and up to a villa overlooking the sea. It was clearly an exclusive part of the city, formerly inhabited by families of naval officers from the French base of Mers-El-Kebir, a fortified position dominating the bay from atop the mountain to our left. We could see it through our binoculars. At the villa, Major Bajtik, who spoke Spanish and had met us at the airport with two other officers, Abdel and Muhamed, introduced us to a small troop of about a dozen soldiers, standing to attention on the lower patio. They would cater for our needs, cook for us, and look after the house security. In short, it was a *petite* garrison with guests.

It was not all admiring the view and eating, however. An intensive training programme had been designed around weekly weapons drills, shooting practice, analysis of their recent war's military strategy and combat operations. We would be examining how the combatants of the National Liberation Front (FLN) infiltrated the French border fortifications and their deployment in cellars and caves around the cities of Algiers, Oran and Constantine. A veteran of the war came to the house to talk about specific cases, and then accompanied us to the actual sites so we could see their strategic importance. We began with the fledgling FLN's first ambush on the edge of the desert, led by Ben Bella, one of its founding leaders. Bajtik took us to a place called Aflud. Other trips followed, and each week we would go over the hills behind the Casbah to a former French army barracks where hi-tech weapons captured from the French during the war had been stored. Celebratory rounds from different calibre rifles, machine-gun salvos, and bomb blasts left our heads buzzing, but it got us accustomed to different types of weapons.

Eventually we were taken on a tour of the French fortifications on the Tunisian and Moroccan borders; it was an incredible experience. The supposedly impregnable constructions were a wasteland of barbed wire, explosives and watch towers which had once been patrolled day and night, but had finally failed to prevent the FLN from breaching them. The fortifications extended in a straight line along both frontiers from the coast to beyond the mountains that descend into the Sahara. Seen from the sea, a cross section of the lines showed first a minefield about twenty metres wide, then a section of barbed wire wrapped round half-buried girders and crossheads, then metallic sheeting four metres high attached to solid iron posts draped with more barbed wire, in the middle a road patrolled by armoured cars, and on the other side the same metal sheeting, barb-covered girders, minefields, etc. Every five or six kilometres, a watch tower with high-powered spotlights lit up the centre road at the slightest sign of alarm and swept over the areas of barbed wire. Patrols from the watch towers would converge on any suspected breach of the fortifications.

Relations between the Algerians and Masetti's group, fraternal from the start, became almost organic, as if we were working on a common project. Although Masetti had re-established contact with Che through coded messages the Algerians sent and received for him, we were in the main isolated from Cuba and our whole stay was coordinated with Algerian staff officers. Not until February 1963, or perhaps March, did Papito Seguera appear, as if following in our footsteps, in his role as the brand new Cuban ambassador to the Socialist Republic of Algeria. There was upheaval while he got the embassy up and running. At first he came to the house every day, but his presentation to the diplomatic corps put an end to his free time and his visits. Papito had brought several belated messages, and reading them, and others he had received afterwards, sent Masetti into a fury all over again. Still no departure plans! Still calls for patience, even messages from Che saying just that. Masetti's mistrust went into overdrive, and he sent Furry to Havana with orders to speak to Che, and only to Che.

The messages clearly contradicted each other. In one that I helped decipher – the phrase is engraved on my memory – Che says: '*Nuestra atalaya se hunde lenta pero inexorablemente*' (Our vantage point is slowly but inexorably sinking), and he added that by now we should be in our zone of operation in northern Argentina. The 'vantage point' referred to was the island of Cuba, the highest point, from where one could see most clearly. By 'sinking', he did not only mean 'defeated' or 'invaded' but also that something unique was 'disappearing', or 'being submerged'. Compared to a message like this, the others – which spoke of waiting, being patient, practising, studying, eating well – did not make much sense. Furry played the diplomatic courier, taking the messages. He and Che examined the collected messages together, one by one. In a meeting I attended when Furry came back a week later, he said that Che had gone through the decoded originals saying: 'This is mine', 'This isn't', 'Nor is this', 'This one is mine', etc. That is, as Masetti explained, 'Colorado is conning us'. Colorado was Barbaroja Piñeiro.

Furry brought precise instructions. Che would take care of finalizing the basic support infrastructure, i.e. buying the *finca* (farm) near the Argentine/Bolivian border, equipment, weapons. He authorized Masetti to draw up his own plans, with the help of our Algerian friends, to travel to the destination as soon as he said 'Now!' Coordination with the Cuban bureaucracy, still indispensable, should function impeccably from now on. Our group had to travel illegally, with Cuban officials making contacts that were problematic in unfriendly countries. A minimum of infrastructure was needed. So that 'Ambassador' Papito did not have to act as messenger, it was decided I would be the link to him, since I was the one with most freedom of movement. Bajtik lent me his car and I went often to the Cuban Embassy, where I was received in all seriousness as the Ambassador's 'Soviet' friend, a good thing to be in those days. The 'Soviet' cover, for the benefit of Papito's staff, was doubtless because of my yellow hair.

Meanwhile, the group still had internal problems. Miguel showed signs of wanting to get out of his commitment. Since he probably could not find a legitimate way of doing so, he invented a kind of personal incompatibility with Masetti. The atmosphere between them soured and a general irritability infected us all. Stupid problems arose, like competitiveness in sport, which was where Miguel was the stronger. This latent machismo gradually led to open confrontation and an invitation to fight, which Masetti was happy to accept in an improvised boxing ring. Fortunately, a series of gastronomic commitments with the Algerian staff officers relaxed the tension for a couple of weeks.

One day Bajtik announced that Boumedienne would be coming to our house for a traditional Algerian meal to celebrate fraternal links with the Cuban–Argentine group. An army truck arrived with field cookers, tables and chairs, firewood and food, including cases of that great Algerian wine Mascará, and a beautiful lamb which defended itself valiantly, kicking to left and right, until a pitiful moan indicated its throat had been cut. The following morning, the truck came back with some army personnel who put together a kind of mechanical grill and lit the flames under it. A metre and a half above the fire, they put the skinned lamb on the spit, stuffed with chestnuts, vegetables, fruit, sweet and hot peppers, and chillies. They opened a ten kilo tin of Argentine fat and began smearing the lamb with a wide brush, as the spit turned and screeched slowly over the flames.

A few hours later, when all the fat was absorbed, an official car arrived with its escort, and out of it got the legendary victor of the bloodiest war ever won by humble peasants and shepherds against a colonial power. Boumedienne was dressed like a university professor in a black suit and overcoat, white shirt and dark tie. He was a very nice, natural man. We were introduced by Masetti, who sat beside him at table, and the banquet began. They removed the lamb from the spit (I thought they had put too much fat on it), placed it in an enormous wooden receptacle in the centre of a long table set up outside on the patio; it was covered with a white tablecloth, plates and bowls of vegetables, fruit and bread . . . but no cutlery. The filling was like nothing I had ever tasted. Perhaps it was the spirit of the desert, something primordial, like a ritual ceremony in which the fruit and the meat were transformed. There was no hierarchy; they were all men of the Sahara at the manna hour, when all are equal under the sheltering sky.

With Bajtik's help, we, the Argentines, organized the next barbecue. He took me to a butcher's where I explained to the owner what cuts of beef I wanted, and showed him how to saw across a calf's ribs, for *asado de tira*. A bed-frame with a squared metal grid served as a *parrilla* to grill the meat. I also asked the butcher to mince a few kilos of the best beef because I wanted to make *empanadas*, with boiled eggs, olives and cumin like the ones we eat in Mendoza; they are baked not fried and the kitchen had a magnificent oven so the *empanadas* turned out amazingly well. Masetti was happy and confident.

Fresh news from Havana precipitated events. Crucial stages of the project were ready. Someone was already travelling to the zone to make contacts to buy a *finca*, and to organize a minimum support network to receive equipment and provide temporary lodging for our group. Masetti, however, had already made arrangements with the Algerians to provide equipment (except weapons), campaign uniforms, boots, medicine packs, gifts of compasses and binoculars from Boumedienne and Ben Bella, and most important of all, as a sign of gratitude and fraternity from both leaders, diplomatic passports (authentic ones) from the newly independent nation. We were overjoyed. Euphoria descended on us like a state of grace . . . or of mind.

Masetti asked me to design a symbolic image for our incipient army, both to save time and so our diplomatic status could protect the sketches we took with us. I went and bought paints, brushes, drawing paper, a geometry set, and pencils, and had a sudden strange sensation of contacting my past, my lost identity as an artist.

I must digress a little. Even at this stage we saw something that became natural as the guerrilla army formed in the jungles of Salta. We were not motivated by patriotism, nationalist clichés, or chauvinist mythologies. For us, history showed how often and flagrantly the people's rights had been usurped, despite some great historical figures. At night, around the radio, we would be more moved by a folksong than by the national anthem. We did not worship emblems. So when we discussed what symbols, flags, colours, we wanted for our image, it was obvious nobody was interested in historical icons. We wanted something distinctive that showed we belonged to our group, and that it represented a break with the past. Masetti said the colours red and black were constantly present throughout the Latin American struggles. Units of Bolívar's liberating army used them, so did some of the national *caudillos*, Sandino's troops in Nicaragua, and the 26th of July Movement in Cuba. Its meaning is so obvious and principled: 'Fight or Die!' After a few sketches, I produced a sun from the national military flag (the Argentine civil flag did not have it then), two light blue stripes, and a white central stripe with a red and black sun instead of a yellow one. The same sun for the uniform insignias, divided horizontally with the red on top and the black underneath.

During one of the last sports sessions on our tennis court, the intensely competitive spirit of some of us, notably Masetti, meant we very unwisely had a long jump competition. People normally use mattresses, not a clay court. Masetti twisted his lumbar vertebrae as he landed, and lay there in terrible pain. Leonardo said he would be alright with complete bed rest and some form of treatment. We were supposed to be moving to another house in the centre of Algiers, from where it would be easier to make our final arrangements. Masetti made the move in silence, in a truss that immobilized him and put him in a foul mood. We installed him on the ground floor of a former French colonial home with a narrow garden round it and railings separating it from four streets, like a small block, in the flat, old part of the city, between the port and the chic French area. When Masetti was a bit better, we walked to the rue Amirouche, a street of luxury boutiques and cinemas.

The house had bedrooms on the upper floor, and dining room and reception rooms on the ground floor, furnished in between-the-wars French style. This was the backdrop to a self-criticism session which I had requested because I was worried about the group's security during our journey. The atmosphere of open animosity between Masetti and Miguel did not bode well; in fact it was a potential danger. The session blew up with no sign of any possible reconciliation. After a huge slanging match, Miguel announced he would not continue with Masetti as leader. Masetti ordered a trial on charges of desertion and operational insubordination which, in themselves, carried the maximum penalty. He named me prosecutor and Federico defence counsel. Furry would preside over the trial, and Leonardo would keep a record.

Miguel was locked in his room until the following day, so he could distance himself emotionally, while Federico and I studied the situation. My position was clear: the fate of a project in which we were all vital elements but subordinate to a higher cause could not be put at risk for personal reasons. Being temperamental and touchy was not a valid argument. This was an army unit and rules had to be obeyed. Miguel did not appear to accept this and seemed to place feelings before duty. He had understood nothing. We all knew the price we had to pay. He did not. His presence put our safety at risk. Our security depended on mutual trust. I no longer trusted Miguel. He acted as if rules did not apply to him: sending postcards, disobeying orders from the trivial to the dangerous. He could not continue with us. He had to be dismissed and kept under some form of arrest, to be negotiated with the Algerians, until we had started our operations in Argentina. Federico said he could not fault these arguments because, although he thought Miguel was a good bloke, it was not a problem of discipline but the destruction of a whole fabric of commitment that was impossible to repair. He asked for the same verdict.

But Masetti, who exercised his right as prosecution witness, argued at length for an exemplary punishment, not so much to punish Miguel, but because letting insubordination like this pass undermined the whole future of the struggle, which depends on us being strong and believing in ourselves. He wanted to set a precedent that would affect all of us, because losing a sixth of our force would be detrimental to our entire project. He insisted on his rights and demanded the death penalty, a decision to be referred to the group. The decision in favour was unanimous.

Coronel Bajtik was informed. A copy of the court proceedings was given to the Algerian general staff, with a request to carry out the death sentence. They accepted the responsibility and a military detachment came to the house and took away the defendant, our *compañero* of seven months of physical effort, illusions and broken trust. That same April morning, I went up to the second floor, opened the door to Miguel's bedroom door – his cell – and told him to prepare himself, it was time to say goodbye. He did not bat an eyelid. Immaculate as always, he asked if he had time to shave. The soldiers were waiting in the garden, and the rest of us were in the hallway. Miguel came downstairs carrying his bags. He passed through the double file, inclined his head slightly to Federico and me, and faced the Algerian officer who took his bag and opened the door for him. He climbed into the van parked in the garden without moving a muscle or looking back. Although he had been informed of the verdict and the result of the vote, he showed no sign of weakness, asked for nothing and said nothing. His bravery was moving.

We had just taken a leap into the void, one that leaves invisibles traces. Objectively, the situation had forced hard choices on us. Possible traumatic alternatives had been studied. But just as abandoning a wounded comrade was unthinkable, so was putting the whole group in jeopardy because of egoism or cowardice. But the philosophy of the behaviour is one thing, the human reaction to that behaviour is quite another.

We filled in the paperwork for our documents, as we had done in Cuba, except that this time the documents were legal. The official Algerian proposal was as follows. The Algerian Socialist Republic would send a delegation to various South American countries to present their credentials and make diplomatic contacts. The delegation would include our two officials, Abdel and Muhamed; two 'assistant diplomats', Masetti and Furry; and other administrative personnel, Hermes, Fabián, Basilio and me. The delegation would use its diplomatic baggage to bring in our military equipment (except for weapons), and protect us through the customs controls at the airport entering the continent, and at our final destination, Bolivia. It was an absolute gift from heaven, or rather, from Ben Bella, Boumedienne and the Algerian Revolution.

On the 1st of May, we were invited to an official event in the National Stadium presided over by the two historic leaders. We watched a good football match between the Tunisian and Algerian national teams. Masetti took the opportunity to thank the two leaders and say goodbye. The departure of the official party was followed by a strident, unstoppable ululation by thousands of women saluting their leaders from the stands. Outside in the streets packed with people, the sound moved like a wave, propelling the procession of cars.

11

Onwards to Bolivia and Argentina: May–June 1963

Our group left Algeria for Rome on 5 May 1963, minus our seventh member. Free of passport worries, I was bent on enjoying the journey. Our Alitalia plane to São Paulo, Brazil, was leaving in two or three days so we had time for walking and looking around Rome. With renewed good spirits, Masetti invited us to dinner in a *trattoria* not far from the Quirinale. We thought it looked a simple family restaurant, but it turned out to be smart. The six of us, without the Algerians, were seated at a large table and, in true Italian style, were waited on with a profusion of deferential compliments and titles. Masetti was addressed as *Commendatore*, a name that stuck with him until Bolivia.

A few unexpected nerves took over as we waited to board the São Paulo plane. Phone calls and confabs behind the scenes between officials holding the pile of passports had us worried. Abdel and Mohamed argued in French. We, the additional personnel, kept our counsel. In the end, we all filed through, not quite sure whether to the plane or a police cell. We always had the nagging feeling our 'diplomatic' delegation was overlarge and drew attention because it was Algerian. Algeria was the hot topic of the day. All the crimes the Western press had been hiding were coming to light. The Organisation de l'Armée Secrète (OAS) was carrying out operations against De Gaulle for having given away France's overseas paradise. And Algeria was leading Africa's independence struggles, together with Egypt's Colonel

Nasser, and the black African countries of Nigeria, Kenya, Uganda, Tanganyika and the Congo, all the way to Cape Town. North to south, east to west, Africa was entering a new maelstrom of change which was to bring millions of deaths, vanquished hopes, and more hunger for its people. We desperately wanted to get to our zone of operation, and take responsibility for our own actions, without any more intermediaries (gratitude apart). In the end, everything went well.

In São Paulo, we began to feel at home, but the train to Bolivia was like a time machine. We left skyscrapers and elevated motorways, crossed the poverty-stricken regions of Brazil's interior, until we reached another century altogether in Santa Cruz de la Sierra, the Wild West in eastern Bolivia. There was mud galore, men on horseback, raised wooden sidewalks, over-laden carts and trucks. All that was missing were gunshots, galloping hoofs, and the bandits' getaway. The journey had numbed our senses. Each railway stop was a catalogue of social dramas reflected in the scarce and humble wares on offer: fritters, *empanadas*, water, orange juice, coffee, bananas and cigarettes. When you get to these parts, there is no room for amazement, you have to hang up your illusion-filled saddlebags and gather up the miserable remnants of neglected humanity, and ask yourself: What am I doing here? What do I talk about? With what right? With whom? You have to recognize that whatever you do, you're not doing it for them, but for yourself, to earn the right to be called a human being.

We had split into two groups: one with Masetti, Hermes and Furry that went by plane directly from São Paulo to La Paz; the other with the Algerians, Fabián, Basilio and myself by train to Santa Cruz; from there we would take the weekly internal flight that linked this forlorn population with the rest of the country. The Algerian bunch were less conspicuous, although no less incongruous: if we met any Arab asking questions, naturally we were to say nothing. We arrived eventually in La Paz, took charge of the ex-diplomatic bags, and said goodbye to our Algerian friends.

Leaving Basilio and Fabián in a café, I went off to find my first Bolivian contact. The address was a mechanic's workshop, and the owner, Rodolfo Saldaña, was extremely friendly and made a favourable impression. He took off his work clothes, and we went in a jeep to fetch the rest of our group and the bags, going back up the road I had come down from El Alto, where the airport is. Driving through the hillsides of the shanty towns which almost encircle La Paz like a funnel, we reached the little house of the modest family of an old schoolteacher, a member of the Communist Party, who with an infinite sense of hospitality offered us everything he had, which was not much. We were given his best room covered in mattresses, while he and his family managed in another. We were to spend an indeterminate time there, not going out or letting the neighbours see us. Luckily it was not too long before Masetti appeared with a plan for moving to the base on the Argentine border.

My group, half of us, took a bus south to Oruro, where we were to meet Furry. He would arrive in a jeep he had bought for his trips as the 'administrator' of the *finca* that had been newly purchased, and we would carry on from there together. I went to the first appointment at an agreed meeting place in the morning, but Furry did not turn up. Nor to the second, nor to a third in the afternoon. He could be having mechanical problems, so we took refuge from the cold in a huge café–billiards hall, checking on the emergency exit every hour. Our presence was too conspicuous in this freezing little mining town.

We stuck it out until closing time, at midnight, and since we couldn't go to a hotel without documents, I decided to try our luck in a brothel on the outskirts of town that had been recommended, and where they served food. We took a taxi down a dusty road in the middle of a barren plain to a ruin of a building, looking more like a stable than a den of iniquity. I decided that we should go back to La Paz, but the taxi driver announced that we would need special passes to go through the police checkpoints, one leaving Oruro and the other at the entrance to El Alto. Not only did we not have passes, we had no documents at all! Masetti had them, because of some incomprehensible security measure he had taken in Havana. Our Cuban passports had been handed back to Serguera in Algiers and the Algerian documents returned to Abdel in La Paz.

As in all wars of attrition, we began negotiations with the taxi driver. He found a solution: the noble institution of the bribe, that popular system for redistributing wealth which, in these parts, lubricates the most intransigent mechanisms and permits the free functioning of private enterprise. For double the price, plus costs, he would act as if we were relatives of his, returning drunk from a wedding in Oruro. We piled into the rear seat, covered ourselves in a poncho, and pretended to be asleep when we passed the checkpoints. We were half asleep, in fact, and dying of cold.

When Rodolfo opened his workshop early next morning, I was waiting for him. We were told that Furry had fallen over a cliff, having lost control of the jeep just before hitting a cement drain on the same road we had driven back on in the night. But it was not simply an accident. If there was one man in Cuba who was right for Che's project, because of his experience and military expertise, his bravery and youth, his intelligence and dedication, it was Furry. But if there was one man who was wrong for it, it was also Furry. His war wound – the shard of anti-tank grenade lodged in his right frontal lobe – had started having secondary effects, causing a sort of epileptic fit, during which he had convulsions for a few minutes, and then fell into a deep sleep. These problems were not caused by anything external, and could not be anticipated. The accident served as a warning. In future, when taking weapons to the *finca* or on any other high-risk trips, Communist Party contacts had to accompany him.

We did the journey all over again, but this time we met in Sucre, the historical capital of Bolivia. Accompanying Masetti and Hermes was a Bolivian *compañero* from the Communist Party in La Paz, who had already helped choose and buy the *finca*. His name was Jorge Vázquez Viaña, but from the very first he was known as Loro, due perhaps to his rather hooked parrot nose. Young and educated, he was very friendly, inspired confidence, and could carry on an excellent conversation. The contact had probably been made by José María Martínez Tamayo (Papi), who had been talking to both the Bolivian and Peruvian Communist Parties about the guerrilla project, at approximately the same time.

We continued our journey south and reached Tarija, Bolivia's southernmost province bordering Argentina where the *finca* was. On the map, the geographical border here looks like a triangle, a fang sunk into hairy skin, formed by the course of two rivers: the Bermejo, which flows southwards down the left side of the fang (facing the map), turns at the tip and flows east for 18,000 kilometres, marking the border between the Argentine provinces of Chaco and Formosa before it eventually joins the River Paraguay; and a broken arm of the River Pilcomayo down the right hand side of the fang which also turns east further up to mark the border between Argentina and Paraguay, before flowing into the River Paraguay at Asunción.

If you stand at the vertex of the triangle and look directly south, you can envisage the more than 4,000 kilometres down to Tierra del Fuego. In between lie the three million square kilometres of Argentine territory containing millions of Argentine citizens that have no idea where this place is. Then you can begin to understand that putting on a rucksack filled with weapons and a few days' worth of food is not an odyssey but a feat of inestimable impudence or daring, and either way pure madness.

We drove southwards from the city of Tarija towards the tip of the triangle on the road which runs parallel to the River Bermejo. The road is in Bolivia, the river is the border with Argentina, and the dense jungle is everywhere. A track leaves the road on the left-hand side and penetrates the triangle, navigating the virgin jungle with great difficulty, fording streams which at certain times of the year can be impassable, under a canopy of huge trees. The trail is marked by tyre tracks in the mud. They disappear into the forest from time to time only to re-emerge further on, until finally arriving, more by luck than design, at the *finca*. In the middle of this inhospitable nowhere, barbed wire suddenly appears, holding back the undergrowth on the right, and the track ends at a gate in a clearing with an orchard of citrus fruit trees and giant avocados. There, behind the canopy of trees, was a stone L-shaped house with a sloping zinc roof, some windows and a corner chimney with a whiff of smoke coming out. The jeep stopped in front of the entrance and the six members of the guerrilla army plus Loro got out. Stiff with cold, and having walked much of the trail, ready to push the jeep out of the mud when it got stuck up to its axle, we still had to unload it. Furry and Loro were returning to La Paz for another load of weapons.

Out of the house came the man responsible for the smoke, drying his hands on a tea towel hanging from his waist, like a housewife. He was Don Benito, an old member of the Bolivian Communist Party, permanently assigned to the Argentine project. His mission would be to stay in the house the whole time, except when Furry gave him permission to leave. He was used to living alone and working the land, so eventually he could supervise farm labourers as well as the house. For the time being, his favourite job was making peanut soup, which took him all morning, much to Masetti's irritation. After morning coffee, sort of Algerian style, he chopped endless vegetables and, using a convex stone on a flat one, crushed a mountain of peanuts he had peeled himself. He fried bits of chicken and rabbit, adding the vegetables to the cauldron and filling it with boiling water, stirring all the time. Chillies and peanuts were his culinary secret and the result was clearly good. In mid-afternoon, when Masetti was looking for a rope to hang him with, he appeared with the cauldron of steaming soup, just in time to change everyone's mind and humour. We ate once a day, to get used to what our future diet would be – at the best of times.

The following week was very intense. We explored our surroundings looking for a way over the River Bermejo, while

Furry made several trips, and not only to La Paz. For security reasons, he had already left weapons in places like Cochabamba and Sucre, helped by the part of the Bolivian Communist Party that was aiding our project. Between the *finca* and the Bermejo were mountains that plunged steeply down to the road, and another river, the Emborozú, also lay between the *finca* and the road. The mountains and the river prevented us from trekking straight from the house to ford the Bermejo. We had to find a place to ford and then use the jeep to transport the weapons.

Furry made repeated trips to another border town, Yacuiba, and even went into Argentina under the pretext of buying provisions, but really to reconnoitre the terrain, and in passing, make acquaintances, like any young, dynamic farm administrator would. Not far south of the border at the tip of the triangle lies Orán, a prosperous town in northern Argentina. The landowning Bolivian bourgeoisie from Tarija often shopped in Orán, finding it more convenient to cross the border and drive on asphalted Argentine roads than to travel, rains permitting, to Sucre.

Masetti was working with Federico on the final details for our clandestine entry into Argentina. The rest of us were unaware of these details, but it would subsequently cost Masetti a long walk. It is useful to recap on our names at this point, because familiarity had given us new ones. Leonardo-Fabián became Médecin, because he had worked as a doctor in a French-speaking country. Federico-Basilio got his original name back, or was Fede, or Flaco. I kept Laureano for strategic purposes, but among ourselves I was Pelado, or Playé for Masetti in his weird French. Neither Hermes nor Masetti changed their names. Furry became Carlos, the administrator.

When Furry finished bringing the equipment, we unpacked the Algerian uniforms made in Yugoslavia. We chose the sizes for each of us and got rid of the labels so nothing could trace us back to Algeria, a commitment fully honoured until now. The uniforms were very well made, out of good olive green material, and we were happy with two lots of underwear, a shirt with big pockets, combat trousers with knee-length pockets, a woollen army pullover, and a fantastic jacket with pockets and zips all over the place. The excellent quality of the uniforms, machetes, cartridge belts, map holders, as well as the binoculars and compasses, which the Algerians had given us, did not compensate for the anger and disappointment we felt when we opened the equipment the Cubans had sent on ahead.

For the second time, we felt we were being made fun of or sabotaged. Every Cuban knows how important good clothes and strong durable equipment is for a guerrilla force. Your backpack is your home and everything it holds means life, survival. Apart from the weapons which Che had helped Masetti choose before leaving Cuba, and to some extent the backpacks themselves, everything else was useless. It was a joke in very bad taste: thin uniforms made out of shiny nylon, awful in the heat and torn to shreds in no time, city trousers, imitation leather Tom Mix–style holsters with stars on them.

We unpacked the weapons, cleaned and oiled them, and Masetti distributed them according to function and experience. There were two FAL rifles with their original cartridge belts for Masetti and Hermes, a Garand which for his height and weight went to Dr Leonardo, a Thompson for Federico, and a .43-calibre M3 for me. Counting stowage, ammunition and spare parts, each weighed more than six kilos. And that was just the rifles. We also each got a 9 millimetre Browning pistol, with magazines and bullets, and three hand grenades. My M3 was made larger and heavier by its silencer, a 30cm iron tube stuffed with metal washers and grilles where the noise of the explosion was muffled into a barely audible click.

We soon realized it was impossible to carry everything we considered indispensable, and we began the inexorable task of unpacking. It was hard to accept, but if we didn't, we wouldn't even be able to lift our backpacks, never mind carry them all day. We took everything we could, up to 35 kilos. We had to repack the load and rearrange our straps, distribute the weight at the bottom, keeping the things we used all the time or in emergencies at the top.

There was an extra load which pleased no one, least of all Médecin who was in charge of communications. We had to help him with the radio transmitter, the electric generator and its pedal tripod, a piece of high-tech equipment the CIA had dropped over the Escambray mountains for the Cuban counter-insurgency, and which Cuban intelligence had always managed to capture. Designed for clandestine commandos, it consisted of two main parts, one the size of a small car battery reinforced with a rubber coating, that could be dragged out of mud and got working, and the other an iron stand for the tricycle that moved the heavy generator. The transmitter was distributed between Hermes and Leonardo, and Federico and I carried the rest of it dismantled. When you included the things stuffed into the dozen uniform pockets, the total weight was indescribable, so that when we camped by a stream, after taking off our backpacks and stripping to change into dry clothes, we felt as though we had to tie ourselves to trees so as not to go floating off down the river.

We chose the ford over the River Bermejo (further north, with less water), and Masetti gave the order to cross into Argentina. On a June night, in mid-winter, the jeep was loaded up with five backpacks and us in full combat kit. The little crazy army set off. The jeep climbed gasping to the base of the triangle, took the road down to the ford, and at around three in the morning, with no moon, we waded the river. Furry drove as far into the water as he could, we put on our backpacks with water above our ankles and with a wave goodbye, we crossed the rest of the river and disappeared into the jungle. Now in Argentina, we climbed a tributary stream, *argentino* like its twinkling silvery water.

12

The Base in the Argentine Jungle: June 1963

We entered an immense country by an unknown door; no one had invited us, no one was expecting us. We were received only by the fantastic sound of water (to become our favourite symphony), and the obscene creaking of the jungle, mixing groans of pleasure and growls of danger: sighs, hoots, trills, thuds, flutter of wings and crash of falling trees. The stream descended impetuously, alternating waterfalls with natural stone dams, a sign of pronounced rises in the water level. Walking in the dark was gruelling, even impossible. At times, when the water route was impracticable, we had to make a detour into the darkness following animal trails, rejoining further up the pale glimmer of the stream we heard rather than saw.

At dawn, Masetti ordered a couple of hours' rest and Hermes, out in front, said he had found a good place. We saw nothing but what the beam of the torch showed us: branches and trunks, weeds and rotting leaves, some crags, a place to collapse exhausted. We set a watch, not so much for safety but to make sure sleep did not rob us of the morning. Every half hour, the sentry would wake his replacement and the last one would wake everybody, with coffee ready. Simple tasks, that would become routine, began laboriously. Making a fire in a damp jungle is not easy. You have to collect dry wood, if there is any, or take the bark off twigs and whittle them down to fine shavings, to find one that is not totally rotten and has at its heart something flammable. You have to improvise a campfire with stones for the kettle, fetch water, huddle the driest material round a tiny piece of paper from your notebook, light it at the first try (or start again), until the flame grows, cheered by bigger and bigger twigs (although wetter), until they finally catch fire.

During those first days, our problems were multiple. First, the weight of the backpacks; second, exhaustion; third, hunger; fourth, lack of sleep. The weight on our backs increased rather than diminished, although we ate a few grams of food every day. Our muscles stiffened, our joints swelled, our legs refused to coordinate their movements, our shoulders throbbed with pain, our feet destroyed, our hands furrowed with scratches, our innards groaning, our lungs wheezing. And all the while sweating, soaking wet, boots inundated, skin blistered. An army of diminutive things stuck to us. Mosquitoes, ticks, lice and diverse larvae wiped our tears and licked our wounds, sipping here and there, nesting in the most intimate regions.

We made camp in the late afternoon, by order of Hermes, who being the expert exercised his authority quite naturally. Although dazzled by the magnitude around us, Hermes began to move around as if he had been born here. We were pretty well lost because our military map bore no resemblance to our surroundings, so although it was almost dark, Masetti ordered a search party to establish where we were.

Leonardo was losing his sunny personality. There was nothing glorious about the harsh reality. There was no room for dreams, and rations were diminishing. Hard work, on the other hand, was ongoing. Daily chores demanded a certain predisposition, even taking a certain pleasure in things like cooking or making bread, and he had neither of them. Hermes, who bossed us about as if the campsite were his house in Cuba, was always having a go at him. Believe me, washing pots in a river or fighting with the fire when everyone else is sleeping is not very stimulating. Once, on his way to the river at dusk, Leonardo came over to where I was on guard duty, and complained bitterly. Curiously, it was not Hermes or the daily grind that upset him. It was Masetti's authoritarianism, the harshness of his military regime, his personal treatment of us which showed none of the camaraderie we had spent months cultivating. The apparent arbitrary nature of Hermes's actions were, according to Leonardo, only expressions of Masetti's tendency to want to subjugate us, to turn us into mere puppets in a campaign for which he would take the credit. I agreed about the harshness of the treatment, although I had not given it much thought, but I knew we could not expect it to be otherwise. Masetti was responsible for a vital part of Che's project: he couldn't indulge in the normal niceties.

After more than a week of exhausting marches, our provisions and energy were depleted, but we still had not left our zone or ventured south. We were moving like a pencil round the fingers of a hand, going up one ravine and down the next, unable to find a pass over the mountains. The end of the ravines met sheer cliffs, impossible to climb, at least in our condition and carrying such excessive weight. Hermes and Federico went exploring every day without success, and we ended up near the River Bermejo again, as if we had been moving in an impassable circle.

That night in the quiet of the camp, Masetti made plans for the following day. We would walk to within a couple of kilometres of the river border and camp before midday in a safe place. From there I would go on and, if possible, go back across the border making visual notes and drawings of the mountain that was blocking our way.

We were very near the chosen site. Around eleven, I left my backpack and guns and changed into creased civilian clothes. I set off with Hermes, walking along the almost dry bed of a tributary that flowed into the Bermejo. Hermes chose a strategic observation point which allowed him to see both where the rivers met and the road on the Bolivian side. He hid there. I crossed the river by an excellent ford, so shallow it covered no more than my boots. You could jump from stone to stepping stone that formed a dam before the two rivers met. There was not a soul in sight. I began walking south on the stony Bolivian road zigzagging between the hillside and the river, in the noisy canyon which this side of the ford regained its voice of stones being dragged along by the force of the water. It was sunny and the birds were singing. But I was detached from the landscape, like a Zulu on a trip to the Arctic. I could see that the mountain peaks on the Argentine side were enormous, and covered by dense jungle, like an impregnable fortress. After walking for an hour, it was obvious to me that only mountain climbers could pass there. I had walked about four kilometres when, rounding a bend, I came across one of those lay-bys beside the road where lorries can pull over. And there, thanks to the other Hermes, the Greek god of commerce, was a kiosk, servicing vehicles and, until that moment non-existent, passers-by. The little hut of corrugated iron had a counter selling fruit, bread and wine, juice, *chorizo*, *mortadela*, cheeses, flour, rice, *charqui*, potatoes, chillies, onions and tins of condensed milk, meat, fish and tomatoes. It was the emporium of a *Colla* who brought contraband goods from Argentina on the backs of his fellow Indians. Like a mirage, it was hard to believe despite seeing it, so I had to prove it by ordering a glass of red wine and a greasy *chorizo*. The man was not very talkative, but filled me in on the unusual whereabouts of his business, and by extension, of ours.

We were some fifteen kilometres from the town of Bermejo, and the last police and customs checkpoint in Bolivia before the international bridge over the River Bermejo. On the other side was the Argentine border police post with more rigorous customs control, and a relatively short distance away, the nearest Argentine town, Aguas Blancas. The area is an easily controlled bottleneck because this was the only road, the only possible pass, down the river canyon. Family contraband was endemic. The *cholas* pass several times a day stacking the merchandise on this side, while their husbands bundle it up and wait for lorries to take them into the interior of Bolivia. Some, however, move some kilometres away from the road, to find more famished travellers to negotiate with. According to the *Colla*, the border police patrol the river banks behind their post, because some people prefer not to pay the *droit du seigneur* or abusive bribes in which the customs officers take a sadistic delight. I explained my presence by pretending my car had broken down a few kilometres up the road and that my whole family was waiting there with no food. A passing driver had promised to bring a spare part and had told me about this kiosk. I asked him for a jute sack and we began filling it with food, including coffee and sugar, cigarettes, all the *chorizo* he had, tins, *charqui*, cheese, bread, and the crowning glory, a two and-a-half-litre demijohn of that Mendoza wine with two glass handles, very popular in the north.

By mid-afternoon, I was retracing my steps, my feet burning, disheartened, and the uncomfortable weight of the bag on my kidneys. I carried it over my shoulder, clutching it with my two hands; the demijohn slung across my chest by string tied to its handles. I might not arrive with the whole sack, but I was certainly going to bring the wine! The kilometres seemed endless. The landmarks I remembered most clearly seemed to have disappeared. Finally I reached the ford, hid behind a crag and waited until I was sure no one was around. Just before dark, with the sack bobbing on my back, I crossed the stepping stones. The river level seemed to have risen, but it was a relief to get in the water to finish passing the ford. I climbed the slope above the stream more calmly now in the last light of the day. Suddenly Hermes jumped out at me, with a radiant smile. I don't know if he was pleased to see me or the load I was carrying. I gave him a *chorizo* as if I were offering him a Partagas cigar. He devoured it, and carrying the sack, set off up the hill. He had seen me arrive and wait patiently, deciding when to cross. He approved.

Our arrival at the camp, with its three occupants dug in on a war footing, and Masetti displaying his best ill humour because we were late, turned into a gastronomic celebration. Nobody commented adversely on the wine, downing it with complete normality, despite it being on the prohibited list. Masetti listened to my report, returning again and again to the nature of the ford and the height of the mountains. I said the mountains were

impassable and the ford was just as good, or better, than the first
one we had crossed, although it was hard to judge since I had seen
this one in daytime and the other one only at night. I could only
go by the depth of the water and that, of course, could vary from
one day to the next. According to Federico, the ford we had first
chosen was the only possible one. 'In that case it's the same one,'
I argued, 'we've gone round in a complete circle.' Masetti considered this possibility. If, as I said, we had gone round in a circle up
there, it could be the same ford. I preferred to leave the matter in
their hands because I was not sure.

By next morning, Masetti had a change of plan. The altitude
indications on the military map showed that the peaks of the
mountain chain coming from the Puna de Iruya were considera-
bly less sharp about twenty kilometres before the town of
Bermejo. So, to avoid the highest peaks, we had to go along the
road and cross the mountains further down, halfway between
where we were now and the international bridge. He would go
back to the *finca* and return with Furry in the jeep to get our stuff
back across the ford. We would hide opposite the ford, as Hermes
had done, and wait for them between two and three in the morning, thirty-six hours from now.

More or less in civvies, with the beard and small backpack
of a tropical drifter, Masetti set off on what was to be a long
walk. He had to walk up to the base of the triangle and down the
track to the *finca*; *s*ome twenty-five kilometres or so. With
Hermes in charge, and having erased all trace of our presence, we
stayed hidden on a slope of dense undergrowth, near a crystalline
waterfall. The hours passed slowly.

On the second night, we took up our position facing the ford.
At the appointed time, a vehicle passed going south, but its lights
blinded us. A few minutes later, another – the same one – came
slowly back and stopped, blinking its headlights. We replied with
the torch and started down to the river. Federico crossed first
without a backpack to verify the identity of the contact. The rest
followed. Masetti did not wait until we were on the bank, even

before knowing who we were; he tore a strip off me in the middle of the river, because it was not the same ford, but ten kilometres further on, and he had had to walk twice the distance. As if it was my fault, as if any of us had been sure, as if I should recognize a place I had only passed once at night, a place the explorers among us had also thought was the same ford! So, if not the same, this one was better, and we would have saved ourselves days of useless, gruelling trekking if we had crossed lower down in the first place. Masetti was showing signs of his subsequent intolerance and his tendency to transfer responsibility for mistakes. In any case, he had decided we would all go back to the Bolivian *finca* while we looked for a way through further to the south.

We loaded the jeep – and with it our bad mood, disappointment at our failure, and general humiliation – and drove in silence to the *finca*.

13

Making Contacts in the Cities:
July–August 1963

Meanwhile, the old political game continued to be played out on the Argentine stage. In March 1962, the coup against Frondizi's developmentalist policies had put the agro-export model back in power, power that had long been undermined by multinational companies wanting to turn Argentina into their own factory farm; a springboard for an expansionist policy that was a precursor to globalization. The fundamental struggle, however, was for the control of power, not for power itself. Trade unionism was one power base. The military was another. The union bureaucracies (right-wing Peronists) would go with the highest bidder. The Armed Forces High Command favoured US hegemony. This was the scenario prior to the general elections on 7 July 1963. But with Peronism proscribed, half the country's voters had no candidate, so they spoilt their ballots. The result was that the winner got the lowest vote ever cast in free elections in Argentine history.

The election result came while we were away exploring on the border. It left our fledgling People's Guerrilla Army (EGP) disconcerted. There had been evidence of pre-electoral fraud and we had naturally expected the 'legal' reinstatement of the military, previously ousted by Frondizi's pact with Perón. Instead, the surprise winner was Dr Arturo Illia, the candidate of the Radical Party. This elderly doctor from Córdoba was seen by many as the symbol of professional and political integrity. The military publicly accepted the election results and Argentina prepared to return to civilian rule. A climate of euphoria and good will dominated the news. It left the infant EGP disconcerted, and necessitated a revision of our immediate plans.

With little discussion or analysis, Masetti decided simply to abandon our planned entry into Argentina. This meant earlier decisions had to be rescinded. Loro Vázquez Viaña was on his way from La Paz to Resistencia, capital of Argentina's Chaco province, to reinforce the contacts Alberto Granado had made with the Trotskyite splinter group willing to work under Che. Masetti now sent Federico, travelling on his Argentine documents, to stop him. Furry would drive to La Paz to send a message to Che that the operation was to be suspended. They set off together so Furry could drop Federico on the road to Bermejo. We were down to four men.

The following night, Masetti changed his mind. He dragged me into the small bedroom where he had a portable typewriter, a radio, some books on farming and other papers scattered on a table, and said words to the effect that: 'What fools we are, Pelao. The elections are a sham, a trap. Nothing has changed, our project must go on. Stop Federico, then carry on to Buenos Aires and the rest of Argentina, and use your contacts to build a support network for us.'

One of Masetti's occupational hazards was his ability to do lots of things simultaneously. He took this monumental decision while listening to his old station *Radio El Mundo*'s nightly news programme and frantically writing a political manifesto at the same time. Speaking in the first person plural, he reminded me of the episode at the ford. We could not accept failure or weakness; we had to be strong, ruthless when need be; or they would destroy us as they had always destroyed the good, the decent, the honest. We could not afford mistakes, and decency is a mistake. This old man, for instance (referring to Illia), cannot admit the scam being perpetrated on the people on the pretext of pacifying the country. Illia is a man of peace, but they will use him to dash hopes and destroy protest.

Masetti finished writing, pulled the sheet of paper out of the typewriter, and gave it to me to read. 'Letter from the Rebels to President-Elect Illia' was a manifesto, calling upon a man of dignity to respect his past, hold firm to principles of honesty and civic courage, not pay 'the price of dishonour' to blackmailers of power, and to ally himself with all Argentines who wanted to be free. It was a superbly written text, with a formidable power of synthesis. It said the EGP had gone into the mountains, explained what had driven us there, and invited Illia to condemn fraud and add his support to the legitimate cause of the people and recover the purity of his youthful illusions. I said I agreed 100 per cent. Masetti, exultant, told me to take the letter to Buenos Aires and get it published. We had a mutual friend there who he was sure would support us.

When I had first arrived in Buenos Aires, aged barely twenty, I had been helped by a well-known artist called Alfredo Bettanín. He ran the art section of *El Hogar* magazine, and had asked me to illustrate the poems or short stories printed in the centre pages. As our friendship grew and work became steadier, he put me in touch with other publications like the cultural supplement of *La Prensa*, one of Argentina's big national newspapers. Its director, a poet called César Tiempo, had also commissioned some illustrations. Bettanín had been Masetti's best friend. He was a draughtsman, not a journalist, but was nonetheless a prominent member of the journalists' union, and well connected to the world of culture and politics. I was to go and see him, and not mince my words, because Masetti trusted him like a brother.

There was just one small snag: I had no documents. Luckily, Federico had taken his passport and identity card but left his army recruitment card: an Argentine's most important personal document. I had a surplus of passport photos left over from Algeria, and I practised the forgery skills I had learned in Cuba. The technique worked and I became Señor Federico Méndez, a man endowed with the miraculous power of passing through the same customs checkpoint twice in two days, with two different faces.

I crossed Bolivian border control, the bridge over the Bermejo, and Argentine customs and border police, and I walked to Agua Blancas. I felt immediately at home on the pavements of a peaceful and orderly village. Unfortunately, there was nothing for me to do there, so I dragged myself away on a bus to Orán, a few kilometres further on, the communications centre for the northernmost tip of the country. Aerolíneas Argentinas, the railway and the bus companies all converged there.

Seated at the back of the bus, I looked out of the window. I was entranced, as I had been ten years earlier, by the crops and the beautiful outline of the jungle (now more aware of how dense it was). The scent of Argentina filled my lungs, I felt as though I had been holding my breath the whole time I had been away. A police van overtook us, signalling the bus to pull over. Two border police got on, acting as if they owned the vehicle. One of them talked to the driver and kept glancing down the aisle to the back. My bucolic complacency disappeared and I focused on how to get off the bus as casually as possible.

As we came into Orán, some passengers asked the driver to stop, and the rear door, right next to me, opened wide. I was off in a flash. I was still quite a way out of town, but the short walk would be healthy and I could use it to go over my instructions in my mind. I went into the first barber shop I saw and got the full treatment. The barber was shocked at the state of my neck and scalp, covered in bites, some of them infected. He carefully applied creams and ointment, gave me a shave, cut my hair, and left me good as new, smelling like a rose. Next stop was a clothes shop, from where I emerged dressed like a sports-car salesman. At the Aerolíneas office, I learned the flight to Formosa and the Chaco had left the previous day and there were only two a week. The same story with the train, not to mention the bus. I would have to do a 100 kilometre detour via Santa Fe.

The girl at Aerolíneas suggested that I went to the airport and find a private flight. I took a taxi driven by another of the Greek gods involved in this story, and we reached the airfield just as a man with a suitcase was walking away from the runway to find a taxi. He had just arrived from Formosa in a Piper. Its pilot was refuelling, then going straight back. With my bag over my shoulder and my best businessman look, I walked into the hangar. The pilot was delighted to take me, 'Let's have a quick coffee and be off.'

Flying in a light aircraft is really flying. Below me I could see the devastation done to the Chaco as we followed the course of the River Bermejo, like a bleeding wound. In Resistencia, the capital of the Chaco, I found a cheap hotel, because I didn't fancy showing my identification card. At a better one, this would have been mandatory. I was shown a large room, with a wide bed covered by a mosquito net, and a ceiling fan. The walls were dark, almost black, or black mottled with ochre. 'Don't you have a brighter room?' I asked in disgust. 'No, señor', said the man, and waved his arm towards the wall. A cloud of mosquitoes rose, exposing bare, ochre-coloured paint. 'I'll be back with the Flit', he said. I needed survival equipment, so I went out into the long deserted avenue and bought some mosquito coils, newspapers, black tobacco. Well supplied, I went to a restaurant for a huge steak, washed down with a bottle of wine, and read the news. Everything seemed normal.

It was after midday by the time I arrived at Federico's house, in a secluded neighbourhood of family villas with small front gardens. The door was opened by a tall young woman, who looked like Federico but beautiful, with that fresh beauty of provincial girls. I guessed she was his sister and, to inspire confidence, simply asked: 'Has Federico arrived?' She looked very nervous, so before she could reply, I added: 'Tell him it's Laureano, we've changed the job, that's why I am here.' Honesty is the best policy. She disappeared but came straight back, inviting me in. And there he was, looking exhausted. He had arrived the previous day but had talked through the night, so had hardly had any sleep. The girl changed from nervous to very friendly, as though we were old friends. I told Federico what had happened and we studied the problem of our shared identity, a problem that could not extend beyond the front door. I could not stay at a hotel, I could not travel with my crude document, and I could not move in with his parents. Federico was meeting Loro Vásquez Viaña that night. They put a camp bed in a small room at the back that had been Federico's electronics workshop, and left me there with some books and newspapers while they both kept the appointment.

Loro understood the gravity of my problem, and promised to get a document from the group he was contacting. The following evening, he received an identity card from the province of Santa Fe that did not need modifying. Its owner looked quite like me: a little stouter, the same kind of bald, but the front view did not do justice to my nose, and our ages did not correspond.

To the sister's dismay, we left the next day. We crossed the River Paraná to Corrientes, where Federico sought out an old friend who had once shared his adventures in 'the Impenetrable' jungle. José Luis Stachioti, a ship's engineer, quickly agreed to join this new adventure. Federico gave him a few days to sort out his affairs and make a rendezvous in the town of Bermejo on the Argentine-Bolivian border. We carried on through Entre Ríos to Santa Fe where Stachioti had given us the name of the captain of a tugboat moored by the Paraná. We slept that night in comfortable bunks and in the morning would go our separate ways.

Over coffee, waiting for Federico's bus for Santiago del Estero, I made my own rather tentative travel plans. Buenos Aires is a jungle: difficult when you don't know anyone, worse still when you know too many people. I was more inclined to go to the provinces, but Mendoza, my home town, was too close emotionally, and further from the guerrillas in the north. That left Córdoba. I had relatives in Bell Ville, a town in the interior of the province, who had close links to the Left and with whom I saw eye to eye on all things. Ademar Testa was a lawyer, passionate about literature, politics, conversation, food and good wine. His wife Clelia was my wife Claudia's cousin and on our first visit we

had formed a strong affectionate friendship. Ademar owned
everything that had ever been published on the Cuban Revolution, Fidel and Che, and made no secret of it. If anyone knew
potential or actual revolutionaries, it was Ademar. I decided to
head for Bell Ville. When Federico left, I took an intercity bus for
Córdoba that stopped at Bell Ville at nine in the evening.

I appeared out of nowhere, and had trouble keeping news of my
arrival quiet. I made Clelia swear not to phone her mother, who
was very fond of me, or let everyone know I was here, while
Ademar kept repeating 'OK . . . OK . . .'. I could not have chosen
a better place. They understood what I wanted and the need for
absolute secrecy. They made up a bed for me in Ademar's study
and, by the time I went to sleep, we had drawn up a plan of action.
This consisted of waiting thirty-six hours for the arrival of a friend,
Oscar del Barco – professor, poet, lecturer in literature and philosophy at Córdoba's *Colegio Universitario*. He was also the editor and
board member of the magazine *Pasado y Presente*, edited in
Córdoba, the most prestigious Marxist magazine in Argentina.

A wavy-haired character with a walrus moustache was introduced to me by mid-afternoon. Oscar inspired immediate
confidence, and disarmed me with his honest and affectionate
expression. I gave him a general run-down of our project, its
origins and its long-term political aims. Oscar asked a few questions, but concluded that the issue was much too important for
him to judge alone. He was not a political figure himself, but
belonged to a nucleus of intellectuals who were influential in the
debate and analysis of events in Argentina. He needed to let the
group know of our project. We agreed I should meet whoever
they considered appropriate. We also discussed the interminable
problem of security. Until we had come to some agreement,
knowledge of the meeting must be restricted to the board of the
magazine. This should guarantee secrecy. Failing any agreement,
the same would apply.

Oscar often stayed the night in the room I was now in, because
he taught in Bell Ville the following day. But that night he

returned to Córdoba while I was closeted in a climate of conspiracy that allowed Clelia to shower me with affection and *empanadas*. Oscar came back the following day with the news that the *Pasado y Presente* board had unanimously agreed to a meeting and we would go to Córdoba that very evening (after dinner, naturally).

José (Pancho) Aricó lived with his wife and children in a neighbourhood of family houses with gardens on the outskirts of the city. It was also where the magazine was produced, and when the latest edition was being printed, work would go on late into the night. The editorial board comprised Pancho Aricó, Oscar del Barco, Héctor Schmucler, Samuel Kiczkowsky – all present on that night – and others I cannot remember now. They published the only internationally recognized analysis and theoretical development of Marxism in Argentina. Independent of the Argentine Communist Party and its networks, the board received information directly from the Kremlin. Getting on for midnight, in a closed room (more for the children's sake than for discretion), I faced what I suspected would be a challenge to my presentation skills and powers of persuasion. I had no political experience, certainly not at the theoretical levels of intellectuals like these, able to hold their own in the Academy of Political Sciences in Moscow, to teach literature and philosophy, and to psychoanalyze a tree. But if I could debate with Che and Masetti, surely I could keep to the bare essentials, and rely on historical and practical facts.

I began with the obvious: the catharsis that the Cuban Revolution had been for the political struggle of the American peoples. Success in the armed conflict had turned all previous argument about the legitimate weapon of the masses on its head. I argued that now we had such an important historical precedent, it was hard to maintain the illusion of being revolutionaries if we remained on the sidelines. We were ready to go down that road, the road the people must take if the Revolution was to succeed. Someone had to take the initiative, and for the time being, that was our main task. Although we had trained in Cuba, our organization's aim was to be organically rooted in our own people. My introduction was followed by a question and answer session, from which concrete ideas and proposals began to take shape. As the discussion progressed, I could see a process of mutual seduction. They were seduced by the idea that an armed nucleus of guerrillas was already on the ground, receiving support and ready to train cadres, that it would not depend on any political party, but on the contrary would create the organic, political and ideological framework to accompany its own development. And I was seduced by their ability to grasp the concept, and their intelligence. 'This will only be possible with Che,' said Pancho. 'Exactly,' I replied.

The magazine had brought together most dissident Communist Party members, and was causing significant rifts up and down the country by defending the Cuban line and supporting the armed struggle. Che's leadership was the ace up my sleeve, and I laid it on the table at the crucial moment. I had been authorized (this was implicit in my mission) to persuade and organize, and to make controlled use of the most sensitive information. For me everything revolved round the presence of Che, and it appeared to be equally indispensable for the others. Aricó spoke for all of them when he agreed to facilitate contacts in other cities and help me set up the urban network of the People's Guerrilla Army.

They would canvass support among their readers, and assumed the idea would meet with immediate approval. Meanwhile, I would travel to Buenos Aires, and establish contacts with similarly serious left-wing groups. The meeting ended on an enthusiastic, quite emotional, note; and with total belief in the importance of our enterprise.

I set off for Buenos Aires, armed with an address where I could stay and a contact in the intellectual circles, connected to the Córdoba magazine, which had already split off from the Communist Party in Buenos Aires. The contact was Juan Carlos Portantiero, working at the University of Buenos Aires, who took me to meet some student leaders. One was Daniel Hopen, from the Arts and Humanities department, and another, Horacio, from Physical and Natural Sciences. The meeting took place at the flat of the latter's father. Lined with walnut and mahogany, it looked as if it belonged to some Saudi sheikh. The revolutionary Left was launched.

I still had to see Masetti's friend, or rather our mutual friend, Bettanín. He was now a graphic designer at the newspaper *La Nación*, which had offices in San Martín Street. I went up to a very elegant floor, where a beautiful secretary asked me questions, spoke on the telephone, and finally took me into another room with soft leather armchairs where I waited. Bettanín remembered me, and was as affectionate as I remembered him. I swear he would have offered me a job if I had not mentioned Masetti. His attitude suddenly changed, he became so agitated that his features altered and he started sweating. So I became more guarded with my information, especially about Che. However, I had already told him about the guerrillas, the letter to Illia, and what Masetti wanted from him. Bettanín replied amicably enough, but so categorically that there was no room for argument, or any point in insisting any further. He said that in the six years since we had last seen each other, he had become deeply religious, and was now *very, very* Catholic. His life had changed, and respect for the commandments of his faith overrode all other considerations. He could not, therefore, participate in a project that involved killing. He said he loved us both very much and had followed press reports of his friend with pride and nostalgia. He wished us luck, assured me that what I had told him would never pass his lips, and advised me to forget this meeting and him. He stood up, embraced me and disappeared. I went down to the street like a scalded chicken and wandered along Florida before taking the metro to Plaza Once, and then a bus to Córdoba. Masetti and I had agreed on a way of communicating which I could use, but he could not. It was time to send some good and bad news, couched in figurative terms, to the *poste restante* in Tarija.

The response in Córdoba was better than I expected. I went to find Oscar del Barco in the Cerro de las Rosas, a leafy middle-class suburb on a sort of plateau overlooking the city, and we set out to find a man was waiting for us on the last street on the hill. Oscar explained how to get back to his house and then left us alone. The thick-set young man was mild-mannered and eager to talk. We strolled back and forth along the street, under the eucalyptus trees that hid the stars. He asked questions and I gave him straight answers, sparing him nothing. I did not sugar the pill, explained the sacrifice required, gave him no false hopes, did not hide the fact that he would be our first recruit, nor how unprotected we were, nor the degree of our madness which had to be seen as a spark of audacity and lucidity in a barren decadent landscape. I stressed that there would be no time for rest, that mosquitoes would eat better (off our blood) in a single second than we would in a whole day, that every time his backpack was emptied it would be refilled twice over, that his bones would ache and his only relief would be the moon over his hammock. Our aim was to be the red-hot ember that would light the fire in the communal hearth. 'Sign me up', said Héctor Jouvé.

In fact, I had first met Héctor's brother, Emilio Jouvé. Oscar had told me Emilio was the leader of a group of young sceptics, estranged from the Argentine Communist Party. Emilo had passed me on to his younger brother when he understood the extent of the physical commitment required; it was beyond him because he only had one lung. Emilio was a quiet young man with incisive and logical arguments that inspired confidence. Illness had forced him to quit medical school but Héctor was still a medical student. The brothers shared political ideals and had encouraged a whole group of medical students and work colleagues to do political work in local factories. Another member of this group, Agustín Gringo Canello, had already qualified as a doctor but, dedicated to the cause of the dispossessed, was ready to leave his post at the local hospital immediately.

Before going on to Mendoza, I wrote to Masetti asking what to do with the flood of applicants willing to join us. We had to set up a mechanism for incorporating recruits without arousing suspicion, so I suggested using the bus to Tarija but staggering arrivals. I cloaked messages to him in the terminology of a construction company: electrical units, bags of cement, bribes and customs. I gave the address of a bookshop in Córdoba belonging to a friend of Oscar's, either to leave letters in the name of Laureano, or to ask for me during normal opening hours.

I took the night bus to Mendoza so that I would arrive in the city during the day. Leaving home is easy; going back is more difficult. As I had done in Bell Ville, I turned for help to a left-wing friend, Ramón Avalos, rather than my family. To do my job safely and efficiently, I needed to block my feelings, limit my emotions, keep a distance from my own self. Mendozans are creatures of habit, so I walked from the bus terminal to the Sorocabana café on Avenida San Martín. I bumped straight into Ramón, a journalist and member of our cultural group. I asked him to find a safe house for me and he found none better than his own. More typically Mendozan than the poplars, Ramón's generosity extended to everyone for no other reason than it was not in his nature to ignore a cry for help. Once the reason for secrecy was revealed (a bit exaggerated in his opinion), we agreed I should talk to his political mentor and our mutual friend, Cholo. Settled in his house, a thick blanket of memories threatened to envelop me while Ramón went about his business, returning at sunset with Cholo.

Cholo was a classmate of my elder brother Avelino and had known me since I was a kid. When he and his friends used to come and study at my house – Marxism, rather than the usual subjects – I would pester them like a tedious bluebottle until one of them, Perelmuter, a bit of a Stalinist, gave me such a huge kick up the arse I remember it to this day. My brother settled nearby in San Rafael but Cholo stayed in Mendoza and we became friends. At the time of this story he was a dissident Communist Party cadre, and the man to speak to about such matters. Although very emotional, he had lost none of his analytical ability. He examined the project using the same criteria we did, and became our contact in the region.

Back at Oscar's house in Córdoba, waiting for a new identity card so I could cross the border and return to the *finca*, his wife Beba said someone was looking for me, or rather, someone was looking for Laureano! In Córdoba I used the name Roberto, but she knew about Laureano. A young man, briefcase in hand like a medical supplies salesman, was waiting in the garden. I don't remember how he got to the house; probably through the usual ritual of contacts and Oscar had sent him over. When he saw me he smiled and said: 'Ah, Pelao, sorry, I mean Laureano!' I had no doubt Masetti had sent him, so determined was he to call me Pelao. He explained that he had come from the *finca*, that he was a friend of Leonardo's from Buenos Aires University medical school. He had brought instructions for me, before continuing on to Buenos Aires. We arranged to meet later in Buenos Aires so I could introduce him to my contacts. His name was Jorge Bellomo, another Petiso because short men meet the same fate as bald men. He was a Cuba enthusiast who on a trip to Havana had picked up the accent and embraced the cause. He was faithful to it until he was kidnapped and blown up by the Triple A (Argentine Anti-Communist Alliance) in 1975.

With Masetti's instructions in my hand, I was able to send the first batch of recruits before returning to Buenos Aires.

14

They All Wanted to Climb Aboard: September 1963

Studies may well be done of all the different social and psychological mechanisms that prompted a generation of young people to make such sacrifices for a revolutionary ideal. With hindsight, it would seem to be an unrepeatable phenomenon. Perhaps you could say that back then there was a future they wanted to be a part of, and now there is no alternative but the present, and nothing matters but living in the moment.

How terrifying, and at the same time remarkable, that those young people were so willing to give up family commitments, career plans, past achievements and future dreams. They scrapped it all in search of a utopia. And they were attracted not by glory or a guaranteed hamper of prizes, but by a journey into the unknown, leading to almost certain death, or at best a slim chance of survival. They all wanted to climb aboard. I did not have to persuade any of them. On the contrary, I tried to paint as bleak a picture as possible of what lay in store: unbelievable hardships, exhaustion and hunger, and insects that give no quarter. But nothing stopped them.

In Buenos Aires, the Anthropology Department of the Faculty of Philosophy and Humanities had become the hub of the EGP, together with the Medical School — Leonardo and Petiso Bellomo's stamping ground. Bellomo was entrusted with coordinating our project in the capital. He took three new volunteers, Pirincho, Pupi and Grillo, up to the *finca* in Bolivia, although he himself asked for time to finish his studies. From Córdoba I sent Héctor Jouvé and another recruit whose name I can't remember, perhaps Colina or del Hoyo. To my embarrassment, I could not go with them because I still had no papers. The problem was solved a few days later, however, when Oscar del Barco obtained from an old Communist Party contact a document I could alter. It came with an added bonus. Oscar suggested I might like to talk to a former regional party secretary who had just split from the national leadership. I felt I was about to hit the jackpot.

The man in question was Armando Coria, who had been one of the Communist Party's most important and authentic cadres but who now led the province's 'revolutionary' current which was pro-Cuban and pro-armed struggle. Mature and reliable, among so many 'improvisers', he stood for solid political thinking, proper analysis of the current Argentine situation, hands-on experience, and links with the working class. His enthusiasm disarmed me, and I asked him to organize our fledgling structure at the national level. I handed him our contacts in Buenos Aires and Mendoza, with a strict internal security plan, and finally I set off north to Bolivia, confident that the organization was really beginning to take shape.

I got off the bus near the trail leading to the *finca*, and walked for a few hours following the jeep tracks, wading swollen streams and assaulted by insects, without meeting a soul. As the sun was setting I found the barbed-wire fence, and arrived at the house. When I reached the citrus orchard, Hermes came out to meet me, shouting over his shoulder: 'It's Laureano, *coño*, it's Pelao!' Masetti welcomed me warmly and enthusiastically, transmitting for the first time something other than praise for military prowess, or recognition of mission accomplished. The house looked the same, but there was no sign of the people I had been expecting. Don Benito was cooking, Furry was away. 'And the rest?' I asked, without specifying names. 'Training with Federico', said Masetti, 'they only come home at night'.

The 'army' had doubled since I had left, but there was one important absence. Leonardo, Médecin, was no longer part of the original group. Masetti explained that he had asked for permission to leave on health grounds (he had *lupus erythematosus*), and had returned to Cuba to be with his family. In his stead, he promised to pass through Buenos Aires and send a friend of his; which he did. This explained the sudden appearance of Petiso Bellomo at my Córdoba safe house. Furry had managed to get a passport from the Cuban Embassy in La Paz, and Médecin had departed forever.

Federico appeared with the 'new boys' who already looked shattered. Uniforms drenched in sweat, gaunt faces and long beards, they looked like the reincarnation of our time training with Hermes; although that was a walk in the park compared to this mountainous jungle. To compensate, Masetti allowed them to sleep on the living room floor with the rest of us. There was a rota of guard duty until morning reveille, followed by a hearty breakfast, the only food until the evening.

Overall, morale was enthusiastic. Masetti had imposed his personal style of leadership: brilliant, severe and playful at the same time. Using my arrival as a pretext, after our meal he called a meeting that established a hierarchical distinction between the new arrivals and the original core group – now four plus Furry – for military and operational purposes. The structure would be as follows: one operations commander – himself; one rearguard commander – Furry; one captain attached to command headquarters – Hermes; one operations lieutenant – Federico; and one intelligence, security and urban relations lieutenant – me.

Masetti and I talked all night, with me describing every step I had taken and the number and attributes of the contacts I had made. But it was not enough to hide his disapointment at Bettanín's reaction; he felt as if one half of himself had denied the other. He was amazed, however, by the great potential of three of the recruits: Cordobés Jouvé, Correntino Stachioti (Federico's friend), and Pirincho Goicochea, a friend of Leonardo and

Bellomo from Buenos Aires. Héctor Jouvé, the fourth-year medical student whom I had interviewed strolling under the trees in Córdoba, was the ideal candidate. His humanity enveloped everyone round him. Correntino was the group's missing link, practically a local man, accustomed to living in the bush, an excellent explorer with unique physical strength. And Pirincho, already a qualified surgeon, was the ideal replacement for Médecin, or even an improvement. He was very calm, with an easy, rather ironical smile, a hard worker, very friendly and willing, although he appeared to think discipline did not apply to him.

In time, being a doctor ceased to be important because we would soon have more doctors than anything else. It might have been copycat syndrome: doctors naturally wanted to be Che. Our main seedbed was the university, and the students who saw suffering and misery at closest quarters were from the Humanities department and the Medical School. The latter in hospital emergency wards, the anthropologists in the shanty towns.

Furry kept bringing in weapons, and we now had more guns than men. The prospects for growth were no longer a dream, it was really happening. Masetti decided to take extra rifles so there would never be men without weapons in the short term. When we arrived in our target area near Orán, I would tour the cities again to establish a line of supply and delivery. Among the new weapons were two Chinese bazookas: a long, thin and light tube with a trigger mechanism. We also had new M1 rifles and Thompson submachine guns, as well as plenty of ammunition and missiles for the bazookas. The house looked like an arsenal, so we stuffed the spare weapons in the ceiling over Furry's bed, hidden by sacks of potatoes and flour. Our precautions were opportune.

One afternoon, Masetti, Federico, the cook and I were in the house, when we heard the sound of vehicles. They could only be approaching along the track to the house. Furry was away on a trip, and was not expected that day, least of all in more than one truck. Masetti sent Don Benito into the bush to look for Hermes, who was training the recruits, to tell him to cover the perimeter of the *finca*, then come back himself with wood for the fire. The noise of car engines was now about a hundred metres away and Federico and I went up to the mezzanine, guns at the ready. We saw two police jeeps from Tarija. They stopped at the gate, and the half dozen occupants got out.

Masetti came out to welcome them like a *finca* owner receiving friendly visitors and, although we could not see them, we heard them talking animatedly on the patio in front of the kitchen window. At one stage, Masetti came into the house and, standing beneath the mezzanine, told us to jump out of the back window if we heard him cough, and hide in the undergrowth behind the house, in order to block their way if they wanted to search the *finca*. He went out again carrying the briefcase with the *finca* deeds, a bottle of brandy and glasses 'to toast the police chief'. We opened a small skylight, climbed out backwards, our rifles slung across our backs, and hung by our fingertips from the edge to shorten the four metre fall to the ground. When Masetti coughed, we dropped one after the other, our rifle butts scraping the wall, as if we wanted to draw the attention of a whole regiment! Masetti persuaded the police chief he was just a regular landowner come to farm pigs. He avoided a catastrophe. The policemen drank coffee, picked grapefruit, and left.

After a reasonable amount of time had passed, Masetti posted sentries along the road and concluded the time had come to leave for good. In the meantime, we had to go back to sleeping outside, except for the legal 'owners and administrators', cook included.

During the final preparations for our second attempt to enter Argentina, two envoys from Che arrived unexpectedly in La Paz. Furry brought them to the *finca*. One was a captain in the Cuban intelligence services, but assigned to Che, called José María Papi Martínez Tamayo (he had fought with Raúl Castro in the Sierra Maestra); the other was Alberto Castellanos, a lieutenant in Che's bodyguard, a comrade of Hermes. It made us think Che was preparing to come himself. But we were nowhere near ready, nowhere near our target zone of operations.

Alberto tried to persuade Masetti to let him join our column, despite strict orders to wait at the *finca* until his boss arrived. He argued, not unreasonably, that the person who would be taking Che into Argentina should already be familiar with the route and any potential obstacles. He would gain valuable experience, he said, rather than staying at home eating. Also, it was an unequivocal token of his good will. Masetti saw the advantages, given the huge load of extra weapons to be carried, so he finally agreed. Alberto was added (but not given a rank) to my rearguard group of Cordobés, Pirincho and Pupi. Pirincho moved to the middle group with Masetti and Hermes.

On a September day, after a pep talk about the whys and wherefores of the People's Guerrilla Army, the growing core of the EGP swore to take the Revolution to Argentina; a disproportionately large aim compared to our meagre forces but not compared to our love, illusions and dreams. We struggled across the frontier into our nation's territory.

The extra men and equipment meant that transporting us along the road was more complicated this time, given the weight on a not very big Toyota. But we did it. Furry worked with his usual cool punctillious confidence, as if detached from the emotional turmoil raging inside the rest of us. He took loads to the main road, hid them, and came back for us. At dead of night, he packed us into the jeep, even on the running boards, and delivered us all in one go. The new ford in the river, further south past the highest peaks, was swollen by the melting ice caps and the freezing water was chest deep. In the darkness we formed a chain to pass the equipment across the river.

First we said goodbye to Furry, who stood on the bank embracing us one by one, like a stage director introducing his actors before raising the curtain and turning on the spotlights. He was gone before we were even out of the water. If all went well, we would see him again soon. We had a rendezvous in two weeks' time at a point on the map where a track branched off the road to Orán, and disappeared into the jungle near the River Pescado (a mountain river that was impassable according to what Furry had seen on his jeep excursions round the area). What is more, the agricultural valley around the city of Orán was also impossible to cross unless the guerrilla army was invisible. So the rendezvous was like a message written on water: a predetermined date and hour which would only be met by the magic of Furry's operational precision and our own superhuman efforts.

We needed to trek through the jungle in order to avoid the border patrols, but we also had to stay in the foothills which, from that point on the map, became lower and spread out to form the wide valleys of Calilegua, Orán and the other agricultural areas fed by the rivers gushing down from the melting snows of the Andes. These rivers span huge differences in altitude, down from 5,000 metres to practically sea level on their way to the River Paraná.

Our biggest problem was the enormous weight we were carrying. Hacking our way through the undergrowth up the hillsides, it became clear we could not do it in one go. We established a system of advancing in stages, leaving part of the load, walking on for while, then leaving the first load and coming back for the rest. We covered three times as much ground, but only carried half the load. On our previous attempt, we had been forced to dump equipment that we never recovered (among other things, the damn generator). But this time, we had weapons and ammunition we could not afford to lose.

Such a situation divides the strong from the weak, the more able from the less able. It is a debilitating process that the military mindset easily falls into, and guerrillas are no exception. It became gradually clear to us at two extremes: while Correntino got stronger by the day, carrying the heaviest loads, doing most of the exploring (walking on while the others rested), Pupi – another of Leonardo's Buenos Aires recruits – was falling to pieces. Although everyone gave him a hand, he was my responsibility, both as the officer in charge of his group and as 'political commissar', so I had my work cut out encouraging him, giving him moral support, and keeping the problems he was causing from Masetti. Apart from Pupi, all the others coped well with the pitiless life of a guerrilla, and displayed qualities and virtues. Enduring hunger and bugs was a personal matter; enduring the workload and discipline (and some injustice) was a question of principle.

One evening while pitching camp, Masetti discovered that according to the map we were only a stone's throw from the rendezvous with Furry. Federico and Hermes went out to explore, and found an old road, just a track really, that looked as if it went down in the vicinity of the river, or even to the river itself if it turned out to be the track that lorries used to carry sand. It proved to be so, and we had indeed arrived at the rendezvous a day earlier than planned. We celebrated the fact with a meagre, almost illusory, amount of food, reinforced by general high spirits.

Dug in at the intersection of the track and the Aguas Blancas-Orán road, we waited for the jeep. It emerged from total darkness at the appointed hour, about two in the morning. Furry flashed his headlights, we answered with a torch, and in silence loaded up the equipment, backpacks and weapons. Half our column got into the jeep, including Masetti and Hermes, while the rest of us stayed to wait for the return trip. The operation was risky despite the late hour. Furry had come from Orán. Although the road had been deserted, and he had checked there were no border police controls, flying checkpoints could be set up at any time if, for instance, the same vehicle was heard passing for a second or third time so late at night. In the solitude of forested ravines and valleys, the sound of a car engine carries a long way and locals know exactly whose vehicle it is. Roaring up to the bridge over the river, the noise of the jeep's engine made us feel as if we were caught in a mousetrap. If we met a checkpoint, we would have to shoot our way out.

Once again we said goodbye to Furry, who would wait until dawn before returning to Bolivia. The reunited group returned to the undergrowth in search of the distant forested hills below Orán and to the west. This was the area chosen for our exploratory work;

it would enable us to move around, without needing to go into the valleys of Tucumán. But man proposes and hunger disposes. The rest in the jeep had not reduced the weight of our load, and as rations became smaller, the march became impossible. Cooking to soothe the hunger pangs of ten exhausted human wrecks meant continually depleting our reserves of cereal, cans and other transportable food. And thirst was even more of a problem. You can spend days without eating, or eat hardly any food for a month, but no one can go twenty-four hours without water. Although big rivers rushed across the region in some areas, the stunted thorny scrub lowlands that we had to cross did not have a single miserable stream, and the heat dehydrated us even when we stood still.

One midday while we rested exhausted in a clearing, I heard someone slashing at the undergrowth behind me. Federico, who was in front of me, leaning on his rucksack against a tree trunk, machine gun on his thigh, reacted like a sergeant and without moving shouted: 'Halt! What do you want?' The man, a poor peasant, followed by a ragged boy in a hat larger than his head, stammered that they were looking for a cow and its calf. 'Nothing else, *señor* . . .' 'Get out of here, these are military exercises, it's very dangerous!' ordered Federico. No one said a word. The miserable twosome crossed the circle of armed men, ragged as they were, mumbling: 'Good day, *señor* . . . good day', and disappeared into the brambles.

We had to get out of the area quickly, but we still needed water. Correntino climbed a tree and said that he could see brighter green towards the south. Masetti told me and Cordobés to keep exploring until we found water. We left our backpacks and, each with our own rifle, hooked all the empty water bottles to our waists and set off. We crossed the brambles, sometimes crawling like snakes rattling their tails. We were about to admit failure when the scrub began to change. Flocks of birds flew screeching overhead. We had found the wide brown Las Piedras river. Héctor and I dived in fully dressed among the bamboo eager to drink the muddy waters.

We returned with the good news and the group moved towards the river. We crossed it and continued towards the hills. Masetti sent Correntino to a hamlet marked on the map to buy whatever food he could find. He returned with flour, tins and cereal from a general supplies store servicing the few sparse settlements. Masetti sent him back time and time again, the distance getting greater as we moved further away, and each time Correntino came back loaded like a pack horse with rice, beans and tinned food.

On one of his errands, Correntino did not return on schedule. Masetti ordered Federico and me back down the path to the scrubland to post a sentry, in case he had been arrested and made to lead a patrol after us. We reached the spot at dawn, hid at one end of the forest with an escape route, and waited. The day passed, and the night brought a persistent drizzle which forced us to lie under our nylon sheeting with branches on top. We took turns sleeping to keep an eye on the bend in the road where whoever it might be would appear. Federico was sure no one would come, and I had an inkling he already knew why.

Correntino never showed up and, back at camp two days and a wet night later, we had to face Masetti's wrath. Fortunately he respected the rules set by the core group which allowed internal discussion. Federico and I argued that you could not demand supernatural efforts from the same man, day in day out, without pushing him to desert. Masetti decided that, from then on, he would apply the rules equally rigourously to the weak and gutless. He also said that on my next tour of the cities, I should find out what had happened to Correntino before talking about desertion because, were that the case, we had to add theft to the charge, since he had taken the food money.

The EGP did not have much money. Masetti had less than 50,000 US dollars and each officer carried a couple of thousand in case we got separated. I had most of the local currency, a few more thousand (in US dollars, I can't remember the exchange rate), that I had to manage extremely carefully. But in all honesty, I don't know exactly how much money we had, or how much

Furry managed back at base. Anyway, Che was clearly not squandering the Revolution's money.

When we reached the hills and found an appropriate place to camp for a few days, Masetti ordered me off on another trip to the cities. I was to travel through the central provinces, developing established contacts and making new ones; buy a van and set up a permanent supply route from Córdoba, run by Gringo Canello who had a driving license. In Buenos Aires, I was to contact an electronics engineer suggested by Bellomo and discuss the price and construction of a generator-powered portable radio rig; begin to stock up on medical supplies, clothes, boots and, where possible, get equipment like hammocks and rucksacks made. I was also to resume relations in Buenos Aires, including this time with the local 'Vasco' Bengoechea group; and above all, send more recruits.

From then on, my trips to the cities became monthly. Sometimes I would arrive back at camp, and Masetti would send me off again a week later.

15

Bringing More Recruits to the Jungle Camp: November 1963

I was now travelling the length and breadth of Argentina, marvelling at its geographic and demographic diversity. It was gratifying to return to the cities where I already had contacts and see how rapidly the EGP was growing and organizing. I made new contacts in La Plata, Rosario and Santa Fe, and I interviewed some of the many hopefuls. We bought an IKA pickup truck and left it with Canello in Córdoba. We created systems of packaging food, clothes, shoes, and all kinds of equipment that guerrillas need, stockpiling it by weight and type, then taking it up in the very overloaded pick-up.

In Buenos Aires, I asked for a girl to accompany me. It fulfilled two important roles. One, to pretend to be my girlfriend (which she did in fact become) so I would not have to travel on my own all the time – this was not normal and could get me noticed. And two, to be an *aide-mémoire*, an unwritten record of appointments and places of contact. Ana María was chosen for this task. She and her friend Susana, both anthropology students, did a lot of the non-clandestine work but adopted the names Paula and Andrea for secret assignments. Another key worker was Bellomo's assistant Rafael who was studying economics. He was an amazing organizer and set up workshops to make hammocks and turn work clothes into uniforms. We rented an apartment where a couple of recruits lived, but all the appointments and contacts were made by rotating meeting places without ever using real names or addresses.

I talked to the radio technician: sworn to secrecy, he agreed to build a transmitter. I gave him a large sum of money to buy materials and we left it that when the time came, he would assemble it wherever we chose. The sociology students, under Daniel Hopen, said they would find out what had happened to Correntino. They organized a market-research project for a type of washing powder, and some *compañeras* from Santa Fe did surveys in a couple of areas, including the part of Corrientes that Correntino's family was from. He was back living at home.

In Mendoza, Cholo had recruited a section of the Vineyard Worker's Union. As agricultural day labourers, they were the most exploited sector of the wine industry, and one of the poorest in the province. The political work he did with them could have been an important platform in the long term, but it was counter-productive in the short term because agricultural workers cannot be uprooted just like that, least of all from production in one geographical area to a completely different kind hundreds of kilometres away. The growth of a guerrilla army depends on local people, who support them in return for protection. Forming advance cadres, the stage we were then at, was something quite different.

Back in the camp, I discovered that Furry was due to arrive on a set date in Buenos Aires via Montevideo; he had been researching alternative ways of bringing in the weapons he had stored there, an operation to be called 'Operation Trampoline'. I had to fetch him and bring him back to the camp. My group accompanied me down one of the trails. I left them my M3 and my uniform, put on my usual creased civilian clothes, and set off on a surreal solitary walk, strolling out of the jungle as if I was leaving a cinema.

In Buenos Aires, when the overnight ferry from Montevideo arrived, Furry and I met casually as tourists might do, and we set off on the 1,400 kilometre bus journey back to our jungle base, stopping in Córdoba and Salta. This gave him an overall view, not only of the huge size of the country, but of how fast our network was growing, and how it worked. At the same time, we authorized four young Buenos Aires recruits to take the train to Salta: Diego, César and Marcos, classmates of Ana María's in anthropology, and another student, Ariel Maudet. Furry was to travel separately from the recruits to avoid making unecessary contact until we reached more favourable terrain. He and I sat in different seats on the bus, occasionally exchanging words as strangers would, sharing a table for a meal, or having coffee on adjoining stools at a bar. The important thing was not to lose sight of each other.

In Córdoba, we arranged to rendezvous with Gringo Canello's pick-up truck at the edge of the jungle where the loggers' track crossed the small river. We reached Salta the previous afternoon and decided to sleep in proper beds. We found a pension, went out for a walk, had a meal, and what better way to pass the time than seeing a film? Half a block from the cinema, facing a hotel, we were standing on the edge of the pavement to let the traffic pass when Furry suddenly clutched my arm. I looked at him. His index finger was raised like a speaker on the barricades, he was stammering, his eyes were rolling and mouth was sagging, as if he was jokingly trying to imitate a moron. I said 'Stop fooling around, let's cross the street', but he kept pointing his finger as his knees buckled under him. His head hit the road hard. He was foaming at the mouth.

All my emergency training clicked into action. While passers-by gathered, I picked him up and carried him across the street to the hotel. With my last ounce of strength, I dumped him in a chair in the lobby where he sat in convulsions, hands and head hanging. The concierge offered to call a doctor. With total calm, I wiped his mouth, pulled his tongue out, put a pencil between his teeth, and said, 'Thank you, there's no need. It's epilepsy, he needs a couple of hours sleep, that's all. He has his medicine.'

The hotel manager wanted Furry out of the lobby, so he got the keys to a room, and helped me carry him to the bed. I offered to pay for the room for a day, although I assured him I would take him to the car when he woke up in about three hours time. I explained that the fit only lasted a few minutes, and now he was asleep. I took the pencil out of his mouth and, sure enough, Furry was sleeping like an angel. I sat in a chair by the bed wondering what to do. No one had mentioned the obligatory registration of hotel guests, but I did not want to risk it with the documents we had. We already had a contact in Salta, a friend of the Philosophy Faculty group in Buenos Aires, and I decided to go and find him, leaving Furry asleep. I told the concierge I was going to get the car. I found Salvador Del Carril and arranged to take Furry straight over there, even though he had no idea who he was. The taxi I took back to the hotel waited while I paid the bill and carried out a drowsy Furry to be taken to the safety of a family home. Promising to be back in time for breakfast, I went to sleep at our pension.

We continued our bus journey first thing in the morning but a tropical storm prevented our getting off the bus at the appropriate place. We could see neither the road nor the jungle through the downpour, so we carried on to Orán to wait for it to subside. In the afternoon, the thunderous crackle of the electric storm receded like a miltary band and, as often happens in the tropics, a parade of black convoluted clouds followed the noisy procession, while light fluffy reddish formations appeared on the horizon, generally a sign of good weather. We took a taxi back to the point of entry into the jungle, pretending to be going to a real *finca* that had a sign on the road (farmers usually hung a flag or piece of white cloth to show passengers where to get off). A long impossible trek awaited us: covering the trail was a mixture of mud, a blanket of leaves and recently fallen branches, as if the jungle had had a haircut. The peaceful stream had become a raging torrent, with tree trunks and drowned animals dragged along issuing dire warnings, their stiff legs pointing to the sky like sailing boats down the gutter. The full force of nature had been unleashed.

We approached our usual fording place with caution, as we had heard shouting from a long way off. The ford had disappeared, but on one side of the now tumultuous waters was our pick-up truck. The river raged between two groups of men shouting to each other as they tried to erect a pully from trees on both banks. A hopeless task: when the water level rose like that, the only thing to do was to wait for it to subside. Furry and I introduced ourselves as if we just happened to be passing by, and took charge. A few hours later, the water level fell as quickly as it had risen and our pick-up crossed the stream.

Furry drove the pick-up while the rest of us pushed, knee-deep in mud. It was already night when we reached the rendezvous with our rearguard. The trail died in Las Piedras river, thundering down in honour of its name, dragging stones and boulders with it. We camped this side of the river, in a clearing hidden from the path, and got food organized. I asked who was responsible for that racket at the ford. Three Buenos Aires recruits owned up and I said they would do guard duty that night as punishment for risking our group's safety with their shouting. It seemed opportune to remind them of the importance of discipline, emphasizing what was at stake here, they were not on holiday.

Next morning, we made contact with the recruits from Córdoba who, lead by Héctor and made up of Henry, Jorgito and Enrique, were crossing the river from the other side. They brought extra empty backpacks inside their own, which meant we could spread the load between a dozen men. After a goodbye coffee for Canello and his assistant, we set off walking again, facing an even harder river crossing: one that descended ever more torrentially, its brown waters frothing and foaming. The experienced men crossed first and the rest followed in single file.

The main camp had one of its best days with the arrival of so many new and enthusiastic recruits. Euphoric under a thick black beard which made him look an embattled crusader, his olive green képi balanced with great difficulty on his mass of unruly hair, Masetti held a series of meetings, starting with Furry. The scene was similar to another I witnessed later when I brought along our bedside Marxist Pancho Aricó, but with an important psychological difference. With Pancho, Masetti was the leader of an important operation; with Furry, a young comandante, a graduate of Che's victorious forces in the Sierra Maestra, he was in charge of their mutual boss's project. The dichotomy was between the done and the still to be done, or more precisely, between reality and dreams. Furry stayed for a few days. I had to make another city trip, so we left together.

However, between our crossing into Argentina and my arrival by pick-up at the target zone, the morale of one of the Buenos Aires recruits, Pupi Rotblat, had deteriorated and become an intolerable burden for all of us. At first, we tried to help him during the treks, lighten his load, encourage him, make him believe he could overcome his lack of ability, careful not to let him lag behind (he was in my rearguard group), cajole him, yell at him, and especially protect him from a Masetti who was becoming increasingly strict and demanding. It was a tricky one. On the one hand, the excess weight, exhaustion and hunger affected all of us, yet we still had to put up with Pupi's constant laments, caprices, sit-downs and generally negative attitude. On the other, Masetti was planning to impose extra guard duties or unpleasant jobs as punishment on the less able when, to be frank, I thought a bit of paternal care might have been more apt.

'It's your responsibility', snapped Masetti if I mentioned signs of despondency in the ranks. It was true that, in some way, I represented the human side of a harsh, sometimes inhumane, reality. Although I never hid how gruelling a test it would be, once recruits got to know and trust me, they felt they could talk to me and discuss political matters, because after all it was a political project. Gradually, more because of my natural predisposition for friendship than my official 'duties', they saw me as the accessible face of the original leadership, to whom everyone went if there was a problem. My visits to the camp were as appreciated as the supplies I brought, and they always had a list of demands and complaints to bring up with Masetti. Letters from family, news from outside, and reminders of home, made me a focal point for them, but above all, it was the ability to communicate outside disciplinary and hierarchical norms. 'Pelado, why don't you make the bread?' they would ask. Hermes had taught us all the technique of baking bread in hot ashes, but mine apparently was tastier, more homely.

I talked to each of them at night during guard duty, and the conversation always turned to the bitter subject of Masetti's arbitrary behaviour towards the *'pan blanco'*, a name he had invented in the Havana house for lads of a more gentle disposition, not out and out warriors, and by extension all new recruits. I tried to combat the idea they had of preferential justice, explaining that Masetti's pedagogical methods came from his strict military formation, inclined to efficiency, will power, etc. In short, a certain machismo. But that behind the facade was an astute politician, a writer of great clarity, and a fantastic guy with total commitment to a common cause. They had to try to gain his respect and overcome the hardships until Che finally arrived, when a new era would begin.

But these arguments did not work with Pupi. His descent into the abyss was of a different kind. He had no pride to cling to, he didn't seem to want to climb back out. He used every possible form of irritating behaviour to hinder our common effort, in which one person's sloppy attitude affected a group already at the end of its tether. He sat down when we took a break and made a fuss when we set off again. He lagged behind and we had to go back for him. He learned nothing, not even how to make a fire, let alone food.

But one thing was clear: we could not abandon him to his fate on a jungle trail nor allow him to be captured. The latter would jeopardize not only the column, but also the support network in Bolivia and the Argentine cities, indeed, the entire project. The idea of getting him out of the region, and if need be, the country, was mooted, but Masetti was having none of it, wouldn't even discuss it. I was unable to argue the toss with him or persuade the others, maybe because I didn't really believe it myself.

In the end, Masetti decreed he be shot. But in the pale reflection of itself our revolutionary dream had become, the sentence was not even carried out properly, and looked more like murder than 'military justice'. A new contingent of recruits had arrived that day, and the scene that greeted them at dusk was dyed a bright red, matching the sunset between the lianas. Masetti separated us into two groups: the new arrivals in one, at a distance from the camp where Pupi lay isolated in his condemned man's hammock; and the original leaders and the earlier intake of recruits in the other.

Masetti explained his reason for the sentence to the new recruits: the need to put an end to a traumatic situation that was undermining group morale. Nobody questioned the legitimacy of the decision, not even those who like myself were against it. Someone had to carry out the sentence. Masetti chose Pirincho, one of his favourites. He admired the way his 'class', his calmness, his ease with people, did not prevent him being an effective trainee guerrilla. He wanted to put him to the test.

The silence expressing the anxiety enveloping us all was broken by Pirincho's hoarse 'Me?' and Masetti's cold reply 'Yes, you'. Pirincho went off, and a few minutes later we heard the shot. He came back even whiter than the rest of us, murmering: 'He won't die, he doesn't want to die!' Masetti sent me to see what had happened. The victim of a tragic personal experience and a seriously distorted collective mindset was lying in his hammock, a bullet in his forehead, shuddering in his death throes, but technically dead. I did what I had to do to finish this macabre spectacle, and the bang has resonated in my head ever since.

Upriver from our camp, where a path climbed from the river bank to a small plateau on which patches of land had been clawed back by the jungle, we came across a group of dilapidated shacks. The chicken coop and goat pens were barely distinguishable from the adobe house with its straw and pole roof, and a front yard which set it back from the slope we had just climbed. The owner came out timorously, surrounded by almost naked children and ragged women, some young, some older, but all of indefinable age. All were barefoot. It was a pitiful sight. I made some attempt to find out who they were and how many people lived there, if there were other houses in the vicinity, if they could sell us an animal and if they would let us camp, but the man's replies were limited to 'Yes, *señor*, no, *señor*'. Masetti took over the 'conversation' and despite his frightening appearance, began breaking down the fear caused by our uniforms, weapons and beards. There were only a few of us in his yard, but he had already seen the others waiting on the path and pointed to them anxiously. Leaving sentries on all points of entry, Masetti signalled to the others to come up, take off their backpacks and put down their weapons.

Relations thawed. Our doctors examined the children for various visible infections, in their ears and eyes. We cooked a chicken stew, made bread, and shared our rations with the family, who ate crouched against the walls of the house like frightened animals. Their story was tragically familiar. They were sharecroppers evicted from their plots time and time again, forced into the jungle, away from their landlords but also from any hypothetical state protection, no school, no doctor, reduced to a state of idiocy by hunger and solitude. We spent the night there, our hammocks hung between the house and the corral, invaded by fleas and mosquitoes.

Masetti made a deal with the man, named Pedro, that when he went to the nearest town, he would buy us provisions, and we would give him money. For now, it was just to find out how good a messenger he was. 'Don't show the money', recommended Masetti. 'No, sir, they'll take it straight off me.' He said there was a 'bloody horrible landlord', who owned most of the land between the valley and the mountains, the route we had climbed. He had a very nasty gang of men and an even worse foreman, who appeared at sowing and harvest time, giving orders and requisitioning, so they couldn't sow what they wanted, and could barely make a cent. Masetti encouraged him to refuse to hand over his crops, but this frightened him even more. 'What?' he said, 'They'd just come back with the army and burn everything.'

Masetti explained that was why we had taken up arms and that when the moment came, we would teach his tormenter a lesson, and others like him, starting with his landlord. To affirm our friendship, and thinking mostly of his family's safety in case something unexpected happened, we agreed that, if the foreman or his gang appeared, Pedro would come down to the river to get water and tie a piece of red cloth in a secret place we chose together. After sharing breakfast, we left Pedro's house and poverty-stricken family. We reiterated our concern for his safety and recommended he did the same for us, especially by making sure his children said nothing.

Meeting this family reduced to almost unimaginable poverty had more impact on us ideologically speaking than any Marxist seminar. We walked on with the image of the miserable family frozen in our minds like a film still, feeling a bit ashamed of our own woes, magnified by our egos, but which were minute and transitory compared to these people's existence. It would not be long before I was back at Pedro's house.

When I had returned to the camp from my last city trip, I'd felt a certain tension in the air. Henry had asked to speak to me alone. He said his relations with Masetti were very bad, not because of anything he had done, but because he felt he was being increasingly marginalized. Henry had not been given any responsibilities, was not asked to do important tasks or to go exploring. He had begun to doubt his own abilities, and worse still, started thinking Masetti was discriminating against him because he was Jewish. I rejected this possiblity – and still do today. Masetti was aware of the marked percentage of Jews in our urban network. In fact, the Argentine Left as a whole were either Jewish themselves or married to Jews. Half the EGP national leadership was Jewish. Masetti knew this but he had never said anything to me, although it was my responsibility. Besides, it was impossible to imagine Masetti being anti-Semitic given his relationship with Che. Pupi was not a good example because it was obvious his fate had nothing at all to do with his being Jewish. I assured Henry I would talk to Masetti because I found the atmosphere intolerable, and I did.

Masetti's view was that we were about to embark on operations that were vital to honouring his commitment (to Che), and although he wasn't worried about anyone in particular, Henry had not shown much enthusiasm. However, he would bear him in mind if, as I said, he had promise. No sooner said than done, Henry was to come with me on an assignment. It consisted of going back to Pedro's house and, assuming his first task had gone well, get him to establish a constant supply line of a few basic products – *charqui*, flour, sugar, coffee, cereals – that he could buy in the area and bring up by mule. The only snag was that this plan was potentially even more dangerous for us than the repeated trips of our pick-up: Pedro was desperately poor and could not be a big spender in anyone's eyes. Masetti wanted me to resolve this problem. Our trip would take one day there and one back, so we could do it without heavy backpacks.

Henry was estatic but I was worried. We had to find a trail we had walked only once. Tracking skills were not my forte, and I never developed them because I was always bringing up the rear. We left next morning, going west beside the stream. Halfway to the river the rain bucketed down and the gentle stream turned torrential, its muddy banks hard to negotiate. At nightfall, way behind schedule, we reached the river now flowing menacingly past, its stony teeth chattering. We could not risk crossing in the dark and spent the night huddled together like Siamese twins in a little hollow we dug for our torsos, the water running over our legs down the slope.

When we finally reached the slope to Pedro's house, there was no red cloth warning of danger. Despite the weather, we were only a day late, thanks mainly to Henry; the storm had washed away all signs I thought I remembered, but not his. Pedro looked very pleased to see us, as if deeds not words confirmed our intentions. He had had no problem buying what we asked, and was ready to repeat it as many times as needed. We considered the risk of him turning up and buying an unusual amount and suggested he do it bit by bit in different places and only buy produce he would use himself. His income was at its lowest at this time of year, having only tree trunks to sell to charcoal burners, and maize and potatoes to barter for fat and flour. I left Pedro an unimaginable (for him) sum of money on condition he hide it somewhere safe, away from the house, and use it only when needed. He wanted to buy rope sandals for his family.

We set off back downriver again, hoping to reach the stream before nightfall. Finding it was a miracle. The torrent had altered the shape of the river banks; whereas before the jungle contour plunged down to a beach of stones and sand, now the water covered everything. A couple of trees, like an arch, showed us the entrance to the stream, but the stream itself was a swamp. The water came up to our chests, except when we stumbled and fell in up to our necks. But this was our path, we had to follow it or we would never find the camp. We struggled on, cursing and gargling mud, until at two in the morning we ran into Córdobes and the rest of my squad coming to look for us. After some high-fives, I shouted 'I'm never going down that bloody stream again!' Héctor said 'Masetti is livid! He was expecting you last night . . .'. 'What? Didn't he hear the tempest?' I asked sarcastically. 'His only tempests are in his head', replied Héctor.

Nonetheless, Masetti greeted us warmly. He handed me some dry clothes and said they had saved some stew for us. He added that we should try to get a few hours sleep because, as if remarking how chilly the dawn was, 'In the morning you're taking your squad to the River Bermejo to collect the weapons Furry is bringing.' 'Left speechless' was hardly relevant since I could barely speak from exhaustion anyway. Henry and I had walked for forty hours in impossible conditions, our muscles were screaming with cramps, our feet were raw, yet here we were being ordered to return to the Bolivian border it had taken us two months to trek away from. (The plan actually included public transport to the outskirts of Aguas Blancas, but only after we trekked to Orán, bought clothes, and found a pension.) The fact of the matter was that, against my most fervent wishes, at dawn we were retracing our steps down 'that bloody stream'.

That night in Orán, we attended to our feet, ate steak and slept in a bed, an unexpected and welcome gift. Early next morning a truck transporting labourers dropped us off at the bridge over the River Pescado. We found the old sand lorry road, where we had met up with the jeep on that oh so distant night, and struck off into the jungle. Only the special exploring talents of Córdobes (with whom Masetti had planned the details of my squad's trip) led us on schedule, after two days' march, to the same ford we had waded to enter Argentina. We were five: Córdobes, Henry, Jorgito, a fourth (I'm not sure if it was Enrique) and me. We spent that night and the following day hiding on the Argentine bank of the River Bermejo, waiting for the first nocturnal rendezvous with Furry. Like a precision stopwatch, his jeep arrived around three in the morning, flashing his headlights as usual. The lights extinguished and the jeep disappeared into the darkness, while we swam the river now swollen into an Olympic swimming pool.

The big surprise was seeing Papi Martínez Tamayo, the Cuban captain assigned to the project, who had come to help carry the consignment. Furry had filled backpacks with weapons, munitions, equipment, and some food for the trek. We had only to put them on. A heavy load no longer helped against the current since the seemingly calm surface of the Bermejo now hid treacherous undertows. The tallest among us could wade with water up to our necks, but Jorgito who was very short could not even breathe without swallowing water and his rucksack dragged him down. We crossed holding hands, but in the middle, Jorgito panicked and went under. He could only come up for air by pushing himself off stones on the bottom, while I tried to hold onto him. I shouted for help, because Jorgito was being swept away and me with him. Papi reached the bank, left his backpack and let the current bring him to us. He took charge of the submerged Jorgito, who was about to drown. Our only gun was my Browning pistol held against my abdomen by my leather belt but which started slipping down my right trouser leg and finally tumbled out and lay, like an offering to the river furies, buried in its bosom. We were not, however, unarmed. We were bringing in more weapons than on any previous occasion, including automatic rifles and plenty of ammunition for all types and calibres of guns.

The march was calm but relentless. We were better fed and more relaxed than at other times, no conflict and no pressure except deadlines and the rendezvous with Gringo Canello and his pick-up for the final lap up. Our arrival at the camp was triumphant. Masetti was ecstatic and gave me his Browning to compensate for losing mine, choosing a recently arrived Luger for himself. The guerrilla army, now well armed with plenty in reserve, comprised about twenty men. We had covered an extensive area and were beginning to master its difficult geography, although the contacts we had made with the local population were poor and of not much use politically. We needed to move our zone of operations nearer the Tucumán sugar cane fields where the exploitation was inhuman, and conditions ripe for raising consciousness and beginning political work.

Lack of relations with our potential social base were not our only problem. Relations within the group were not good either. Papi was not there on the offchance. He had arrived at the *finca* with Miguel Ángel Duque de Estrada, a personal envoy from Che, who had orders to wait and enter Argentina with him. Papi had not only come to lend a hand, but also to check the route, see how well things were functioning and ensure tight security. (He travelled throughout the zone and eventually went all the way to Buenos Aires where Ana María escorted him round – she played an important role for the EGP there developing contacts and chosing recruits.)

Masetti put on a show for Papi. He conferred the rank of lieutenant on Cordobés and I passed on to him responsibility for

my squad (to which he belonged) so that, as personal delegate
of the guerrilla command, I could concentrate permanently on
strengthening ties with the cities. With my frequent trips away
from the camp this was de facto already the case. Now that the
network had a life of its own, my trips were used both for coordination purposes and to carry out special missions for Masetti.
In this way, he commanded the whole organization. We created
a permanent base in Salta so that new recruits rendezvousing
with Canello's pick-up did not have to register in a hotel.
Responsibility for this was given to Enrique Bollini Roca, an
architectural student from Córdoba, who always used to ask me
if I needed company on my trips. This job, possibly rotating,
would be an urban vanguard, prior to eventually forming local
supply centres and ending the long-distance dependence on
Córdoba and Buenos Aires.

Masetti wanted a series of meetings with the political cadres
who supported us. He decided to start with the group in Córdoba,
and on my next trip I passed on the invitation. The *Pasado y
Presente* editorial board immediately accepted and chose Pancho
Aricó and Armando Coria. We went up to Salta in two groups. I
advised them on appropriate clothes and footwear and gave them
some pointers, although for the uninitiated there are no valid tips
for trekking in the jungle, except take lots of bandages. The pick-
up took us as far as it could into the jungle, and from then on we
started the usual trek upstream. Enthusiasm, however, is not
waterproof. Armando's strength gave out halfway. His feet in
ribbons, he could not continue, and we had to evacuate him with
Canello who luckily was climbing part of the way with us.
Pancho, who was younger, adjusted to the rigours of the trek
despite his professorial aspect. We reached the camp without
further problems.

For Masetti, the conversation was a success in all respects,
although the surrealist nature of the situation may not have made
a strong enough impression on Pancho to mitigate the eventual
disaster. Pancho shared the vicissitudes of the campaign and

endured the daily hardships, but he also glimpsed the possibility of an integral revolutionary education, and discussed with Masetti the idea of creating in our camps some kind of Maoist 'cadres' school' like the Yenan Forum. There were also discussions with the rest of the *compañeros* sitting round the fire. It was the high point of the Salta political debate.

16

Defections and an Execution: February 1964

Enthusiasm spread throughout the urban network. This was both exciting and a cause for concern, since we needed to absorb new recruits gradually, not overload our capacity to supply them. Otherwise our main task would soon be how to feed a troop of hungry exhausted men wandering aimlessly around the jungle. We also had to guarantee enough weapons to arm our column and to create a strategic stock. So Masetti planned to stop using – at least not exclusively – our rearguard border with Bolivia, thereby guaranteeing the security of the *finca*. He devised a new method of bringing in weapons and equipment through Uruguay, which would rely on the navigational skills of Pirincho, an atypical representative of the Buenos Aires bourgeoisie who had left his yacht anchored in the Tigre delta and embraced the revolutionary cause.

Pirincho had told us about his excursions to Punta del Este, Uruguay. He and his friends sailed to and fro, bringing back cigarettes and booze. He didn't give it much thought, and it was certainly not a business. No one ever questioned him when he moored his sailing boat at the Yacht Club. We deduced that for the Coast Guard, a young playboy's bit of fun and smuggling were two quite different things. In the light of this new focus on his favourite sport, Pirincho would have to study the possibilities *in situ*. He and I would then would meet up in Buenos Aires to plan the rest of the operation.

We moved with ease through an area from which we could expect nothing but solitude and increased knowledge of our environment. The exhausting treks posed no problem for the established explorers like Hermes, Héctor and Federico, but left new recruits ready to quit. The fateful experience with Pupi made us only too aware that physical aptitude was essential, in fact a priority. We could not keep carrying weights that might end up 'dead'. A tacit consensus was rigorously imposed. Hence, a trio of young Córdoban lads from Héctor and Emilio's home town of Bell Ville, who arrived overflowing with enthusiasm, were packed off home after three days when they proved useless. They swore to accept responsibility for not putting our safety at risk.

It happened again with a 'top notch' heart surgeon sent from Buenos Aires, the golden boy of the university contingent. Like Masetti, his name was Jorge, and like him, he was very cocksure. But it lasted only a day or two. Before the week was out, he had melted like a candle, and began showing signs of increasing disintegration, conjuring up the unbearable spectre we all wanted to leave behind. Nonetheless, he was ordered out to explore with me. 'Take the surgeon', barked Masetti. After a few hours trekking through the tangled and aggressive undergrowth, the surgeon's desire to die turned to panic when he realized we were – I was – lost. His sobs, interspersed with convulsive hiccoughs in the best melodramatic fashion, kept on and on. I opened a couple of the tins of sardines I always carried in my uniform pockets, and made him eat while I talked about tomorrow being a new day, and that we would find the track again. To really encourage him, and get rid of his fear and stop his hiccoughs, I pointed my pistol in the air and fired between his head and mine. It must have sounded sweet to him because he calmed down, and even slept.

By next morning, his moaning, whining and complaining was back, and he refused to budge. To show I knew what his game was, I took out my pistol again and stuck it in my belt. I grabbed his collar, pulled him to his feet, and kicked his arse to get him walking. I promised to kick him all the way if need be, and ask for his immediate dismissal. The trail I had not been able to find the previous day was suddenly obvious. Halfway home, at about ten, we bumped into Hermes coming to look for us.

Masetti was hopping mad, but I played down the problem: getting to the river took longer than we thought and we would not have got back before dark anyway. I insisted, however, that we get rid of the heart surgeon without more ado, to avoid a new case of Pupi, something we could not justify to our urban base. The people who sent him had made a mistake and we had to reject him. I don't think it was my debating skill that convinced Masetti to sack the surgeon. He had come to the same conclusion but I had been tasked with the final test. The 'golden boy' left in the same inept bunch as the lads from Córdoba.*

Among the recruits, the sudden separation from their families, added to the hardship of camp life, caused depression which was not treated with much compassion, except perhaps from the *compañero* next to you. It could even produce hallucinations. One night about eight, a noise came up the slope to the camp. 'People are coming up the stream!' shouted the faltering voice of the recruit on guard duty. Federico and I stampeded down the bank. Our search exposed nothing but the sounds of the stream, the creaking of the jungle, and animals. Masetti punished us with eight hours of guard duty for acting off our own bat, after which we would all comb the area since any intruders would have fallen back to wait for dawn when they heard the sentry. Two patrols set out at four in the morning. Federico said a pair of tapirs could make more noise than a border police platoon and we would probably find their tracks. The only tracks found were those made by Federico and me earlier. No tapirs, no border police. Hallucinations.

---

* When I told this anecdote to John Lee Anderson in 1995, the only one of Che's biographers to come and see me about the Argentine part of his project, I confused Jorge with Pupi. However, thinking over the memories that were filtering out, emerging from the shadows, I realized the mistake and wanted to send him a fax telling him this person was not Pupi but another recruit. It was too late, however. So the mistake is not his.

When Héctor took over my squad, he inherited my duties of political commissar, psychologist and shoulder to cry on, and brought his considerable professional skill to the job. I became the 'former squad leader with influence' to whom recruits still turned with latent problems they wanted me to bring up with Masetti on my return to camp. As a result, I learned that another division between 'the favourites' and 'the spurned' was assuming dangerous proportions. A couple of recruits were confined to hammocks: Grillo was on a course of antibiotics after an infected spider bite but Nardo was under 'house arrest'. Henry was in charge of them both. Nardo had deteriorated very quickly, and the understanding and solidarity that tried to save him from Masetti's 'sights' was wearing thin. Masetti's 'liberal' period was over and he had invented his own military codes of conduct. That dangerous mentality that spreads like a virus in exhausted organisms was already gnawing at our principles. We had to act before the crisis came to a head. We were all desperate to get Nardo out.

Under the supervision of our architect Enrique, before he left to set up the base in Salta, Masetti had dug a refuge in the ground with a roof of branches. In this 'commander's headquarters', he escaped the mosquitoes that devoured him as he tried to write and held his private meetings, including those he had with me before and after my trips. I passed on anxieties and concerns. The *Pasado y Presente* group in Córdoba, our most supportive political structure, had already rejected (through me) the repressive 'court martial' as not conducive to the ideals of a liberation project. Now I used practical arguments. Masetti had already agreed to five dismissals, plus the one confirmed case of desertion, and no harmful consequences had ensued. However, we were talking at cross purposes. His arguments were military and mine were political. Nonetheless, Masetti finally bowed to my experience and made me responsible for organizing Nardo's departure, on condition he did not return to his former haunts in Córdoba. That was the deal.

Pirincho had gone to Buenos Aires at the end of January to prepare the ground for his maritime operation. He was to go back to his family and friends with some credible story, take up his privileged life again: yacht club, sailboat, excursions to Tigre and Punta del Este, and his girlfriend. I was to meet up with him on my next trip to evaluate security in terms of Customs and Coast Guard. Charged with these tasks, I set off again in February 1964.

My stopover in Córdoba was devoted to meetings with contacts, and plannng Nardo's transfer to some remote part of the province. One possibility was Gustavo Roca's *finca* in Ongamira. Roca agreed to have him there as an 'administrator'.

I carried on to Mendoza. Cholo knew of a workshop (one of his former Communist Party colleagues worked there) that designed secret compartments in vehicles smuggling goods from Chile for select clients. We needed a vehicle to transport 'compromising material' and Cholo found a Ford 350 pick-up with bodywork covering the back and a large part of the total space hidden under this imposing facade. Commissioned by a smuggler who was now in jail, it was on sale at half price. I authorized its purchase. Cholo would take it to Buenos Aires as soon as the paintwork was finished.

In Buenos Aires, I met contacts, travelled to towns in the immediate vicinity, and discussed supplies and potential recruits with Bellomo and Rafael. Among the candidates were a couple of militants from a Communist Party cell in Matanzas, a town in the province of Buenos Aires. Che's firm stance was 'not to pinch people from the CP' so as to avoid international relations problems unconnected to the project. Contact with these two had cooled, and they had never had access to home addresses or phone numbers. Neither did they know who the political leadership was. Nonetheless, they kept insisting they wanted to join. The fact that one of the candidates was a pedicurist was very tempting, a gift from heaven for feet on forced marches. They were told to resign their party affiliation and finish their studies, then we would see. But the expectations raised back at camp by the possibility of such sophisticated health-care boosted the decision to let them join. They were told they would be contacted at the appropriate time.

Finally free of other engagements, I phoned Pirincho. He sounded a bit ambivalent, but I attributed it to family reasons. We agreed to meet in a café in the Barrio Norte, a smart area near the centre. He did not come. I phoned him and he apologized, alluding to family problems. He asked me to phone the following day. We arranged to meet in a tea room opposite the Belgrano R train station, another elegant area slightly further from the centre. I went with Paula (Ana María), as usual. Ten in the morning was 'family hour' in those circles. From a café across the road, we watched the crowded tea room. I told Ana María not to wait more than half an hour. Crossing the road, I went inside.

Couples and youngsters were sitting at tables against the windows and walls, encircling the centre of the tea room where Pirincho was sitting alone at a table, a coffee in front of him. Intangible criteria that you feel rather than see indicate whether a clandestine meeting will go well or not. The phone calls, the failure to show up, the excuses, had put me on my guard. Pirincho, also obviously wary, had chosen a table in full view of everyone in the café. As I sat down opposite him, I felt apprehensive. His reaction was distant, he showed neither enthusiasm nor surprise.

I don't recall the exact conversation, but the content was memorable. He began by saying he was there out of loyalty to me and our *compañeros*, not to explain anything to Masetti. He was not going to do the Uruguayan operation, nor returning to the guerrillas, nor staying in Argentina. The day I phoned he had just married his girlfriend, and they were leaving for Europe that very night. If any part of him remained sane, he preferred to put it in his own hands and not in Masetti's, whom he no longer respected. The most important part of the project had been completed and he promised never to betray that. He preferred to wipe the whole thing from his memory, although there were some of us he would always remember.

Bellomo, Pirincho's old friend from medical school, promised to make discreet inquiries. By the end of the day we had confirmation of the wedding and the trip to Europe. Another fellow student had been to a private goodbye party organized by Pirincho's family. The episode was over and irreversible. I would have to wait and see the effect when I presented my report to Masetti.

With such a philosophical dilemma weighing heavily on my mind, I started back to Salta. The impact of what had just happened was incalculable, but, analyzing the facts and circumstances, I understood Pirincho, just as I had understood Correntino. They had both taken a gamble, leaving behind a good life for a dodgy offer: beast of burden and totalitarianism, instead of adventure and moral revolutionary. We may all have had, at some time or other, a desire to end such arbitrary and soul-destroying effort. But, for me, personally, still central to everything was a commitment to the ideal and its progenitor – Che – rather than the vicissitudes of its development. The problem was that while some people were ultimately joining a political project, others of us were embodying a myth.

As I approached the camp, I began to get that sense of freedom again, of being more sure of myself, on my home ground. So, telling myself I was happy to be back was not untrue, but it was better not to show it too much, because in the eyes of those welcoming me, I had the privilege of coming from the easy life, the air-conditioned city world, full of flavours and news. And the news I was bringing was bad. It was hard, then, to believe I would receive news that was even worse – Nardo had been executed!

Only days after I left, having solved the problem of Nardo's evacuation to Córdoba, Masetti had set up a military tribunal. Nardo had been tried for moral decline and setting a bad example; in short, as a cancerous, counter-revolutionary infection. At nineteen years of age, he had been found guilty and executed. The fascist mentality had triumphed and struck another fatal blow to our liberating utopia.

Fascism is a state of mind rather than an ideology: the mentality of the absolute exercise of power over the individual, unrelated to age, the environment you're born in, or political affiliation. It is not limited to the Right, nor is the Left immune. Power is an instrument of coercion, blackmail, humiliation and crime: a synthesis of pathological sadism and fundamentalist fanaticism, it is the raison d'être of the owners of the truth, from the miserable torturer in the Navy Mechanics School in Argentina to the sinister Pol Pot. We were impregnated with this *fascistoide* mentality, and we didn't even know it. We thought we were imbued with revolutionary truth but we were just naïve, enamoured of the idea of imposing justice by force.

There is a black hole in my memory at this point, I don't know how the bad news was exchanged. Usually, I was immersed in news long before I reached Masetti, and obviously for the camp the shocking news I brought this time was Pirincho's defection. The other news, about Nardo, only affected me, like a metaphysical implosion. Masetti took my news as a personal affront, he did not believe Pirincho would desert. I must have misinterpreted the facts out of vanity, perhaps to get promoted. It was pure revolutionary infantilism. One phrase echoing this accusation of vanity stuck with me: 'I was waiting for you with your captain's stripes. You'll have to win them again.' No doubt I thought I would not be promoted and I might have said so. Anyway, the subject was closed.

I was to set off again to fetch Furry in Buenos Aires (they were receiving coded messages via Radio Habana, or locally through Radio Tarija) and, in passing, bring back Pirincho. The incongruity of the order, a mixture of security mission – the highest level of risk – and impossible fantasy, seemed like a joke. I don't remember how the discussion continued. There were several other convoluted yet serious suggestions, like beginning military operations by attacking some objective, as yet unidentified but in the pipeline.

Such a plan was diametrically opposed to our project's strategic goals. And that meant, in fact, we would not be able to do it.

It would take only one armed clash to jeopardize the whole programme of exploration, control of territory, growth in manpower and expertise, that was crucial if Che were to come to Argentina. Masetti wanted to strike a blow and then leave the zone, in effect making the anticipated move to a more agricultural region with a larger population, but without doing any of the required groundwork. It was the equivalent of burning your boats without any idea of where you were going. And with a group of men, traumatized by the laws of life and death, showing signs of strength and disenchantment simultaneously. Despite everything, there was one bright spark: Furry's visit might be related to the pending delivery of weapons or, in the best possible scenario, to transcendental news – the arrival of Che. That was what I was hoping for, and I decided to postpone the battle with Masetti until I came back with Furry and found out what our future was to be.

The news of Nardo's fate caused indignation in Córdoba, muted in part by the trust we had built up and the prospect of a discussion with the national leadership when Furry arrived at the camp. I requested lodging for the latter and carried on to Buenos Aires. Things did not have the same immediacy there, not only because of the geographical distance, but also because the group in Buenos Aires was a clandestine cell organization, not a splinter group of a recognized party like *Pasado y Presente* in Córdoba. Bellomo was a de facto 'military cadre' waiting to join the guerrillas once the Buenos Aires infrastructure was firmly in place and Rafael had completed his plan of operations. Meanwhile, they had just dispatched a new group of five volunteers, among them the pedicurist and his friend, the two Communist Party militants from Matanzas. They had left just as I arrived. Of Pirincho, of course, there was no news.

It was the beginning of March 1964, and Buenos Aires was a Turkish bath; boiling hot streets and everything dripping with humidity, even the walls. Furry arrived by plane from La Paz. A prudent conversation, full of things not said but implied, coded and silent, occupied our waking hours. Furry listened and asked questions but gave no indication of what he thought, or let slip anything that he needed to discuss with Masetti first, although the latter's change of plans and a few clues intimating Furry's interest in certain things and not in others (like Pirincho's desertion, the frustrated Uruguayan operation, etc.) made me think the changes were more serious than arbitrary and that perhaps Masetti's dilemma lay in having to do something to justify our existence.

We took the bus together to Córdoba at the crack of dawn. Oscar had arranged for Furry to stay at a relative's house. He said someone from Mendoza wanted to see me at another house, where I could sleep to avoid having to leave at night. We agreed to meet the following day. I was told which buses to take. After eating a *parilla* in the garden of a restaurant in La Cañada, we were both taken to the house. The visitor was my ex-wife Claudia. The whole night was spent in a long overdue conversation. Ramón, in Mendoza, had given her the contact.

We were going to Salta by plane because, as well as saving time, it was less conspicuous than the interminable highway going north, with its endless stops. Oscar would buy the tickets. There was a flight at midday.

17

Sudden and Total Disaster: March 1964

I left the house in Córdoba early in the morning and went to the bus stop. I bought the newspaper *La Voz del Interior*, got on the bus, installed myself in a seat and opened it.

On the front page was a blurred photograph with a heart-sinking headline: 'Border Police Raid Guerrilla Camp in Salta'. Reality suddenly interrupted the dream. The information, provided by the police, was sparse. It spoke of men in charge of a supply camp being surprised and taken prisoner without offering any resistance. Bearded, dressed in olive green uniforms, one with a foreign accent, they were there to light the flame of Castro-communist intervention. The news had to be true: it was Alberto and the *compañeros* of Camp No. 1. I kept my rendezvous with Oscar del Barco and we went together to fetch Furry. We had an improvised meeting and took urgent measures.

Police operations in the north had temporarily blocked the road so we cancelled our flight and our entire trip. Furry needed to leave Argentina immediately and get back to the Bolivian *finca* in Tarija. The people most visibly connected to the EGP had to leave the cities and go into hiding. I had to stay in Córdoba and wait for a pre-established emergency contact, so I could resume our internal links. We organized Furry's return to Buenos Aires to catch an international flight. One of the girls from Córdoba, Jorgito's girlfriend, would accompany him. This was obviously not to nanny him, which he would not want, but an extreme security measure. His being a Cuban comandante would create a diplomatic scandal if there were any incident involving the police, his Cuban accent drew attention like a neon sign, and his unpredictable fits meant it was not safe for him to travel alone in Argentina. The girl would put him on the plane, and then make the necessary contacts in Buenos Aires to raise the alert and take emergency measures. Claudia was to do the same in Mendoza.

Between March and May 1964, the border police occupied the whole guerrilla operations zone, gradually capturing all its members, alive or dead, with the exception of Masetti and Atilio. Those responsible for the EGP infrastructure in Salta were also arrested, and, thanks to the typical error of writing down names and phone numbers, so was a member of the *Pasado y Presente* group, the psychiatrist Samuel Kiszkowsky. The only other civilians to be detained were Eugenio Franco and his wife Nora Levin. We were unable to establish any contact at all with the guerrillas, so our only source of information about how events were developing, week by week, was the press.

Meanwhile, we got together a team of lawyers headed by Antonio Lonatti and Gustavo Roca from Córdoba who, with the help of Farat Salim, Norberto A. Frontini (Grillo's father), Silvia Bouvier and others, interceded for the lives of the detained and acted for the defence during their subsequent trial in Salta. Through them, we were able to piece together information from the survivors and reconstruct the events. It turned out that rumours of suspicious activity in the guerrilla zone had set in motion two lines of investigation, independent of each other and a thousand kilometres apart, by two separate repressive agents of the state.

In Salta, landowners and tenant farmers in the area had heard stories from their day-labourers of mysterious armed men in vehicles moving about the area. They lost no time in informing the border police of the rumours, mainly because they were afraid of losing the exclusive control of the territory they enjoyed, if, as they thought, the men were rustlers or smugglers. Aware of the continual changes to smuggling routes, the border police decided to patrol the zone.

At the same time, in Buenos Aires, three factors coincided: the Secretary of the Argentine Communist Party, Victorio Codovilla (an Italian CP leader imposed by Stalin), was told 'confidentially' by the Secretary of the Uruguayan Communist Party, Rodney Arismendi, that the Bolivian Communist Party 'had confided to him' that they were supporting an Argentine armed group linked to Cuba that was operating in the north of Argentina. As I have already mentioned, Rafael, our man in charge of recruitment in Buenos Aires, had long been in contact with two members of a CP cell in Matanzas who wanted to join. One of them was the pedicurist who had interested us for obvious reasons. In fact, both men were undercover agents of the DIPA, the Argentine secret police (*División de Información Política Antidemocrática*), and had been embedded in the Communist Party for a long time. They had received the same order from both the Communist Party and the secret police: infiltrate the EGP, find its base, and return with information.

Getting the thumbs up after being fobbed off for so long took the couple by surprise, so they had not been able to leave a contact in Buenos Aires. They had no choice but to follow their orders: go to Salta and keep a rendezvous. Their police handlers, however, had them followed in the train until they met their Salta contact. When they learned the new recruits would be continuing the journey in a pick-up, the DIPA decided to continue the operation without informing other parts of the force. An unmarked jeep followed Canello's pick-up (driven by Enrique) with the five volunteers under a tarpaulin in the back. The pedicurist signalled to the jeep with his torch every now and again, but Enrique had perfected his security technique and routinely changed direction when he stopped to fill up at a petrol station, losing the police jeep that was tailing him. The would-be infiltrators were alone and unprotected when Canello's

pick-up turned off the road up the trail into the jungle to where
their reception committee came out of the undergrowth to greet
them. Armed men with beards distributed the heavy loads they
had struggled to carry and ordered them to start marching.
They had no option but to obey.

Diego, with my M3, was in charge of the group and very
friendly to the new arrivals. When they stopped to rest, the pedicurist, who had agreed with his mate to escape before they went
any further into unknown territory, showed an interest in Diego's
gun and managed to wrest it from him. DIPA assault units use
PAM submachine guns, a smaller calibre version of the M3, so,
being familiar with the weapon, he slid the bolt without hesitation, shot Diego in the thigh, and to everyone's astonishment
took charge. An exchange of insults and threats followed, in
which Diego assured them they would be surrounded when the
rest of his *compañeros* heard the shot (the silencer had been taken
off). The pedicurist responded by hastily tying them all up, and
beating a quick retreat.

The border police patrol that had gone that same day to investigate sightings (of smugglers) had not seen Canello's pick-up.
They must have taken another route, following animal tracks
running parallel to the stream, checking places where activity had
been reported. They found nothing until they bumped into a
couple of uniformed men with beards. Not quick enough with
their guns, Grillo Frontini and Marqués del Hoyo were arrested.
With some information about Camp No. 1, the patrol advanced
and surrounded another dirty uniformed man with matted hair,
who looked surprised to see them. It was Alberto Castellanos,
Che's former bodyguard. They made him shout to someone they
could hear chopping down a tree somewhere but could not see.
Alberto did so, but the axe man made a detour round the hill
carrying his Thompson only to stumble upon another policeman
who was hiding. Caught off guard, he handed over his weapon. It
was Henry Lerner.

The group of five new recruits led by Diego had left Camp

No. 1 at dawn for the main camp, a day's march away. When the pedicurist and his colleague, the two police infiltrators, had escaped, they were soon lost, having opted to scramble down the mountainside willy-nilly for fear of either being caught or ending up back at the camp they had left. Their dilemma was resolved at dusk, when they accidentally bumped into the border police patrol combing the zone after having occupied the camp. The border police, now on a war footing, took them prisoner and gave them a good hiding for pretending to be policemen. Detained and beaten, they were taken to Orán with the other prisoners.

The anti-guerrilla operations, begun in this almost accidental way, were continued until there were no guerrillas left. In practice, manoeuvres were limited to detaining small groups or isolated individuals moving about the area looking for stocks of provisions, or the few peasant contacts who had sold them food. Being taken prisoner saved their lives.

Survivors' accounts indicate that Masetti had no plan for armed resistance, only for abandoning the area with enough provisions to enable them to move further south. To do this, Masetti had sent out a series of exploratory missions that were physically and morally debilitating. They not only achieved nothing but meant that, on the verge of exhaustion, his men were either killed or taken prisoner in ambushes set by the police. That was what happened in the only combat incident. Hermes and Jorge had reached a *finca* where they were ambushed together with the foreman. Hermes returned fire, killing a policeman before he himself was shot dead. The guerrilla army was so totally dependent on outside supplies that previously vigorous young men were soon so starved and weak they could barely move.

Two anthropology students from the original Buenos Aires group, fellow students of Ana María, died of hunger: César Augusto Carnevalli, twenty years old; and Marcos Szlachter, born in Viña del Mar, Chile, twenty-five years old. Others who died were Diego Miguel Magliano, twenty-one years old, who despite being wounded in the thigh reached the main camp to warn Masetti; Antonio Paul, an oil industry worker, who died falling over a precipice, when he and Héctor went to help Masetti and Atilio who were stuck on some cliffs, according to Héctor; Jorge Guille, Jorgito, twenty-four years old, a medical student, who died fighting alongside Captain Hermes Peña, the twenty-one-year-old Cuban *guajiro* who Che had sort of adopted in the Sierra Maestra and who became head of Che's bodyguard when he was in government.

Then there were the two recruits who had been executed earlier: Adolfo Pupi Rotblat, a twenty-five-year-old student; and César Bernardo Nardo Groswald, a nineteen-year-old bank employee. To them have to be added the unknown deaths of Oscar Atilio Altamirano, a twenty-three-year-old employee, and Jorge Ricardo Masetti, Comandante Segundo, a thirty-four-year-old journalist, both lost in the jungle. Also Pascual Bailón Vásquez, fifty-one, *finca* foreman, and Juan Adolfo Romero, a border policeman.

Twelve poor dead men, with no tributes or fuss made.

Thirteen guerrillas were taken prisoner and put on trial in Salta: Federico Méndez, lieutenant, car mechanic, aged twenty-five; Juan Héctor Jouvé, lieutenant, medical student, twenty-four; Henry Lerner, combatant, medical student, twenty-six; Jorge Bellomo, initially evacuated to Uruguay, medical student, EGP organizer in Buenos Aires, twenty years old; Erique Bollini Roca, combatant, architectural student, aged twenty, in charge of the Salta base; Alberto Castellanos, Cuban, combatant, one of Che's escorts, aged thirty-one, in charge of Camp No. 1; Miguel Colina, employee, aged thirty, would-be guerrilla; Federico Fronti, student, eighteen years old, would-be guerrilla; Oscar del Hoyo, bricklayer, twenty-four, aspiring cook; Alberto Moisés Korn, bank employee, thirty-one, would-be guerrilla; Wenceslao Jorge Paul, Antonio's brother, mechanic, twenty-one, would-be guerrilla;

Carlos Bandoni, florist, eighteen years old, would-be guerrilla; Fernando Gallego Álvarez, twenty, would-be guerrilla.

Others went into exile in Montevideo: Emilio Jouvé, in charge of supplies, Héctor's brother; his wife; Porota, Héctor's wife; Agustín Gringo Canello, doctor, in charge of transport and contacts. Jorge Bellomo went with them initially, but disobeying orders, went back to Buenos Aires after a couple of months to see his family and was arrested at his home. He was taken to Salta to stand trial, together with José Luis Correntino Stachioti, whose name had come up during questioning.

People's desire to write things down, which is impossible to control altogether, meant that Kichi Kiczkowsky was arrested, although only temporarily since he was the family doctor of the owner of the address book in which his telephone number appeared. Others arrested were the Francos, a married couple from Córdoba; in Salta, the notary Carlos H. Sánchez; Delfor Rey, as well as the owner of the pension where the latter lived. Salvador María del Carril and Ariel Maudet, both of the Buenos Aires university group, had different experiences. Salvador was detained for a short time in Salta where he was the main EGP contact, but Ariel managed to escape through the Chaco province. Our peasant farmer friend and provisioner from upriver in the forest, Pedro Guari Apaza, was also detained. The last three were all released during the trial.

The bulk of the organization in the rest of Argentina, despite its importance in both political and human terms, did not suffer any repressive measures. I continued moving about and being given a bed in various cities, while we appraised the political reality evolving around us, without our security having being affected or my name having been mentioned. Laureano became Mauricio. Looking back over this whole episode, the only saving grace was the humanity and dignity of the recruits who joined our project, ready to give their lives for a revolutionary ideal that was more difficult to implement than to simply support. Without men of this quality, it is hard to explain the capacity for sacrifice and, paradoxically, their acceptance of extreme hardships, and the negative options that they faced. This includes those who left the group early but who never betrayed it.

Part Three

China

18

A Post-mortem with Che in Havana: May–July 1964

Argentina as a whole heard almost nothing of these events. A few small articles appeared in the press but the news moved gradually towards the back pages until it fell off them altogether. At the national level, the superficial response was the publication of various derogatory comments, although the head of the border police, General Julio Alsogaray, warned that it was the beginning of the continental revolutionary war and suggested it be taken seriously. Among grass-roots student movements, and union and political groups, however, the news provoked loosely organized solidarity and a burgeoning spirit of struggle. Apart from the obvious need to regroup and reassess, our provincial leadership increased its efforts to establish contacts and to create a political organism to respond to the demand.

I renewed my contacts with Havana, via the embassy in Montevideo. In May, a message came from Che, asking me to go to Cuba and to bring an appropriate member of our organization with me. I was to let him know which one. The provisional leadership in clandestinity was composed of Cholo, Armando, Oscar and Mauricio – my new persona – and we met in Córdoba. We decided that Pancho Aricó would fill the role, so that he could give Che an analysis of what had happened and the political repercussions. We obtained two passports which I had to modify, adding our photos, stamp and perforations. The fakes turned out perfect. We left Montevideo on an Air France

flight to Paris, at the end of May or June, I don't remember
which exactly.

In those days, travelling to Cuba was a complicated business.
There were only two or three options available. On this occasion,
we went Paris – Prague – Havana. Pancho had a briefcase full of
books with him and, after take off, he spread them out and scheduled our work, discussion and rest hours, as if we were at a
conference. His methodical intellectual passion proved a great
boon: I was the lone student taking an accelerated course on the
economic interpretation of capitalism as an inexorable way of
constructing communism, according to Marx and Pancho; a
theory which, he added, was being adversely affected by the
wishful thinking and pre-emptive expressions of victory from the
writers of Marxist 'manuals'.

A friend was waiting for us at Havana airport. It was Papi
Martínez Tamayo. He helped us through the official red tape
down a special channel away from public view and, joking and
asking questions, took us to a government guest house in Miramar. We would have two free days, unless otherwise informed,
but at night we had to be on call. Papi would be looking after us
all the time. We were still sifting through the pile of newspapers,
magazines, speeches and interviews to bring us up to date with
Cuban politics, a hot potato as usual with Cuba's revolutionary
prestige facing the American continent and the world, when Papi
came at midnight to fetch me for a meeting I was to have alone
with Che, prior to the one Pancho and I would have the following night when Che would have more time. 'Tell our guest not to
be upset', Che had told Papi. But Pancho had no intention of
being upset, thrilled instead that Che even remembered him,
thereby recognizing his existence.

The car sped away to the bowels of the Ministry of the Interior,
and I went from the underground car park to the little kitchen
beside his office where I had to wait for a few minutes. The meeting itself only lasted an hour. Che had made time between other
important commitments because he wanted answers to two or

three questions. We would look at everything else afterwards. He had already had reports from Furry and Papi, but he needed to understand even more. He was very relaxed, as if we had seen each other the previous week; and made a somewhat jokey reference to the fact that I was still alive. He came out from behind his desk as if to stretch his legs and we sat in front of a little table in the corner of the room. Papi went to get some soft drinks.

He had three main questions. How could people possibly die of hunger in a forest full of wild animals? Why had we stayed in the same spot for three months? And what had Hermes thought of it all? I did not have any definitive answers, except to the first, maybe, from my own personal experience. Once the border police were in pursuit, hunting became impossible. Even under normal circumstances we could only do it intermittently: wild turkeys would suddenly appear between the legs of our vanguard group or of lone explorers, then take flight and disappear before we could shoulder our guns. Hunting meant becoming hunters, merging with the undergrowth, laying in wait for prey and having the appropriate rifles. Our weapons were useless in retreat (hunting rifles were the first to be discarded). On one occasion we killed a tapir but its meat made us all ill. Apparently, it had to be cooked for a very long time to counteract the acid effects. The absence of anyone living in the vicinity was a fatal handicap. Hermes moved around better than anyone, but this was not the Sierra Maestra with its abundance of fruit. In the Argentine jungle he was as lost as the next man, although he learned much more quickly. In the end, it became clear there were insufficient reserves of food in the forest, or we could not get to them; the exit route – never fully explored – was impossible to cross and the attempt exhausted everybody. And Masetti's back pain became so bad he could barely walk and had to disperse his men.

As for having stayed too long in the same area, I understood the dilemma. We needed to fully exploit being near the frontier so we could bring in the equipment being stored in the Bolivian *finca* – something we had already done in part – and consolidate the Argentine bases before being left with no strategic exit. We all admired Hermes for his efficiency, but he never disagreed with any of Masetti's decisions, on the contrary he always argued for them. His advice was only taken on practical things like terrain, marches, camping, exploration and discipline, which boiled down to banalities like obeying orders about making too much noise, looking after equipment and doing guard duty. But, in reality, Masetti's was the only opinion that counted. I tried to explain how I failed to convince Masetti of my concerns, like the constant to and fro of the lorry, but he cut me short with 'forget about what you did or didn't do'. I wasn't sure if it was because it was not relevant or because he had already made up his mind about certain things.

We did not discuss the executions, but we did talk about the recruits and their virtues, and he seemed to have a clear picture of Héctor – Cordobés – who he said 'confirmed the law of fifty in five hundred; five in fifty; one in five'. We brought no news of Masetti's fate, except Héctor's ultra-pessimistic opinions, trans-mitted via our lawyers. He had been the last person to see Masetti and Atilio, and said Masetti could neither go up nor down because of the physical pain he was in. Héctor thought they must have died of hunger, since none of the details sent out with food were able to find them. Without Héctor, it was like finding a needle in a haystack even supposing they could get to the haystack. Che then postponed the conversation until the following night, when he hoped to have more time.

The next day, Furry arrived at our house on a police Harley Davidson. He did not have much time either. He had taken a short break from an army course to come and see us. I had no idea what he had gone through after we had said goodbye in Córdoba, but he told me he had managed to remove all trace of us from the *finca* before putting it up for sale in La Paz. We would meet again at the weekend, near the beach, in a small house belonging to the Revolutionary Armed Forces. Papi took us there after we had spent the morning practising shooting at a range near the

Ministry of the Interior. Papi and I shot in tandem with powerful FAL rifles at an iron sign 200 metres away. He made it spin to one side and I to the other. Pancho too was remarkably good at this new (to him) sport. At the house, the wives of the officers present prepared a simple meal of *congri* (beans and rice), with yucca and tomato salad, and we spent the afternoon trying to keep out of the sun, baking despite the sea breeze.

Papi told me Che had asked him to go over codes, keys and concealment techniques with me again. They were going to give me, appropriately hidden, a book of Soviet encryption keys with which to communicate directly with their security team. The short week we spent in Havana brought back memories of October 1962, when the world seemed about to split into two.

That night, Papi took us both to see Che, in his same MININT office. I remember the sensations more than the words, because added to my own feelings were Pancho's, so anxious to meet the myth, so legendary yet at the same time so familiarly Argentine. Pancho knew some of Che's friends and family from his Córdoba days. One of them was our lawyer Gustavo Roca who had joined our prisoners' defence team without a second thought, on the basis of his long-standing friendship with Che. But Pancho also took a critical view of the Salta experience. Because of its geography and isolation, he thought it was like making the fire in one place and putting the stockpot in another. An analysis of the situation on the basis of this critique, face to face with the leader promoting the armed struggle, promised a very illuminating debate. But the magic of Che's presence produced an altogether different result.

The meeting lasted over three hours – during the night, of course – and Pancho forgot what he had meant to say. They talked about a bit of everything: Argentina, the world, real, unreal and desired socialism, China and the Stalinist, anti-Trotskyist, ideological paradox, the interpretative currents, the founders and forgers, Gramsci and Rosa Luxembourg, transparent socialism. Che spoke practically the whole time, not imposing criteria but – as if confirming historical rather than theoretical conclusions – relegating Pancho to the role of technical witness. Yet Pancho seemed increasingly enthusiastic and in total agreement. We did not study future plans or projects that night: everything was clear and when things are clear, you just get on with the job in hand. 'When you finish your training,' he said, 'we'll talk some more. Meanwhile, tie up all the loose ends here with Papi.'

There was much work to be done in Argentina. But just then something happened that, if we had been Greeks consulting the oracle, would have augured disaster. Manresa, Che's secretary, came into the room with a piece of paper. He gave it to Che who read it, and re-read it. Then with a gesture of dismay, but without a word, he passed the paper to me to read. An explosion in an apartment in the centre of Buenos Aires earlier that evening had caused a five-storey building to collapse, killing several people who had been using explosives. Among the dead was the leader of a Trotskyist revolutionary group, Ángel Bengoechea, aka 'Vasco', who had been planning to merge his group with the EGP since Loro Vázquez Viaña and Federico had first met him in the Chaco. His death meant that I was now the main contact.

19

Beginning All Over Again: August 1964

A Cuban intelligence services photographer came to teach me microphotography, which I needed to know in order to send encrypted messages, documents, pages from newspapers or books, all to be photographed and reduced to a ten millimetre negative. Armed with a Minox camera, equipped with a flash, tripod, developing tank and appropriate chemicals, we spent hours practising taking photos very quickly, in bad light, with improvised scenarios, interiors and exteriors.

He taught me how to take apart objects made of leather or synthetic material (key rings, shaver cases, watch straps, purses, wallets, briefcases, or slippers) and then how to reconstruct them using the original holes and stitching, after stuffing them with tiny negatives, dollars, parts of firearms, etc., so they could be sent, or taken, from one country to another. I became sufficiently skilled in these arts to later receive praise from my Cuban instructors, who, according to Papi, said I had done 'some of the best concealment work they had ever seen'.

Then, suddenly, seats were reserved for us on a flight to Prague and I was to be 'on call' at any time. Meanwhile, I was taken to see the immediate boss of the Latin American intelligence teams, an old acquaintance, Comandante Barbaroja Piñeiro. He asked me how our prisoners were being treated, the possible outcome of the trial, and if the lawyers needed anything. He gave me a sum of money for them – I don't remember exactly how much, between three and five thousand dollars – and on Che's request, the secret encryption book, appropriately concealed in a tube of toothpaste. It is worth pointing out that I met Che alone on more than one occasion but he took no part in these economic transactions, leaving that in the hands of the Revolution.

Shortly before our departure, earlier than usual, around ten in the evening, Papi took me to the MININT building again. It was not a long visit. Just after midnight, Che and I went to fetch Pancho and have a few goodbye beers with Papi. The conversation was more relaxed. I remember Che showing a nostalgic interest in details, and being more disposed to hear the whys and wherefores of views that might even contradict his own. As in those far-off nights in the Country Club, my humble opinion centred on the fact that we were operating in the utmost isolation, not only from the political masses, but also from our own immediate environment. Our nearest source of support, or potential support, was Furry, a foreigner, on the other side of the frontier. This meant we failed to respect the most elemental rule of constant mobility and awareness of our surroundings that would have enabled us to survive in an uninhabited zone and develop the project, with which all of us, including the new recruits, were obsessed.

The Salta Chaco was not the Sierra Maestra, an area of peasant farmers, where crops may have been meagre but where fruit grew wild on every hill. The Chaco was a solitary wasteland full of insects and bands of howling (and thieving) monkeys. The territory we operated in was larger than the Sierra Maestra and the whole of Oriente province put together. The province of Salta is 40,000 square kilometres, larger than the whole island of Cuba. In six months, we only met one family – not poor peasants but best described as complete human wrecks. In that jungle solitude, there was no political work to be done, and someone from Buenos Aires was totally out of place.

At one stage, Che asked 'And what kind of work is there to do?' As far as we in Argentina were concerned, we had to carry on preparing for his eventual arrival. It is hard for me to accurately reproduce what I said then without inflating or diminishing it. I only remember the ideas, not how they were expressed. The main points were: evaluate previous experience; justify the struggle; choose the most appropriate region for an armed vanguard, given the variety of the population and their political maturity; make strategic alliances with like-minded groups, or better still, transfer trained cadres into the zone, so they could integrate socially and economically and set up food supply routes, with transport companies operating normally, and medical services, etc. Beyond that, there was a need to develop the clandestine political infrastructure to provide a network of intelligence, safe houses, depositories and security.

Obviously, a project of this kind also has to have military actions, but they have to be strategic and linked to training and ideological education. Establishing another guerrilla base in the same area was unthinkable, given the enormity of the disaster suffered and the proven inappropriateness of the location. Also to be considered was the potential of young people in the cities, students and workers, who were conscious of the inequalities of capitalism, and open to the ideas and examples of struggle, and masters of their destiny. Che thought that while young people might be receptive to the idea of armed struggle, we had actually tried to run before we could walk. We should not have taken extreme military measures, like executions, without military actions that could possibly justify them. He himself had not been able to come, although he had told us to expect him, and he did not want to sit in judgement on what had happened.

'You have to begin all over again', said Che. There was no point talking deadlines, we had to develop our own strategies and act on the outcome. 'Put your plan into operation.' He told me to continue my contacts with disaffected Communist Party cadres without ruling out other groups, but I should not make organic political commitments to any party in particular. He urged prudence: I should remain in clandestinity, not take on any public role, and lead a quiet normal independent life. He wanted better means of communication, clearer and more stable, and assured me I would receive news from him directly when the time came.

The time he had available was up, and we said goodbye until the next time.

20

Encounter in Uruguay with Raúl Sendic:
September 1964

A few days after we had passed through Rome the first time, in June 1963, Pope John XXIII had died. He was pejoratively called the Red Pope by the scribes of the system who did not approve of his attempt to drag the decrepit ideological structure of the Catholic Church into the twentieth century. The second time I passed through Rome, with Pancho Aricó a year later, another Pope had just died, this time a truly communist one: Palmiro Togliatti, leader of the strongest and most independent Communist Party in the non-socialist world. Posters bearing his photo still adorned the walls and red banners hung over the balconies of practically the whole city, except of course in the historic ruins, reminders of times when powerful Caesars became no less powerful Popes. To paraphrase Clausewitz: the Church is the continuation of power by other means.

Pancho Aricó's head was full of ideas from Einaudi, the Italian publishing house that published a great deal of current Marxist thinking, from which he used to translate articles for *Pasado y Presente*, but we had no time for browsing. Our stay in the beautiful city lasted only long enough to go to the Minox camera shop where we bought an entire semi-professional spy kit with plenty of instructions, packed in a box as small as a shoe box. The Alitalia flight left us in Montevideo, where Pancho retrieved his Córdoban identity. I stayed for a few days tending our small colony of exiles.

Petiso Bellomo had rented a bachelor pad so we could avoid hotels. It was in Yi Street, half a block from the central police station. Being well educated and of an inquiring mind, Bellomo had already made friends in journalistic circles and at the Café Sorocabana in the Plaza Cagancha. It was a wonderful Madrid-style café, with soft armchairs under wide windows, where you could sit and read the newspaper, write, or have business meetings.

Among Bellomo's friends was a young journalist called Eduardo Galeano. A member of the editorial board of the left-wing magazine *Marcha*, he was a sure-fire contact with the most radical pro-Cuban left. Galeano introduced him to other socialists, like Andrés Cultelli and Javier Furidi, a former director of the Communist Party newspaper *El Sol*. He suggested introducing Bellomo to the leader of the cane-cutters' union, a young lawyer called Raúl Sendic. He was already known internationally for organizing marches of agricultural workers from the northern provinces of Artigas and Paysandú, demanding agrarian reform under the slogan 'For land and with Sendic'. According to Furidi, Sendic was interested in meeting Lieutenant Laureano, the only survivor of the Salta guerrilla group not in jail and proof that the armed group was still organizing in Argentina.

We studied the proposal and I finally agreed to meet Sendic alone. It was a Sunday, after lunch, on the deserted beach at Cerro, a poor industrial area of Montevideo. The simple operation involved a series of people out strolling, normal behaviour for a Sunday afternoon. Bellomo walked in one direction and received instructions as to Sendic's whereabouts from someone coming towards him in the other, which he then passed on to me when we crossed paths at the end of the beach. Omar (aka the now exiled Emilio Jouvé) arrived to sunbathe about fifty metres from some rocks half in the river where a solitary fisherman was standing. I strolled along the edge of the beach looking for flat stones to skim on the water. I passed Omar without looking at him, until I reached the place where a poorly dressed man, in a crumpled shirt and decrepit black felt hat, appeared to be fishing on the rocks with an improvised rod. 'Caught anything?' I said, in my limited language of the sport, and he answered 'It's very windy, but if you like, we can chat and have some *maté*.'

Sendic had a very strong personality. After a few short minutes, I sensed I was in the presence of an important man. Years later, I understood that I had indeed been talking to an extraordinary individual. He propped up the rod between some stones and prepared *maté* which we passed between us until the water in the thermos ran out. In an open and friendly tone, he asked about the abortive experience in Salta. His questions were ordered and systematic, leaving out 'secret' details, although the origin and imminent leadership of the project naturally floated between us like the smell of the river.

The hours idled by placidly. The conversation lasted several hours. A little way away, young fishermen, his people, alternated fishing with playing football. For his part, Omar remained motionless, behind me. Sendic's questions centred on the errors committed, to which I answered 'the fundamental error of isolation'. We were the fish out of water; the negation of the Maoist motto. I don't remember everything that was said, but I know we talked about the importance of organizational growth in the city and the implicit receptivity towards the armed struggle in an environment very far from where we had directed our efforts. We needed workers and students, rather than monkeys. He intimated that they were currently developing a worker-peasant alliance, which students and professionals would also join, in a broad front determined to initiate the armed struggle, although without as yet a clear idea of what the nature of it would be. It was clear that the poverty in the Uruguayan countryside made revolution a more favoured option, perhaps because the peasants had less to lose: the cows lived better than they did.

We offered each other assistance, and he immediately asked for weapons and basic security and intelligence training for one of his most trusted men. This meant I would have to come back to Montevideo, since I had only stayed on in the city to lay low while Pancho went back to Argentina. I was carrying dollars and secret equipment so I had to plan my own return a little later. But I told Sendic we had weapons in Montevideo that we had not yet managed to bring into Argentina and that they would be better off in his hands. Transferring the weapons and picking the trainees could be done while I was away.

The EGP's national leadership met whenever and wherever it could. For me, it meant travelling from Buenos Aires to cities in the provinces. Ana María and I had set up house in Buenos Aires where we remained until, among other things, Bellomo was arrested. We were advised to go and breathe the fresh air of Córdoba.

Cholo moved to Buenos Aires at the wheel of the contraband pick-up truck we had purchased. In terms of parking and petrol consumption, it was clearly inappropriate for clandestine living, and it was soon exchanged for a manageable low-cost runabout, easy to park and cheap to run. We decided to invest the remaining money in an electronic communications shop, a business coming into vogue in those days. It would help stretch our money and give us cover. Through an old friend now working in the Mendoza Police Department, Cholo obtained my personal police file. It showed no links of any description to any guerrilla group, so he was able to get me a range of completely legitimate documents – including identity card and driving licence. This meant I could travel openly and participate more or less fully in our organization's meetings. Our leadership had broadened to include David Tiefemberg and an oil workers' leader, Petiso Zárate, who brought with them further grass-roots political and union contacts.

I went back to Montevideo with Ana María to keep the promise I had made to Sendic and we installed ourselves in the Yi Street apartment while Bellomo moved to the house of a friend. He arranged for me to meet the man whom Sendic had chosen to do the intelligence and security course, a prior requisite to delivery of the weapons.

I worked with my trainee alone in the apartment for a couple of weeks while Ana María went for walks, to lunch, cafés or the cinema. We also carried out various tactical manoeuvres in the street: simulating being followed, checks and counter-checks, drop-offs, signals for contacts, individual and collective security. If I had learned anything, it was that extreme compartmentalization, reinforced by rigorous individual safety measures, assured one's own survival, as well as that of the group. Every militant thinks he knows someone he can trust with his life, but that person also knows someone he can trust, who in turn totally trusts some family member, who has a best friend, etc., until they reach some rarefied place where their safety lies with third parties they don't know. The undeclared armed struggle is a conspiracy that develops outside the law and societal norms and, as such, society will respond with all the repressive means at its disposal, legal or otherwise, exercising its monopoly on violence and lack of ethical considerations as it always does. Spontaneity and too much trust lead to disaster.

The trainee was very serious, capable and responsible. A methodical economics student, he understood immediately that the training was worse than useless without intense rigorous practical sessions. His name was Jorge Notaro. Twenty years later he told me they had been very useful, at least to him.

Omar (Emilio Jouvé) set himself up in a kiosk selling magazines, cigarettes and sweets. Our contact in the Cuban Embassy had delivered us a cache of weapons months before he returned to Cuba, when Cuban-Uruguayan diplomatic relations were broken off. The Organization of American States (OAS) had pressured Uruguay to act quickly, so we did not have time to carry out our plan properly and the weapons ended up in a sort of semi-cellar Omar had discovered under the kiosk; unsuspecting antecedent of what the Tupumaros called hidey-holes. There was no time to lose. Omar could not stand on top of such a volcano day after day, no matter how much worn carpet was covering the hideaway. Omar closed the kiosk for 24 hours for refurbishment and we went to paint it. I divided up the arms cache at the same time. There were half a dozen P38 revolvers, two or three Uzi machine guns, and a large amount of ammunition and equipment. There were also an appreciable number of incendiary bombs which Cuban counter-intelligence forces had collected after the daily aerial drops the CIA made by light aircraft from bases in Miami for counter-revolutionaries on the island. The 'Revolution in the Americas' Department had then redistributed them throughout the continent. It was only fair; the Yankees fomented counter-revolution and the Cubans fomented revolution. I kept half the pistols and the incendiary bombs for future use.

We did the handover on a corner quite a long way from the kiosk. Bellomo arrived with the weapons on the back seat of a taxi. He invited Sendic's emissary to get in and took him to another part of town where he got out taking the bag of weapons with him. All went well. Ana María and Rafael left for Buenos Aires to arrange to bring in our share, and eventually a happy group of young couples crossed the River Plate by ferry with a cargo of bombs, a sort of diabolical cigarette of inflammable grey plastic gelatine. They only needed a hard squeeze in the middle to break a glass receptacle that released some sulphuric acid, which, after corroding another compartment for a controlled number of hours, combusted into a huge blaze, similar to a small flame-thrower. A single one could burn a set of thick wood shelves in a shop or warehouse. We never used them, but years later they were passed on to a group that, in time, would become an armed organization called the Revolutionary Armed Forces (FAR), whose first operation made spectacular headlines in 1974 when, shortly after closing time, they destroyed the first chain of Mini-max supermarkets, owned by the US magnate Nelson Rockefeller. There were no casualties.

Meanwhile, the survivors of Masetti's group were on trial in Salta. The plaintiff in the case was the National Gendarmerie, that is, the border police. The defence was jointly in the hands of two Córdoba lawyers, Antonio Horacio Lonatti and Gustavo Roca. Roca was Che's childhood friend from Córdoba; they had studied together and spent their holidays in the Córdoba hills. Gustavo was the son of Deodoro Roca, who had led the fight in 1918 for radical reform of the Argentine university system. He succeeded in getting independence and autonomy for university courses, syllabus decisions put in the hands of teaching staff, students and alumni, and territorial immunity for the major universities.

Our working relationship grew into a close personal friendship with both of them, although different in nature. Lonatti was a man who never sought the limelight, the epitome of generosity and commitment. He was the ultimate professional, always delving into the Penal Code to recommend the line the defence should take. Roca was a brilliant wit, a tad anarchic and extrovert, seemingly irresponsible, but efficient, bold, brave and a good friend. He knew everyone who was anyone in political, trade union and cultural circles. They filed through his office and his house, and continued to do so even years later when the repression started and the Triple A was operating and it was nothing short of suicide to be seen there. The office he shared with the labour lawyer Garzón Maceda was eventually blown up. But all of us went there.

Lonatti's house, on the other hand, was a temple of peace and tranquillity. They opened it to me, making a bed on their sofa among scattered law books, briefs and files, that neither he nor his wife Sara – also a lawyer – ever found time to clear up. Alone, at supper time, when the hustle and bustle died down, we ate in the peace of the kitchen. They were back to being a young couple enjoying a visit from their friend. I sometimes accompanied Lonatti and Roca to the prison in Salta, driving Gustavo's car, a powerful Ford Falcon, the model which would later be the vehicle of choice of the military 'task forces' operating during Videla's dictatorship. Roca's eldest son, Deodoro, used to come with us too.

The two lawyers were earning nothing but their legal costs, but they were supported by other lawyer friends and representatives of the prisoners' families. The aim was to get the case tried as a political rather than criminal matter so that they could use as evidence the underlying social causes, and the impatience felt by the younger generations at the deceit and corruption of the current political class. It would be a hard slog and there would be no happy ending, but solidarity and support could help get the prisoners better conditions, political prisoner status, justification of their struggle and vindication of their names. Whether they got out of prison or not depended on the vicissitudes of national politics, or our potential military capacity in the future.

The confused fabric of left-wing politics comprises a variety of threads. Politics is an activity of the intellectual, economic and religious professional elites, who answer only to themselves and attempt to manipulate the working masses. Only atypical 'revolutionaries' successfully break the mould, until they fall victim to the same rigorous rules of the political game. But for every law, there is a way round it. Enthused by socialism, many young people passed through the ranks of the Marxist parties, but many then abandoned them, sick of theories that bore no relation to everyday life on the factory floor, and fed up with the opportunist behaviour of their leaders.

21

A Decision to Suspend Guerrilla Activity in Argentina: 1965

Poets are like the landscape; there even though no one is looking. Without them, man could not exist. Poets appear when drizzle or nostalgia, joyful spring, truth or deep sorrow, prick the conscience. Then, they search the layers of your soul like an electrician after a storm, tying cables, changing fuses, isolating bare wires with a cloak of verse. Like a covering of snow over the landscape, smoothing out the bumps, levelling the hidden depths, opening the distances to memory, and making the sun sparkle in their reflections. There have always been poets, their metaphors making magic of facts, with that existential wisdom they seem to be born with. What is more, poets are always poor and, even if they may one day get published successfully, they retain that touch of tenderness that men who make fortunes do not possess. They become politicized, I think, to try to serve as lightning conductors in reverse, sending out into infinite space all the bad vibes generated by political parties and their followers.

My friend and favourite poet in Mendoza, Víctor Hugo Cúneo, intellectual mentor and literary adviser, creator of my first serious library by recommending authors, special editions, and translations such as Faulkner's *The Wild Palms* by Borges. He appeared one day with Herman Melville's 'Bartleby', and on another with Joyce's *Ulysses*, recently translated into 'Argentine' by a bank clerk. He insisted I had to have them, buy them, and take advantage of special offers, like a bookshop salesman. Cúneo was a much-loved character. Thin as a suit on a coat hanger, tie all twisted, black hair and moustache, bright incisive eyes that, somewhat alarmed, flickered from side to side until his gaze settled on you. Cúneo killed himself in Mendoza's main square in 1969, setting himself alight like those bonzos who did so out of impotence and indignation at the massacre perpetrated by the Americans in Vietnam. I heard about it years later when I came out of jail in Bolivia.

Other poets, before and after, influenced my appreciation of life. In Argentina, from dictatorship to dictatorship, poets had always sided first with the poor, and later with their armed organizations, their sensitivity a shield against exasperation. One militant publication, edited by another friend and political contact, José Luis Mangieri, was called *La Rosa Blindada*.

Through my liaison work I got to know many poets, the first of course being Oscar del Barco himself. A hermetic poet, he was more of an existential philosopher, suspicious of people's illusions of grandeur. A note from Oscar brought me to the door of another disturbing and already remarkable poet, subsequently to become one of the great poets of Argentina and the Americas. Near the Plaza Once, a few metres from the house of the radio technician who was constructing the guerrilla's communications equipment, was the office of the Chinese news agency, *Sinhua*, the representative of which was this poet, a journalist by profession. We had arranged the meeting on the phone, and no sooner had I tapped discreetly on the door than I was ushered in. In the centre of a large room which constituted the agency's entire journalistic operations, was a desk at which was seated the poet Juan Gelman. Initially our relationship was purely political, there was no place for friendship; but friendship is like mature wine, once it is opened it spreads its sense of well being and you cannot resist it. Juan explained the areas where he agreed with me and those where he had doubts, although there was already a common denominator linking us and spurring us to action. That, of course, was the Cuban Revolution. Juan provided me with a whole series of contacts (useless to recap at this point), and he also helped me send my first messages to Cuba, the indispensible condition for which was absolute trust. Invited to Cuba to attend a *Casa de las Americas* conference, he personally took an encrypted report stuffed inside one of my embossed leather gifts – a key ring in the form of a gaucho whip, or a cigarette case with a tango motif, something like that – to be delivered to Che.

Other contacts were with the 'trade union elite' of the independent Left in Buenos Aires, like the pair of *EJ*s, Emilio Jáuregui and Eduardo Jozami, leaders of the journalist and print unions respectively, small in numbers when compared to the powerful Peronist unions, but important politically.

The next poet belonged to the generation after Gelman, but with a poetic style along the same lines, much appreciated in the most influential literary circles in the university from which he had graduated. He visited the prisoners in Salta, demonstrating solidarity with them by embracing a common ideal. He edited the cultural section of Jacobo Timerman's newspaper *La Opinión*. His name was Alberto Szpunberg, Albertito.

Alberto introduced me to David Viñas, a well-known writer who travelled widely, both to receive literary prizes and to serve on the juries awarding them. We went to his apartment in the centre of Buenos Aires, in Reconquista Street, and found him fresh out of the shower, wrapped in a towel, his wet hair sticking to his body. In his big loud voice, he questioned the serious intent of the mission I wanted to entrust to him (only solicited, in fact): to deliver a folkloric gift to a certain person. I had to convince him that handing it over personally was of the utmost importance, and he accepted. His brother Ismael, who headed a small left-wing Trotskyist party, an offshoot of Frondizi Radicalism, was closer to the revolutionary ideal politically, but David was an important cultural figure.

Alberto Szpunberg spent that period torn between a passion for poetry and the revolutionary struggle. He, Octavo del Valle (aka Manuel o Cristóbal, the EGP's new Buenos Aires organizer) and Roberto Mario Santucho created the Masetti Brigade, the urban successor to the EGP. The impact of the youth and total commitment of the Salta guerrillas on Alberto's life meant he eventually chose the most resonant metaphor. Juan Gelman and he would end up as militants of the two big revolutionary organizations of the time: Juan joined the Peronist Montoneros and Alberto joined the Marxist ERP (People's Revolutionary Army).

I got in touch again with 'Vasco' Bengoechea's group, not only to find out how the accident had happened, but also to determine the status of our common project. As it turned out, my usual contact Carlos was one of the survivors of the explosion in Posadas Street, so he was able to tell me what he knew about it. Carlos was a calm, reflective, militant Trotskyist, who had been a member of Bengoechea's group since it had opted for the armed struggle and split from Nahuel Moreno, founder of *Palabra Obrera*. Santucho would later do the same, and his own vision of armed struggle would become the ERP, Argentina's most important Marxist revolutionary military organization. It was the fat, balding Carlos who had lent his identity card to Loro Vázquez Viaña in the Chaco, when I was following Federico into Argentina on my own spurious document. So, you could say we were almost brothers.

According to Carlos's story, the group had received a shipment of explosives, material that was easy to work with as long as you took adequate precautions. They were making land mines or grenades to be shipped out to operational zones when the time came. A supposedly well-trained technician was teaching them the last part of the assembly process. Hence, five or six people, including 'Vasco' Bengoechea, were in the apartment sitting round the dining table with a box of detonators on it. At this point, Vasco reminds Carlos that he has an appointment to keep. Carlos goes to the toilet, picks up his jacket, says he'll be back in a couple of hours, and leaves the building. A couple of blocks away he is waiting for a bus, but instead of the bus comes a huge explosion. Like everyone else in the streets in the Barrio Norte, he runs towards the sound of the explosion and finds the apartment block he has just left is no longer there. As the dust clears, he can see that six stories of apartments in the middle of the block are now a mountain of rubble. Carlos thought someone must have dropped the box of detonators. On the subject of whether or not bombs should be assembled in a building full of family apartments in a densely populated suburb, Carlos expressed no opinion. Total lunacy had descended on the Argentine political landscape.

The Córdoba section of our support network, headed by the *Pasado y Presente* group, also had links with the progressive sector of the trade union movement: for example, with Argentina's most prestigious workers' leader, Agustín Tosco, secretary of *Luz y Fuerza*, the energy workers' union. They were also in contact with the metal workers of SITRAC and SITRAM, who a few years later would be at the heart of the *Cordobazo*, the famous popular insurrection that began in Córdoba in 1969. Our Córdoba group preferred the political actions of these unions to guerrilla tactics.

Our Mendoza group, as I already mentioned, had been formed by dissident Communist Party leaders looking for grass-roots support and organic political development. One was my friend Cholo, of course, but others like Antulio Lencinas, Fuad Toun and Armando Camín also had considerable prestige and influence among workers both in the cities and in the countryside. The latter's brother, Gustavo Camín, had been about to represent the Mendoza group on a visit to Masetti in the guerrilla camp when the tragic events of March 1964 prevented him. The organizational abilities of the Mendozans had been bearing fruit: they had been making uniforms, collecting weapons, enlisting recruits and preparing them to go to the mountains. But the defeat of the Salta guerrillas also altered the way they thought, and at a national conference in Córdoba the Mendozans agreed with the Córdoba group that there should be no further attempt to undertake guerrilla activity.

However, opinion in Buenos Aires, La Plata and Rosario was divided. Peremptory demands were more passionate (often opportunistic) than rational. So it was decided to hold a plenary session, to be held in Uruguay for security reasons. Sendic's people lent us a little house, or a shack to be more precise, on an immense empty beach on the Atlantic coast up near the Brazilian border. We had to get off the bus at some God-forsaken town and walk towards the sea to find the house. There was nowhere to sleep, except for old man Tiefemberg, who occupied the only bunk. The rest of us were in permanent assembly. We passed a resolution to suspend all guerrilla activity – de facto non-existent since the collapse of the Salta base – until such time as conditions were ripe for us to move into a more populated area with access to, and the participation of, an organized workers' movement. It would be my job to transmit this resolution to Che.

However, something happened in that year, 1965, which sowed confusion and uncertainty. For a prolonged period, Fidel and Che had been the undisputed heads and spokespersons for Cuba's active revolutionary leadership of the Latin American peoples. Then, suddenly, Che began to withdraw. He had played no part in the conference of Latin American Communist Parties in Havana, even though in November 1964 he had just returned from his second trip to Moscow, where he had met the new premier Leonid Brezhnev. In December, he left on another trip, leading the Cuba delegation to the United Nations General Assembly. His speech in New York stirred up passion and hatred among his admirers and enemies, respectively. From there he went directly to Algeria, and then on to the rest of Africa, China and Europe, on a seemingly interminable tour. In February 1965, again in Algeria, Che gave his last public speech, almost, it might be said, his political testament, together with an article, 'Socialism and Man in Cuba', originally sent to Carlos Quijano, editor of the Uruguayan magazine *Marcha*, where he openly criticized the non-revolutionary positions of the socialist camp. On 15th March, Che landed back in Havana and was officially received by Fidel, by all the important figures of the revolutionary government, and by his wife Aleida. He appeared before the press for the last time, and then he disappeared.

A whole wave of rumours, some sinister and all tendentious, swamped the world's media. Depending on the sources, versions had him being assassinated in the corridors of power after a disagreement with Fidel, being imprisoned on the island, being deathly ill, or committing suicide. The most 'authorized' sources, linked to the Argentine Communist Party, gave a political scientific interpretation, based on the dialectic of historical materialism, according to which good sense had prevailed and reined in the petty-bourgeois adventurism that undermined the inexorable march of the world's proletariat towards socialism, under the banner of the Soviet Union. The same sources talked about Che's 'overt provocations', his pro-Chinese, even Trotskyist sympathies. There was talk of a shoot-out in the middle of a meeting with the Castro brothers and other 'important party members' on the very night he arrived in Havana. Some recently arrived exiles, self-professed witnesses to the dark deeds, told stories of a cleansing operation throughout the country, dismantling support for the charismatic comandante. There was even a message asking for help, supposedly scribbled by Che on a scrap of paper, stuffed in a bottle and thrown into the sea through the bars of a cell in Havana's La Cabaña fortress, where he had previously been commander. Cuba kept its counsel. The world's intellectuals looked askance. When and how would the alarm have to be raised?

At the end of April, Fidel had referred ambiguously to Che's whereabouts – 'he is where he thinks he will be most useful to the Revolution' – to try and scotch the rumours. Unlikely as it may seem, I was not at all worried. The rumours were so absurd they ran off me like water off a duck's back. Colleagues thought I was so calm because I knew what he was doing and was keeping it to myself, but the truth is that I had absolutely no idea where Che was, although I was certain he was up to something and we would learn about it very soon. The silence from Cuba did not feel like a catastrophic drama, more like a manoeuvre combined with disinformation. The situation worsened, however, with the death of Che's mother in May. There was no word of his reaction to her death, even though it was common knowledge that they had a very close relationship. The Cuban government published an official message of condolence for the death of the mother of the beloved Comandante and Minister of the Revolution, but no reference was made to the why and wherefores of his absence.

Around the middle of 1965, news started emerging from Africa. Insurgent struggles were breaking out all over the place, especially in the Congo after the death of Patrice Lumumba. Guerrilla groups were fighting the troops of his successor President Tshombe who had been installed in power by the Belgian multinationals that controlled diamond extraction in Katanga province. Newspaper articles made mention of the presence of foreign advisers and white officers leading combat units for the government forces: Belgians, South Africans, North Americans from the CIA and the Pentagon, ex-OAS Frenchmen, Miami-Cuban pilots post–Bay of Pigs, etc. Western journalists were filtering out news. One day, came a surprising news flash: a column of trucks carrying government troops had been ambushed north of Katanga. Attacked with bazookas, the convoy was stopped and dispersed in a perfect tactical manoeuvre. According to the journalist, commands were shouted in a mixture of the local language and Cuban Spanish, specifically Cuban. So, there were Cuban officers there, Cubans from the island, not from Miami, concluded the report. For me, the mystery was solved.

In October of 1965, in a public act to celebrate the creation of the new Cuban Communist Party, Fidel Castro finally announced Che's departure from Cuba, and he read out Che's famous letter bidding farewell to the Cuban people, resigning all his army ranks as well as his government posts.

22

Summoned Back to Havana: May 1966

Six months later, in April 1966, a contact passing through Buenos Aires and Montevideo, where the Cubans still kept a trade mission, told me I was to go to Havana. He asked me for my personal details and intended travel dates so that airline tickets could be left for me at the mission. Che's name was not mentioned, but to me it was obvious; only Che could send for me without further explanation and his were the only orders I would accept.

Emilio Jauregui, of the journalists' union, had just returned from a trip to China and he also wanted to see me. I went to his office and he said he had an official invitation for me from the government of the People's Republic of China, handed to him personally by a Chinese civil servant during a private meeting in Peking. Emilio insisted that, at the Chinese Embassy in Paris where I would have my first contacts with the Chinese, I would have to make sure that the flight to Peking went via Karachi and not any other city, supposedly to avoid Soviet surveillance on other routes. The significance of his concern did not strike me then as it would later, especially since I was excited about visiting the land of Mao, leader of the greatest peasant and guerrilla revolution in modern history. But first I had to go to Havana.

While preparing for my journey, I also had to think of my family responsibilities. I now had two children. Paula was born in January of 1965 and Andrea in February 1966. Ana María had to bear the burden of bringing them up when I was away, which was all too often. My trips were like the journeys our forefathers made into Indian territory in wagon trains: the date of departure was known but not the return journey. I might suddenly leave for a few days, a few months, or even years. That was my agreement with Ana María, but it had not been ratified by our little girls, and I had at least to consider them. A revolutionary should be a solitary soul, but history shows they all had lots of children, as if the starting point for revolution is love.

As usual in those days, a trip to Havana involved a flight to Paris and Prague. In the Latin Quarter of Paris, in the rue Cujas, was a small hotel run by a certain Madame Sauvage, who had been a painter's model for, among others, Picasso. Her friendship with Fontana, Berni, Spilimbergo and other Argentine painters on their European pilgrimage had made her the protector of waves of Argentine students in particular, and Latin Americans in general, who arrived in the city with heads full of illusions, but pockets short of cash.

One of Madame Sauvage's former protégés was our lawyer Gustavo Roca and, holding his letter of introduction, I climbed the interminable stairs of the Hotel San Michel until I met the lady herself, fat and affectionate with *les Argentins*. She was indeed happy to have me stay and installed me in a single room two floors up from the loo. Not far from the hotel, in a student attic, Toto Schmucler and his wife Miriam were spending a year in Paris on a study grant.

When the day of my flight to Cuba arrived, Miriam and Toto took me to Orly airport to continue my journey via Prague. Alejandro, an intelligence officer who wore his pistol hanging over his right leg like a Wild West gunslinger and whom I had met on my last trip with Pancho, was waiting for me at Rancho Boyeros airport. He sorted out passport control, then as we sat at the bar waiting for my luggage and sipping a welcome daiquiri (they did especially good ones), he ran through our immediate plans.

For starters, there would be no hotel, only a house as on the previous occasion. 'Protocol houses' they were called, 'for security'. None of my friends were around: not Papi, nor Olo, nor

Furry, who was now head of Cuba's Western Army Command. There were only Barbaroja Piñeiro's people, who I would be seeing shortly. 'Relax, *chico*. You have to wait . . .'. Alejandro took me to an American-style house in Marianao, with an (empty) bar with stools in front of a glass display cabinet at one end of the huge lounge/dining room. The bedroom had wall-to-wall carpeting and a king-size bed. After the usual warnings (always say where I would be, avoid people I knew, etc.), he left me Cuban pocket money, cigarettes, cigars, newspapers and political material to study: recent speeches, updates on campaigns, etc. There was a lot about the Congo, Patrice Lumumba, Amílcar Cabral, Africa in general. To make my stay even more comfortable, Alejandro announced that a '*compañera*' would come every now and again to tidy up and clean. I roundly refused, saying I could take care of all that. We were arguing about that when an official jeep arrived with enough provisions, including beer, to fill both fridge and kitchen. My waiting started.

The jeep came by, not even every other day, but every single day, ostensibly to drop off the canisters containing my meals from the Ministry canteen, but also insisted on leaving crates of Hatuey, the Cuban beer, cold cuts, cheese and other provisions, as if I were dutifully eating for an entire regiment. I eventually complained vigorously and asked to see someone in charge: Ariel, Iván, or Piñeiro himself. I had not come to Cuba to get fat. I kept complaining until Alejandro reappeared with an explanation of sorts. It was true I had been sent for but 'you know how things are, *chico*, it's not that easy. Your (work) plan isn't available yet, be patient, *coño*!' That being the case, I asked him to put me in touch with Furry. After all, he had been my immediate superior and as far as I knew he had not resigned from our group. Alejandro promised to pass on my request, and left with considerable tension in the air.

A day later, Alejandro returned with permission for me to fly to Santiago de Cuba, in Oriente province, and back. My reservation was for the following day. From what I have read recently, my account may seem to contradict others concerning the supposed date of Che's secret return to Cuba (from Czechoslovakia, after the Congo) during his disappearance from the public eye. What I still think to this day might be wrong, of course, because I don't remember the exact dates and I have no way of comparing them with anything. But there are a couple of facts that lead me to think I am not mistaken.

Cubana airlines had renewed its domestic fleet, and a brand new medium-sized Soviet Ilyushin took me from Havana to Santiago. In an area of cyclones, this normally peaceful journey was liable to be dangerous if there was a tropical storm. And this is exactly what happened. In the air again after a stop in Santa Clara, over Sancti Spiritus, halfway to Santiago, the plane turned into a cocktail shaker. As the plane lost altitude, the cabin hubbub died down, and the passengers, mostly men and women in some kind of uniform, began frantically making the sign of the cross rather than praising the quality of socialist industry.

Over Camagüey, we were just coming out of the storm when the plane suddenly shuddered as if it had hit an air pocket, and dropped vertically, in free fall. The journey abruptly changed destination, not so much physically or geographically, but psychologically. Sitting by the window, I watched what I believed to be my last sight of earth. The plane was falling like a stone, and the countryside below was rapidly coming up to meet us. I could see we were heading straight for the mill or hacienda of a sugar plantation because of the carts loaded with cane. There were people too, looking up at the sky, then scattering in all directions. I could even see some details: women carrying children as they ran, the dirt road bordering the plantation, the relative height of the palm trees. I still have a clear image of the moment in my mind's eye. The machine started to shake and vibrate as if it were trying to grab hold of the clouds, suspended in the air as in cartoons. Just above the tops of the palm trees, it recovered its horizontal position, pinning us to our seats as we regained speed and height, and the sugar mill disappeared from sight. A chorus of wailing and clapping made it hard to hear the captain announcing our immediate landing in Camagüey. On the runway, we were told that a piece of ice had destroyed the internal blades of one of the jet engines, suddenly causing the plane to lose altitude. We could not continue our journey, and had to wait for the arrival of another plane the following day. The airline invited us to rest and regain our composure in a hotel, meals and tranquilizers included.

I walked through the streets of the old city of Camagüey, delighted to be able to do so, but also astonished at how little there was to buy. There was no longer a café on every corner, as there had been four years earlier when I used to drive by in the pottery workshop truck. There was the odd one every now and again, but they had neither coffee nor rum. Shop and office windows were empty except, very surprisingly, for one. On display in the office of INRA (the National Institute for Agricultural Reform) was a brand new car, made in Argentina for use as taxis, small and white, peculiar-looking next to the six-metre-long Yankee models that Cubans were used to seeing. A placard explained that the car was first prize for 'cane cutter of the year' during the province's current sugar harvest. Che was noticeable by his absence.

We arrived in Santiago in the afternoon, twenty-four hours behind schedule. A soldier in olive green greeted me as if I were an old friend. 'Hey, Pelao, cheer up, *chico*! You've arrived, *coño*? I've been here since yesterday.' I had never seen him before, but his cheerfulness was contagious. We got into an army jeep and left in a hurry, because, he said 'We've a long journey.' 'Where to?' I asked. 'The north coast', came the reply. That is, across the Sierra Maestra, past Bayamo and Holguín, the journey I used to do at weekends when I lived in Holguín and gave art classes in Santiago! It seemed like a nostalgic joke. He had orders from Furry that, as he told it, implied a level of trust and secrecy: 'Go and fetch Pelao and bring him straight here to me.'

When we got to Holguín, I knew we still had to get to the coast, near Gibara. The roads were not good and we were running very late. Nonetheless, I asked if we could cross the city instead of taking the road round it, and the soldier agreed. What I wanted to do was drive past my old pottery workshop. We had been talking about cyclones and especially Hurricane Flora which years earlier had been so disastrous for this region, and I was curious to see the roof of the main part of the workshop, held up by columns only one brick square, designed by my architect friend, son of the dreaded engineer Fontana, despite doubts on my part.

The jeep turned down the main street, past the new hospital building (the Revolution's handiwork), the Central Park, in front of my old house, and stopped at the gate to the workshop. Without getting out, I could see the corrugated iron roof shining in the afternoon sun, reflecting its green plastic sides. It was intact. The gate opened and Braulio, the clay maestro, stuck his head out. He looked up and down the street without giving the jeep a second glance. So the workshop was still running? Was it doing the job as planned? 'Let's go', said the soldier. Or did I?

It was already dark when we reached a military zone, where we were detained briefly at checkpoints. I could see in the headlights that we were driving towards some hangar-like canvas constructions. The soldier had me wait in an empty canteen and disappeared for a long time. When he came back, he said Furry had left orders that I be given a meal and a bed. He did not know when he would be able to receive me but would see that I was woken up. I could not sleep at all; the four o'clock reveille coincided with someone coming to fetch me.

Furry was at his post, in a low building – half map room, half radio transmitter room – onto which had been tacked a camouflage tent like a wing, obviously intended to prevent a quagmire in front of the door. Other officers were working in the room, absorbed at their tables and radios. Furry had not changed. Thin, well shaven, dressed in his campaign uniform, he was his usual friendly self, no indication that our relationship had been so dramatically interrupted a year and a half ago. He explained that he had had more time to give me the day before, but the 'bloody plane' had put paid to that. I understood that he had a final troop movements exercise for a visiting Soviet Army delegation to start 'this minute'. 'Come on, tell me what's wrong', he said.

We sat at his desk and I explained the following: 'I received an encrypted message from Che, to which I have responded as quickly as I could. I've been in Havana for two weeks, being fattened up in a luxury cattle pen, without anyone telling me anything. I have to be back in Argentina by mid-July to deal with the financial needs of the prisoners on trial in Salta, but first I have been invited on an official visit to China, not of my own doing, which I consider an obligation.' And I added: 'You see?' We examined the matter in detail and, eventually, he made a radio phone call, which was not easy.

Military communication language is cryptic and, as would be expected, I understood nothing, but a few odd words were helpful. First, he wanted to talk to X, who was in Z, not there. Sent to Z, the problem was M, Q or something worse. 'It's 4.30 here too. Proceed', said Furry, implacably. Eventually, a more normal conversation was had, but full of innuendo. Something like: 'I've got Pelao with me, what's going on?' Ending with: 'No, *chico*, sort it out, put him onto *the man* and be done with it.' And a heated exchange ensued, still over the radio – in fact very heated indeed for Furry who usually said yes or no, leaving no room for excuses or discussion with subordinates. Furry said he had been talking to Barbaroja Piñeiro.

I looked out through the entrance tent, which framed the rising sun through the mist, disturbed only by a restless group of officers with enormous peaked caps and rain capes – impatient Soviets – in the best tradition of the calm before the great battles of the Second World War. Summoned by Furry, the jeep's driver appeared, rubbing his eyes. He ordered him to take me back to Santiago. We said goodbye affectionately, before I passed in front of the nervous group watching the Soviet Military Command out of the corner of their eyes.

Back at the house in Marianao, things began to change. Within two days, I was visited by Ariel, who had 'got himself up to speed' with the situation. He said it was not possible for me to see Che for the time being. I had to wait, but Che knew I was here. To save time, Che wanted me to write a full political report on Argentina: parties, groups, contacts, relationships and organizations with common goals. They brought me a typewriter and paper. I protested that, typing with one finger would take me a month to write the analysis. 'No problem, *chico*, tomorrow you'll get a short-hand typist, *coño*, that's better than a dictaphone.' True enough, the next morning a middle-aged lady in an olive green uniform arrived, turned the splendid dining table into a desk: chair at its right height, carbon paper for the typewriter, ashtray on one side, cigarettes on the other. And, like a pianist to a dancer, fingers in the air over the keyboard, she nodded her head at me as if to say: 'Shall we begin?'

I had prepared a brief outline of the points I had to make. This included a separate analysis of our organization after the catastrophe: a description of the different political sectors and groups; potential capabilities; the role of the General Labour Confederation (equivalent of the TUC) and the army, with the (apparent) internal crises within both these power blocs. They all appeared to be split by an inability to define themselves ideologically, but were actually split by the desire to define themselves once and for all: pro-imperialist capitalist right or nostalgic nationalist right; principled traditional socialism or popular pre-revolutionary socialism; combative Peronism or nationalist populism. Each party split into two: Radicals, Peronists, Socialists, and even the Communists and Trotskyists (it was said 'there are two tendencies inside every Trotskyist'). The grass roots were beginning to break away from the party bureaucracies and a whole range of small groups were proclaiming the road to revolution, while the conservatives and the oligarchs went to their estancias to drink *maté*. Capitalism's international pressure groups had dug in their claws strategically and the organisms for extorting wealth from the Third World – the World Bank and the IMF – slowly and simultaneously squeezed the neck and the testicles of the national economy and the ruling class. Meanwhile, the armed forces, beloved and feted by the US School of the Americas, made alliances, ready to put themselves at the service of the higher bidder.

My improvised analysis – inexpert and precociously daring – based on reading the abundant Argentine daily press, ended by predicting a military coup against President Illia, the old anachronistic and honest Radical who, I thought, had no way of surviving. (The coup by General Onganía happened a couple of weeks later on 28 June 1966, before my return to Argentina.) The typist came every morning for the next few days. We ate together, she made very good coffee, and we talked, though she never let slip a single ill-considered word. She didn't mind altering the original as many times as necessary, but she was frustrated by the 'Argentinianisms'. We finished. She tidied everything up, and Ariel swept her away: typewriter, copies of the report, and all.

Ariel returned a few days later, in a better mood. Apparently, Che was very pleased with my report. There were a few more matters to tie up before I could go home, without seeing him, given the hurry I was in. 'As you know, he's not available at the moment.' I did not know, but I never questioned measures taken by superiors or outside my control. At no time was the mystery surrounding Che's absence, or the campaign of rumours, ever mentioned. Both they and I had total faith. Between us, there was a tacit knowledge that he was not being manipulated by anyone.

We talked instead about the financial problems of the trial in Salta, and what the prisoners could expect. If the trial went against us, appeal included, we would have to get them out some other way, and for that we needed support and planning. Ariel promised to study the alternatives. Meanwhile, I had to continue making political contacts, monitoring the situation, and reporting back periodically. For the first time, they gave me one of their own contacts in Buenos Aires. I was to meet a certain Hellman, secretary of a dissident Communist Party youth sector in the city, and help him with whatever he needed to send people to Cuba for military training. Now all that was left was my interview with

Comandante Barbaroja Piñeiro. He would sign me out and give me money. So I went on waiting for another couple of days.

Alejandro came to fetch me after midnight and we drove around various parts of Havana, from Marianao to the other side of Vedado, as if we were lost and were looking for a restaurant or we were not sure of an address. We stopped at the Ministry of the Interior in the Plaza de la Revolución, where I waited in the car, then continued on through areas I did not know on the outskirts. Guided by a radiotelephone, the car finally stopped at what seemed like an Argentine-style police checkpoint. There were jeeps and patrol cars across the road, blocking the traffic. Alejandro got out, walked towards them, and came back immediately with a group which stood under the street lighting in the middle of the street. They gestured to me to come. As dawn was breaking, I went up to the group to find the Head of the Cuban Intelligence Services, Comandante Piñeiro, holding court.

He put his arm round my shoulders protectively, and said that he still had a long night ahead of him so it was best not to make me wait; that they would give me 5,000 dollars and a plane ticket for the following day; that Che wanted me to constantly update instructions for how I could be contacted, and to wait in Argentina for his next message; that I should discuss the contact details with Ariel and leave everything clear; that Che was pleased with the written report and did not think I needed to wait for a meeting which would be hard to arrange now, because he 'was in the mountains' and nobody could take me there; that I should go back to Buenos Aires, without more ado; that I talk to Hellman and help him send people to Cuba for training. 'Have a good trip, Pelao!' It seemed appropriate to tell him that I would not be going straight back to Buenos Aires, because I had an official invitation to visit China and the ticket was waiting for me in Paris. He was interested in the details of the invitation, but he had no qualms about it. We said goodbye and Alejandro took me back to the house in Marianao.

Time was now short and I spent the rest of the night finalising details with Ariel. Córdoba would be our contact point via a shop selling books, records and photos owned by a friend of Oscar del Barco. A special password (I don't remember it now) was the only way to reach me. Ana María and I were planning to move to Córdoba, with the agreement of the EGP's national leadership, so that all contacts would be centralized in the middle of the country.

Alejandro, my official guide, drove me to Havana airport, where we repeated the welcome ritual of the daiquiri, waiting for the Cubana flight to leave for Paris. We only had one, and afterwards in Gander (Nova Scotia, Canada), I regretted I had not accepted a few more rounds. My seat was on the right-hand side just over the wing, from where I could see the plane's engines. The European route was still served by Britannias, a formidable British machine with turbo-propellers, which had possibly over-spent its flight hours.

23

The Terraces of the Rising Sun: June–July 1966

Once I was in Paris, Toto Schmucler accompanied me to the Chinese Embassy. We had to explain the reasons for our visit, leave a phone number, and wait to be advised. We got a call the very next day. This time we were ushered in (with Toto as interpreter). They took my false passport and we waited a few minutes. A secretary from the embassy appeared holding a paper with my data on it, and asked me: 'Are you Laureano?' 'Yes, I am'. 'Do you have any other name?' 'Yes, Mauricio'. 'What is your name?' 'So and so'. 'And what do people call you?' 'Pelao'. A very Chinese smile that we would see often during the coming days illuminated his face. He asked when I would be ready to leave and I answered: 'Tomorrow, *via Karachi*, please'. I did not need to insist on the route. It was clear that the Chinese had information that could never have been given them by Emilio Jauregui, who did not even know my real name. The invitation had come from a previous source.

After another couple of days, Toto and I were saying goodbye at Orly, and so began my most extraordinary journey into the future. After a stop in Rome, and a couple of hours in Beirut's amazing duty-free airport, the first leg of my journey ended up with a night in Karachi, Pakistan. We had to leave the plane and sleep in a hotel paid for by the airline. Going through immigration control, a bearded policeman explained something in English that I didn't understand and kept my passport. I reacted vociferously, gesturing at him to give it back, and we got into a fierce mutually unintelligible argument, while the queue of passengers looked on impatiently. The policeman, with plaited black beard, abandoned his courtesy and me my calm, swearing in Spanish and hanging on tightly to the corner of my passport. If I lost it, it would not be for want of trying not to. Then a young Indian, just behind me in a smart Western suit and tie, asked me very politely in perfect Spanish, if he could help. He argued with the official animatedly until, coming back to me, explained that the documents of all passengers continuing on the same plane the next day, are kept and only returned on board the following day. His included, since he was also going on to China. My unexpected interpreter turned out to be a Colombian student with a scholarship to study in China.

The journey went smoothly after that, despite our exhaustion and a few surprises. We were in Asia and the Pakistani Airlines plane also landed in Dacca, West Pakistan until 1971, when it became Bangladesh. The most terrible face of poverty was everywhere, even invading the airport lounge.

When the plane finally landed in front of the airport building in Shanghai, our first stop in China, there began what seemed like a comedy of errors. The Colombian and I watched anxiously through the window as a group of people invaded the tarmac, among them children in uniform holding flowers and lining up beside the steps being placed at the front of the plane. The air hostesses asked the passengers to wait in their seats until requested to disembark. Outside, a red carpet was being laid from the foot of the stairs to where a line of officials in typical blue Mao tunics were waiting.

An air hostess approached my seat and invited me to get off first. As astonished as the Colombian, I barely managed to say goodbye before following her to the airplane door, where the whole crew with wide smiles were waiting to say their farewells. I descended the steps, convinced there was some mistake, waiting for the moment for them to drag me away, but as soon as I set foot on terra firma, hardly daring to touch the carpet, the children ran towards me offering me their flowers. One of the Maoist officials spoke emphatically in Chinese and an interpreter repeated a welcome that explained how grateful the Chinese people were to receive a South American revolutionary who was fighting to build the road to socialism for his people, just as the Chinese people had achieved it under the leadership of Chairman Mao. There was obviously some confusion as to who I was. I was of course me, but I was by no means as important as they believed me to be.

They took me to some VIP rooms on the upper floor of the airport, where we sat in armchairs and they offered me the first round of the several litres of tea I had to drink in China, prepared before me with boiling water from a huge thermos and a mixture of herbs and flowers. Remember that it was midday at the beginning of June, mid-summer, and you can understand how little desire I had to drink hot water. But it was the first lesson I learned. Dying of thirst and heat? Remedy, boiling water. You don't even need the tea. Boiling water by itself will do. From then on, everywhere I went, they repeated the thermos for the tea ceremony and the exchange of greetings, hopes for future achievements, and compliments.

Arriving in Peking towards the end of the day meant another reception, more tea and sympathy, and making official contact with a representative of the Chinese government, a member of the Committee for Relations with Other Peoples in their Fight Against Imperialism, and with a couple of interpreters for my exclusive use for the whole of my stay: a calm professional middle-aged man; and his tall, young, enthusiastic assistant from a translator's school. We moved as a group to a huge Western-style hotel, the old and respectable Hotel Peking, on the big avenue in front of the Imperial City, in Tiananmen Square (Square of Celestial Peace). On the top floor, they left me in an enormous suite, with bedroom and lounge, and the most modern of bathrooms. The chief interpreter gave a brief rundown of our plans for the following day. Breakfast was from seven onwards, because at eight someone would be coming to discuss the schedule of work, visits and receptions.

The hotel served foreigners, or rather, Westerners. There were English, French or American breakfasts, with impeccable silver cutlery, crystal glasses and bread. The coffee was awful, so I made do with fruit juice. At eight on the dot, there was a knock on the door of my suite. But my visitors got the first surprise. The previous night in the shower, I had taken off my wig. It had become veritable torture in the summer heat and I had no intention of using it until the return journey. The official and interpreters stared at me, then between giggles and greetings, sat down in the armchairs and took out their papers. My schedule was to start the following day: a general of the People's Army would explain his experience in the victorious people's revolutionary war, going back to the struggle against the Japanese and the Kuomintang nationalists, and as a commander of Chinese troops in the Korean War. Every day I would be given relevant material in Spanish, so I could read up in my spare time. Later, we would go on a tour of the Chinese interior to learn about the development of both the army and the party, from the early days in Shanghai, the Long March, and the first liberated zone in Yenan. The programme would take a month, after which, we would visit North Vietnam: two months in all.

I told them I only had a week, that I needed to be back in Argentina in time to organize support for my comrades who were standing trial; that I considered the invitation from the Chinese authorities a huge honour, but it was my imprisoned comrades not myself who were worthy of such a distinction, and my commitment to them was precisely why I could not prolong my stay. In their name, I was ready to meet any appropriate official to show my gratitude for the invitation and for the political support the People's Republic had shown to the peoples of our continent.

Unfortunately, then, I had to decline the invitation to participate in such a long programme. It is impossible, almost forty years on, to reconstruct from memory the details of the ensuing discussion, with its arguments, counterarguments, coercions, concessions and conclusions all expressed via interpreters, before we reached an agreement that was hard to better: they cut a month from the programme and I would extend my stay by over a week – what was left of the month of June and some of July, some twenty some days in all – but only in China, without going to Vietnam. In passing, this controversial session gave me a sense of the ways and means of parabolas, metaphors and adjectives in Chinese language and culture, and of their transforming and symbolic power. I was astonished how, for example, the more I humbled myself, the more my prestige grew. It was obvious to them that I was an integral part of a project lead by Che. I understood that it was Che they were honouring through me.

The next day after breakfast, again at eight sharp, there was a knock on the door and a large delegation came in, entailing a small ceremony to introduce the general and his assistants. The general was about sixty, relatively young given his trajectory. His history class was delivered almost automatically, not creatively as a teacher would, but schematically and rigidly, as if he were forcing an idea into the brains of his troops, like a instrument of ideological battle that had to be used in an implacable and precise way. He continually referred to the central role of Chairman Mao, the source of all wisdom and leadership, to the ideological work of the party as an indispensable link to the masses and, above all, to the masses themselves, origin and raison d'être of the revolutionary class struggle. The general's story did not linger on anecdotes of suffering or heroism, of which there were no doubt many during the Long March.

When the general left at the end of each day, I was handed a pile of theoretical material which could politely be considered – in terms of kilos, more than anything – excessive. I could do no more than leaf quickly through them like reading a cartoon, stopping at chapter or page headings, to help me eventually formulate some sort of question.

We visited all the sacred sites of the Revolution's heroic deeds with the same religious intensity. The face of Imperial China was, in fact, being changed into that of a more equal society, determined to carry out the Five Year Plans, and leap from feudal backwardness into a future of unimaginable achievement. The changes in peoples' expectations and their confidence in the political leadership were tangible at every step.

The programme of visits included sites outside Peking. The Great Wall was being restored at a point near Peking and was only open for official visits. There was nothing accidental about this. There was no charter-type tourism, as there was to be later on, everything had to convey a message: the Chinese were an ancient people and were planning to leapfrog over contemporary history because they were armed with the legendary patience and wisdom of the people, accumulated generation by generation over four millennia.

Towards the end of the week, it was announced that I had been invited to dine with the Mayor of Peking. Doubtless, this was a big step up the hierarchical ladder, but I did not know exactly how far. I began to get a sense of his importance when they showed an interest in the state of my clothes, and took my suit off for dry cleaning, shirt and tie included. The two interpreters also appeared in elegant but proletarian blue Mao jackets when they came to fetch me that afternoon. Our car headed for the old most populated part of the city, with its grey brick houses and tree-lined pavements, and a few motorised vehicles but a multitude of bicycles and rickshaws. A distinct smell of shit, which I had noticed before, filled the air and infused our car. The interpreters explained they were collecting the sanitary waste, which was left in large drums to be picked up by trucks during the night. The journey ended, however, in an elegant and salubrious area.

The banquet was at a famous restaurant specializing in traditional Chinese dishes. I was welcomed by a group of men dressed in that indefinable attire, a mixture of military uniform and gala evening dress, of a jeans colour, except for one tall imposing figure in an impeccable pearl grey suit, buttoned up to his bull neck and shaven head. It was Peng Chen, the Mayor of Peking. The restaurant had closed its doors to the public to wait on our official table.

Mayor Peng Chen began the ceremony by explaining the role played in Chinese tradition by the placement of guests at table. According to this, my place was reserved for the person showing most praise and courtesy. The back of my chair pointed towards one cardinal point and faced another one, and these together apparently represented a specially auspicious place. I don't remember the reasons given, but I was suddenly anxious about the confusion over my person, feeling I could end up being tried for fraud if I did not explain it soon. Toast after toast only served to highlight the incongruity between my modest presence, the political expressions of revolutionary sacrifice and devotion, the bourgeois glitter surrounding us, and the series of toasts. I was seated immediately to the right of the mayor, and although the table was round, we were obviously at its head. At our shoulders behind us sat the interpreters and their assistants. The rest of the guests made up a kind of Greek chorus to the speech, in which the mayor continued dropping informative morsels about the place, origin, development and importance of food in Chinese culture, while continuous waves of plates arrived with different tastes, colours, flavours, smells and consistencies, each one palate-teasing by virtue of its sweetness or saltiness, bitterness or tartness, hotness or coldness, liquidity or solidity.

The mayor's speech was a lesson in gastronomy, an extraordinary thousand-year-old tradition about which I knew nothing. Everything was related to the people's wisdom, which had gradually merged through knowledge and the need for food, until it had turned disgust into pleasure and routine into art, making it possible for ants or snakes, properly seasoned, to taste exquisite. One after another, people got to their feet, raised a small glass and proposed a toast. Peng Chen set the pattern. They filled glasses of a determinate colour and size with a liquid which could be made of roses or potatoes, distilled grains or seeds, or something of the sort, but never grapes, and proposed a diplomatic toast, not forgetting the brother land of the Argentines, because 'the compatriots of a great revolutionary like Che are our brothers'.

I eventually began to understand the frames of reference: seated at table, the talk would be of culture in general; on our feet, out of temptation's way, about politics; and facing each other, we would praise the example of absent but exemplary leaders. At one point when we were sitting down, I suddenly felt a reply to previous toasts was in order, and I stood up again. Everyone got to their feet. The liquid was taking effect, and I resorted to childhood memories of the time my mother dressed me up, as children did at Carnival, as a Chinese mandarin. I had a droopy moustache drawn with a burned cork, and a pigtail of black wool falling down my back from a conical hat, and some 'typical' dark silk pyjamas with vividly coloured dragons painted on the front and back. This was our image of China when it was seen as a far-away world, admired more for being different and exotic than for its reality, which began to set us an example with the long victorious march under Chairman Mao, to whom I now wanted to raise my glass on behalf of myself and my comrades. The toast was a success and the dinner became visibly more animated, whether on account of my speech, or the glasses of soft rose wine, or who knows what, I wasn't sure.

The restaurant staff began clearing away the innumerable pieces of empty china (some still containing tasty left-overs which ideology did not allow us to eat, worse luck), and others arrived with trays full of steaming hot towels. But to my surprise, when I tried to praise the food and thank the mayor, who by the way was always the president of the Communist Party in Peking, he told me that it was now time for the serious food, that what we had just eaten was merely the hors d'oeuvre. During a pause in the eating, there was time to talk of my activities for the coming weeks and of our future relations. I would be leaving in a couple of days for a tour of the interior, to visit places of historic importance for the future of the revolutionary struggle, like the base in Yenan. Until now, I had only heard of the strength of the Chinese Revolution, but now I was going to meet the worker and peasant masses, the fount of all wisdom. I looked at the mayor, impressed by the exercise of power emanating from him, like a mandarin of the new communist dynasty.

Looking back at this period, four decades later, it seems extraordinary that the Chinese leaders offered our organization, which had just suffered a calamitous defeat, what numerous representatives of armed groups had tried unsuccessfully to obtain. The key was that they believed in and set great store by the same catalyzing element that we did: Che's politico-military leadership.

I had been told that before I left Peking for Shanghai I would be meeting a very important figure. I was uneasy because it seemed disproportionate to me. The person in question was no less than the Vice Premier of the Permanent Committee of the People's National Assembly, Comrade Kuo Mo-jo. That is, the acting chief of the People's Congress and the government. The Premier of the Permanent Committee was Chu Teh, one of the legendary revolutionaries.

We left the Peking Hotel early because the meeting was to include a tour round the People's Palace and the People's Assembly Hall afterwards, about two or three hours altogether. We arrived on foot at the Palace's grand staircase and, for the first time, there was a photographer among the officials milling around. He was taking photos of the reception committee and my humble yet elegant self, in suit and tie. I would rather have been swallowed up by the ground, however, than appear in the photo. I was hostage to these thoughts when a new group came into the hall accompanying an obviously high-ranking personage in a pearl grey Mao jacket. He was of an indefinable age, thin, with the look of a company director or hospital administrator. The photographer did his job and the introductions were made. An exchange of greetings was translated by the legion of interpreters by his side and my two at my shoulder. Vice Premier Kuo Mo-jo invited me to pose beside him so the photograph could finish documenting the meeting, before we moved to an equally large salon, where we sat in a semi-circle of armchairs, facing small lacquered tables with an impeccable china tea service.

I have a vivid memory of us sitting at one end of the salon, under yet another embroidered portrait of Chairman Mao dominating the scene, but I don't remember the exact conversation, except its memorable end, so brusquely terminated. The Vice Premier was on my right, in front of his individual table, flanked by other government officials and his interpreters. I was in front of another table, my interpreters a little distance away. A mass of people in white jackets and gloves were serving tea. Another exchange of courtesies took place, with a little more detail, references to my visit, my appreciated stay in China, the Revolution in motion, the thoughts of Chairman Mao. He spoke specifically of the hopes Chairman Mao had for indigenous America, that the great aboriginal cultures could not remain oppressed forever, or something like that. I managed to argue that colonization had wiped out those diverse ethnicities or at least subjugated them indefinitely, imposing a new power elite, unified and exploitative, which was ultimately controlled by the United States. He told me we had to fight these usurpers and their lackeys. He said I had witnessed what the energy of the masses could achieve when led by the correct route of the Revolution and the thoughts of Chairman Mao. And that the Chinese people, its government and its Communist Party were very pleased to receive the visit of a representative of the revolutionary project of their friend and comrade Comandante Che Guevara, and hoped that it would bring mutual benefits. He then said words to this effect: 'When you go back to your country, you must lead your comrades in a campaign of public denunciation of the revisionist role, in its complicity with imperialism, played by Fidel Castro, who has betrayed the revolution.'

When the Vice Premier spoke, my interpreter translated; when I spoke, his interpreters translated. I looked at my nice interpreter, practically my friend by now, with incredulity. I asked him to repeat what had been said. He did and I said there must be some mistake; that he must confirm the correct translation of the Comrade Vice Premier's words. There was an agitated exchange between the interpreters, with a dry comment from the Vice Premier. My interpreter repeated exactly what he had said before. I took the floor and replied, more or less, that Comandante Fidel Castro was the founding father and natural leader of a revolutionary current that included the whole American subcontinent, one to which myself and my comrades belonged. That I assumed the Vice Premier's statement was an error of ideological interpretation that we could not share. That while our project was independent of the Cuban Revolution and our commander was Che and not Fidel Castro, for us and for all Latin Americans engaged in the revolutionary struggle, Fidel's Cuba was an example to follow.

The Vice Premier of the Permanent Committee of the Chinese People's Assembly, Comrade Kuo Mo-jo, stood up – as did all those present – to indicate the meeting had finished. He bid a dry farewell, although he invited me to continue with my programme of visits, and left the room, followed by his assistants and interpreters. My interpreters, the major-domo and I remained in the middle of the salon, perspiring. The audience had lasted barely twenty minutes and one solitary cup of tea.

Contrary to what I expected, after the lunch and a nervous pause, the official from the Committee for Friendship Between Peoples came to my hotel room, not to arrest me, but to tell me the time of my flight to Shanghai the following day; and to give me a donation from the Committee to help the organization I represented. It was $1,500. In addition, I was given pamphlets in Spanish, some books on Chinese Art, and a just-developed print of the photo posing with Kuo Mo-jo. My official programme, similar to that in Peking, carried on as if the incident with Kuo Mo-jo had not happened.

Shanghai was already a huge over-populated city, with 16 million inhabitants. Built on the estuary of the Yang Tse Kiang, or Blue River, it is one of the longest rivers in the world, a thousand kilometres of it navigable by deep draft ships. It is the vital artery of the Chinese industrial economy. Shanghai's park had a iron grille entrance gate and to one side was a monolith with a carefully preserved bronze plate with the following inscription in English, French, German, Japanese and, of course, Chinese: 'Entry prohibited to dogs or Chinese'. It was a sign of the cultural arrogance of the empires that dominated China through the cunning – or dubious morality – of the British, who resorted in those days to a weapon of mass destruction called opium and the corruption that went with it.

I left China with the sensation of having been through an exceptional experience in an extraordinary country bringing fundamental change to the history of humanity. The energy of millions of citizens was being mobilized to produce the Great Leap Forward. However, great leaps can bring great catastrophes, when the leadership concentrates more on the fancy footwork of the action and glory than on the creative object. The Chinese Revolution was finding its way: first came the Cultural Revolution which razed any vestiges of bourgeois society; then the current socialist road to capitalism and, no doubt, one day it will find the capitalist road to communism, and prove the young Marx right.

Part Four

Bolivia

24

'Che Wants to See You': January 1967

When I first lived in Salta, I shared a house with my friend Ramiro Dávalos in a town called Campo Quijano. The house was borrowed and we lived there in winter, but when the owners came for the summer, we moved to the hills where we set up camp in a couple of tents and held open house for Ramiro's friends. They became my friends too: well-known poets, folk musicians or artists like him, and all enthusiastic drinkers of the unique Cafayate *Torrontés* wine, one of Argentina's best (if not *the* best), grown in the Calchaquí Valley. I needed a place to paint too, so with the compensation I got from being laid off at the sugar mill, I rented a shed a couple of roads away.

Among the regular guests were two guitarists. One of them, Eduardo Falú, aka El Turco, from a Turkish family that settled in the north of Argentina, had perfect technique and was already challenging the reputation of Argentina's folk legend, Atahualpa Yupanqui, on the airwaves. Eduardo was put in my tent, since Ramiro occupied the largest one with his wife Negrita and their children. Every day at around five in the morning, after a long night of singing and imbibing, I awoke to the sounds of paradise: gentle strumming, musical scales and miraculous chords. Guitar in his arms (like a woman, he said), Falú honed his technical skills and emitted the purest and most harmonious of sounds. The other maestro of the 'viola', as he called it, was of Spanish descent. He did not quite have Falú's mastery of the instrument, but was nonetheless a fine musician and an inspired poet. His name was

Ernesto Cabeza or Cabecita, and he became my closest friend. Cabecita fell on hard times at one stage and came to live in my Campo Quijano studio for a while, despite the cold.

Hence, in the silence of the night, or at dawn, I witnessed the birth of two of the most famous sambas in the Argentine folk repertory: Falú's '*La Candelaria*', composed in our tent, and Cabecita's '*La nochera*', created in my workshop. Romantic verses were added to both later by Jaime Dávalos, Ramiro's brother, another friend and habitué. The miracles there were endless. Ramiro was the greatest *cantor* in the memory of the region, certainly the best I ever heard. A *cantor* by vocation of every folk tune in South America and especially of our precious northern Argentina, he rejected all professional or commercial offers, refused to sing in public and performed only for friends, despite being the envy of every *bagualero* and gaucho troubadour in the interior. There was only one amateur recording of his voice, made without Ramiro's knowledge by our common friend, Alberto Burnichón, but it was such bad quality that it did not do him justice. His fame spread, however, and youngsters would come to listen to him in Campo Quijano, where he organized duets, trios or quartets with his brothers, Arturo, Jaime and Hernán, or with Cabecita and even myself, since he insisted I sing the fourth part.

Two things came out of these Salta gatherings. The first was a group of students who had formed a quartet and needed a guitarist. Cabecita accepted, collected his stuff from my studio and joined the group. They already had an offer of radio work in Buenos Aires, and they went on to launch the folk boom of that period, providing a showcase for the musical wealth of the interior, overtaking the audiences for tango and foreign artists (jazz included) for the first time. This first internationally famous Argentine folk quartet was called *Los Chalchaleros*. The second related thing concerned a young neighbour who was so bowled over by Ramiro's songs that he asked to come to the house and listen to him. He too became a close friend. Following the success of *Los Chalchaleros*, he formed a group which had the good luck to be advised by a musical genius, another friend of the Dávalos family; the lawyer, musician and electrifying personality Cuchi Leguizamón. (I was the beneficiary of some of his legal advice.) This new group was called *Los Fronterizos* and achieved popular and international acclaim with 'La Misa Criolla'. They wore black ponchos in contrast to the *Chalchaleros*'s red ones, and became their most serious rival on the folk scene. Our young neighbour and friend, Negro López, was their lead singer.

Arriving in Montevideo from Paris, on my return from Shanghai, I had to wait for passport control in a small room, which was soon inundated by passengers off another international flight from the US. The public furore outside alerted me in time: among the new passengers were *Los Chalchaleros*, back from performing in New York. The situation was very dangerous because I was travelling on false documents, in disguise, and carrying a lot of money, secret codes and the Chinese photo, enough to unleash a scandal. The room was so narrow there was no way of avoiding them. I knew all four of them through my friendship with Cabecita, which had continued when we both moved to Buenos Aires.

Fortunately, the logic of fame took over: if Pavarotti enters a room, people see him, but he doesn't see the people (unless Plácido Domingo is among them), and officialdom attends to famous people before anyone else. A military dictatorship – that of Onganía – had recently taken power in Argentina and controls were stricter by the day, with the primary objective of making transit passengers with something on their conscience feel constitutionally defenceless. The logic of fame was also aided by my sudden interest in the Customs and Excise notices stuck on the walls. Immigration officials did not follow the order of arrival, and this meant I could wait until the end before going through, contrary to my usual security tactic which was to get myself at the front of the queue. The situation was still precarious in the baggage hall, but I could not leave without my suitcase and everyone knows the free-for-all there is when luggage arrives in airports. But in the end, nothing untoward happened.

Our last days in Buenos Aires before moving to Córdoba were hectic. Some problems were very urgent. The Buenos Aires section of our organization was going through a crisis because, to the crucial loss of Bellomo was added the departure of Rafael, our logistical lynch-pin, who was caught up in a family drama. This meant further compartmentalization of the organization. We concentrated on our own work, and for me this included getting in touch with Hellman, the contact the Cubans had given me. As seemed to be the norm among the leadership of the Argentine Communist Party, he was waiting for me on the pavement in front of his house which had a huge wrought-iron gate giving onto a garden. He did not invite me in. The pretext was that he didn't want me to be seen by other people he was meeting, and that houses were less safe since the Onganía military coup. He was a big blond man, a typical specimen of the Argentine upper middle class, educated and well mannered, who immediately recognized the password and acted like we were old friends. The Cuban intelligence services had told him I would be contacting him on my return to Argentina. Hence, I modified my 'door-to-door book salesman' cover, and offered him another meeting if he wanted one. But he told me with unruffled calm that he was already sending people to train in Cuba, and he did not understand why Barbaroja Piñeiro was worried. As far as I was concerned, the less contact we had in the present circumstances the better, so we said goodbye.

Ana María and I had rented a house in Maipú, on the outskirts of Córdoba. It had just enough furniture to be habitable, and we moved in with little Paula and Andrea. With our local contacts re-established, a series of heated discussions ensued. There was a clear consensus for abandoning the guerrilla struggle. Our lawyers Lonatti and Roca also told me that the prisoners in Salta wanted me to come to the prison personally to discuss internal organizational matters, future political strategy and the role that we – I and they, as former guerrillas – would play in that strategy. We studied the viability of borrowing a document for me from one of the lawyers named as part of the 'official defence team' the judge had authorized. We did not look a bit like each other, but with a wig and Gustavo's verbal diarrhoea, it might work. I would have to go to Salta during the military reorganization of the country, under the notorious Internal Disorder Plan, an old repressive mechanism the author of which was none other than the new dictator Onganía. I would not be going as the lawyers' chauffeur, as I had done on previous occasions, but actually usurping one of their identities. The idea was that I would wear a wig and have the meeting with the prisoners in the room allotted to the defence team for interviewing their clients.

We reached the prison, an old yellow building resembling a medieval castle, situated on one side of the city between the park and the hills, and began a series of routine security checks – negotiating these was the job of Lonatti and Roca, who had already been joking with some of the guards. A succession of sliding iron doors opened and closed behind us in a noisy concerto of metallic banging, chains clanging, bolts locking, and resounding echoes. The prison warden was given papers certifying me as an additional lawyer. He authorized a pass for me as part of the legal team, established the number of prisoners to be interviewed that day who, because we wanted to agree on the text of certain written documents, would be seen as a group, and finally we negotiated a dark passageway to the interview room. Gustavo had come by himself the previous day to organize the meeting, and decide who would make up the prisoner's delegation. Federico and Héctor were named, and two others, Petiso Bellomo and Henry, were elected by democratic vote.

We had never been very good at expressing our emotions, but now our repressed feelings hindered us, contaminating the air. I had not seen Federico, Héctor and Henry since I had walked out of the jungle camp to fetch Furry two and a half years ago. Bellomo I had not seen since we delivered the weapons to Sendic in Montevideo. We all felt a certain embarrassment, like a guilt complex: them, for being in prison; me, for being free. We dealt with matters one by one. First I presented a report on my trip to Cuba and China, a report which did not hide my personal enthusiasm, nor disguise how bright their star shone there. Sharing their lives was a way of valuing their experiences collectively. For them, petty political problems no longer existed, theirs was a principled vision, they were not some prize to be awarded to the highest bidder. Let each follow his own path. If it coincided with ours in the end, we would be millions; if not, we would be on the pavement opposite. They rejected the gossip that reached them like a vaguely irritating noise, questioning our passivity, our inaction. They knew the reason, and that nothing could be done openly.

We looked at our finances and decided to maintain what had been allocated for the trial, transport costs and keeping me in clandestinity, and if possible, help for families and comrades in exile. The meeting could not go on indefinitely so we said goodbye, our mutual trust and solidarity confirmed, and went out. That is, *I* went out, into the fresh air. Your sensory understanding of the world and of life changes diametrically when you lose your freedom, although your awareness is heightened and your intellect is sharpened.

Roca and Lonatti went back that same afternoon to continue the legal work, but when we met later that night they said a problem had arisen between the prisoners. It risked destroying what we had achieved and creating a climate of conflict. Alberto Castellanos, Che's former bodyguard in Cuba, in prison under the name of Raúl Dávila, had been hysterical, and then depressed, because he had not been allowed to see or speak to me. Alberto was one of the first guerrillas to be captured by the border police patrol when they stumbled on our supply camp. Since then, although he had saved his life by protecting his real identity, he had suffered from the 'Cuban captured without a fight' complex and was terrified of what his former victorious *compañeros* in the Sierra Maestra would think. And, especially, of what his boss, Che, would think. Both lawyers and friends thought that, to avoid any greater risk, I should do something for Alberto that they could not do.

The following morning, I put the wig on again and went back to the prison. I ran the gauntlet of iron railings and gates, again accompanied by Gustavo, who asked the guards if we could see Alberto. We waited in the interview room, and he came in looking really miserable, very much the victim. After listening to his laments and protestations of loyalty, I told him as truthfully as I could that in Cuba I had heard nothing but expressions of concern, appreciation and friendship. In actual fact, I had had more news from the previous trip to Cuba than from this recent one. Then I had met his friends and *compañeros* who had asked for news of him. This made Alberto feel much better; he regained his confidence and even his rather ribald sense of humour. He was very emotional when he saw me and swore he would never forget that I went back to the prison just for him. We watched him leave the interview room almost a happy man. Alberto Castellanos regained his freedom less than a year later, in December 1967, but lost all memory of what I had done. A couple of months earlier, our positions were reversed. The military tribunal in Camiri had sentenced me to thirty years in prison.

In Córdoba, we lived a quiet family life, connected to the world through Armando Coria and Oscar del Barco, the only people who knew where we lived. My periodic, but irregular, sorties corresponded to the rhythm of a door-to-door book seller. Our immediate neighbours were Irene and Elías, former university friends of Ana María's, who had found the house for us. One day, at lunchtime, Oscar arrived in his mother's car, and we went for a walk under the trees, in search of a fresh breeze. '*Peladito*', said Oscar, 'someone is here looking for you.' We agreed that he would go to the first afternoon rendezvous and fix another meeting for later on, after we had discussed the matter. The city was like a sauna, and we met in a beer garden in the centre. Oscar told me of his meeting with a woman who 'looked like a commissar from the Soviet Politburo'. Her password was in order, but I did not know it, as it was not even in the canons of the Cuban secret services. Oscar thought she was from the KGB. I designed a counter checking operation. She was asked to meet me at ten the following morning at a place on one side of the city and, at eleven, if there was no contact within fifteen minutes, at another emergency meeting place, to which she would have to walk since it was only five or six blocks away. Finally, to be absolutely sure, she had to go to the other side of the city, to the park, three hours later.

The route between one point of the morning rendezvous and the other crossed a square, but there was also a short-cut with three successive observation points. If anyone contacted her or was following her, we would be bound to see it. At two in the afternoon, in front of the park, I finally met her. My impression was worse than Oscar's. She looked like a 'kapo' in a concentration camp. Dressed in old-fashioned clothes, all that was missing was a stiff uniform collar and whistle on a chain. She spoke from irrefutable positions, like an executive delegate from Vulcan in Star Trek. I invited her to a nearby ice-cream stand with tables in the shade, to lower the temperature a bit. After the obligatory passwords, she said without more ado, 'Che wants to see you'.

She spoke in an Argentine accent learned outside the country, which she quickly substituted for her Cuban accent, also learned. She was neither Cuban, nor Argentine. She was Tania, born in East Germany. She said I should get ready to leave. I would need a passport, because I was going to La Paz, Bolivia, by plane. She suggested I take my time, because if I didn't go within the week, it would be better to go in March. Getting and altering a passport cannot be done in a rush. She also indicated I would need clothes and shoes for the mountains. She herself would be my contact in La Paz and I would find her in more or less the same way she had found me: a particular photography shop with a password we would memorize now. 'Except I won't have to check you out', she said ironically. She gave me to understand that she had to return to Buenos Aires because she had not yet found someone else she was looking for.

This message from Che called for a meeting of our group, restricted for security reasons to Pancho Aricó, Oscar del Barco,

Armando Coria and Petiso Zárate from Buenos Aires, in place of Cholo who was away. You did not have to be a clairvoyant to imagine what Che was planning, although we did not rule out the possibility that it was just a meeting to discuss future plans – possible but improbable. If they had told me in Cuba that Che 'was in the mountains', it was because he was there already, or should be soon. And if I had to go and see him in Bolivia, he must have already left Cuba. And it would not be a return ticket.

There was unanimity on the kind of report I should make to him. While the political base was fast taking a radical turn in a revolutionary direction, it was nonetheless still wishful thinking to embark on armed struggle, given the ideological diversity that tended to divide rather than unite us. We thought this was at the very heart of what Che was proposing: unity through action. The only thing that could untie the Gordian knot would be if the impetus came from the working class, that is, on the back of their struggle, rather than being peripheral to it. To us, insisting on a guerrilla foco was unrealistic. Our position was absolutely clear. We did not want to sacrifice lives before we had created cadres of young people to raise awareness among the masses. And even less did we want to sacrifice Che's own mythical figure as potential overall leader. The political conditions would have to be right objectively, practically and contextually, to justify embarking on revolutionary armed struggle now.

Oscar del Barco, as a member of the editorial board of *Pasado y Presente* and the EGP national leadership, had put forward an idea in which a sum of money had been invested. Héctor Schmucler was still in Paris and knew Julio Cortázar, so it was suggested to the famous author that he be recorded reading some of his own work, chosen by him, and we would turn it into an LP. Cortázar was enthusiastic about the idea. Héctor arranged the recording, sent us the tapes and Oscar did the editing, with the help of publishers *La Flor* and *La Rosa Blindada*, using professional recording studios and commercial distribution networks. Oscar asked me to design the sleeve. I cut a full face photo of Cortázar horizontally below the eyes, and moved the halves a few millimetres to the side without separating them. The title, *Cortázar reads Cortázar*, was printed in red and black. Oscar thought it a perfect synthesis of the author. When I passed through Buenos Aires on my way to Bolivia, I took the corrected proofs to Mangieri, publisher of *La Rosa Blindada*, and he gave me back the original photo of Cortázar. I put it in my suitcase on top of my clothes with a copy of his latest book, *All Fires the Fire*, which I wanted to take to Che.

Punctuality is the basic ground rule of the militant. I was to meet someone in a Buenos Aires bar at five in the afternoon on the dot. I got off the underground at Congreso and walked slowly since I was a few minutes early. I went into to an L-shaped shopping gallery with exits on two streets, window shopping my way to the other side. I found the iron grill already closed, however, and retraced my steps. As I turned the corner on my way out, I saw a bloke pull up short in surprise and turn to study a shop window full of women's underwear, putting his hands up like blinkers, his face stuck to the glass. I remained calm. It was time for my appointment and I could not confront the impromptu transvestite who was still bent on staring at ladies' knickers. I passed beside him, walking normally, as if I had not seen him, and went out into the street. It was Miguel, our man condemned to death in Algiers, a picture of health. Only years later did I discover that he was now working for Barbaroja Pineiro, the Cuban spy chief.

One of our group, Manuel, was charged with finding an impeccable passport. That is, one recently obtained from an acquaintance without a police record, who was willing to lose it and wait for a few months to report its loss. He secured one from among his personal friends, a civil engineer, a little older than myself, but with similar physical features, called Carlos Alberto Frutos. Lodging in a family home Manuel had found for me, I worked on replacing the photograph so that the passport did not lose its virgin document smell. The dry stamp over my photo, the little dots of the number running vertically along its right side and the corresponding part of the page, were all perfect. The dots were a certificate of credibility, applied to the new photo after it had been stuck, like a surgical operation, using the finest dentist's drill passing painlessly over the perforations of the page.

My flight to Bolivia went direct to La Paz from Ezeiza airport in Buenos Aires. From sea level in Buenos Aires to the 4,000 metres of El Alto airport in La Paz, the only thing the plane can do is climb. In the morning, I went to the first rendezvous in La Paz. Nothing. I had lunch there in a market then walked to the next rendezvous. Again, nothing. At the third, Tania appeared. Walking together downhill for about a hundred metres, she gave me another rendezvous for two days later on the corner where buses left for Sucre, formerly Chuquisaca, capital of Upper Peru. Tania had changed her appearance to that of an archaeologist setting off for the ruins at Tiahuanacu, in a military-style jacket and trousers. She looked much the better for it. I never understood why she had disguised herself as a Puritan jailer to go to an Argentine city. To avoid complications, she gave me the money for the fare to Sucre. We would be travelling on the same bus without appearing to know each other. She got into a taxi and disappeared.

From a security point of view, things had not started well. Three days wandering around a small city like La Paz, seemingly without any good purpose, was dangerous. I devoted myself to history tourism, climbing slopes and steps. I don't think I left a single site unvisited, although tourism wasn't very organized in those days. However, like a good tourist, I bought two Oruru devil masks which I put in my suitcase, like guardians. At sundown, I went to the Café de la Paix, almost in front of my hotel in the Avenida Camacho, an obligatory ritual for all types of local conspiracies.

The bus for Sucre would be leaving after midday. The bus company was in a leafy street with a wide pavement near the corner of Avenida Montes. Its office was the size of a billiard table, just a ticket booth and luggage store two steps up from the street. The pavement outside under the trees served as a waiting room. Passengers were already lining up against the wall, sitting on the ground or on their boxes and bundles. I don't remember the exact time the bus left, but for simplicity's sake, let's say it was three o'clock. Once I had bought my ticket, there was nothing for it but to wander around waiting for Tania. Soon I noticed another stranger, doing much the same as I was, passing the time by strolling from one end of the piles of luggage and passengers to the other. He looked out of place, idling aimlessly about. Tall, thin, and wearing an elegant bottle green padded windcheater, of a kind not available in Latin America in those days, he would have looked foreign not only in Bolivia, but in any of the neighbouring countries. I could see he had noticed me, just as I had noticed him. We were, then, in the same boat, and this could indicate some common cause. My brain started putting two and two together. He did not look North American; having neither the physique nor the clothes of the Yanks. I imagined he was European, but he had none of the characteristics of an Italian, Spaniard or German. Ah, but that discreet gentlemanly air, that polite way of letting unruly children pass, that savoir-faire, smacked without a doubt of a Frenchman. A young Parisian literary figure, a disciple of Althusser, came to mind. He had got himself noticed about two years earlier with a thesis on the Cuban Revolution, and his distinctly pro-Cuban book on revolution had just been published. If I was not mistaken, it was Régis Debray, author in the first instance of *Castroism: The Long March of Latin America*, a European view of the influence that the guerrilla struggle initiated by the Cuban Revolution was having on the new generation of Latin American militants, and also of a theoretical manual of *foquismo*, *Revolution in the Revolution?* which had also just been published.

With fifteen, ten, five minutes to departure time, Tania had still not appeared. Both the Frenchman and I were glancing furtively at the clock. The bus company staff had finished loading the luggage bundles onto the roof and tying them to the roof-rack. That done, and after an argument about whether the chickens belonging to a woman passenger had the right to travel with her in the bus or on the roof, the staff locked the doors to the office, handed the keys to a third person, and got on the bus in their new roles as driver and ticket collector. Loud shouts and a peeping horn urged the dejected passengers saying goodbye to their loved ones to get on board fast. With one last glance at the clock, I decided to get on the bus. After all, the real story was waiting in Sucre, not in La Paz. The Frenchman followed me down the crowded aisle, as if this last-minute manoeuvre had been planned.

Standing in the middle of the bus, among a ruckus of restless passengers suddenly discovering an urgent need to move from one seat to another, passing packages and belongings to and fro, we looked at each other in silence. The roar of the engine merged with the passenger hubbub and we set off. The bus carried on down the avenue, weaving in and out of the traffic, the standing passengers hanging on to the backs of the seats for dear life. Friendly *Collas*, old men and women, informed us 'you'll only have to stand as far as El Alto', because a lot of people got off there. The driver kept his finger on the horn and all manner of carts and wagons gave way before his strident hooting. Another horn was in competition behind us, however, like a cortege of newlyweds. It turned out to be a taxi which managed to overtake our bus and brake slowly in front of us, a handkerchief waving out of the window as if an injured person were being taken to hospital A&E. Our driver was forced to stop. The taxi door opened, a hysterical passenger got out, still clasping the handkerchief, lugging a bag, camera dangling from her neck. She got on the bus with no attempt to disguise the fact she was looking for us. It was Tania.

25

The Camp with an Absent Comandante: March 1967

On that journey, Tania did the exact opposite of what the tremendous responsibility she had been given demanded of her. She was a 'mole', and a mole should only operate structurally, keeping strictly to her role, not mixing with foot soldiers or hangers on. I don't want to sit in judgement after the fact. I only want to highlight the succession of minimal but indispensable security norms that were not observed during that mission, for which she was responsible.

Tania's triumphant entrance onto the bus was missed by nobody, not even the chickens. Nor was the fact that she was following us pale-faces; already part of the passengers' collective consciousness. The absence of greetings or reproaches, our silent acceptance of a sudden group symbiosis, united us in the eyes of the jostling audience. It was indeed true that there were seats to be had once we reached El Alto and, freezing and tired, we sat down to face a night's drive across the Altiplano, bringing back unforgettable memories for me of our previous time in Bolivia. I imagined we were retracing our steps, that we would end up at the *finca* in Emborozú which had not been sold after all, and that I would find Masetti there, like a uniformed Moses showing me the Promised Land, undefeated, peeling a grapefruit.

It was getting dark when we got to Sucre. The sight of the narrow winding cobbled streets of the old town was like taking a step back into the colonial period. The *Colla* population crept along the walls like shadows, the women with their multiple petticoats, bowler hats, sandals and children, their babies' vicuña bonnets peeking out of the colourful woven cloth tied across their chests. Crawling through the melée of carts and pack mules, the bus finally stopped in a small triangular square, blocking the road. We got out.

Tania motioned us to wait and disappeared round a corner, only to reappear a few minutes later with the news that she had found a hotel room not far from there. Each carrying our own bag, we advanced through the crowd of peddlers, onlookers and passers-by to the hotel, or rather more of a boarding house. The manager said he had a room with eight beds free. Alternatively we could share three- or four-bed rooms with other guests. Tania preferred the first option. The window-less space looked like a junk room or, to be generous, a war or catastrophe emergency zone: a bunker. While we went out to eat, they put sheets on the first three beds, separated from each other by a mere fifteen centimetres. The Frenchman chose the furthest from the door, got into it, turned his back to us and lay there immobile. I was in the middle, my bed pushed next to his. Tania, who came back from the WC smiling, was assigned the first one, next to the wall. The space between our beds was so narrow that she had to take off her boots on the bed, where she then preceded to get undressed slowly, in an unexpected bout of striptease. With a smile she alerted me to the possibility of *vinchuca* bugs, then flexing her powerful legs in the air she slipped her body, not beautiful but well endowed, between the dubious sheets. As she stretched out her hand to switch off the light on the wall beside her, she wished me an amiable good-night before we were both plunged into darkness. We were not to know that it was the last time she would sleep in a bed in the long and painful last six months of her life.

In the morning, we were the butt of gossip in the hostel canteen. The local clientele were used to families cohabiting, but they didn't think it normal for a gringa to share a room with two men.

Tania went out again to organize the next part of our journey, the right thing to do but with no very satisfactory results. There was no public transport between Sucre, where we were, and Camiri, our destination, a subtropical oil town in the province of Santa Cruz. There was nothing for it but to hire a taxi, or rather, look for a driver prepared to cross a mountain range which, as we were to discover, was an almost impossible safari due to the recent rainy season. Tania found one, argued, insisted, doubled the rate and ended up bribing the driver to take us to Camiri that same day. The owner of a canvas-topped Fiat, a wheeler-dealer of uncertain origin, settled in the area since God knows when, he was one of the 'motorized class', which allowed him to behave with aggressive arrogance towards the 'pedestrian' locals, though he was docile with his gringo 'bosses'. Anyway, prematurely drunk, he said we had to leave at once if we wanted to get to Camiri in daylight, because the road was very bad. It was about ten o'clock. We put our stuff in the car and left.

Sucre sits astride the Central Cordillera, which marks the boundary between the high Altiplano and the tropical valleys below, and the Bolivian Chaco beyond. Its foothills run down into Argentina, parallel to the great exodus of Andean water via the Bermejo and Pilcomayo rivers: the region that would be our new 'Salta experience'. We had to cross this cordillera, a difficult task at the best of times because the roads are mountain tracks with precipices on either side, frequently blocked by land and rock slides. After heavy rain the road disappears altogether, becoming an impassable mud channel, only attempted by lorry drivers and guides with winches, or by the irresponsible. In our case, the latter. The guy drove at top speed in the passable stretches, as if he were taking part in a rally, and in the muddy sections, the jeep lurched from side to side, totally out of control. The wheels sometimes hovered over the abyss, while the gearbox crunched, trying to engage the four-wheel drive to get us out of trouble. Tania roared with laughter in the front seat, enjoying it as much as the driver, who was toasting her health with swigs from his bottle. The Frenchman and I, our bodies and heads battered about in the back seat, could only grip the metal door handles to try to protect our backsides.

I finally reached the end of my tether and yelled at the guy and Tania to stop. I leapt out of the back door and asked Tania for a word alone. Without a fuss, but with authority, I told her I was taking over the operation, since the guy was clearly a danger and I hadn't come to Bolivia to fall down a cliff face because of some drunken idiot. Tania concurred, as if she had suddenly come to her senses. I then talked to the driver and made it clear that if anyone was going to end up in the river, it was not going to be me, and least of all not at his hands. I confiscated the bottle and threw it into the void. I said I could drive if he didn't feel well, but he claimed dolefully: 'No, *señor*. You have to know the road, *señor*.' The rest of the journey was exhausting, but calm. We all rode in silence, me in front, beside the upright driver.

We arrived in Camiri at twilight. It was a town surrounded by low densely wooded hills, and inhabited by a heterogeneous population of Quechuas migrating from the Altiplano, Chapacas from neighbouring Tarija to the south, or Cambas from Santa Cruz in the east, mixed with the descendents of the native Guaraní from the Chaco plain who have always lived in this area. Camiri was a garrison town, the headquarters of the Fourth Army Division. But it was also a fiefdom of the state oil company, the YPFB. Both institutions stemmed from the Chaco War (1932–35), fought because of the thirst for oil, urged on by two big international oil companies, US Standard Oil and Anglo-Dutch Shell. The region became the bastion of Bolivian resistance, and spawned the new army. The presence of both institutions was immediately noticeable in town: soldiers, police, military personnel of all types, oil company technicians and workers, all enjoying a minimal, but lively, commercial and entertainment infrastructure.

Among the businesses which had flourished was the Italian restaurant to which we headed after Tania had made her contact. The Marietta, named after the owner's daughter, belonged to an

Italian who was getting rich by being able to turn his hand to good pastas, sauces and other peninsular food. The place was not very big but had an open-air patio, tablecloths, and good family-orientated service, typical of a Roman *trattoria*. Not surprisingly, everyone ate there, from army officers to oil workers, either with their families, or alone before they plunged into the darker reaches of the town's nightlife, drawn from a broad international spectrum, but mainly Argentina.

Tania had returned to her role as hostess and guide, and had also picked up a jeep 'of her own', a bullet-proof Toyota, that she had left on a previous visit. We left all our bags in it, except for our documents and personal stuff, books, etc., and the jeep returned from whence it came. We walked the few blocks to the Marietta, to stretch our legs. The streets were furrowed with craters, a sign that the storms carried everything in their wake. The square was full of people, and music from a military band accompanied the locals as they walked their dogs or stood chatting. It didn't inspire much joy though, more like depression.

Sitting at a table in the Marietta while we waited to order a pitcher of wine, Tania and I twittered away like parrots about silly things. We had introduced ourselves by now, more or less. I knew who Régis Debray was, a young French philosopher and writer, but he did not know who I was, except that I was called Carlos, an Argentine *compañero*. On second thoughts, maybe he knew who I was, and I did not know him. While Tania and I talked, he said nothing. We jumped from topic to topic, from the weather to oranges, to tropical food to vegetarian cooking, from bread with tomato to wine boiled with lemon, from cars to the immortality of the crab . . . It was Tania's most appropriate behaviour to date and I was seconding her enthusiastically. Suddenly Debray shattered the mood, and revealed the personality he had chosen for himself and would try to construct throughout his life, inspired by the hero and author of *L'espoir*, André Malraux, his alter ego. In a fit of Jacobin rigour, he banged the palm of his hand down hard on the table, making the plates and cutlery jump, and shouted to our and the assembled audience's surprise: 'Please, *señores*! I can't stand it . . . Let's talk about something serious.'

We were finishing our ice cream in silence when Tania's contact appeared. He came in, greeting some of the diners as he passed, and sat down at our table, as if we were old friends. It was Coco Peredo. He was coming to fetch us but now discovered Tania wanted to be part of the group too. We left the Marietta together. That meal was the last Tania would have sitting at a table with napkins and glasses, desert and coffee. We got into Coco's jeep, its headlights piercing the darkness as it sought the road. It was eleven o'clock. It had taken us twelve hours from Sucre, but Coco said we would be able to rest in a couple of hours if there were no problems on the road. As a precaution, we had to flatten ourselves against the sacks of flour, rice and potatoes he was carrying in the back when we passed a barracks or a village, or, later on, any curious neighbour. The road was just a track cut through clay earth, a bush trail, and the jeep shuddered and whined. At about two in the morning, the trail died in the patio of an adobe house with a bright zinc roof. We had arrived at the *Casa de Calamina*.

A man came out, covering his eyes from the glare of the headlights. According to Coco, he was the *finca*'s 'caretaker'. We went into the house while they unloaded the jeep, and were soon enveloped in the aroma of freshly made coffee and a worrying tale of a row with a neighbour, who had threatened to fetch the army if he wasn't let into some imagined 'business' that he supposed was drugs. This threat altered the situation and our plans for a night's rest. Tania needed to change her plans too. Coco suggested she go back to Camiri with him, but she was determined not to. So Coco decided we should spend the night in the forest, in a so-called 'emergency and contact camp'. He would go back and show his face in Camiri, and try to use his contacts to stop any repressive action. One of the caretaker's men would show us the way. So, in the dark, we transferred the jeep's cargo to a place in the woods near the river, and Coco left before dawn.

Lying in the undergrowth against the trunk of a tree is not ideal for a tired traveller, but it was not impossible to sleep for a few hours despite the mosquitoes. Halfway through the morning, the caretaker who was keeping watch with one eye on the path up to the house and the other on the trail to the river, spied the group he was expecting: uniformed with beards. If I still had any doubts about what I was going to find, they disappeared completely. Leading the new group, carrying a M2 carbine and wearing a cowboy hat, was Captain Olo Pantoja, our former instructor in the house in Havana. He embraced me warmly. It was now clear. Che was not simply passing through; he was implementing his project. It was not a complete surprise, since I was here to meet him, but all the same I was astonished that military action was a fait accompli.

Perhaps in retrospect I should not have complained about the time I was wasting in Havana. I should have abandoned my trip to China and just waited for his orders. The China trip had not materialized out of the blue, of course, but I should have waited to learn the details of his plans. According to Olo, Ramón (Che's name now) had taken the bulk of his men, most of them Cuban, on a long exploratory training march. Papi Martínez Tamayo, who had been with us in Havana and Salta, was with them. I was supposed to have come in January or at the end of March, not at the beginning. It was 6 March 1967.

The group who had come to fetch the provisions consisted of four or five men. This was something they did regularly between Base Camp and the *Casa de Calamina*, an operation they called the 'gondola'. Gondola is the name country folk in Bolivia give to the buses which do the round trips between provincial towns and cities. People use them not only to travel from place to place, but also to carry their produce, animals, furniture, everything they need for family life and commerce. The gondola carrying food and equipment between the Base Camp and the *finca* was done two or three times a week. Including us foreigners and the care-taker's men, it was a pretty big column. We began by fording the

Ñancahuazú river a couple of times because it made an S bend at that point before heading northwards. The river was rough and difficult, sandwiched between rocks and jungle-clad cliffs. Once the S bends had been left behind, the river itself became the path, against the current, to the north east. In a few places, trails ran along the river bank, otherwise the main part of the journey meant wading from one side of the river to the other, over stones and the odd sandy beach.

We did not have rucksacks, so we carried our stuff in jute sacks on our backs. My lack of training, and a few extra kilos, began to make itself felt and, after a couple of hours, I was on the verge of collapse. As often happened to me in Salta, just when I was about to throw in the towel, Olo called a halt. We did a bit of shooting practice and the Frenchman showed he knew how to use a gun, shooting a turkey or some such. In the late afternoon, after about eight hours marching, we reached a place where gentle rocks rose from the river and embedded themselves in the jungle, like a beach of pink granite. There, on the right-hand side, the column left the river and climbed into the trees, skipping from stone to stone, leaving no tracks.

After a few metres, we reached an almost invisible path, like an animal track, turning leftwards, and another hundred metres further up was a vantage point from which you could see how the river below took a right-angled turn to the left, and on the bend out of the forest appeared the crystalline waters of a stream. The path continued to climb steeply along the right-hand side of the stream, until it delved so deeply into the jungle that the roar of its waters disappeared. We noticed trenches had been dug there to control the passage up the path. There was also a sentry post that the column passed with brief greetings and jokes.

We came to the first installations of the Base Camp, set up on a kind of plateau between the hills and the stream. It comprised areas of cleared land, new ditches, a *criollo* bread oven mounted on tree trunk trestles, the outline of a corral, some *pahuichis* – rudimentary huts of poles tied together – and a wooden table and benches under an awning. A little further away was a kind of amphitheatre which served as an *aula magna* for meetings, and in between each bit of infrastructure the ground had been cleared of undergrowth, and hammocks hung from trees with room for rucksacks underneath.

There were not many people about, doubtless because of guard duty and the gondola itself, but those who were there gathered together, and introductions, via nicknames, were made. We became Danton (the Frenchman, obviously) and Carlos, the name on my passport. The caretaker's name, Antonio, was the same as Olo Pantoja's pseudonym, but two guerrillas could not have the same *nom de guerre*. So the real Antonio became León, because he had defended the *finca* bravely all this time, like a lion. As well as Olo, there was another Cuban, Arturo, the telecommunications man, who turned out to be Papi's brother. Then there were old-timers, like Ñato and Camba, and some new arrivals who nobody knew anything about except that they all belonged to a pro-Chinese group led by another Guevara, Moisés, a miners' leader; and a trio of Peruvian 'internationalists': a doctor El Negro, Eustaquio, and their leader El Chino. While food was being prepared, Ñato, the quartermaster, handed out hammocks, mosquito nets and blankets, and we made our nests.

After the meal, everyone bar the sentries got together on the steps of the amphitheatre for a bit of socializing, music courtesy of a portable radio tuned in to Radio Habana Cuba. The mood created by the rhythmic *guarachas* was a bit surreal, as if we had been transported to the gardens of the Tropicana. In the middle of this fantasy, Tania suddenly delved into her bag and brought out a packet of photos that she handed to Antonio (Olo), the camp commander. He handed them round to those present, most of them bewildered Bolivians, and the people in the photos were identified, as well as the time and place. When the photos reached me, I could not believe my eyes. There was Che in various guises, without a beard, with a few weeks' growth, with his head shaven, with short hair. Also in the photos, all perfectly recognizable, were Papi and lots of others who were mostly not Bolivian, but also some rather inopportune Bolivians like Mario Monje, secretary of the Bolivian Communist Party, young Loyola Guzmán and Rodolfo Saldaña, our contacts in the city. Even some of those present were there – Antonio, Ñato, Arturo, Coco, and Tania herself – taken in the very places we had come through.

For me, acting instinctively was an occupational hazard. I was not a professional intelligence officer, but the little I knew about security and the responsibilities I had been given made me jump up immediately and take Olo aside (Olo *did* happen to be in Cuban intelligence.) I told him I thought what was happening was outrageous, a really dangerous mistake. I said there were would-be guerrilla recruits present, who should not have access to information like that, let alone pictures, and I wanted to register my disapproval. It amounted to a potential threat because if there were subsequent problems, nobody could say they didn't know. Olo was petrified and ordered the photos returned immediately, making Tania responsible for checking they were all there – not an easy task because there were four or five rolls. Olo undertook an immediate public self-criticism. Debray confessed to having been astonished by a whole series of violations of the most elementary security norms, saying that the journey had been a comedy of errors, except when 'Carlos' (me) had intervened, then and now. He supported my intervention.

The next morning, during breakfast, hunting groups were organized. The Frenchman and I were in the same team and we set off upriver accompanied by Julio, a young Bolivian doctor. We went as far as a place called Pampa del Tigre and spent the whole day there without bagging anything; we returned, dying of hunger, in the late afternoon, to help with the evening chores. It was Tuesday the 13th, and if it had not already been an inauspicious date, it certainly deserved to be now. When we sat down to eat at six o'clock, some of the hunters had still not returned. An hour later, we found disturbing signs indicating that Moisés Guevara's men had deserted. They had left a note for another of

their group to the effect that they were leaving. The two of them
had been sent off alone with a special .22 calibre Winchester hunting rifle. Antonio was beside himself and yelled at Moisés,
supposedly responsible for his people. After a few nervous deliberations with Ñato and Arturo, he ordered someone to return to
the *finca* immediately – against the wishes of Moisés who wanted
to go himself – and tell León to go to Camiri to warn Coco, unless
he came across the deserters first, that is. Moisés would go with
him as far as the *Casa de Calamina* and bring back news.

What on earth had gone wrong? How could something like
this happen to a project of such magnitude, with such experienced
revolutionaries? The explanation could be the one Moisés prof-
fered, somewhat incoherently. During Carnival, people go
missing and when the time came to leave for the jungle, he could
not find the men he had organized to join up with. 'Indians are
like that', he said. Moisés had replaced them with just anybody he
could find, dragging them away from their traditional fiesta.

But you cannot deny other factors which turn political decla-
mations into something closer to wishful thinking than reality. A
wave of revolutionary dreaming and individualism swept away
all vestiges of seriousness, because the political 'struggle' became
a way of life that gave militants prestige. In many cases, the
personal sacrifice was genuine and they paid for frustrating experiences with their lives, but their hopes and yearnings distorted
reality. After the dazzling example of the Cuba Revolution, the
tendency to imitate zoomed off into the realms of the absurd.
Moreover, links to 'the island', 'contacts' and 'revolutionary' ties
were flaunted – they brought invitations and other advantages –
because the official Cuban connection was always with the
Communist Parties. And to achieve these links, abilities, resources
and offers were often embellished. When the time came to honour
obligations, they had to show not only the purest of convictions,
but also short-term promises of glory and immediate gratifica-
tion. If principles failed, there was nothing for it but to recruit the
unemployed in *chicha* bars, for money.

Moisés returned at dawn with no news from the front. There was no sign of the fugitives at the *finca* so all we could do was wait for the return of León from Camiri. Antonio mobilized our scarce manpower to keep lookouts on the river and to devise an emergency plan in case of invasion. He started to worry about the 'visitors', as they began to call us – Debray, Chino the Peruvian, Tania and myself – and wanted us out of any potential harm's way until Che came back. A team lead by Ñato went exploring and found a place for a rearguard camp by following the trail Che and the absent guerrillas had taken upstream to the north. Depending on León's news, we would either stay at Base Camp or evacuate it and move further up into the mountains.

León appeared with Coco a couple of days later and we learned that the deserters were already in the hands, first of the police and then the army, so Coco had decided to fall back to Base Camp with León. I learned the full details of this episode many months later from León while he was sharing one of the brand new cells in Camiri jail with Régis and me. However, given its crucial importance, I'll describe it now, modifying my aim of writing only about what I have seen myself.

What happened was that when Antonio sent León after the deserters, he told him to follow their trail (León was from the Beni, the cattle-ranching region in the north, and was a good tracker) and to kill them if he found them. He gave him a .38 calibre revolver which was easy to carry. The order could be considered a normal military action in time of war for agents trained in the art, but not all the requisites were present in these particular circumstances. The war had not started and the recruits were still peasants or miners, who had taken up arms for a political ideal of justice and fraternity. León, who had hardly slept for the past few days and had twice done the journey upriver to Base Camp, managed nevertheless to catch up with the two men. He left the *finca*, passed surreptitiously by the treacherous neighbour without seeing anything amiss, and carried on to Lagunillas, a small village halfway to Camiri. Figuring that the fugitives would be as exhausted as he was, he went to the hostel, a big old house where a *Colla* family rented out space on the floor to travellers, who might arrive in the middle of the night and then settle up the next morning. He found the two men sleeping in the interior patio, huddled up together on the straw.

León was not prepared for a mission of this kind, I don't think anyone is: these were not proven criminals or torturers, after all. He shone his lantern on them but they did not move, so he lay on the floor between them and the door, gun in hand, and waited for daylight.

When the cocks crowed in the dawn, he talked to the frozen deserters, who attempted to trivialize the situation: 'We couldn't bear all that menial work and guard duty; there was barely any food and no money. We were hired for more important work so we could send wages to our families, but all they did was boss us about all the time.' León tried to convince them to go back and demand that promises be kept; those responsible would surely keep them. No way. They wanted to go home. They did not even have the bus fare to Oruro, however, and were going to sell the rifle. León proposed giving them money for the journey in Camiri, because selling the rifle would cause problems. He appealed to the miners' traditional solidarity in the struggle against exploitative bosses and asked them not to do any more damage because it would rebound on them afterwards.

They agreed a rendezvous in Camiri, and León left to get there as fast as he could. A lorry driver may have given him a lift part of the way. Luckily he found Coco quickly in Camiri. But Coco had no money either. Che had ordered all the money to be kept by the guerrillas since the police had already searched the *finca*. Coco borrowed money from the woman who was his cover in the town but the deserters did not turn up at the rendezvous. The police had already arrested them when they tried to sell the rifle to someone, who then denounced them. Coco asked around and found out that the army had claimed the prisoners were under their jurisdiction. At this point, he and León decided to return to the camp.

Clearly it would only be a matter of time before the army advanced on the Base Camp, the whereabouts of which would have been described by the prisoners. Antonio carried out his plan of retreat for us, and Tania, Debray, Chino and I left the Base Camp accompanied by Julio, and someone else I can't remember. The route was easy along the bed of the stream which provided the Base Camp with water and ran through the jungle without obstacles. Then, about halfway along, where there was a waterfall called 'the elevator', the stream disappeared into the sand in places, only to re-emerge, filtered. Its source was at the head of the ravine about three hours trek away, in mountains that lose their jungle cover as they go northwards. There, to the left of the nascent trickle of water, in a discreet hollow in the hillside, plagued by insects and thorn bushes, we set up our refugee camp, at a spot we called '*El Oso*' after a bear that Debray had killed during the days of waiting and hunting. It was duly stewed with maize and eaten despite its strong wild taste.

26

The Prophet in Tatters

Antonio decided that our presence in the rearguard should be of some real use. Our role would be to maintain an advanced post that Che's vanguard group would come across before it descended the ravine to the Base Camp. What we had to tell them might influence their decisions and save them the trouble of going down and perhaps coming back up the steep slope. So, early the next morning, Debray and I took on this task. On the right side of the stream, emerging at the foot of the hills, was a path that may originally have been an animal track but which was now used by men in boots who left their imprints in the mud. The climb was diabolically difficult, aggravated by the mass of bald tree roots which made the slope very slippery, as the vegetation struggled to get a hold on the almost vertical wall and extended its roots underneath the trunks.

Just when we thought our lungs would burst, the jungle began to thin out, and we set up our observation post. We saw the path continue upwards until it disappeared from sight and we thought we were near the summit. It was a dry but very hot day, and it seemed as if the only water around was that dripping from our own bodies. A cloud of mosquitoes, or rather, of countless species of mosquitoes, enveloped us all day. We tied handkerchiefs round everything, smoked, and furiously waved branches, but all to no avail.

We went back down in the late afternoon and found all hell had broken loose. Apparently, the advance guard of Che's column had followed the course of the river and had gone straight to the *finca*. When the group leader, a Cuban comandante called Marcos, came up to the Base Camp, he ordered it to be evacuated. He also told three men, including El Negro, the Peruvian doctor, to take food and emergency supplies, and to go to meet Che's column. The weather had been appalling and the column had suffered a series of catastrophes, including deaths. Heavy rains had made the river crossings dangerous: rafts with equipment on board had sunk; a third of the column had lost their boots, and even their clothes; and the effort had sapped their energy. The men's health had been affected by lack of food. They were suffering the physical effects of malnutrition which meant that their legs and feet were so swollen some of them could barely walk. At dusk, a solitary guerrilla called Rolando came by. He had managed to swim the river and he too had orders to send food urgently. Fortunately, someone, perhaps Tania, knew him. Rolando confirmed the bad news. We were all worried about the state of our *compañeros'* health.

The slope now seemed even steeper, tougher and interminable than before. On the second day, we had reached a higher lookout point than on the first, but now we needed to climb to a plateau even further up, double the distance, to get the clearest possible view of the route the guerrilla column would be returning by. We wanted to see them the minute they appeared in the distance and perhaps receive some signal. After over an hour of very hard climbing, leaving the tropical vegetation behind, we reached the crest of the hill, to be faced with a most unusual spectacle. A sea of hillocks, like dunes in the desert, as far as the eye could see, floating in a kind of watercress salad – the jungle – which seemed to waft towards the summits or flee from them chased by the wind. The whole panorama spread out before us, although it was not clear if this gave us an optical advantage or just made the experience surreal.

The hours drifted by slowly and peacefully, like the clouds. The only things that seemed to have any life in them were the sun's shadows which moved over the hills and ravines, defining the topography of the landscape. In the late afternoon, we saw two little figures, like cartoon ants, walking on two legs and carrying a backpack with the other two. Silhouetted in black, they appeared and disappeared between the dunes, far away, at the very back of the picture. The Frenchman and I ran down, took up our positions and lay in wait. When they were a few metres away I cried 'Halt!' I had no doubt they were *compañeros*. But we did not know how they would react, since the first thing they saw of me was the weapon pointing at them. As if it were the most natural thing in the world, they said they had been 'sent on ahead by Ramón', to prepare food, and asked after Rolando. I let them pass, telling them they would find more people down below, and maybe Rolando in the stream. They carried on, saying the main body of the column would not be long in coming.

The column was gradually taking shape and, despite the distance, we could see how it was organized, and we noted the rapid energy of a small advance guard which from time to time disappeared off to the sides, returned to the path, and then stopped and went back, yet always advancing. At the same time, an Indian file of men followed slowly without stopping. Members of a phantasmagorical platoon approached us, as if from another world. We had got to our feet, and were standing motionless, leaning on our rifles, with no thought of any absurd ritual of passwords or greetings. And the feeling was mutual. The first men passed us as if we were statues and went to sit on the largest stones behind us.

One man walked straight up to me. He had a rifle on his shoulder, a 1930s anarchist's cap on his head, thin beard and pipe hanging from the corner of his mouth. It was Che. His clothes were torn to shreds, a trouser leg was missing, the right sleeve of his khaki shirt hung in tatters but was perfectly buttoned at the wrist. It was not just any old combat uniform. He was wearing the clothes of universal misery, threadbare and filthy. Pockets bulging with papers and pencils, map holder crosswise, and rucksack full to bursting.

Behind him, the only person emitting annoying noises, incongruent and rather vulgar, was Papi, who as soon as he thought I could hear, that is, at about thirty metres, walked along proffering abuse: 'Pelao, you're fat . . . ! *Prrr, Prrr* . . . You'll soon lose that flab here . . . and *Prrr Prrr* . . .', with irreverent raspberries and snorts.

Che came up to where I was standing paralyzed. I hate formal expressions of affection, and my usual reaction is to say nothing. He took off his rucksack, leaving it on the ground, his M2 leaning against it, and (I didn't know what to do with my rifle) we fell into a prolonged silent embrace. Neither of us said anything, nor did the spectators; I thought I heard the beating of at least one heart. Head on my shoulder, his mouth next to my ear, he said, breaking the silence: 'That must be the Frenchman.' Debray was behind me, still standing among the rocks. As I took a step back, I managed an unnecessary gesture of introduction. Che greeted him cordially, then walked on a little and sat down on a stone to rest. He seemed to gather strength, or rage.

A series of deliberations with his men demonstrated what we would be seeing from now on: a mechanism of command that worked with a minimum of discussion. Uppermost in his mind was to reach the camp at the bottom of the slope and eat. I heard orders given to someone going to the Base Camp: 'Send enough provisions to cook all night . . .'. After a few playful hugs, Papi presented me 'to society', introducing me to the rest of the troops. It was amazing the expectations that our presence raised, not as individuals, but for what we represented in Che's subsequent plans.

Papi gave me a rundown of what had happened on the march: some events were tragic, like the men who drowned and the sinking rafts; others were pitiful, like guerrillas reduced to their underwear and walking barefoot, their feet wrecked. But Papi was an inveterate optimist and, for him, catastrophes were mere contingencies of the struggle. A significant change was palpable now. The atmosphere was electric and orders were given and executed as if we were on a boat in the middle of a storm.

The guerrillas headed off down the path leading to the carpet of jungle below, but we had to wait to be relieved of our duties, since the rearguard with the men in worst physical shape was yet to arrive. When our guard duty finished, before night fell, we slid down that damned slope and, guided by the light of the campfire, arrived in time to witness a terrible scene.

Che was not mincing his words. He was haranguing his group of silent men, men who had moved heaven and earth to get back to camp only to discover that, in their absence, things had kicked off, that now the war would be won by fighting, that the maximum sacrifice would be required, that they had not been chosen to come on a picnic, that no one was to retreat without fighting the enemy, and that anyone not in agreement should say so now and be expelled immediately, because from now on, anyone leaving would be shot.

He told Ñato: 'Go and tell everybody I forbid them to come up here, I want everyone back at the Base Camp, or even further back.' I had guard duty at two in the morning, so after eating my ration of stew, I took refuge under my nylon sheeting, in the concave space reserved for my private universe: my hammock. Come what may, I needed to sleep.

27

A War Is Won by Fighting

The outlook was gloomy. There was no longer any room for doubt: this was an immediate and operative guerrilla army, not a long-term project. And the man who had unleashed revolutionary passions throughout the continent, like a gust of wind whisking up dry leaves, was back in charge.

It was incredible to see those around me acting with such carelessness, and excessive confidence. Battle was about to begin prematurely and, although it could be argued that this was not only inevitable, but also this army's raison d'être, there is no doubt that the actual decision to enter the fray, to fight, was the strategic prerogative of the commander, in order to keep the initiative and march on to victory.

At the stage of preliminary exercises and accumulation of forces, prior to establishing long-term emergency plans and becoming independent of its urban support network by consolidating different contact and supply routes, a guerrilla force is inward-looking and stuck in a dilemma. Contact with the outside world is the guerrilla's Gordian knot. It has to exist but is always the weakest link in the chain. In this case, all the intermediaries between the guerrillas and the outside world were now up in the mountains, incorporated into the guerrilla nucleus. That is, they no longer existed as external operatives. Tania, the strategic contact who should have been fulfilling her most important role during the prolonged buildup to military action – staying buried in enemy territory – was also in the mountains. There was

absolutely no way of communicating since the radio was not
working. The panorama was depressing.

The Cuban combatants, however, were enthusiastic and optimistic. They were fresh from a remembered victory in the Sierra
Maestra, and although some of them had also been involved in
the failed operation in the Congo, they had come out alive and
more determined than ever. Nevertheless, they did not hide the
differences they observed, especially since they now had experience of the huge distances involved, and the other overwhelming
geographic factors. But the Cuban victory and its subsequent
success had filled them with a fatal sense of omnipotence that
would not brook pessimistic assessments, or even realistic ones. I
heard more than once that the struggle would be intense, but that
victory was certain, in no more than three or four years, against
Yankee imperialism and the armies of its neighbours. This
tendency to hugely underestimate the task was not of Che's
doing. He never tired of saying that in all probability none of us
would live to see the victory.

The reason for Che's rage was the decision taken by Marcos,
commander of the vanguard column, to move the lines of defence
away from the Base Camp, thus abandoning it to its fate. Marcos
had previously ignored Che's orders by allowing a group of oil
workers to see his column deep in the jungle by the river, and
then disobeying express orders by continuing on openly to the
Casa de Calamina, which had already been raided by the police.

Che had originally hoped to establish the foco in the region
clandestinely, but with local people reporting the presence of
bearded men drying clothes, banknotes, weapons, and military
style footwear, it was not surprising that within a week news had
reached – by various routes – the Fourth Army Division headquarters in Camiri. Such reports gave additional credibility to the
version told them by the deserters, taken prisoner only a few days
after Marcos' piece of theatre by the river.

Che could not know this for sure, but he guessed it pretty accurately. The army had put two and two together and started

investigating these reports and other connected rumours. Within a couple of months, despite some initial setbacks, the army had taken control of the military situation.

The strategic initiative of the guerrilla foco could not be implemented. Che was on the defensive before he had even finished drawing up his plans. If security norms are ignored and you are put on a premature war footing, if you don't want to retreat in disarray, and hand over a strategic position, then you have to fight. That is the reason Che was so livid. It meant his basic plan to continue on to Argentina had been put in jeopardy. It was not a cold fury, chewed over alone. No, the outburst was reiterated to any emissary arriving from outside. 'I forbid you to come here! A war is won fighting . . .'. His fury made his voice hoarse.

The kitchen, or centre of operations, was a constant hub of agitation. But there was little comfort to be found, and the line of guilty parties waiting to see Che was long: Tania, who had arrived and stayed without permission; Antonio, who was in charge of the acephalous camp; Arturo, the radio operator without a working radio; and various furtive food thieves, some moaners, and some real complainers. The expedition now had more losses than gains: two fatal accidents, weapons and equipment sunk, and half the men in bad physical shape, with serious symptoms of malnutrition, swollen legs and feet, intestines full of parasites and constant diarrhoea.

None of this was insuperable for the Cuban veterans, or for anyone with time to get used to the physical and mental demands of this kind of life. But it coincided with chaos in the camp, and only a rigid exercise of power could put the project back on course. From now on, what was needed was not distance from the camp, but a return to it. Not fleeing from the enemy but facing it.

When we arrived back at sunset, the camp was almost empty, although another hammock was hanging where mine had been. I looked around for a new place, one with two good trees spaced far enough apart. I was considering the advantages of a new spot between two big trunks, albeit covered in thorny undergrowth, when a Cuban, who had arrived with the expedition the previous day laden like a mule, came up to where I was assessing the spot and nodded his approval. There was room for two hammocks, so he took out a machete from his rucksack and attacked the undergrowth with the efficiency of a true gardener, turning the inhospitable place into a first class suite with his well-aimed blows. He talked incessantly: '*Coño, chico?* So you're Pelao? Let me tell you . . . the big man was really happy . . . knowing you were here . . . now we can start work, he said . . . you know . . . I don't want anything to happen to him, he said . . .'. Urbano, aka Captain Leonardo Tamayo Nuñez, was one of Che's bodyguard-cum-assistants. He had been with him since the Sierra Maestra, where he was known as the Comandante's 'wing-footed messenger'. He was one of the survivors. His enthusiastic confidences showed me the way the wind was blowing.

28

Back at the Camp on the Ñancahuazú

From the moment Che returned to the Base Camp, it lost its former peaceful and bucolic air, as if the chief electrician had suddenly illuminated the stage. The actors entered and exited on cue, without changing the dramatic tension centred on the figure of the furious commander. Some were dispatched on exploratory missions and others were summoned urgently. When Marcos and Antonio arrived, the mood of exacerbation reached unusual levels of violence.

I had often tried to imagine the strength of character that a legendary figure must have in order to maintain, in moments like this, a degree of influence over tough men with strong characters. Not only prestige, which in Che's case was perfectly clear because of his own ethical behaviour, but also uncompromising rigour, regardless of hierarchy or rank. I had thought of the thrall in which Alexander the Great held hundreds of thousands of starving men, prostrate before him before he was even twenty years old. Or the young Napoleon. I'd always assumed that there is a mixture of intelligence, example and justice to which men react unconditionally. And this was the case here.

They knew him, first and foremost, as a just leader, who never demanded anything he was not prepared to do himself. They knew he was impartial when it came to applying rules and meting out punishment, even when he himself might be affected. They had seen him accept the most difficult challenges and had grown accustomed to seeing that, in the end, he would be right. At this late hour, in his ragged clothes, moving around a circle formed by his motionless, dejected fighters, he seemed totally alone. Facing an irreversible fait accompli, not caused by incompetence, as might have been expected, but by carelessness and pride, was more than he could tolerate. He was there because of a grand ideal for which he would fight to the bitter end, to end injustice at the cost of his own life. If those who wanted to join him could not leave aside their personal ambitions, he would prefer to be alone.

But just because certain behaviour is normal – even common among campaign commanders – it does not mean that expressing anger openly, even crudely, causes any less bitterness. Che's former subordinates, those closest to him during his Cuban exploits, some of whom came to Argentina and some who could not come because they were black, and even comandantes of other columns in the Sierra Maestra, all wilted spiritually at his outbursts. Yet all followed his orders devotedly and were ready to give their lives for the privilege of fighting with him. It is hard to remember the past without falsifying the moment. It is not legitimate. I try to stick to the emotion I sensed, the tension I felt as a spectator, what I remember vibrating in the air like a harsh reproach. No one tried to escape the rage being unleashed, instead they tried to make their presence felt somehow, and guess where the needle of the barometer was pointing. Some felt tears of life streaming down their cheeks, disappearing into their parched beards, as if their souls were watering the relentless drought. Others looked in solidarity at the victims. Then they closed ranks around their leader, bruised but happy.

The crucial thing, then, was to regain the initiative, and this needed some good field work, to find out exactly what was happening, what the army's movements were, and to what extent these had affected the guerrillas' control of their positions. Che devoted what was left of the day to planning meetings with his commanders, who immediately went to see that tasks were carried out, while the night fell upon the camp as military preparations intensified: some cooked, some mended clothes or cleaned their guns, or made inventories of the ammunition and equipment coming in and going out. It was back to work.

I was part of the protective ambush set up at the entrance to the Base Camp, between the rocks and branches at the bend in the river. There was so much work to be done simultaneously that it was all hands to the pump, guerrillas and visitors alike, all except the very ill. It was not the ideal place to digest the heavy stew we had just eaten. Legs soaked from the knees down, boots like compressed ice, and horseflies and mosquitoes acting like a fifth column, it was torture to remain in a crouching position. To cap it all, as soon as the sun goes down, it is freezing in the jungle. I was shivering. Was it just the cold?

29

Che Reiterates His Strategic Objective: Argentina

Sleeping curled up in a hammock under the nylon sheeting an inch from the face, held by a taut rope down the middle creating a sloping roof with the four points attached to the nearest undergrowth, was a very gratifying experience. When it rains, the rhythm of the raindrops lulls you to sleep, and your dreams soften the implacable harshness of reality. The pleasure does not last: a shift of guard duty breaks it in two. Sleep is reduced almost to nothing, the voice of the sentry saying 'Reveille . . . !', with a more or less amiable shove, wakes us from our warm reverie.

The first around the fire would stress their voluntarism and accept tasks immediately. But the order of the day would be transmitted by Pombo (one of Che's bodyguards) or someone else, after Che had met with each of his commanders. A group charged with exploring the *Casa de Calamina*, now in army hands, was to leave immediately, together with those relieving the advanced ambush. There were other tasks too, but the four visitors were at Che's disposal, and he wanted to begin a round of discussions that same day.

The first to be summoned was Chino from Peru, with whom Che had already started talking when he arrived at the previous camp at '*El Oso*', but the conversation had not been finished. An hour later, Debray replaced Chino. After midday, Che came to get me, the *conférence* with Debray being over.

He said: 'Let's find a place over there in the shade.' We walked towards the stream and found a clearing to sit in, like a picnic lunch. Tiny midges were standing in for the mosquitoes. They are perhaps even worse, although mosquitoes seem to be like the Republican presidents of the United States, the last one is always the worst. Without more ado, he asked me, already in work mode: 'I want you to tell me what Tania told you when she met you in Córdoba.' 'That you wanted to see me', I replied. 'No, no. I want you to tell me how she said it to you. In her own words.' 'Ah, well. She said: 'Che wants to see you.''

His reaction was devastating. He jumped up shouting: 'Tania, Tania', and went back towards the camp. 'Tell Tania to come here, right now.' As if to show he intended to compare the versions, he walked back to where I was, although he remained standing, while I asked myself if I might have changed the wording. But no. I was sure, also because I remember being surprised that some meticulous codes created for our contacts and communiqués had been passed over just like that. Tania arrived a couple of minutes later, crashing through the under-growth with gusto as she smiled happily, doubtless thinking she had been invited to the conclave. Her face changed from enthu-siasm to consternation when Che started to question her angrily: 'What did I tell you to say to Pelado when you met him in Córdoba?' 'That you wanted to see him', said Tania. 'No, no. Repeat what I told you to say. In the same words.' Tania tried to recall, unsuccessfully, a moment that, in all probability, had escaped her among the thousands of messages, recommenda-tions, security norms, passwords and phone calls that she had to remember when she left on one of those missions. 'What was it you had to say . . . ?' he insisted. 'Who wanted to see him?' 'Well . . .' remembered Tania. 'Your former boss wants to see you.' Recalling the words literally only made things worse for Tania. 'And why the fuck didn't you do it? What the fuck do I tell you things for? It's the same old indiscipline, not listening to my orders . . .'

And he went on with a tirade of insults against such practices. Tania had begun to snivel apologetically, explaining that she thought it was alright to talk to me frankly because she had never been checked out so thoroughly as she had been in Córdoba, when he started off again, more harshly: 'Just like now, you've come here, where you shouldn't be. Overriding my orders. We're going to have to have a serious talk . . .'. And he sent her off angrily, implacable, despite the fact that Tania was going, dragging not only her wings, but her soul.

There was a pause for him to fill his pipe and savour the strong Santa Cruz tobacco, and for me to devote myself to the tribulations of an exploring ant, which served as environmental relaxation. We sat down again, and renewed the conversation. 'And what would you have thought?' 'That Masetti had risen from the grave somehow, or that it was you', I replied. 'And what would you have done?' 'Come, of course', I replied.

Such a surreal scene deserves some explanation. Readers may be surprised by the excessive importance given to semantics. The key is the ambiguity surrounding the sender of the message. If I thought that Masetti, rather than Che, had been resurrected and had rushed to see him – as I would have done – imagining him to be in a state of utter helplessness, with no documents, in hiding, or planning to return to the armed struggle, it would mean, in fact, that the project in itself and my participation in it was important, despite the defeat of the Salta guerrillas and my disagreement with some of Masetti's mistakes. If, on the contrary, I understood that Che had sent the message, and I came – as I *had* done – it meant explicitly that the project and the leader were indivisible, independently of what had happened in the past. It is not difficult to see that he had hoped to see in my reaction a response of much greater scope. My arrival, after that cryptic summons, would have been an implicit and explicit response to that expectation of his. Che began: 'Strategic objective. Seizing power in Argentina. Do you agree?' 'Of course', I replied. 'I want to enter Argentina through the area you were exploring, with two columns of about a hundred men, Argentines, in the space of no more than two years. Your work from now on will be to send them to me; I want you to coordinate what needs to be done to get the people here, the logistics of it. Try to maintain your cover as long as you can, before you are forced to join us as well. Do you agree?' 'Of course', I repeated.

Actually, I didn't know what else to say. The decisions taken by the EGP leadership in Argentina before I left for Bolivia were clear, but confusing. My mandate stressed the fact that, after the Salta disaster, we were not in a position to send inexperienced youngsters to a region without a political or military infrastructure to guarantee a minimally functioning guerrilla force. The area was immense and riddled with border police, lords of the frontier passes, and of course the terrified minds of the few inhabitants. To start in that area would be to immediately confront the best-trained combat force in the country's repressive apparatus with one that had only moderately good training and firepower. It would be repeating what had already happened: being isolated, without military capability, supply infrastructure, and, even worse now, without a rearguard. Our national leadership in Argentina rejected the idea of a foco. They were not, however, thinking of a plan like this, under Che's direct leadership. This is what, for me, complicated the mandate I was charged with. Moreover, I was bound by the personal commitment I had made in Havana.

Was finance available for putting into action a project of such importance? Che was reluctant to go into this. He said he did not want his plans to depend on money from the Cuban Revolution, but understood that it was inevitable at this stage, which was why we had to look after every cent. There must on no account be a repetition of the money squandered in Venezuela, which had cost Cuba millions of dollars. The main task was to reinforce and sustain the base here in Bolivia, where he thought columns from different countries could receive their baptism of fire, then, when the moment came, go home and continue the struggle. The idea would acquire mythical proportions.

Truth to tell, however, we were at an impasse. Tania came under fire again when I told him that she had wanted me to come either immediately in that week in January, or at the end of February, beginning of March. Now they could not get me out until they saw how the situation with the police or army was unfolding. But there would be no contact with La Paz unless someone went there personally, so I would have to do it. But Papi and I needed to 'tie up all the ends' to do with Argentina, and I had to work with Pombo on supplies.

Tying up the loose ends was not a problem. It was a question of creativity, ingenuity: passwords, drop boxes, variable methods of contacts, what to do in emergencies, checking and security systems, indirect communication, appropriate symbolism, classified ads instead of telephone numbers. Papi and I agreed on a basic system that we would try out and keep polishing. It was a great help that he had been in Argentina with us and knew our urban network.

Harry Villegas, or Pombo, the nickname he was given in the Congo, was another veteran of Che's column in Cuba. He would also be one of the survivors. In the camp, he was chief of logistics, and called all the shots by being in charge of supplies. The work conversation I had with him was like being in a surrealist play, and we let it go after a while. On the one hand, the guerrillas' indispensable priorities: food, footwear, uniforms and medicine. On the other, the ideal amount of goods to be stored, in batches. For example: ten sacks of flour, ten of lentils, ten of beans, ten of sugar, tins of coffee, fat, oil, 100 pairs of large size boots (Bolivian soldiers generally wear small boots), 100 rucksacks, well . . . Two or three tons at least, with a military cordon around us and no fixed abode. My question was: 'What tree do I leave it under?' We stopped there, because we were already into realms of fantasy. What with contacts with La Paz and the rest of the world cut off indefinitely, and nobody knowing where the guerrilla would be next week.

When we finished our chat, Che had told me to go after Tania, because he thought he had been hard on her. 'Comfort her and help her . . . I'm in no mood for niceties', he said.

There was a different, more animated, mood in the air, a sense of fair weather in the offing, calm and enjoyable; the feeling you get, without knowing why, when spring is on its way. Che gave orders that we be supplied with our own weapons, not borrow them for guard duty or hunting as we had done previously. I got an M2 automatic rifle and a hundred rounds of ammunition, which I had to carry in a sock, and the rest of the visitors, including Tania, got an M1. We walked round the camp checking out the infrastructure. When we passed the amphitheatre, Che announced that classes would be starting. He told Tania to take some photos. Anecdotes and comments about his presumed disappearance from the Cuban scene, and the surprise that his reappearance in Ñancahuazú would be, took the place of champagne bubbles.

30

The First Battle: 23 March 1967

I was on guard duty until midnight and Che kept me company, reiterating quietly what we had talked about that morning. We gradually turned to more personal matters, however, as if this kind of family stuff could not be dealt with during working hours.

He said that, obviously, he could not give me letters to take, but I could perhaps visit his father, if I could find a way that was 100 per cent discreet. His mother had died while he was in the Congo and he had been unable to make a single visible gesture of grief for her. The same thing could happen in reverse. I could also contact his sister Ana María and tell her 'everything she wanted to know'. He suggested I visit Ana María Oliver, a prestigious Argentine writer whom he had met in Havana and admired very much. She could, he thought, represent him with dignity among Argentine intellectuals in order to promote the revolutionary struggle and its aims. The conversation was very nostalgic, and unusually intimate. He talked about his Cuban family too, his children, whom he had barely had time to kiss goodbye. He asked me about mine, about my daughters, ending with a paradox: the ideal situation for a revolutionary guerrilla is to be single, with no family, despite the fact that everything that moves us to take action is related to life, and family. The change of guard duty shift sent us to bed.

At around nine the next morning Coco Peredo arrived, all agitated, with the news that the army had fallen into our ambush. A provisional report indicated there were several dead, some injured, and a major, a captain and many soldiers taken prisoner. It looked like a big military victory. Che, sitting on a log in the kitchen, banged his thighs with both hands, and getting to his feet, stated, as if he'd just been told he'd won the lottery: 'The war has started. I'm going to smoke a pipe of the best tobacco.'

The statement sounded a little untimely, but it was no doubt said to lift the spirits of the new recruits, all waiting for something to happen. Personally, deep down inside, I knew a chapter of my life had closed, that I had to leave behind those precious things: love, life and the mere curiosity about man's fate. Another chapter had begun, one fraught with dangers, with no option but to fight or die. My plans had been knocked sideways, and what should have been a mission of huge responsibility for me – tied to the Argentine project – had been stymied by harsh reality. I had some experience of getting out of a conflict zone against the odds, like someone transplanted from one century to another, completely removed from the social and geographic context. But crossing the lines of an army thirsting to revenge some unexpected deaths was something altogether different.

A synchronized buzz of rapid activity began. Messengers came and went. A couple of doctors left to attend to the injured soldiers and a group of porters went off to fetch captured equipment and bring it back to camp immediately. Che called Alejandro, one of the Cubans in the sick bay, and told him to take charge of interrogating the captured officers. Looking at me, a useless spectator just standing there, he said: 'Go with him and listen to what is said. I'm afraid there may be some confusion because of the way Bolivians speak. But don't open your mouth or they'll immediately know you're Argentine.'

With his brown beard and light eyes, Alejandro was an impressive figure. His real name was Gustavo Machín, a Cuban comandante, Che's deputy at the Ministry of Industry, and now our camp's head of operations. He was wearing a coffee-coloured fedora he had no doubt worn on the flight to Bolivia and had not yet resigned himself to jettisoning. It gave him a romantic air, which tied in nicely with his amiable manner. His legs were very swollen and the difficulty he had walking meant we didn't get to where the prisoners were being held until after midday. It was in a sort of gully, where the river was boxed in by crags and cliffs eroded by the current which had uncovered the roots of huge trees and left them hanging in the air, ready to fall at any time. A scene of chaos greeted us. The sonorous reality of nature, rhythmic and secret, was broken by the groans of the injured and fearsome voices of the victors.

Alejandro established his 'interrogation room' in a clearing. We agreed I would play the role of assistant and look after security. Some fallen logs were arranged a bit like an open-air tribunal and he sat down on one of them. He told me to bring in the prisoners one by one. We started with the major – major not only in rank but in age and girth – who suffered from depression and tachycardia. In my efforts not to say anything, I communicated with him by signs, helped by grunts and the barrel of my gun, to indicate the way he should behave and what he had to do. But the method had too many police connotations and I disliked it more than he did. Alejandro inquired after his health, since he seemed about to suffer from apoplexy, and talked to him very calmly, as if reprimanding him for taking a wrong turn at his age and keeping bad company. The good man agreed, and promised to leave the army. He swore his mission was surveying land for road construction. Alejandro scolded him gently: 'In the river . . . ? And since when have mortars been used to build roads?' The major ended up explaining the army's operational plan. Accumulated reports of sightings and denunciations had indeed confirmed the presence of guerrillas at Ñancahuazú.

'Take the major away and bring the captain', ordered Alejandro. I returned with the latter, younger and thinner, also more frightened, and manifesting a disposition to collaborate fully, which he proceeded to do because, he said, he had a brother studying in Cuba and he himself was a member of the Communist Party. He allowed himself a critique 'between friends'. We had been very careless, he said: '*Caramba*, Fourth Division command knows all about the armed bearded men who dry their clothes on the river bank, and had begun sending search patrols out on a war footing.' He gave details that in no way contradicted the major. Wailing, fainting, and swearing sympathies, they told us more than they knew. I was witness to it all, something that would have unexpected repercussions later on.

We requisitioned documents showing the enemy's plans. They coincided with the detained officers' statements and, in short, established the existence of two exploratory groups, one of them led by the two officers now our prisoners, and another that was following the same route in reverse, combing the river from above and descending it until the two groups met. This information represented an imminent danger so a messenger was sent to Che.

By the time we returned to camp, the necessary measures had been taken on the opposite side of the river to repel troops, who were either very late or had already been alerted to the first confrontation. We had to set up our 'reinsurance' ambush in the river again, at the entrance to the camp, to compensate for our lack of numbers. We arrived back at nightfall like a pack of ravenous wolves, only to find we had to share our meagre portions with the prisoners; fourteen empty stomachs craving food.

We spent all of the next day bringing up the weapons and ammunition harvested in the ambush. Twenty soldiers carry a lot of heavy equipment, when you take into account their machine guns, mortars, grenades, ammunition. The 'visitors' had to do their bit to help, mitigating the lack of effort and negative attitude of the slackers.

Che made Inti Peredo the 'Bolivian leader' of the guerrillas. He was Coco Peredo's brother, and he made his debut visiting the prisoners to tell them they were being released and giving them a deadline, within the terms of a ceasefire, to take away their dead. The major and the captain left in full uniform. Not so the soldiers; some left barefoot and in their underwear, although with their dignity intact. They had been persuaded that *force majeure*, the necessities of war, meant the guerrillas had to dispossess them in order to equip themselves.

The war had begun with the deaths of five soldiers – 'almost children' as Che wrote in his diary – a lieutenant and a civilian guide. They were representatives of the poorest sectors of society, in whose name, paradoxically, the struggle was being waged. Another forty would die.

The logic of any war, including a revolutionary war, is constructed on behalf of the victims: victims of exploitation, victims of hunger, victims of tyranny, and victims of liberation struggles. Without victims, there is no reason for the struggle. Without the struggle, there are no victims, nor liberation. The local population saw events from a different angle, and political resonance mediated the impact it had: first, horrified rejection; then, heroic mythology. But the army's losses in the first battles were bound to affect the guerrillas adversely. The state propaganda apparatus used it to the hilt, to their advantage: 'the deaths of innocent conscripts were caused by criminal hordes of alleged foreign liberators, come to disturb our peace and national development'.

The military government, facing the chronic crisis all Bolivian regimes throughout the century have faced, affirmed itself through violence. What people on earth did not support a regime, no matter how bad, when their frontiers were breached by a foreign invader and their sons killed fighting for an army that had a populist discourse and used land reform to prove its good faith to the dispossessed? Bolivia was the only country in South America where (in 1952) a nationalist revolution had introduced agrarian reform, giving land rights back to its peasant farmers, descendents of the ancient Inca empire. The miserable inhabitants of the area where the guerrillas were fighting actually owned their shacks and strips of land – with more bugs than fruit on it, but nonetheless theirs. At the slightest sign of outside interference or latent threat to their possessions, they would inform the army.

31

Bombardment, Che Calls a Meeting, and a Night March

A furtive peace had descended on the camp. Everything appeared to be working according to a new rule of efficiency and division of labour.

Part of the advance guard had accompanied the released prisoners the previous afternoon, and on Che's instructions had set up a forward ambush on the hill almost directly in front of the *Casa de Calamina*. The officers' statements had revealed that the army might approach from both directions, so another group was positioned upriver, a few hundred metres from where the stream flowed into the river. Men from the rearguard and the centre columns would occupy the existing fixed positions in the lines of trenches and access to the hidden pathway leading from the river to the camp.

Manning all three positions meant using every single available person, including the visitors. So although we might rotate tasks, positions and *compañeros*, we were always engaged in some furious activity or other, from collecting wood for the cook, to helping the officers in charge of the mortars or machine guns. All of them Cuban, of course. Added to which, we had to carry the booty seized in the ambush back to camp, classify the equipment, guard it and prepare new caves to store it.

The person in charge of the arsenal was the efficient Ñato, veteran of the Puerto Maldonado disaster, on the Peruvian-Bolivian border, where many Peruvian guerrillas were killed in

1963. He was a man of little humour, but with a great capacity for hard work and multi-tasking. Coming from the region of the Beni, gateway to the Amazon, he could do all the jobs typical of a man from the tropical jungle, from hunting an animal and dissecting its carcass, to making wearable shoes from its skin, like the pair Che was wearing when he was captured. He had an amazing ability to organize his time and play to his own strengths and was, right from the start, the person the guerrillas turned to for resolving practical matters. He was not intimidated by the Cubans and their propensity to omnipotence, a reciprocal quality which led to friction.

While exploring the hills, Ñato had found a good spot for a new cave to hide equipment. The digging would be done under the technical supervision of Moisés Guevara who was a miner, but the job of moving the equipment fell to the so-called '*resaca*' (the dregs), the group of Bolivians who were to be expelled for lack of '*firme*ẓa', revolutionary fortitude. We involuntary tourists would help them, but in case something came up that meant Debray and I would have to leave immediately, we were only asked to carry the supplies to a particular point upstream, and Ñato's men would take them on from there.

The coffee ceremony in the mornings was our daily communion. Gathered round the oven, wiping sleep from our eyes, seeking warmth against the dawn cold, and smoke to banish the insects of the day, it was the only moment of spontaneous gossip, an expectant audience monitoring any slip of the cook's attention, the concretion of the only daily privilege Che required. While each man readied his tin cup, the cook placed a measure of coffee in it before adding the sugar. Che drank his coffee bitter.

One morning, Debray and I were sent to the guard post at the entrance to the camp, on the line of trenches. Our lot, and this included work, seemed linked to our abnormal situation of visitors passing through. Hence, we often went together. On this occasion, an old Hunter fighter plane flew over the river, machine gunning the forest, firing blindly at any possible site for a camp, still very far from ours, but not so far from us. When the plane passed overhead, we could hear the taca-taca-tac of the impact on the tree trunks, and afterwards, the dull sound, like distant thunder, of the guns they were firing. I quickly ducked into a trench, urging the Frenchman to do the same, and we both ended up flat on our stomachs. The plane did another couple of turns then flew off. The habitual silence, broken by the frantic cheeping of the birds, gradually returned.

Food is a crucial subject in guerrilla life. Men have different reactions to the lack of food and giving in to pangs of hunger is an indicator of the level of moral weakness. Some, despite physical weakness or flagging energy, were disgusted by rotten meat, floating insects or other particular taboos. For example, veteran fighters in Algeria told us that Boumedienne used to have to threaten to execute men in order to get his troops to eat whatever was available, even if it were pork. Even then some pretended to swallow it and spat it out as soon as no one was looking. Personally, I refused to drink milk. I don't like milk. And I always took out bits of horse fat. Oddly enough, the taste reminded me of the smell of the blood in the hammock of our victim, shot in Salta.

Papi, a crafty conspirator who did not miss a trick, had noticed my selective manoeuvres, and began sitting beside me. He would threaten under his breath: 'Give it here or I'll tell on you!' As *compañeros* from Salta days, our relationship went very deep: for him I was not an honorary visitor, but a link between a dramatic past and an uncertain future. He had proclaimed himself heir to my private guerrilla belongings, like the boots I had bought before coming in Grimoldi, a shop in Buenos Aires. They were not special army boots, which since I had come by plane in tourist class, I avoided, but he liked them and we wore the same size. Whenever we were assigned to the same task, we would talk nonstop. He asked insatiable questions about the *compañeros* in our Argentine network whom he had met: especially the EGP girls who had accompanied him when he travelled; and families who had put him up for the night. But mostly about the political progress we had made, the contacts with other organizations, those I had established and could tell him about in detail. His passion for conspiracy was total, and that was precisely why he was upset when his preparatory work in La Paz had been questioned, and Che had criticized him. For his men, being criticized by Che was humiliating.

Papi told me a lot about their African adventure. He had been one of Che's stalwarts in the Congo, especially in their few successful military operations. In his opinion, the Congolese experience had been negative in more than one sense, and the only good thing about its failure was that it speeded up Che's return to his main project which, with a bit of luck, would take him back to Argentina. For a Cuban veteran of the Sierra Maestra, the recalcitrant passivity of the so-called African revolutionary fighters, with no combat morale or discipline, enveloped in a mixture of voodoo and corruption, dependent on leaders who were never present, had meant there had been no option but to leave. Che never managed to be in total command and, therefore, could not use his military skills. African internal political contingencies bore no resemblance to solidarity and internationalism. These were Papi's own conclusions; he never attributed a single opinion to Che.

Che was not very explicit on that subject either. Although we had sometimes talked informally about the Congo, and he recalled anecdotes about this or that, or such and such a situation (no resemblance to what was happening now), with a certain nostalgia.

Our conversations were not very numerous and occurred on the spur of the moment. More than once Che called me over to his hammock just to chat, and once to play chess, although I had to confess I didn't really know how to play, only how to move the pieces. On other occasions, he appeared when I was on guard duty, at night, and settled himself against a tree, 'So there's no danger of you falling asleep', he said. It was not so much a conversation as him asking questions about Argentina, not specifically about politics, but about things in general, from the humidity in

Buenos Aires to what comments people in the street were making about newspaper headlines, magazines, television programmes, jokes. All mixed up with anecdotes about what ordinary people were thinking and the judicious opposing analyses of the prolific Argentine intellectual class. I told him of an interview with Lobo Vandor of the metal workers' union, in those days the strongest union in Argentina. The journalist asked him, apropos Che's disappearance from public life in Cuba and the rumours which put him in different places on earth, in heaven (or in hell), something like this: 'Do you think Che could fill the gap in leadership of the masses left by the General?'

Vandor grimaced sceptically and answered: 'There's only one Gardel.' It was one of our rare funny moments, and Che laughed heartily. Our country was Peronist.

Che did not want me to include any Peronists in my recruitment plans. He said: 'It's too risky, they're too infiltrated.' But I already had contacts with grass-roots Peronist groups on the left of the labour movement. We had a cordial relationship, respectful of security norms, and they did not give me any trouble. I could not say the same about the socialist groups, who questioned everything and wanted to take us over, or of certain Trotskyists, who demanded permanent assemblies. In any case, proposing a project at some imprecise future date is not the same as saying: 'Want to fight? OK, buy a pair of boots and off we go.' And that is what I would be doing if I ever got back to Argentina. The scenario was not very clear from where we were sitting on the steps of the 'auditorium' built for the classes Che gave to his legionnaires. 'You were only supposed to spend a day here. Now everything has changed and you'll have to stay until we figure out some way of getting you out.'

Che's rage when he came back from his exploratory trek and found the Base Camp evacuated and chaos reigning – the intensity of which could still be measured in the anxious glances of the guilty parties – had calmed down, and in our intimate conversation (more of a monologue, with me as the mirror) was more like bitter resignation at the turn of events. There were now no precise plans, only hypotheses. No clear decisions could be taken on how new recruits would come, or how we would bring in supplies. Che gave me the name of an alternative liaison in La Paz, a certain Dr Rea, whom I should convince to put me in touch with Rodolfo Saldaña. Rodolfo already knew me and together we could try to re-establish links with the guerrillas unilaterally. Aspirant recruits could converge in the area near the Cochabamba–Santa Cruz road and in some magical way, guided by news of events on the radio, move south to join the guerrilla forces.

(Two months later, in July, while I was detained in Camiri, I was allowed fifteen minutes with my wife, Ana María, in the presence of an officer and guards. I took advantage of our embrace to whisper in her ear that she should seek out Dr Rea in La Paz, but the doctor was no longer in Bolivia.)

The members of the network in La Paz were supposed to be taking other measures, like transferring money and documents to a safer place, and advising Havana of the seriousness of the situation, especially the loss of radio contact, and get them to send as many as possible of the volunteers training in Cuba (Argentines, Cubans) to join the struggle in Bolivia. For my part, whether I was able to make the contact in La Paz or not, I would certainly have to inform Havana when I got back to Buenos Aires.

In the end, however, no one was ever able to inform Havana of anything. Not from the mountains, not from La Paz, and nor was I. And even if we had, Havana had already taken off its earphones and pulled down its antennae.

The scope of the project emphasized just how disastrous it was for the guerrillas to be incommunicado at that particular juncture. Until that problem was solved, nothing could be organized for the future. Our conversation verged on the surreal, the magical. We had no idea how I would get out of the area, what I would find in La Paz, what contacts would work, nor how, when, or where. Until those mechanisms were reactivated, there was no point giving orders. It was all just wishful thinking.

The spotter plane flew overhead almost daily now, machine-gunning and dropping bombs. No one was affected, apart from our nerves. Che did something, however, that soothed nerves and calmed spirits. He called a meeting of all his men. Recent exploratory work had convinced Che that the army had no plans to advance on the Base Camp, so the ambushes were lifted to allow everyone except sentries to attend. People started arriving in the evening and the atmosphere was electric with expectation. There had been no time for informal gatherings since the return of the expeditionary force and the start of armed action, so the veterans and new recruits were meeting for the first time. It was a unique occasion and, as often happens at international congresses, people tried to do some lobbying in the 'corridors' to glean extra information.

Antonio (my former trainer in Cuba, Captain Olo Pantoja) assumed that being a survivor of the Salta EGP gave me some special status, and so possibly some influence. Nothing was further from the truth, but it was no use telling him that. Olo's world was falling apart. He had lost the confidence that came from having been in Che's column, at the battle of Santa Clara, at the victorious entry into Havana, and from having carried out special confidential tasks, such as training Che's group for Salta. His morale at rock bottom, he told me he could not sleep, rest, or swallow his food. He had come to give his best, to die if necessary. Beside Che, for what Che wanted most, his constant dream from the Sierra Maestra to the Ministry, was to fight in Argentina. 'We've been waiting for it all along, on the alert in case we got left out.' Olo thought he had done the right thing: not risking combat with untrained recruits, assuming this was a preliminary stage, and that there could be no action without orders from Che. Moreover, it was not his fault that Marcos had come back to the Base Camp after being seen at the river, had taken command and organized the retreat. Fighting back his tears, Olo wanted to convince me, as if absolution depended on it.

In my role as spectator, I reflected in amazement on how seasoned fighters, used to commanding other men through crises at critical moments, now collapsed and were crushed by them. Marcos, in a more imperious tone, but more nervously, circled around me in the same way. I felt like an unofficial mediator, placed unwillingly in the centre of the battlefield. Marcos's tale took on epic proportions. He was a combatant, a Cuban comandante who had come to offer his life for Che's cause, as he had done before for Cuba. His only wish was to be first in the line of fire.

It would not have occurred to me, or anyone in their right mind, to expect to exert influence or proffer any suggestion. Everybody, including the victims, thought Che's indignation was justified. The project that Che had worked so hard for, that all the participants were offering their lives for, was about to fail because of mistakes that Che put down to general indiscipline. We had already seen dangerous examples at the camp and it was impossible not to notice that the root cause lay in that omnipotent insouciance, that scorns security norms, underestimates the context, and belittles the enemy. Perhaps in an attempt to stem the tide of approaching failure, Che talked to his men.

The tone of the meeting changed more than once. It started informally with a review of the defensive measures taken. Then Che went over what had happened on their trek, emphasizing the positive behaviour of the participants, among whom four or five were singled out for special mention, but also pointing out the extremely negative attitudes of others. The bottom line was that a project like this, a revolutionary struggle intent on victory, is only possible with an iron discipline that inspires respect. Discipline plus personal and political responsibility for actions; or chaos and failure. He had no hesitation in saying that any violation of these principles was betraying the cause. The tone of his voice rose with his rage. In the middle of the jungle we were living a Greek tragedy, in which a thundering God reproached his petrified unbelievers for their sins. Marcos was relieved of his command and demoted, Miguel replaced him as leader of the vanguard column, and four of Moisés Guevara's men were expelled. Until their departure could be arranged, they would be stripped of their guerrilla status and, as the *resaca*, would only do menial tasks.

I was shocked by the violence with which he spoke to tough, armed and physically and psychologically exhausted men. But the only protests heard were reaffirmations of undying loyalty. Apparently, no one doubted that, behind such harsh words, a greater layer of tenderness protected them as individuals. Some new energy eased our tasks, and us as well, as if we had been reinvigorated by a transfusion of fury. Those who had been reprimanded hovered diligently around Che, ready to volunteer for anything, desperate for some sign of benevolence to help them to swallow the bitter pill. A glance. Anything.

The number of exploratory missions increased. Alone or in pairs, men set out every morning in various directions, before daybreak but after coffee. They returned exhausted at sunset, and went straight to Che with their reports, only to be told they might have to do it again the next day, because the information they had got was not precise enough, or because something else had come up that they should know. They ate and then slept like tree trunks – unless, that is, there were some other sort of 'voluntary' military or educational class it would not be politic to miss.

In the middle of the camp was a shelter, a sort of open-air canteen, with a large table made of poles tied by lianas, in the purest jungle design style. All items from the evacuated cave had been piled there, ready to be transferred to the new storage places, after the men had chosen what they wanted to carry with them, or leave behind in the storage cave until later. The communal library was there, for example, for whoever might want to add a few extra grams to his backpack (full of essentials like spare food, ammunition, clothes, etc.) by taking a book. Needless to say, not a very popular idea. I was sniffing around the pile of books when Che came up for the same purpose. In his hand was the present I had brought him from Buenos Aires, Cortázar's latest book of short stories *All Fires the Fire*. At the time I had commented: 'There's an amazing story'. 'Which one?' he asked. 'The Southern Highway', I replied. Now at the 'jumble sale' he pointed to the book: 'You were right, it's the best story in the book.' Between the first conversation and the second, enough things had happened to destroy his plans, but not his love of literature, nor the effort he made, amid mosquito bashing, to read every day, and part of the night, by the light of a miner's lamp on his forehead. The by now old tradition of insomniac leaders of the Cuban Revolution was alive and well in the Bolivian jungle. And there was a suspicion that others around him were awake too, for fear of being caught sleeping. But for the lucky ones who could sleep, it was an obligation.

When he deemed our explorations had delivered all the necessary information, Che announced an operation to take out the visitors and buy food. A false press pass and safe-conduct was fabricated for me using a photo left over from those taken in Buenos Aires for 'my passport' and one of the blank pages signed and stamped by the president's press office that Tania had obtained from a secret source in the government. This and my passport was all the documentation I had, as false as the illusion that it would pass as genuine.

We hardly slept a wink. At three in the morning, we drank coffee prepared by the sentry on duty. We tried to disguise recent footprints to conceal the date on which the camp was being abandoned, an impossible task since hammocks, for instance, left indelible marks showing exactly when people had slept there and how many. The sick guerrillas were 'interned' in a hidden camp with a doctor and a couple of other fit guerrillas.

The advance guard set off, and an hour later it was the turn of the middle group. We had a few hours trek in total darkness in front of us. Most of the torch batteries had run out, and anyone who still had any guarded them jealously. I was just behind Che in the column and, since I did not have a torch, I kept as close to him as possible to take advantage of the brief flashes of light in front of his feet. To lose visual contact was to be totally lost.

Visibility improved when, guided by its liberating roar, we left the forest at the river, but the walking was harder, wading over the stones.

Pausing for ten minutes in every hour, with messengers going back and forth between the vanguard and rearguard columns, we continued walking until the dawn sun rose majestically accompanied by the symphonic awakening of the jungle. We reached the spot where the ambush had taken place twelve days earlier and, passing in silence, saw the abandoned corpses still lying there. On the river's left bank, on a little sandy beach, lay the skeletons of an officer, five soldiers and a guide, uniforms in rags, picked clean by vultures.

The advance guard sent back news that the area around the *Casa de Calamina* had been occupied by the army, and also that we could 'expropriate' maize and a cow there. So the rendezvous was there, a gastronomic one, with beef stew.

32

Way Out Where There Was No Way Out

The jute sack that Ñato had made for me, because of the shortage of proper backpacks, began to take its toll. It was a simple design: two knotted ears at the bottom and one in the middle at the top. A cord from one side to the other, top to bottom and bottom to top, formed the straps. While such a gem of improvisation meant I was not able to carry as heavy a load as the others, it did not save me from the individual minimum: hammock, mosquito net, blanket, civilian clothes, spare food, ammunition for my M2, extra shared goods, medicine, maize, etc.

Listed like that, it already sounds a lot, but when the weight hangs from your shoulders by quite a thin cord, it digs right into the clavicle bone, and feels as if it will keep going till it pierces the ribs. Meanwhile, jumbled up in the bottom of the sack, the bulk of it hammers the kidneys and the spine, turning the vertebrae, discs, sacrum and even coccyx, into mush. When there is a pause and you take the sack off – carefully peeling the ropes away from the bones, to save your arms from falling off and your spine disintegrating – and you manage to stand up and walk a few steps free from this terrible torture, you feel your soul is moving all by itself. The ability to bear physical pain is not related to morality, ideology, or intellect, but to a masochistic corner of your personality that allows you to prematurely savour the moment you will rub raw sores and burst blisters with some kind of ointment, either recognizable or invented en route from horse grease and saliva. Putting the sack on again the next day is even worse. And worse still is climbing interminable hills, tangled up in lianas and prickly branches, slipping on mud or bald roots, stumbling and falling, with that damn dead weight on your back. At one point that first night, I tried to improve things by wrapping the cord in pieces of bark tied on with strips of a T-shirt, to cushion my mistreated shoulders.

The march continued, always at night to penetrate the army's cordon. For some strange reason, the army units communicated their positions by bursts of machine-gun fire or isolated gunshots. Every now and again, a platoon's fire would be answered by others further away, and others in front of or behind us. This meant we could follow our own trail, almost parallel to enemy positions, in relative safety. Leaving the river behind, we walked eastwards through a field of sugar cane, crested a hill, and finally descended into a valley at dusk. Part of our rearguard dug in and Che said he would try to take the village of Gutiérrez, on the Camiri–Santa Cruz road, steal a truck or jeep to drive Debray and me out of the area, and buy whatever we could.

We made camp and waited for nightfall. Debray and I handed over our equipment, guns included, changed clothes and shaved. In crumpled civilian clothes, we waited for the order to walk to the village. Che, who had alternated resting and reading with a succession of conclaves with his commanders, suddenly heaved his rucksack onto his back, got laboriously to his feet, and came over to where our group was waiting. Looking at me as if I were some kind of weirdo, he asked: 'Where's your rifle?' I said we had left our equipment with the rearguard, along with those going to buy supplies. Those had been his orders. He called Pombo and barked: 'There are not many of us, I want him armed. Give him Tania's rifle, she can bring it back.' Tania protested, but I ended up with her M1.

Silently we followed the path that at one stage ran beside a fence, an indication of how near the village we were. We stopped to wait for the liaison with our advance guard, who arrived with news that the village was in uproar. A company of soldiers had camped there only a few hours earlier, and some of the poor souls had barely got over the fright of seeing lots of armed soldiers, when they panicked all over again as bearded guerrillas came out of the night and, uninvited, took over their patios, houses, corrals, and closed off all the exits.

The Bolivian guerrillas chatted calmly to the houses' occupants, who said the army would be back the next day. So the idea of getting some kind of transport out was dead in the water, and our departure was postponed. We bought some pigs and they were slaughtered and shared between the vanguard and rearguard columns, beginning a day of Pantegruelesque excess. The cooks worked non-stop. When we came up the ravine from the river, the army was going the opposite way on the crest of the hill. This prevented a surprise encounter. We would return via the hilltop and, hopefully, they would take the ravine. We ate ourselves silly until around three in the morning, then set off again.

My technique of following Che's footsteps by the light of his torch had its advantages and mysteries. The flashes of light allowed me glimpses of where to put my feet. The sound of his footsteps, the swish of the branches as they brushed his body and whipped back again (lashing me hard from time to time, as punishment for getting too near), and the odd curse, gave me some quite precise information about obstacles ahead.

But something had me worried. I thought I heard a continual muffled sound, like a litany, although my senses could not distinguish what it was. In the dark, full of crackling and crunching – human, animal and vegetable – it was almost supernatural. The sound rose and fell, then faded into long periods of silence that seemed to bear no relation to the lay of the land, or the noises of the jungle. On a flatter stretch, where walking was easier, the mystery revealed itself. The noise began taking shape: I could hear words; harmonious, suggestive, beautiful rhythmic words. It was Che reciting poems by León Felipe as he walked.

When we got to the river, we bumped into a squad of soldiers. Luckily for them they did not see us. Squatting on an island of sand and rushes, I was astonished to hear the soldiers, who were crossing the river in the opposite direction, come and sit right beside our hiding place, chatting ten to the dozen. If any of the frozen, motionless but gung-ho guerrillas had sneezed, battle would have been on. After a few long minutes, the soldiers continued crossing, moving away with the water up to their waists. We did the same, in silence.

We advanced northwards on the crest of the hill. It is easy to say it now. Northwards. At that time, except for Che and his group of explorers, I don't think any of us had the slightest idea where we were going. As far as I was concerned, we were marching blindly, back and forth, up and down.

We knew the vanguard column had met some drovers bringing their cattle home. Since they belonged to Ciro Algarañaz, the nosey neighbour beside the *Casa de Calamina*, responsible to a large extent for the precocious actions of the army, we confiscated some cows and they joined our column. Abandoning the river again, we headed up into the jungle following a trickle of water up a ravine. We camped an hour later. On the menu was piebald cow.

We stayed there for a few days, while we explored. Two of the explorers, Urbano and Julio, went to the refuge where Joaquin was guarding the sick men and came back with bad news: the army had taken the Base Camp and was searching the hills all around that area. A few days later, in a censor-authorized radio programme, a Chilean journalist called Héctor Precht from El Mercurio described how the camp had been taken. Che would write in his diary: 'A Chilean journalist gave a detailed account of our camp and discovered a photo of me, without a beard and with a pipe. We'll have to investigate further.'

Language, history and basic economics, explaining the method and degree of exploitation in the region, were taught in the improvised camp. Usually the teacher was Che, although Aniceto, a Bolivian, taught Quechua. The students' morale was good. We went down ravines, up paths and trails, breaking cordons this way and that, with total disdain for the shooting in the distance and the catastrophic news on the radio, bursting with confidence in our leadership and our own strength. If Che ordered one of his key men to go to the farm to collect maize, or to the Base Camp to see what the army was up to, or to the 'clinic' to tell Joaquin something – all places inside occupied territory – no one gave it a second thought. Off they went without batting an eyelid.

They might walk for a whole day, scrambling up impassable slopes, hungry, drenched, and knowing they had it all to do again on the way back. You would have to be a deranged superman to do it. Yet it obeyed the logic of the free spirit: the explorer made his own decisions, and took responsibility for his actions. He was outside the anthill, obeying his instincts, overcome by a boundless feeling of autonomy. As Cordobés put it in an interview: 'Exploring, alone, on the summit of a hill, leaning on my gun, I was God.'

Che gave orders for the day. Inti and I had the first tour of guard duty at the ambush observation post. Coffee finished, we set out. The climb was pretty tough, and we were gasping by the time we reached the spot, very well chosen for its perfect view of the river on both sides. As a lookout point it was perfect, with a clearing under big trees, where tracks left by previous sentries invited us to sit comfortably facing each other, leaning against the solid trunks. In front of me was a stretch of river, perhaps a kilometre to the south, upriver. Inti looked over my shoulder to the north, downriver.

Seeing a river from a distance, up above, discovering the twists and turns of its bed, divided by islands and sandbanks, gushing between rocks, forming waterfalls, seeing it but not hearing it, is like watching dancing in a silent film. It was the unreality of the real, under a diaphanous silence. Birds glided over the water or dived into the forest in serene harmony. Inti placed a handkerchief on the ground and stripped down his M2 to clean it. Nobody could surprise us in this place but if I had wanted to clean mine too, I would have had to wait until he finished. We chatted amicably, always with an eye on the river.

At mid-morning I saw, there where the river described a curve from the right, a little figure come out of the jungle, cross the quietest part of the river, to the left-hand bank. I was wondering what I had seen when another silhouette started to cross, followed by another. It was not my imagination. They were men, probably soldiers. Inti passed me the binoculars and I could see them clearly. Soldiers. The first were almost across, water up to their knees, rifles raised over their chests, when others began wading across. I counted them. One, three, five, they kept coming. A total of fifteen. They did not seem very cautious, as if they felt safe, in good company, so we waited for the rest. They regrouped, and continued advancing on the right, downriver, towards us.

After a brief exchange of opinion, we decided I would go down to the ambush to warn Rolando the army were coming. Excitedly, taking great leaps, halfway down the slope I bumped into Papi and Negro coming up to relieve us. Telling him what was happening, Papi stopped mid-joke ('Did you fall in an anthill, Pelao?') and exchanged his mocking tone for one of sudden military efficiency. He gave me an order: 'Go and find Rolando, give him details and take up your position.' And to Negro: 'Go back to camp and inform Che.' He climbed quickly up to find Inti.

Finding someone who is lying in ambush is not easy, but Rolando was a God of War who was everywhere, so I found him – or rather he found me – emerging from a thicket. He listened attentively to my news, then showed me my position; the first on the right, facing the enemy. It was in a ditch, full of branches, undergrowth and even dried animal carcasses, left there when the river overflowed, but separated from the noisy waters by a few dozen metres of trees, reeds and rough grasses. In the ditch lay Rubio, alias Jesús Suárez Gayol, captain in the Sierra Maestra, deputy minister of sugar in Che's Ministry of Industry. There was not much room among the debris, so I was barely two metres from him. I remember him asking me, avid for news: 'Have you see them, Carlos? How many are they?' There was a sudden exchange of gunfire, followed by another, with shouts and howls

and prolonged distressing wails of someone invoking his
mother . . . '*Ay, mamita, mi mamita!*'

A moment of panic seized me, but I was more concerned with
doing something concrete, although I did not know what exactly.
I could not even see the river because of the thicket in front of it.
I remembered something Furry had told me in Czechoslovakia.
'I'd go into battle trembling like a leaf, but my nerves calmed
when I fired the first shot.' I fired at random in more or less the
appropriate direction, and began to take stock of the situation. I
could do nothing; my field of vision was zero. Tactical preoccu-
pations took a back seat, however, when the undergrowth parted,
and a young soldier came staggering out in tears, rigid with fear,
dragging his rifle by the barrel. He advanced towards us petrified.
The image was truly pitiful, so far removed from the textbook of
warfare, and so clearly an innocent in need of protection that,
without prior agreement, neither Rubio nor I fired. The soldier
kept coming. He did not see us and almost stamped on my head
as he jumped the ditch, disappearing behind us in search of his
mother's womb.

Reality returned, however. Rubio nodded to me. I left the
trench and went after him. The battle abated and we could hear
only isolated shots, threatening shouts, or cries of pain. I caught
up with the soldier on the hillside, in the wood. I disarmed him in
mutual incomprehension: he murmured something in Quechua,
and either my voice was not martial enough, or he did not hear it.
I took away the rifle he was still clutching by the barrel, and,
nudging him with my gun, returned to the scene of combat. The
ubiquitous Rolando appeared, and said with obvious delight:
'Did you catch one, Carlos? I'll take care of him. Get back to
your position.'

The first thing I saw on my return was Rubio lying outside the
ditch, with his right arm stretched out over his head and his left
arm trapped under his waist, shaking with convulsions, as if the
only bits of his body alive were his thorax and fingers, which
moved as if honey was sticking to them. I crossed the ditch and

bent over his body, putting a hand on his shoulder as I said: 'Rubio, what's the matter?' I tried to prise his face away from the ground. His mouth was full of dust, so were his open unblinking eyes. His unseeing gaze would never see again. When I moved his head, I saw that the part of his skull above his right ear was missing and there was bloody encephalic matter on his arm just below his shoulder. I noticed a small wound on his left temple, a hole with hardly any blood. I ran to get help and bumped into Rolando for the third time. He shouted for a doctor, as we went back to Rubio's body. Rolando was distraught; he talked to him, knowing there would be no reply. Kneeling on the ground, he tried to cradle him in his arms.

I lowered my gaze and went over the scene. Beneath the first tree, a little to the right of our position, a metre and a half from his motionless outstretched hand, I see a grenade. Without thinking, I bent down and picked it up. It was activated but had not gone off. Fortunately, I did not throw it away and risk an explosion, but put it back carefully, not so much wisely as paralyzed by fear.

The doctor could do no more than confirm Rubio's death. Rolando took command again. We did a clean-up operation and recovered weapons that were stacked on the river bank, and attended to the army's wounded, even operating on a lieutenant, who died nonetheless. Rolando showed his obvious military skill when, as we withdrew, he ordered some of the guerrillas to set another ambush 500 metres to the south of where the first patrol emerged, in case reinforcements came. The rest kept searching the rocks and undergrowth on the river banks. Rolando told me to take as many rifles as I could carry and return to camp to inform Che.

With the extra weight of six rifles, I arrived at the camp and went straight to Che. I laid them at his feet like an offering, with no symbolic intent, just exhaustion. 'How many were they?' he asked. 'Fifteen', I replied. 'At last some reliable information', he commented. He listened to my report of what had happened. Then he wanted to know the details of Rubio's death. I told him bluntly: 'His was the first position on the right facing the enemy, but we couldn't see anything because the vegetation was so thick. After the first soldier passed us, Rubio must have left the ditch to throw the grenade, to stop the rest following. The bullet went through his head, the right side of his skull was smashed, and there was a little hole on his left temple.' 'From your description of the wound, the bullet is from a Garand, Braulio's rifle, the shot was ours', declared Che.

The body of the first guerrilla to be killed arrived at camp at midday. It was wrapped in his hammock and tied to a long pole carried by several of his *compañeros*. We had camped on a narrow bank of the stream, so our hammocks had been hung in a kind of oval shape, more or less in the order in which we had arrived. Che's hammock was in the middle of one curve, and mine was on the other side. Che ordered Rubio's body be laid between the two of us. And there it stayed for the rest of the day and throughout the night, until it was buried the following morning. There was no ceremony. Just a camp with the body present.

The rest of the day was devoted to bringing back the weapons, which would be stored nearby. At around five o'clock, we heard another gun battle. It eventually turned out that Rolando's ambush had inflicted the biggest defeat on the army so far. A whole company, in fact: dozens of prisoners, among them a major and other officers. We had captured so many weapons it took the whole of the next day to collect them. Ñato was again in charge of hiding them and, again, our status as visitors meant Debray and I could only go halfway up the trail, back and forth along one of the many gullies that join the stream, carrying rifles, mortars and ammunition, enough to arm another two guerrilla groups.

As we trekked back to the Base Camp, we met Joaquín and his sick guerrillas. Sadly, they had made the effort to join us in vain, given that we were going back. Joaquín's charges showed no improvement, and in fact were increasing in number due to the many cases of debilitating diarrhoea. There was a belated funeral in memory of Rubio, underlining the fact that the first casualty was Cuban, and honouring the willingness of peoples to unite their blood in the struggle for a common future.

At midday, Che divided our central column to speed up the march, which was being held back because so many men were exhausted. I was in the faster group. Debray and Tania brought up the rear. It was a terrible climb. Pombo was chosen to go on ahead to the camp, and I was to go with him. He waited for me patiently when I got tired and when we stopped to rest we talked about our families. I told him how sad I was not to be there to see my two little girls grow up at this important stage of their lives.

We arrived at the Base Camp to find it pretty much intact. The oven had not been destroyed, nor had the wooden constructions, so we reoccupied it. I was reclaiming the spot where I had previously slung my hammock when Che came up. I asked his permission to go down to the stream to wash, because I felt sticky with sweat and dirt. He told me to go, but not to overdo it.

Steering clear of the spring that we used for drinking water, I took off my clothes and gave myself a therapeutic treatment with mud and fine sand, being careful to wash it all off properly. Climbing back up was exhausting. Staggering into camp, gasping like a legionnaire dragging himself to the oasis, I told Che, paraphrasing the Cubans: '*Tengo un cansancio de tres pares de cojines . . .*'* His eyes were smiling, but he rebuked me unceremoniously: 'Don't joke about feeling disheartened. We have to avoid that kind of demoralizing joke. We're here to set an example all the time . . .'

---

* Bustos says: 'I'm as tired as three pairs of cushions (cojines)', whereas the common Cuban phrase is more vulgar: 'I'm as tired as three pairs of balls (cojones).' The translation would be something like 'I'm knickered' instead of 'I'm knackered.'

33

Leave-taking and Farewells

In the darkness of the jungle, in the glow of the campfires, what sparkles is not ideology or political passion, but the flash from the barrel of a gun.

Fifty men moved around in the shadows, exhausted by their loads, hunger and illness, yet did not shirk their tasks even though they had barely slept. The insanity of their surroundings did not affect them. They were here to give of their best, offer their lives generously in the struggle for human dignity. They were not forced to come, had no contracts, just volunteers tied by a pact of loyalty to a man offering them, at the very least, death. Many had followed him since they were boys, from a country where their horizon was the edge of a cane field, only to discover that on the other side of the battlefield was a world that did not want to share its treasures with the poor. At his side, they had learned that what mattered was not nationality or skin colour. Here, there, everywhere, society was based on theft, usurpation. People were not born rich or poor. To become rich, you had to steal from someone else. And to put things right, you had to fight; it was as simple as that. It was not about faith or believing in saints but about being true to oneself. It was not about praying, but about sharing; about making a choice.

Equally simple was the moral code of the group. The hardest task here was to make doing the banal and boring a source of personal pride. Quiet daily sacrifice was rewarded by more demands being made on you. Only hunger would produce fissures in this wall of virtue, and Che was implacable when it came to punishing this kind of weakness. The first thing Ñato reported on his return from inspecting the stores was that two dozen tins of condensed milk were missing. The large number suggested they had not just been misplaced.

The morning had been hectic but the men worked with enthusiasm, relieved that the army had left the Base Camp in good condition. We now appeared to be sharing the camp since the soldiers had left their individual 'Made in USA' rations to use at a future date. When I returned from guard duty in the line of trenches, where I watched Pombo install a mortar to reinforce our defences, I found Che composing a communiqué addressed to the Bolivian people. He suggested dictating it to me since, being an artist, I must have decent handwriting. To disguise my apprehension about my spelling, I protested that on the contrary my handwriting was illegible. It was true; it was so bad I couldn't even read it myself. That was precisely the point, my hand was a painter's hand.

While Inti took charge of the communiqué, Che and I got into a conversation which gradually attracted an audience. I was amused by his jokey tone, but there was something suspiciously naïve about Che's argument. I realized that he was drawing me out, looking for information. I remember the conversation clearly. I defended modern art in all its abstract variations because, I said, not concentrating on the purely figurative was exactly what creative freedom was all about. Che maintained that the people have the right to understand art; that it should not be the exclusive domain of the elite. I replied that art is not something you understand: you either feel it or you don't, you like it or you don't, and there is no art more popular or accessible to the masses than the black African art that influenced Picasso's most avant-garde work; whereas previously he had been a 'classical' master. Che argued that art should serve the Revolution, by teaching. I agreed, but said that technology in the form of photography and film had taken on this more graphic role. Art itself is transcendental, more abstract than a manual, I said. As the debate became more political, I said I regretted the Revolution had surrendered its avant-garde banner in art; that this was like renouncing poetry, regressing to grotesque 'socialist art', which was neither one thing nor the other. If revolution was the vanguard of society, then avant-garde art should reflect the Revolution and in fact almost all the painters, sculptors, writers and musicians of the avant-garde movement were revolutionaries. Many were Russians, or rather Soviets, who joined enthusiastically in the first phase of the Revolution, believing that they had found creative freedom, but were then harassed, banned, exiled: Malevich, Rodchenko, Kandinsky, Mayakovsky, Stravinsky . . .

'And in Cuba? What happened in Cuba?' asked Che, malevolently. For the time being, we can only speak of pre-revolutionary art, I conjectured. Cuba had been very advanced artistically, given the influence of the US, but nearly all the artists had left. Yes, he said, the cultural minority who lived off the Americans left with them but there are Cuban artists who are with the Revolution. 'I'm not sure,' I insisted, 'there is a horrific "social realist" artist who paints *guajiros*, in straw hats, holding machetes with sugar cane in the background and he is the official favourite.' 'Was it so bad? I rather liked it', he said, suspiciously seriously. 'I liked Portocarrero', I said. He was not only not figurative, but homosexual. His elongated mural of Venetian mosaics on the facade of the Habana Libre hotel was the most beautiful part of the building. Was, because it was no longer there.

Years later I realized from reading some of Che's writings that not only did he know more about modern art than I did, but he had used our conversation as an opportunity to have a natural non-academic debate, knowing we were being listened to, as if at Mass.

But the real hot topic was the disappearance of the milk. A final inspection of the storage cave unleashed Che's anger, and suspicion again fell on an Aymara lad, Eusebio, because of some rather contrived evidence. Funnily enough, Che did not have a bad opinion of him, because he had performed well on the march (even though he ate his reserve food thinking that was what it was for). When Che's ragged column had first returned to camp, Eusebio was accused of stealing various tins of milk because there were empty tins under his hammock, which he swore had been there before. He had been expelled from the guerrillas and sent to the *resaca* group, humiliated and made to do menial work until our return to camp. Now he was being accused of stealing another twenty-three tins of milk (perhaps even the same empty ones), which had disappeared from the cave. It seemed quite odd. Eusebio had come with us to Gutiérrez, taken part in the action on 10 April and come back with us, loaded down like a pack horse the whole time. At what point did he raid the cave, carry away the loot, and drink it?

Che called me over for a chat, to tell me of his latest plan for our escape. This time we would walk to Muyupampa, a village on the Sucre road. We would occupy the village to give us time to get food and medicine for the sick, then Debray and I would stay there and find a way to travel on by ourselves, if that was at all possible. Failing this, we would have to stay with the guerrillas until they had escaped the army dragnet and found space to dig in between Cochabamba and Santa Cruz to the north.

His assessment of the situation in the short term was pessimistic. The group's mobility was minimal because lack of food had reduced them to a state of physical collapse, and this would not change until they contacted their urban network. Nor were there enough supplies to consider lying low until the sick could recover. With the death of Rubio, the countdown for the guerrillas had begun, and there was no hope of new recruits for quite some time. Meanwhile, behavioural problems had arisen, the thing that Che feared most. These problems would not be resolved unless he imposed the full force of his authority. The missing milk was an example of the sort of thing that could happen, and each incident was like a cancer gnawing away at revolutionary morale; if, that is, his own patience was not exhausted first. He gave the impression of having a lot of pent-up anger caused by similar events, left

over from the Congo perhaps, which undermined the possibility
of forging the 'new man' who was essential to the super-human
project he dreamed of. In addition to the disputes over food, there
were more serious ones about indiscipline. Che did not agree
with the results of the investigation into the missing tins of milk,
and doubted the accusations. He said something terrible: 'I have
no proof, and I don't want to start shooting people like you did in
Salta. But if we get out of this hole and on our feet again, I'll crush
the balls of whoever it turns out to be, even if it is a Cuban.'

It *was* a Cuban. So I learned nearly a year later from León
when we were in jail together: a Cuban who was a terrible problem in the final stage of the march.

About this and other events he mulled over and thought worth
mentioning, Che said something that should be taken into account
because it suggests a reason for the inexplicable omissions in his
diary: 'I have to be careful what I write. We might be surprised at
any time and backpacks containing inconvenient information
could be left scattered around.'

This moment did not come until he was captured and killed
while we were on trial in Camiri. But it had always been on my
mind because it would have meant the end of the laboriously
woven farce I had constructed after capture. The fact that he
hardly said a word about me in his notes meant I was able to
maintain my role as an idiot caught in a trap until the very end.

The intimate tone of the conversation, not confined to work,
made me feel comfortable enough to ask a question that had
occurred to me before leaving Córdoba. What would have
happened if, having organised publicity beforehand, Che had
flown in directly to Ezeiza airport, Buenos Aires, where hundreds
of activists would be waiting for him (like a football hero or film
star) to guarantee his safety and his life? Of course, I ventured, he
would immediately have been arrested. But that would have been
illegal since there were no charges against him in Argentina, and
his arrival would have demonstrated how his charismatic presence could mobilize hundreds of thousands of potential young

revolutionaries in a flash. Or maybe not? Che looked at me searchingly and, before walking off towards his hammock, replied in a hoarse voice: 'I don't believe in science fiction.'

We stayed in the Base Camp for two more days before leaving it for the exclusive use of the army. These were tense and silent working days for Che and his officers. Telepathic communication seemed to be sending out the same nostalgic messages. Tania, who was having serious difficulty keeping up on the marches, probably because of parasites, talked about La Paz and her favourite café. Papi talked about how he avoided taking taxis in La Paz since he seemed more Cuban than usual in a taxi. The Bolivians talked about the fabulous spicy chicken dishes at food stalls in the market. I had become good friends with one of them, a young doctor called Mario Gutiérrez Ardaya, aka Julio, and we would sit and chat whenever we could. I remember his warmth and humanity, more of an apostle than a fighter.

We left at dawn, following the course of the Ñanchuazú upriver. Tania and Alejandro, who were ill and therefore unable to stand the pace, walked separately with two *compañeros* in support. At nightfall, we bought abundant amounts of food from a hamlet: pork and corn, and some potatoes for a change. Hidden in the forest, we sat around an overflowing stockpot and had an 'end of festival' banquet that took us all night to finish.

The following day, Che decided to divide up his forces, for two unavoidable reasons: first, so that the sick could rest, and second so we could move on more quickly to the village of Muyupampa where they could buy supplies and finally offload the burden of us visitors. It is tempting to speculate now about what effect Che splitting off from a third of his force might have had on the final catastrophe. We passed the confluence of rivers where (as when roads converge) people are most likely to settle, and had to take extra precautions not to be detected.

The next morning we came to another larger hamlet where several bridle paths crossed. We posted guards in all directions, resulting in the capture of various peasants. We wanted information, so we had to detain them while we cooked, to stop them giving our presence away. This precaution was a bit tardy because over the previous couple of days quite a few children and adults had managed to slip away.

At midday, one of the guards apprehended what Che called a 'Greek Gift': an Englishman guided by some Guaraní children who had run off three days earlier when the guerrillas passed their house. The astute Englishman had found them when they reached the village of Lagunillas and persuaded them to re-trace their steps that same night.

The so-called Englishman was George Andrew Roth, a free-lance Anglo-Chilean photographer, who had accompanied the army to the Base Camp when it made its first incursion. He was a maverick, intrepid and enthusiastic, interested only in a scoop to enhance his journalistic reputation. He arrived in the dark grey summer suit, white nylon shirt, and blue tie he had been wearing in Santiago de Chile when he heard the news that guerrillas were operating in Bolivia. With just his camera bag and a toothbrush for luggage, he got on the first plane to Buenos Aires and introduced himself to the US news channel CBS who gave him an advance to travel to Ñancahuazú.

In La Paz, he went to Army Command headquarters and managed to get himself a permit, signed by General Juan José Torres, which allowed him into the zone of operations as a war correspondent. While we were trying to escape via Gutiérrez, he was at the Base Camp. When the Guaraní children appeared in the village of Lagunillas where the army was billeted, he immediately hired a horse from them and offered them money to take him to the guerrillas, avoiding the army cordon. This was despite the fact that the already restrictive security measures imposed by the army had been tightened since the disaster of 10 April. And here he was, in his city suit and tie, wearing slip-on shoes, his legs dangling down the flanks of his horse. He had done what we had failed to do: connect with the local population, make them serve as guides, and break through the military cordon.

The first thing Roth asked was if he could interview the guerrilla leader, and if he was in fact Che Guevara, a rumour circulating round the army. Roth recounted in detail his stay at the Base Camp with the troops, the discovery of Braulio's diary, the alleged photograph of Che with a pipe, the discovery of the Cubans' luggage hidden at the *finca* and Tania's jeep in Camiri. A depressing scenario. The discovery of the jeep meant Tania's cover was blown, as were her years of working as a mole to embed herself in the ranks of the government, the armed forces and the security services. One thing was clear. The guerrillas were no more than what they appeared: a group of sick, exhausted men, alone against the state.

Che discussed our escape with me again. He said that Debray had outlined a plan whereby we could use the Englishman to make our escape, taking advantage of his status as a bona fide journalist, with a safe-conduct from the military top brass. But there was the problem of the Englishman's real identity and whether we could trust him. Among his papers and documents were personal details showing that in Puerto Rico he had at one stage belonged to the Peace Corps, a US civil society organization used by the State Department and the CIA to penetrate indigenous Latin American communities (they were active in much of Bolivia, inspired by Kennedy's Alliance for Progress). His passport had been altered from student to journalist. He had lived in the United States. He was English. He was Chilean. He was a photographer. The guerrillas suspected he was an infiltrator, so I questioned the plan and said to Che, 'What's the point of putting ourselves into the hands of an enemy agent? Nevertheless, Ramón, I shall follow your orders.'

We left it there for the time being; the outcome would depend on Debray's conversation with Roth. He would ask him to help us find a way out in exchange for an interview with the Bolivian chief, Inti. The negotiation went ahead and Debray thought Roth was sincere, that his willingness to take risks on our behalf was genuine. He had weighed everything up and wanted to be the

Herbert Matthews of Ñancahuazú. It sounded credible. Che
noted in his diary: 'Carlos reluctantly accepts'.

So we re-organised the escape. Che wrote an apocryphal interview text, which, if everything turned out well, Roth would know
was his. We had said goodbye to Tania, Alejandro and Joaquín,
Negro, the doctor, Braulio, Marcos and some of the Bolivians,
Moisés, Pedro, Ernesto (also a doctor), Apolinario, Walter,
Victor and also to the *resaca*, Pepe, Paco, Eusebio and Chingolo,
who remained behind under the second-in-command, Joaquín.

We carried on marching till dusk, when the middle section set
up camp and the vanguard went ahead to explore the area until
they found a track. While I shaved and changed my appearance
from filthy militiaman to a supposed journalist, who was nearly as
scruffy, another argument arose between myself and Inti. Che
asked Pombo how much Bolivian money there was so that he
could give me some to replace my funds and my Buenos Aires
tourist clothes which I had left in Tania's jeep. I had to get to La
Paz and then travel on to Argentina looking reasonably present-
able. Pombo had 5,000 Bolivian pesos available. Inti said that was
extravagant. It did not seem very much to me, since there was
transport to be paid for and eventually bribes at some point. Inti
trivialised the problem: 'In this country, you can buy a general
for 400 pesos.' I told him that was a stupid underestimate, since
even before firing a single shot, Tania had given a 500 peso bribe
plus expenses to the driver who brought us from Sucre to Camiri.
And now the whole area was at war. I had to get out of there, and
I could not bribe by credit card. Che agreed with me and Pombo
gave me the 5,000 pesos. In Che's diary entry of 21 March he
wrote: 'I will give 500 pesos to send off and 1,000 to get around
with', but he is talking about the dollars needed for Argentina,
not about local necessities in Bolivian pesos. And anyway, the
amount was increased, without my saying a word, to 2,000 dollars.
He said, 'I think 2,000 dollars should do it.'

It was a very cold night and, without a jacket, my clothes were
not warm enough. I looked suspicious, so Che spontaneously

presented me with his jacket, an imitation sheepskin with an artificial wool lining, made in Czechoslovakia. It was the one he was wearing when he arrived in Bolivia and in the photo of him and Tuma beside the jeep, waiting to board the barge en route from Santa Cruz to Gutiérrez. In this jacket, I changed from criminal to construction engineer. Papi and Pombo were present when Che gave me my last instructions and we had our last conversation. He said he was almost certain we would be arrested, but since the opportunity to get out had arisen, we should take it. He had thought of giving me a pistol, but if we were detained, it would be worse for me. Che said: 'You take command of the group and go over the hills. Try to avoid villages and walk at night. Mount a rearguard guerrilla action. If you manage to get out of the military zone, go as far away as you can in whichever direction possible. If you're arrested, the most important thing is to conceal the presence of Cubans here and my presence too, for the time being.'

He thought for a moment, his fingers stroking his beard, then with a gesture of disdain, as if he were chucking ideas into the rubbish bin, he said in a loud voice: 'But, if you see they know everything, go for it, try and make as much noise as possible. So I can be myself again, and wear my beret.'

Returning to Che's diary, what relation do those words of advice, and his concern that I might be cold, bear to what he writes on 30 April in his monthly analysis: 'Danton and Carlos were victims of their haste, their desperation to leave'?

We embraced again in silence. I turned and walked to where Papi, Chino, Pombo, Urbano and Tuma were waiting their turn to say goodbye.

34

Under Arrest in Muyupampa: 20 April 1967

Some nights when the moon is full, the light on open ground is so clear you can read a newspaper. So, emerging suddenly from the dense forest, to drop down into the valley, I could see obstacles on the path quite clearly. It gave the landscape an eerie quality, like a black and white film, and together with the relative silence of the jungle, heightened the drama of our march.

At midnight, when the group accompanying us reached the path to Muyupampa (the village we intended to capture), they made contact with our advance guard who told them a couple of things that forced a change of plan. The tip of the advance guard had bumped into a group of village people patrolling the area on a self-defence mission. They were quickly disarmed and provided some valuable information. The reason they had mobilized was to act as a buffer between the army, which had occupied the village, and the guerrillas. They wanted to avoid any confrontation that might bring death and destruction to the village. Miguel, commander of the vanguard operation, set up an ambush, assigned the prisoners to Inti, and sent Ñato to inform Che.

When the rest of us arrived, we made a mistake that was to have serious consequences. In the light of the splendid moon, we saw the prisoners talking animatedly to Inti, trying to convince him of their good faith. We did not immediately realize that by the same token they could see us in the exact same detail. Inti tried to repair the damage and, having explained that we three 'journalists' were also prisoners of the guerrillas, ordered the two groups to be separated, on different sides of the path. Ñato returned a couple of hours later with Che's latest orders. The operation was to be abandoned again, given that a dozen men could not fight a whole company of soldiers for a village without knowing where its sympathies lay. Che ordered the Englishman released, and left it up to Debray and myself to decide our course of action before the guerrillas withdrew from the area. Inti took the two of us aside and explained the choice we had: go back with them, or stay and try to make it out ourselves.

Che wrote a personal diary in all his campaigns, and his 'Bolivian Diary' has become a cult document and a testimony of irrefutable historical value. But a diary is only a diary; a mere a record of circumstances, emotions and everyday events. It reflects feelings rather than rigorous political, military or moral judgements, a task he would leave as far as he could to the future, as he did with his diaries from the Sierra Maestra and the Congo. They were intimate jottings, written not to be published but for him to evaluate by himself at a later date. Although he took precautions in case it got lost – as he himself told me – he was not worried about semantic exactitude or strict logic. There were occasions where his honesty even made him doubt the justice of his own actions, if there was not enough proof to back them up, but this did not prevent him using irony and humour. Che had seen my reaction to Debray's plan to leave with Roth, but he did not see Debray's reaction now, there on the side of the path. He was not there to see it. He was told about it. But he was told wrong.

If we consult Che's diary, when he explains the exit plan, it says as follows: 'The Frenchman asked to talk the problem [our leaving] over with the Englishman and as a sign of good faith, ask him to help get us out: Carlos accepted grudgingly and I washed my hands of it.' The same day, 19 April, he writes: 'Ñato reported to me at 1 o'clock . . . He asked for instructions and I told them to withdraw, given that it was now late, to release the English journalist, and let the Frenchman and Carlos do whatever they

thought best. At four o'clock we began to withdraw even though
we had not achieved our goal, but Carlos decided to stay and so
did the Frenchman, this time it was he who did it grudgingly.'
What actually happened was that, for Inti, Debray was not only a
philosopher but also French, whereas I was only an Argentine –
nothing strange in that, the whole Latin American Left, the
Argentines included, would react the same way in the short term.
So he goes up to Debray to explain Che's orders. But Debray (I
can still see his face lit by the moonlight) says: 'I agree with whatever Carlos decides.' He passes the ball to me, and not for the last
time. So it is my opinion Inti hears. And my opinion is that the
guerrillas are making a great deal of frustrating and exhausting
effort just to get us out, because we have missions to carry out on
the outside. What is difficult now after the recent battles will get
more and more difficult as the army turns the whole area into a
military zone. If we have to leave, we have to do it now, it is our
last chance. Che has given me urgent orders and, to my mind,
that is because they need to be carried out straight away. At the
same time, I tell Inti: 'These guys have seen our faces, you can't
release them at the same time as us.' Inti assured me he would
bear it in mind and promised to hold them until Che gave orders
to the contrary. I added: 'If the village is a couple of leagues away,
we need a few hours start.'

   'OK, fine', said Inti. We said goodbye in the half-light. The
moon was disappearing behind the hills surrounding the valley.
The only thing left visible now was the road to Muyupampa. So
there we were, the three of us, the Englishman, the Frenchman,
and me. We began the crazy moonlit walk, each carrying a small
bag – the Englishman's camera, our few crumpled clothes.
Following Che's instructions, I proposed getting as close as
possible to the village before leaving the track and going into the
forest, because the first shock of being on our own was that we
had not the foggiest idea where we were, nor where we were
headed, nor where the track we were on (which a map of the
region would call a road) was located. When Che met with his

commanders they poured over maps, but we didn't see a map the whole time we were in the camp. The absurdity of it is that for thirty years I thought we had walked westwards from the camp, until I read in books published on the thirtieth anniversary of Che's death, that Muyupampa was to the south, almost on the same latitude as Camiri, further down than the *Casa de Calamina* or Lagunillas, on the other side from Gutiérrez but further south. If I did not know then where I was, now I know we were totally disorientated.

There was immediate opposition to the 'rearguard guerrilla action' that Che had outlined, and I put forward. Roth said a categorical no, because he had a safe-conduct signed by the Army High Command in La Paz to travel in the war zone and it was crazy not to use it. I argued that that should be our trump card, but if we did not need it, so much the better. Falling into the army's hands was always going to be bad for us. The Englishman replied that he had promised to help us legitimize our status as journalists and get us out of the area; not to leave one lot of guerrillas and form a mini group of our own. He had a point. That was what he had promised Debray, but he had not been given the full picture, like my false papers and the dubious nature of Debray's claim to be an innocent French journalist. It was better to tell the truth and I proposed we say that we had come to the area before anyone knew anything about guerrillas and before military requirements for safe-conducts and special passes were in force. This was undeniably true, and the situation was just as dangerous for him, being taken prisoner with us. Like it or not, our fates were interlinked, and it was best to minimize the risk. The further we got without having to use his documents, I argued, the better it would be for all of us. Moreover, by this stage in the discussion, we were in complete darkness.

The moon disappeared and the track turned into a black tunnel in which we could see nothing. I stopped and insisted, in a whisper, on the need to avoid the village, but objective conditions were against me, and so was Debray. His argument was that the

army would shoot us like birds if we moved about at night in a
military zone we were not familiar with. He insisted his idea of
taking advantage of Roth's legitimate status was still valid: it was
the only bona fide thing we had. And he was right. I had to admit
that if we came across a soldier on guard duty, we were dead men;
but the same was true on the track in total darkness because we
could not see if there was a bend, a stream, a house; nothing. So I
proposed, and they agreed, we climb the hill above the track, and
look for lights that would indicate where the village was. But in
the pitch black, finding a way through the undergrowth up a steep
hillside we were not familiar with was impossible. Our dejection
was manifest. I tried to think of some logical way out. We would
have to wait for daylight, carry on up the hill, locate the village,
skirt round it, and find a road out the other side. The situation
obliged the two reluctant parties to accept the plan, but not neces-
sarily go through with it in the morning. Roth refused, and
Debray agreed with him.

Meanwhile, the temperature started to drop and the Englishman shivered in his light summer suit. Humour found a chink in
our misery and we joked at the way our teeth chattered, like tap
dancers. I only had the jacket Che had given me. If I gave it to
Roth, I would be worse off than him, in a white dress shirt, an
addition to my leaving outfit from one of the Cubans, so I passed
him a stick to bite on. But Debray had a jumper under his padded
jacket and lent it to him. Huddled together like old women at a
funeral, we spent the rest of the night sitting in the undergrowth,
leaning against a low fork in a tree to stop ourselves sliding down
the steep slope into the dark. Soon afterwards we heard the sound
of angry voices, getting louder as they approached. A group of
men were walking rapidly down the track we had left to climb the
hill, shining torches and talking at the top of their voices, either
because they wanted to be noticed, or to ward off evil spirits. We
began to make out words and realized it was the locals the guerrillas had captured, and whom they were supposedly going to
detain for some hours.

The Frenchman and I were just about to lament their release so soon after we set off, when the Englishman tore himself away, leapt up and rolled down the bank before we could grab him. He went crashing through the undergrowth, making a terrific rumpus, hurtling down the hill like an avalanche, and landed up on the track, in the path of the chattering locals who, stunned into silence, commended themselves resignedly to God. Roth got to his feet, brushing his clothes, and said in a loud voice that we could hear perfectly from where we were still hugging the trees: 'Good evening, *señores*! Could you please tell me how many kilometres to the village, and if I can find a taxi there?' as if he were coming out of a bar in Santiago or Buenos Aires. The petrified locals, fearful of shapes and shadows that wander around at ungodly hours, stammered in an incoherent chorus, as they shuffled around him, and fled in terror: 'Good evening to you too, *señor*! Just over there, about a league . . . No, *señor*, no taxi. At this hour! Maybe tomorrow, *señor* . . .' and disappeared into the night.

Debray and I climbed down and, sitting by the track, we may have chided Roth for not asking if there was a bar as well. The darkness gradually morphed into fraying wisps of mist clinging to the forest, and the rising sun silhouetted the solitary track we had to follow, or not, according to the prevailing opinion. My arguments were even stronger now, I thought, given that the inconvenient witnesses to our connivance with the guerrillas were now in the village, instead of behind us. But, strangely enough, this fact reinforced the others' idea of normality. They imagined that emerging from the middle of the jungle, like honest journalists with nothing to hide looking for a taxi, proved we were bona fide. Their underestimation of the Third World, and crass ignorance about the susceptibility and intelligence of its peoples, with long experience of having to defend themselves against everything and everybody, told us a lot about how untouchable the white man from educated and opulent societies feels: even failing to recognize the signals the locals sent out by coming to look for guerrilla forces ten kilometres from their village, as if they had been sent a telegram with the day, time and route chosen.

Roth walked down the middle of the track, followed by the Frenchman, who made a declaration of independence by throwing in his lot with the Englishman, and I brought up the rear, pissed off and pensive. In all revolutionary organizations, armed or not, you never challenge the leader responsible for an operation whatever the circumstances. You do not have to have a machine gun to impose a decision. In this case, I was leading only myself. In our farewell talk, Che had told me to take command, but we were alone and I think that was the intention: 'Take command and go over the hills. Mount a rearguard guerrilla action.' If he had meant to include Debray, he would have said it in front of him. Che, like poets, had a great ability to predict things: 'I think you'll be arrested, but you have to take your chances.' The problem was that I did not know (but did not like to say) where I was, where I was headed, the time it would take to get out of the area across the mountains if need be, how I would survive, without even a penknife to cut branches, dig, or skin an animal. 'I thought of giving you a gun, but it might make things worse.' I could not, then, dictate any plan to the Englishman, nor to Debray.

The landscape began to show signs of human activity: cleared land, plots of maize, some distant shacks. The track widened and turned right, circumventing adobe houses with tiled roofs emerging out of the mist. Before the bend, I stopped one last time, asking Debray to reconsider, saying that I was going over the hills. He said exactly what I had been mulling over in my mind: we would have no chance of surviving in the jungle; we would need to go to villages to buy food and the filthier we got, the more suspicious we would look. The logic was irrefutable. Only someone with suicidal tendencies would deny it, and I certainly did not. At that moment, I had to choose between the 'perhaps' and the 'nothing'. I chose the remote possibility we would get out of this.

The widened track was an avenue leading into the village, lined with typical low colonial adobe houses, their small windows hidden behind blinds or wooden shutters, a stone step at the door and a narrow flagged pavement along the front. The avenue ended some 200 metres further on at a house that made a right-angled turn, closing the block and creating a long rectangular space, in which the shadows of the night still clung to the corners, while the first rays of the sun sought out the cornices of the roofs. When we entered, walking down the middle of the road from the south, soldiers appeared from the north with a curious symmetry and, on seeing us in the distance, stopped short and fell over each other. They obviously had orders to split into two columns and began spreading down both sides of the street, sticking to the walls like limpets, or rather like the shadows projected by their silhouettes, as they advanced towards us, their rifles cocked and taking aim.

We continued walking gingerly, in a line, avoiding brusque movements so as not to shatter the nerves of frightened recruits fingering the jealous triggers of old Mausers. No one said a word. The only sound was soldiers panting and weapons clattering. After the first soldiers had passed us, to our left and right, they closed ranks behind us in a pincer movement. Only then did a rather hysterical or martial voice order us to halt, announcing we were under arrest. The Englishman became the group's spokes-man and declared we were journalists but, as was to be expected, the officer did not believe in press freedom. He shouted 'Shut up', and ordered us to empty our bags on the ground, which we did. The man was not stupid; he did not want to run any risks. He then told us to undress and pile our clothes in front of us. We undressed to our underwear. 'Everything!' he shouted impatiently. It was the first time I had practised the art of public striptease without music, before a platoon of stone soldiers and an impassive officer. 'Socks as well!' he exclaimed. He ordered a soldier to collect the documents and Roth's camera, summarily inspected everything, then allowed us to get dressed again and put our things back on.

Then, surrounded by soldiers, we were taken to the town hall, where the army platoon was stationed. It was an old building with a verandah, a few paces from the corner of the small square. Suddenly our ruse seemed about to work: the prefect (or mayor), roused from his bed, arrived at his office with his staff to represent the civilian administration. He took charge of the documents and, with the military commander, set up an emergency tribunal to clarify the reasons for our presence in the area. The Englishman mounted his legal case, referring to the permits signed by the Army High Command in La Paz, and by General Torres himself, as more than legitimate and valid, while Debray began to assume the same natural level of importance, requesting a telephone – there were none – to call his embassy in the capital. I said nothing, trying to pass unnoticed.

The prefect asked the women in the crowd to prepare some breakfast, since we would not get a taxi before nine in the morning, and in any case, the officer had to wait for instructions from Fourth Division headquarters before anything could be decided. The whole thing looked more and more like a hectic work meeting. The Bolivian-style breakfast arrived in the prefect's modest office, and like castaways we devoured the mincemeat with fried eggs and freshly baked bread and coffee. Sitting on a bench in the corridor, Debray used the apparent normality of our situation to ask me to help invent a contact in La Paz that we could both use. Standing in front of him, as if we were discussing lost cows, I said off the top of my head: 'Thin, tall, high cheekbones, big eyes, black hair, slightly Indian-looking, name of Andrés'.

But the bonanza was short-lived. In the course of the morning, among the growing number of onlookers, came the ex-detainees from the previous night, witnesses to our having been with the guerrillas. Like old acquaintances, we recognized each other's faces, somewhat marred by exhaustion and the crude light of day. 'Those idiots are guerrillas!' shouted one, and lunged at us, forcing soldiers to intervene. Pandemonium broke out in the crowd egged on by our accusers. The army restored order and we were transferred to the building's interior patio, a paved square surrounded by a verandah supported by ceramic pillars. The officer separated us, placing each of us by a pillar with a guard so we could not speak to one another. We did not see him, but a reporter from the La Paz newspaper *Presencia* climbed onto the roof of the house next door and took our photo, an act which saved our lives. My photo, which appeared in the Córdoba daily *La Voz del Interior* wearing Che's jacket, smoking, leaning against the pillar, right hand hooked in my belt, in a recognizable pose of mine, reached Ana María, Oscar and the other Córdoba *compañeros*, although they did not know the name I was travelling under. Less than a week after their initial appearance in *Presencia*, in an amazingly effective race to offer journalistic protection, these photos of Debray, 'Frutos' and Roth provided irrefutable proof that we were alive and prisoners of the Bolivian army.

Hours on your feet are not recommended after several nights walking. Exhaustion took over and we slumped against the pillars. But the little soldier had orders that we stand: 'Stand up, you shit!' he said, but with more respect than fury. The day went by like that, while the village returned to its habitual drowsiness. The joint civic-military command decided to take us inside again but still incommunicado. We had no chance to discuss strategy or develop any line of argument, except the invented figure of Andrés and the fact we had only seen small groups of guerrillas, a decision we had taken in the nick of time. A small helicopter, making a menacing noise, landed in the patio. Debray was led to it and it took off again. At dusk, the roar of blades breaking the air announced it was back. This time it was Roth's turn. I remained alone with the same guards. Friendlier now the danger had diminished, they told me that Colonel Rocha, commander of the Fourth Army Division in Camiri, had demanded the prisoners be handed over: he considered them guerrillas, carrying false documents. The news, as recorded in Che's diary on 20 April, said: 'They . . . told us that the three who left had been arrested in Muyupampa and two of them are in trouble for having false documents. Bad news for Carlos, but Danton should be all right.' Debray had his valid passport, but the army was obviously referring to the false press passes, with the false authorization from the President.

In the days that followed, I could see that my passport was standing up better than I had hoped. Apparently I had to wait for the helicopter to return before I could be transferred and I spent the time putting my emotions in order and preparing a minimal plan of action: events were way beyond my control but I had to adapt to them with clarity and forethought. First, I weighed up the general situation. Clearly my first mistake was not obeying Che's orders to the letter and striking out on my own over the hills. It is useless to speculate about its viability now but it led to the worst error a revolutionary can make: not to die at the right time.

I have before me a letter from one of my closest *compañeros* at that time, Oscar del Barco, written thirty-five years later apropos of a certain documentary film. 'Your arguments are valid, rationally valid, but the Left, *that* Left, is not interested in rationality; they would rather you had died and not come out alive. That Left can understand you, but will not accept that you didn't die.' Yet saving their lives – the members of that Left – was one of my concerns at that time, and I decided to make sure they were safe, no matter what it cost me personally. But the Left always demands martyrs, because it does not live in the real world but through iconography, like all religions.

Moreover, I had important instructions to carry out that were, to my mind, still urgent despite the fact that I was in jail.

The guerrillas' situation was disastrous for three main reasons: total lack of communication; isolation from the local populace – made worse because guerrilla successes in battle meant the deaths of young soldiers, the sons of the nations' poorest people; and the deplorable state of the guerrillas' health, which could only deteriorate because of the first two reasons and progressive debilitation. The tasks Che asked me to carry out, given my previous experience, were aimed at alleviating this perilous situation. I was to re-establish contact with the clandestine grass-roots and outside support networks that could supply human and material resources. If this failed, there was no way for them but down. Obviously they could not incorporate defeated army units, as the Romans used to. But the numerous volunteers who had been trained, and/or were being trained in Havana to join the liberation struggle generated by the guerrilla foco, needed to be called to action.

Overcoming these hurdles did not depend entirely on me, of course; mine was only one of several attempts that were possible. But I had to do my part, even if it was only to communicate what was actually happening, because the united Left was intent on glorifying the guerrillas. As it happened, mine was the only attempt made. To my mind, as long as I was alive, I had to play the card of asking for legal assistance, and pretending that events had overtaken 'my innocent intentions'. If I could see a lawyer – I thought obsessively about our Argentine lawyers, Lonatti or Roca – I could pass on Che's instructions and things would take their course, regardless of what happened to me. Having come emphatically to this conclusion, I had to put it into practice. But I needed to be alone, I couldn't think in the midst of all this civic-military hysteria. I faked intestinal colic, due to the freezing nights, spicy food, and nerves. They took me to the toilet, in a corner of the corridor. I reviewed my belongings, miraculously they were all intact. It was vital I save the 2,000 dollars which, if I was able to, I would give to the lawyer for Ana María and to cover any expenses incurred. The problem was how to keep them safe. I knew we would be searched any time now; incredibly they had not already done so. Despite forcing us into nudism, they had not so much as put their hands in our pockets, nor taken anything from us. I was ready to lose the 5,000 Bolivian pesos, but not the dollars (after all, it was what I was worth, according to Che's calculation), so I tried putting them in the soles of my moccasins – also inherited from another of the Cubans – but it made them very bulky and I could not get them on. The soldier guarding me was banging on the toilet door so I had to go out without finding a solution. To my surprise, the time at my disposal was extended when I learned the helicopter would not be making another journey that day because of the mist. My turn would not come until the following day.

From that moment, my brain worked non-stop for the next two months. The colic turned into fully fledged diarrhoea and I kept asking to go to the privy. I had invented a way to hide the dollars and everything depended on the time I was able to spend alone with Che's jacket. Where the collar met the synthetic wool padding of the back – where the label usually is – I made a hole by ripping the seam about three centimetres. I inserted the rolled up notes and worked them down between the lining and the fake leather to the bottom hem. It was not easy because the rolls got stuck and I only had a few minutes for each visit, during which I had to make all sorts of onomatopoeias and appropriate sounds. Two thousand dollars, in twenty- and fifty-dollar notes, means innumerable little rolls that refuse to pass inadvertently. I had to spread them out along the hem which, fortunately, did not have any seams. It took me most of the night and several visits to the toilet to complete the task.

The next morning, I dozed on the bench in the corridor until the guard changed and new more excitable military behaviour made life harder. They did, however, offer me a coffee. The helicopter arrived at about nine. They tied my arms and led me to the waiting machine.

The transfer technique was self-explanatory since the helicopter had only two seats with a narrow space behind where I was put, on the floor tied to one of the supports. As well as the pilot, there was a guy from the Criminal Investigation Department who pointed a gun at me. The machine made an infernal racket as it took off. It was like travelling in a noise bubble pulled from above. I was twisting my neck to see the scenery below when we entered a dense totally impenetrable white mist, and my interest turned to panic. Nerves also affected the crew, rightly so, and they forgot about me. We flew blindly for a few minutes when, suddenly, the pilot pulled back on the controls. The layer of cloud lifted and five metres (or ten at most) in front of the helicopter was a wall of rock, a mountainside we would have crashed into had it not been for the pilot's instinctive reaction. The helicopter turned its tip and, instead of stamping us on the rock like hiero-glyphics, flew away like those suicidal folk who hurl themselves into the abyss tied to an elastic rope. Coming out of the white carpet, I saw the contour of a hill disappearing into the jungle. We would never have made it that far.

We landed in a clearing used as a football pitch. They took me unceremoniously from the helicopter, like a pig tied to a rope, and led me to some nearby huts. It was a barracks: Choreti, on the outskirts of Camiri. I was handed over like a parcel to some offic-ers in campaign uniform who already had my documents, doubtless brought on the first flight. 'You! What's your name?' shouted one of them. The performance was about to commence.

During my training courses in Havana, we touched on coun-ter-interrogation techniques. The officer with whom I did the intelligence course repeated over and over again: 'Deny every-thing!' 'Don't stray from the memorized text and deny everything that doesn't fit it, even when it's obvious.' 'You know nothing. We don't know you.' Of course, it is one thing to be taught on a course, and quite another to know what will later be required politically. I knew that I had to play my role myself, and I could not expect anything from anybody to make it sound convincing.

The idea, broadly speaking, was this: I, under the name of Carlos Alberto Frutos, was a volunteer member of a committee set up to defend political prisoners of meagre means in the prov-inces. I was an engineer by profession, and I helped the committee by writing articles on the subject for limited circulation journals. This was why, or so I thought, I had been contacted by a Peru-vian, Bolivian or Central American woman called Edma or Elma, and invited to a meeting on the rights of political prisoners in countries ruled by dictatorships where human rights abuse was rife and undeniable – apparently there was money for expenses, flights included. I had agreed to participate as an independent journalist and we were to meet in La Paz at the end of February. I was then told the meeting would be in the interior, and I had to travel to Sucre; a French journalist, Debray, an international observer, was on the same bus and that to me that gave the whole thing credibility. In Sucre we learned our journey was not over and we ended up in a guerrilla camp, disguised as a farm, where the first thing I did was to complain about the deceitful method used to bring me there – in other words, I had been led to believe I was attending a semi-clandestine but legal meeting, not an armed conference. I demanded to leave immediately but events had overtaken me; both Debray and I had only been in contact with a small group of guerrillas in charge of supplies. I wanted a lawyer to defend me.

The defeats the army had suffered made the officers in charge of the interrogation angry and bitter. Their tone was persistently violent, and their threatening behaviour suggested the outcome had already been decided. That same day, 21 April, Che wrote in his diary of '. . . the news on the radio of the death of three mercenaries, a Frenchman, an Englishman and an Argentine. There must be a response to this disinformation campaign so we can teach them a lesson.' The officers talked of Che and Cubans leading a 'foreign invasion'. 'Your accomplices have already confessed', they said, 'don't waste our time'. The tactic followed the manuals: set us against each other, get us to accuse each other. I had to stick to what we had agreed and deny everything.

Meanwhile, there was another strip-tease session. As I was getting dressed again, the officer going through my clothes picked up the jacket from the floor and emptied the pockets. Then he went on to check the sleeves, lapel and seams. As he ran his fingers downwards pressing the edges, I sensed catastrophe. He started on the bottom hem, squeezing it with his fingers, until he came across something strange. Scrutinizing the lining, he eventually found the hole. Using his fingers as pincers, he dug down to the bottom of the jacket and found something. Widening the hole to get his entire hand in, he began fishing out rolled-up dollar bills, like a magician taking rabbits out of a hat. The shouting that broke out was confusing: I could not tell if they were cries of indignation or joy. Two thousand dollars could be spread around quite nicely; the *cantina* would soak up the 5,000 pesos. (It has to be said in passing that Pombo had counted wrong: there were 1,980 dollars, twenty short.)

They ordered me to be handcuffed and a captain, or perhaps a sergeant, a big black guy, put my hands behind my back and tightened the steel handcuffs as far as they would go, to the sound of a cricket announcing bad weather. I was practically dragged over the entrance to the barracks where I was locked in a shed full of debris and rubbish; it had even been used as a shit house. They threw my jacket and bag in after me, in an effort to respect my property. The window had been boarded up with wooden planks separated by millimetres and nailed from the inside. The door, also of wood, was locked and secured with chains. The flies buzzing above the shit provided the mood music. Standing in a space two metres by two metres, I reflected that they had not given me time to pee, something I had wanted to do all morning; and now that I was finally in the appropriate place, I could not do it.

35

The CIA Takes Charge

I could not see my arms but the pain became proof they existed. It began to span the whole of my back, especially my shoulders and neck. My hands, it seemed, had swollen and each pore pricked from inside with a permanent neuralgia that sent spasmodic electric shocks not only along my arms but in a straight line down my body. I felt it pass through my buttock, my calf and die at the bottom of my foot, or negotiate my ribs upwards, and dig into my neck, behind my ear. My hands had gone to sleep, and the pain came from my wrists where the steel handcuffs were tightest. They were the sort that got tighter the more you moved, an error I could not commit because there was no margin for it. Buried deep in my flesh, they became so completely fused with it that the steel ring emitted pain like an external bone tumour, and throbbed through each link of the chain between the hands.

Between muscle cramp and stomach cramp, I saw the dawn break through the gap in the door. The barracks sprang to life, soldiers lined up in some kind of uneven and unwilling order, only to later disappear, and I imagined them having breakfast of heaven knows what. I made a few futile attempts to get the attention of each new guard. At midday, twenty-four hours after being incarcerated, they came for me.

During the morning there had been some movement of vehicles and men, and I had seen tables and chairs being set up in the garden opposite. And that is where I was taken, handcuffed and wet as I was. There were no introductions, of course, but among the group of soldiers waiting, were two civilians who appeared to be in charge. The tallest, an authoritarian Bolivian whom I came to know as Major Quintanilla, had organized my first interrogation session, but the professional asking the questions was the other one, a Dr González, who as soon as he opened his mouth proved to be Cuban, the other kind of course, in the pay of the CIA. His technique was completely different from the terse Bolivian, and he demonstrated it straight away by asking the major to unlock my handcuffs. A sergeant brought the key and fiddled with the lock until my liberated arms hung by their own weight. I could not move them, not even to look at my hands.

Dr González, a pale-skinned man with a high forehead and black hair, the collar of his white shirt over his jacket in tropical sporty style, adopted a paternalistic stance: 'No, not like that, major, that's not how we do things. Just look at this!' And raising my hands, he demonstrated what 'this' was: two pieces of swollen meat as big as feet, sliced by bloody purple furrows where my wrists should be, and fingers like sausages. Still protesting, he began massaging my arms, from fingers to shoulders. He asked for ice, there was none, alcohol, none either, and continued for a good half hour until he restored my circulation and I could feel my fingers. After making me drink a jug of water, which he held for me like a Good Samaritan, in a strange tense atmosphere that I could not call totally farcical, they sat down at the other side of the table, took out papers, documents, notebooks and a tape recorder.

There are two elementary interrogation techniques, based on contrasting principles: the use of violence to get information while the subject clings to life; and the intelligent use of facts to confront the subject and push him into a corner until his defence collapses. They both start from identifying the prisoner's personality and behaviour in any particular circumstance. But, while the former is a dead end, because the prisoner's death is also a failure, the latter works on the simple logic that the accumulation of contrasting information leads to success. Information can be exaggerated and/or false, but using it and following the thread can get to the truth. In a nutshell, the technique has to demonstrate the futility of denying known facts and the advantages of collaboration – an end to the pressure, restoration of identity, final respite, including prison or death. It was the way of the KGB school, whereby the victims thanked the party for allowing them a glorious death by firing squad.

But like any theory, this technique can be turned on its head and have unexpected consequences. The professional interrogator starts from what he knows, he is not operating in a vacuum. If the prisoner has principles or reasons that motivate him, he finds out more than he tells, and rations what he says in order to maintain a secret balance in his favour. One big lie is made up of innumerable small truths that end up creating a splendid illusion, like a jigsaw. I don't pretend that I had mastered the technique in those days. But when I read real professionals later on, I was convinced that the fixed idea I had of omitting everything to do with Argentina and insisting on contacting my own lawyer was instinctively the right thing to do.

The picture I painted of myself was not at all flattering, or even relevant, but it was very effective. You only have to compare my final statements to the interrogators with the story told in this book of the real role I had played. However, I base my success on two things: one, my total denial of any link with the events in question and hence my repudiation of them – following the advice of my Cuban military intelligence instructors – and two, the amount of knowledge Dr González had was evident in the way he channelled the interrogation in certain directions, his accuracy and precision, the names he introduced, and the gaps he left. It was like driving a car with two steering wheels. One was mine, a secret one, and I gave it an inadvertent twist whenever I could.

Some things were undeniably true. I was arrested after the first three battles, the bloodiest defeats the army suffered at the hands of the guerrillas. From then on, all I could hide was my past, not the existence of the guerrillas. The army already knew where, when and how to fight them. I could only accept or deny what was more or less known, and use that knowledge. If, for example, the question was about the number of Cubans, it was because their presence was worth knowing about, and any Argentine presence was not. If they name Antonio and Arturo, it is because they already know their names; they cannot invent them off the top of their heads. I can delay my recognition, accumulate shared facts and release them when some route is blocked, knowing that it will not be news or do anyone any harm. The questions also helped in the sense that they provided information about what was happening. If details came out that they could not have known about, they must have come from another source.

So, there were signs of other detainees, although they were not confirmed until much later. (Loro, Jorge Vázquez Viaña, had been arrested on 22 April. My real identity was safe, because apart from Che and some of the Cubans, only Loro knew, and he did not reveal it.) My initial aim was to gain time with my false identity – Carlos Alberto Frutos, civil engineer – in the hope that Manuel in Buenos Aires would raise the alarm among our *compañeros* in the three or four cities most involved in the EGP, and that would give them time to put in place the necessary safety measures. You can never know where an interrogation that starts with a massage will end, but the assumption that we were dead ducks hovered over us like the trump card in a poker (or *truco*) game.

In the first session, I merely identified the person in the passport and reiterated the story I gave when arrested in Muyupampa. But it gave me a clear idea of how to weave threads into a fabric: I did not know Frutos and his family circle so I had to invent everything and, more importantly, I had to remember what I invented, because a basic knowledge of police techniques shows the interrogator may suddenly return to previous questions looking for inconsistencies. The first round of invented names I got from conjuring up groups of old friends, lost in time but not in my heart. This gave me a certain flexibility and the chance to create the organogram: parents, children, brothers, relatives, friends, family anecdotes; it was a particular social milieu and space/time framework that was easy to remember.

My main worry was how quickly I would be identified. In Argentina, all six-year-olds get a *cédula*, a police ID. It is based on Civil Registry records and the fingerprints of both hands, and is kept in the police archives. It was not until the second or third week that they began this process.

I was also worried about hiding a very hot potato indeed. In the years following the consolidation of power by the Cuban revolutionary government, the primary aim of US intelligence in Latin America was to undermine that power and destroy the example set by the Cuban model. Naturally they were anxious to capture informers who had come out of the Cuban programme to export the Revolution across Latin America. Every so often some bureaucrat or other took the plunge and fell into their net, but they were usually tram salesmen looking for a way into exile or counter-intelligence agents persuaded to get into bed with the US. In me they had a first-hand source that was potentially an unimaginable diplomatic and military propaganda coup, a real complication for the Cubans, and worse still, it implicated other countries. But they did not know it, nor could they imagine it. I, on the other hand, *did know*: it was a time bomb I had to swallow even if it exploded inside me, or in the best of cases, would take so long to digest that it would ruin my life anyway. The alternative was to make them kill me. But I did not want to die. So I sacrificed my vanity, and passed myself off as a first-class imbecile, consistent and believable.

The boarded up shack became my cell. They furnished it with an old wrought iron bed, probably from a rubbish dump. The iron and bronze supports were kicked into place, but nothing could sort out the sagging rusty wire mesh base, which did not even have a mattress. Before bed, I ate the *plat du jour*, which was what the troops got every day: a sort of soup of potatoes and maize flour, with bits of fat or crackling floating in it, served on a tin plate accompanied by a tin beaker, both dented, for my own personal use. I also got a piss pot, a narrow-necked milk bottle. When the night sentry arrived at seven o'clock, my right wrist was handcuffed – with difficulty – to the wire mesh base. I used Che's jacket to cover the part of the mesh without holes and lay down, able to change position painfully. Twelve hours later, with the change of guard, I was given breakfast: my beaker full of *maté*, and a piece of bread. They also took off my handcuffs, so settling myself by the crack in the door I observed what was going on.

In mid-morning, I saw them setting up that day's tribunal: Debray and Roth were to be questioned together, instead of devoting a day to one person as they generally did. After that everyone disappeared, for the weekend, I supposed, and came back from La Paz with renewed gusto. But, despite Quintanilla's tendencies, our treatment did not change. We were never tortured. After Debray's initial kicking and my mashed wrists, they did not touch us again. A mantle of protection had suddenly fallen over one of the prisoners and extended to all of us. The Guardian Angel was General Charles de Gaulle, irrefutable hero of the Second World War, founder-president of the Fifth French Republic. We did not know it, but Debray could have expected it. His mother was a Gaullist member of parliament for Paris.

General de Gaulle's prestige stemmed from having granted independence to Algeria (an historic role), despite fierce opposition from the most reactionary sectors of his armed forces, who had been losing influence since Vietnam. Yet paradoxically it was this sector that had most influence over the Latin American armies. It is wrong to think that it was only the North Americans who were ethically 'corrupt'. It was the ex-generals of the OAS (Secret Army Organization) who introduced anti-subversive methods – no holds barred violence, torture of prisoners and civilians – widely practised in those countries where they trained local armed forces, including the US. Years

later, Argentine torturers were their model students; some of
the generals recognized that the French techniques had been
successfully applied in the Dirty War of the 1970s. In our day,
the pro-US cupola of the Bolivian army, which included President Barrientos and generals Torres and Ovando, was being
challenged by the pro-French sector, led by the Oruro garrison's General Banzer, over its proposal to negotiate over the
lives of us prisoners. And again paradoxically, the negotiations
were with that very same French government.

Meanwhile, I clung tenaciously to my story of the deceptive
invitation. It was one thing, I argued, to participate in a legally
organized Latin American conference in solidarity with peoples
daring to fight oppression, and quite another to end up with a guerrilla group that had been forced into military action before we had
time to leave. I had done nothing but refuse to participate and wait
until I could leave. I had not seen the leader who, it was true, they
called Ramón. I did not know if the men in charge were Cubans. I
could not tell their accents from others, possibly Central Americans or Ecuadorians. We had only seen small groups of guerrillas,
since they kept us foreigners away from military operations. There
was, however, an iron rule in place: if you did not work, you did
not eat, so we had to help collect firewood and water, and carried
our own sleeping equipment and other general loads.

The Argentine part was of special interest to them, and there I
could let fly, based on what I remembered from all kinds of magazines and pamphlets in Buenos Aires endlessly analyzing details
of politics, the unions and the clandestine struggle, and naturally
I overdosed on reports from conferences on human rights, freedom of expression, and culture, until my interrogators got tired
and changed the subject. I needed to remember my gradual introduction into those circles, quite normal in a more or less
democratic Argentina in a permanent state of political ferment
since the fall of Peronism, but without straying from what was
common knowledge: union meetings, fashionable study centres
and seminars, which in actual fact I had avoided like the plague.

They wanted to find a link between those activities and the guerrillas in Bolivia; it was like playing cops and robbers.

One morning, out of the blue, they took me and the Frenchman to a runway. A little Cessna landed and we were pushed into the seats behind the pilot, handcuffed together. The other front seat was occupied by Major Quintanilla, a Colt .38 in his hand. The plane took off towards the north, or so I thought, seeing the jungle-covered hills to the left and the desert plains to the right. We were flying directly over the area where the drama of armed ideology was being played out. Debray and I could not talk to each other, but some telepathic communication must have gone on. It was the first time we had been together since our arrest, although I had seen him almost daily through my crack in the door. We both sported the authentic prisoner look: a few scratches, a lot dirtier, but basically intact.

The plane landed in Santa Cruz de la Sierra, probably at a military airfield, and truckloads of troops were deployed to accompany us to a barracks. We were still the responsibility of Major Quintanilla who finally introduced us, a tad theatrically, to the Eighth Army Division's head of intelligence, Major Saucedo. Quintanilla was a police major and head of intelligence for the Ministry of the Interior. Only rivalry between the Commanders of Divisions Four and Eight explains this prisoner transfer operation. Instead of the chief of the interested section doing the interrogation – in this case Section Two (Intelligence) of the Eighth Division from a neighbouring military region where the guerrillas were expected to be heading – the individual sessions remained where we had finished the previous day. Here they merely took personal stock of the statements we had made so far. The prisoner interrogations were still in the hands of the team based in the Fourth Division barracks in Camiri, controlled by the CIA.

Halfway through the afternoon, we got into the Cessna and returned to the Choreti barracks outside Camiri. We sat in the same seats for the hour's flight and for the very first time a viable way of escaping occurred to me. Why not relieve Major

Quintanilla of his revolver? The major, a typical example of the South American macho, freed from the critical eye of his boss Dr González, was keen to exercise his power. So, twisting round in his seat, instead of speaking – as if we did not understand Spanish – he used the barrel of his cocked gun to indicate he did not want us to move, speak or look at each other. But every now and again, his attention was distracted and he looked out of the front window at the scenery.

With my hands together, I thought, I could lunge forward, wrest the gun from his hand, press it to the pilot's neck, and get the flight plan altered, or rather, carry on down to the Argentine border. But this was not Hollywood, I was not the star of a film, and my impulses were subordinate to my reason. I tried to move my arm, but it was anchored to Debray's and we had no visual contact. Any action that depended on being able to move freely – without being able to – was crazy. The imponderables were: a stray shot might hit me; he might have another gun for his right hand; he might be stronger than he looked; and most probably, the plane might not have enough petrol.

One morning a third person appeared. Wearing a dark grey suit, a white shirt and a tie, he put a briefcase on the garden table and took out several things. From the few words I heard him say, I detected an unmistakeable Argentine accent. He was from the Argentine Federal Police's special political brigade. He took ten fingerprints with professional expertise, like a manicurist, then handed me a petrol-soaked rag to wipe the ink off my fingers, which given their recent treatment were still like half-peeled bananas. He said goodbye to the interrogators and went off to get his plane without a word to me.

Almost immediately I started on a new version of my story. The Buenos Aires police would clearly not tolerate being made fools of, and had sent an Identification Section expert to make absolutely certain. Now all I could do was wait for the results. The dry, threatening tone the interrogators used became ironic, insisting on family dates, details, ages; the questions were as fictional as the replies. We were all pretending. The weekend went by gloomily. In the next session, all hell broke loose.

I was sitting in front of the interrogation table. The day was sunny, but cold. The interrogators came out of the office. Quintanilla stormed towards me, furious, hurling insults, kicking the air, and knocking over chairs. He was over-reacting, of course, but behind him Dr González seemed livid too. It was the only time I saw him lose his cool. While the major shouted for the firing squad – something he could not do – Dr González swore at me between his teeth: 'Bastard! You little shit! You made me look like a fucking idiot! You tricked me like a kid.' The racket they were making was ridiculous. They must have already travelled from La Paz together knowing who I really was. Or maybe not. The telegram may have come straight to Camiri. I did not know. The point was that, while Quintanilla said 'We have to shoot this fool!', Dr González pointed out that while I had wasted their time, from now on it was plain sailing. 'We're going to listen to what Señor Bustos has to say to us!' he said, and let slip a few signs of what they now knew.

They knew my real identity down to the last detail: a painter, from Mendoza, well-known leftist, friend of communist artists and painters, travelled around Argentina making contacts in political and cultural circles dominated by international communism. 'Let's start again', I said. And we started again: date of birth, parents, brothers and sisters, last address, education, jobs, political activities. It was easier. I could describe a concrete past, not at all subversive, full of famous people known for their pacifism and concern for human rights. Artists and poets, musicians and writers, actors and bohemians who had never held a gun or so much as a firework, committed to the struggle for peace and nuclear disarmament. That was my world, and they knew it.

I exchanged the false history for my real life, more romantic than combative, or both things interrelated. However, I retained my basic reason for being in Bolivia. I was active in peace and human rights movements, and supported political prisoners fighting for justice and against exploitation. 'Didn't you do that in 1952?' I asked.

The false passport was normal political behaviour too. When I went to Buenos Aires to meet the person responsible for the invitation – a certain Isaac, a name given me in Córdoba by Elma – I discovered I was going to La Paz and needed a passport. I did not have one and getting all the proper documentation from the police would take too long, so I gave Isaac a photo and he got one for me. The newspapers were full of politicians and union leaders flying to Perón's house in Madrid under false names, so I took the risk. The web I wove, a mixture of truth and lie, was unravelled daily, and my heart was in my mouth each time my secret came perilously near to being uncovered.

Some (police) information cropped up about my trip to Cuba in 1961. I made it as far-fetched as I could, saying that I had planned a trip with my then wife Claudia, but that we had split up and wanted to hide the fact from her wealthy family, so we left Mendoza to keep up appearances and eventually parted company in Chile. I went south to Osorno, to manage a seaweed processing factory; a job offered me by a friend in Santiago. The story was true, except that it had happened ten years earlier, and never got past the project stage. The friend was called Maruja (María) Moragas and I met her at a Continental Culture Congress. I hoped Claudia's family's visceral loathing for revolutionary Cuba would prevent that lead being followed, and that was in fact what happened. But it was not all so dangerously easy. It did not make sense that an armed organization involving Cuba, and leaders of the status of Fidel and Che, would invite me by mistake.

On the other hand, it was all so preposterous that it could be an error or overestimation by the Cubans of the level of commitment of the Argentine Left (this had happened in Bolivia, after all). There were too many false trails and Dr González was already suspicious. When he thought he had all the facts, they turned out to be false. 'OK, how the fuck do I know any of it is true? Painter? How do I know you're a painter? OK, draw something, damn it. Draw a guerrilla!' I felt the parachute open. Instead of diving into the abyss, I could descend gently, and keep pulling the ropes until I finally landed.

Dr González sent someone out to buy a small pad of drawing paper, and a thick pencil. I drew a 'guerrilla' who looked more like a tramp. The impact was as instantaneous as the image was useless; the power of the virtual was more real than the bloody actions they had taken part in. Things moved fast after that. I had the opportunity to reinforce my own story, probably at the cost of my own honour. I did not hesitate. The choice between my own image and the secrets of the Revolution was simple, and I made it. The public might be suspicious, but my *compañeros* would be safe. It all hinged on credibility; they had to accept that I was a genuinely neutral witness, willing to collaborate so as not to be linked in any way with the other side. Who had the soldiers seen? I asked myself. After the ambushes, the prisoners not only saw but talked to various guerrillas, they were treated by guerrilla doctors, they confessed to other guerrillas. Managing more than just a coincidental likeness would be a miracle anyway, and that boded well for me. A good draughtsman can repeat from memory a face he has drawn numerous times, but he cannot make a faithful copy of faces that rush in and out of his memory in chaotic situations. I drew what they might find recognizable: beards, a certain look, recognizable features, the order was not important. Deep inside I had a clear idea of where I was heading, I could almost guess what they would ask me to do next.

In the days leading up to this watershed, it had become clear that they knew the composition and leadership of the guerrilla group. They made me listen to other interrogations, so I could not go on pleading ignorance. Subsequent speculation, for reasons of press or murky interest, about who did what when, did not change what the army knew. It did not matter what Debray or I said, nor when we said it: they already knew. To get a picture of the chronology, best examine the statements of the defectors: they had already established the presence of Che under the alias

Ramón, a group of Cubans under his command, some Peruvians and, naturally, Bolivians led by members or ex-members of the Bolivian Communist Party. All of them were shielded by pseudonyms, which was their purpose. As for our being there, the reason fluctuated like a kaleidoscope. Debray, who had arrived with his own passport and cultural baggage, was in fact more illegitimate than the person who had arrived illegally, because his being 'important' was worth something, whereas mine was insignificant. When they found my suitcase in Tania's jeep, it contained a few clothes, catalogues of Buenos Aires publishers, a photo of Cortázar and two Oruro devil masks bought in La Paz. When they opened the Debray file, they found Cuba, Fidel Castro, Masperó (French publisher), world famous philosophers and writers supporting the great journalistic adventure to find and interview Che Guevara.

Shortly after my real identity was established, Debray wrote a letter to Dr González (signed by him on 14 May) in which he clarified and corrected details and dates of his previous statements, the circumstances under which Castro told him he could see Che: how, when and where. 'I realize under these circumstances there is no point hiding today what will be headline news tomorrow', he writes. Neither knowing the truth nor speculating about it would alter the drama of an isolated guerrilla army prepared to fight to the death.

Or would it? When we said goodbye, Che had said: 'but if you see that they know, blast off, spread the news, make as much noise as possible. Then I can be myself again and use my beret . . .'. That was not some throwaway phrase; he had hit the nail on the head, the importance of his presence. But my unconscious drive to self-preservation initially buried the possibility of making such pronouncements. When I began to see the need for them, I found the crucial element was missing – the press, the indispensible medium for 'making a noise', however great or small.

This was consistent on the part of the army. In the almost four years I was a prisoner, I was not allowed a single contact with the press. And this applied exclusively to me. The only 'article' was written without my knowledge by the Argentine magazine *Gente* when we were taken to Camiri in July. But from our perspective in Argentina, our hopes of success were always based on Che leading the struggle, his ability to get the masses to join him. Without a base in the people, against a powerful army, in an immense country, the struggle was an illusion; more than risible, impossible. Our project could be saved by informing the people, and they would choose whether to accept or reject it, on the basis of their own yearning and the historic merit of the figure proposing it. Keeping his leadership a secret meant denying him support. That was the view taken years later by Bolivian journalist Humberto Vázquez Viaña, Loro's brother, in his book *A Guerrilla for Che*, and also intimated by General Gary Prado in his book *How I Captured Che*.

The next step was difficult, because it meant a dual challenge. Drawing Che would be both risible (pretending the drawings were a weapon against the guerrilla is nothing more than that) and a commitment, not only of memory but also of emotion. If I had no voice with which to 'make as much noise as possible', I had to use my other talents, and I was prepared for Dr González to say: 'And Ramón? Draw Ramón.'

The drawing was a rough sketch. The important thing was not the outward appearance but the inner strength, which I was unable to capture. It looked more like a hungry poet and bore no resemblance to Ramón, or to what he represented. Yet he was considered the success of the guerrilla drawings. Nonetheless, Dr González was soon removed. Of all the drawings I had to do, those of Chino and Ñato were the best (as it happens they were the men I had most dealings with in the camp). Better too was the drawing of Papi, of whom I was especially fond. There still remained the strategic objective I had to carry out, to protect my network by drawing Argentine contacts that did not exist. But I had to let them force that out of me.

I don't think the drawings changed the interrogation process, but suddenly one night, we were dragged out and piled into a jeep that took off along a mountain track. In the middle of the night and the middle of nowhere, the jeep stopped behind an army truck and we were pushed out. I thought our final hour had come. But it was just a change of vehicle. We were hauled into the back of the truck carrying a load of soldiers and continued our journey to a mini barracks in the jungle. It was a camp where a Bolivian ranger unit were being trained by US instructors, an eventual Green Beret regiment. I was put in an empty store room, the sort used for harnesses or tools, where I could only stand or squat in the space between shelves, with my knees against the wall. The old wooden door was chained shut, but it had a few opportune slits at eye level.

During the day I could see a lot of troop movements and US officers talking to Bolivians in a kind of pidgin cowboy-Caribbean. They seemed to be the technical directors. We only spent a couple of days there, but it was clear we had been abducted clandestinely because even going to the WC had to be done when no one was about.

We were eventually taken in a US military helicopter to *La Esperanza*, an old sugar mill to the north of Santa Cruz. A prison had been improvised in a dilapidated house in the old administrative quarter, surrounded by a covered verandah in the best tropical colonial style, with a corridor separating the rooms where we were quartered. Debray was to the right, and I to the left in a corner room, with boarded up windows and torn mesh mosquito netting. I don't remember where Roth was.

Debray suggested we exaggerate the strength of the guerrilla contingents to more than a hundred fighters, of which we had only met two or three small groups, the ones they already knew about. This coincided with what I had been telling my interrogators. The idea was to dissuade the army from searching for them because that would be dangerous for the small groups of guerrillas in their present state. In the short term, exaggerating their size could be favourable. I was not sure how many men the army could mobilize. The US general staff theory was: more troops, less mobility, but greater ability to encircle the enemy. In practice, the poorest army in the southern cone relied on its human resources to multiply its activities.

We did not know it at the time, but, for the first time in Latin America, the Bolivians were using a theory that was both new and appropriate: creating their own guerrilla groups acting independently and simultaneously. The strategy of isolating the guerrillas was decisive in the struggle. The US-trained troops did not join the action until the very end.

Two things happened in this peaceful place which gradually brought an end to the interrogations of Roth and Debray, though they continued with me. The first was that Dr González was replaced by another Cuban exile, Gabriel García, also a CIA agent. He was more energetic, more obviously an employee of the 'Company'; he tried to control everything. He told me that Dr González had finished his work and returned to the US, my interrogation was only just beginning; it would depend on me how long it lasted, and whether it would have a happy ending.

He was mainly interested in my contacts in Argentina, and in the links between them and La Paz. My line of 'collaboration' was clearly defined. They seemed receptive to my arguments since everything seemed to fit the political preconceptions the CIA had about local and regional left-wing politics: the Communist Parties were openly against the armed struggle in Latin America, and Argentina was no exception. Young people there were abandoning the party ranks and the political scene was dominated by the power of the Peronist labour organizations. The masses had not supported the Cuba-backed guerrilla experience in Salta for that very reason. The Left was only united through solidarity with their jailed militants, and I had been very active in that campaign. Nevertheless, someone had been behind the invitation I had received and that person must be the bridge to a continental-wide project, like the one now taking place in Bolivia. Gabriel wanted to know who it was.

He asked me to provide a written statement, which I did. My mistake was to hope my statements would 'make as much noise as possible', but that I could keep my secrets at the same time. I more than achieved the second objective. But the CIA stymied my first objective by not publishing 'my statement' (a version appeared in English many years later). They used the figure of the defeated collaborator, that I had laboriously created through my drawings and my 'lacking in content' statements, added information to it gathered from other sources, and then finally presented it as a great work of CIA intelligence.

Yet the work – of counter-intelligence – was done by me to protect the information I had accumulated: the direct implication of Cuba in 'continental subversion', the complicity of other states, and the safety and freedom of all the members of our organization in Argentina.

I pretended to be on the sidelines politically, even against the project I worked for, ceding a little information each day, until I 'broke' and delivered the names and drawings of the two contacts crucial to the CIA investigation: Isaac Rutman in Argentina, and Andrés in La Paz, neither of whom existed.

When I lived in Buenos Aires in the 1950s, I met a guy who later became my best friend in the city. We met in the 'Chamberi', a café-bar on the corner of Córdoba and San Martín, where in the late afternoon artists and literary people gathered in a *peña*. In fact, there were various *peñas* going on simultaneously. The *peña* next to ours centred round film and socialism, and at the table alongside us sat a film critic called Leo Salas who was always banging on about Ingmar Bergman, in the years when the Swedish director was more famous in Argentina than in his own country. Leo's friend, who became mine too, was called Isaac Shusterman – or Isaquito – a Jewish socialist who dreamed of adventures, faraway and improbable rather than political, and managed to join the crew of an Argentine merchant marine ship going down the Atlantic Coast to the south. On his return, sailor's bag over his shoulder, Isaac came straight from South Dock to our *peña* in the Chamberi. We spent many enjoyable times. I did not become friends with the critic, because for me the film genius in those days was Orson Welles, not the remote Viking, and that particular heresy was unacceptable to his ears.

My friend Isaquito came to mind the first time I mentioned someone called Isaac in Buenos Aires in my interrogation. When the moment came, broken by my 'defection', I gave his face to Isaac Rutman, so I could draw a Jewish face properly. The name, Rutman, came from another Jewish friend, from Mendoza, called Roitman, but I changed the spelling. Next I drew the Bolivian contact created to help Debray, who we 'knew' only as Andrés. These two people became famous at my expense, despite never having been born.

One day I was writing the résumé of my statements that Gabriel García had asked for. I was trying to clarify what I had really said, and divest it of the rubbish other people had said that García wanted me to approve. There was sudden agitation at the entry checkpoint when a couple of vehicles passed the barrier and drove down the avenue of jacarandas in front of our house. A jeep, followed by an army truck full of soldiers, advanced slowly until it passed the house and stopped a little further on. In the jeep sat General Ovando Cándia, Commander in Chief of the Bolivian Armed Forces, whose photo we had seen on scraps of newspaper in the bathroom, or in magazines the soldiers on guard duty had lent us. It was an unmistakable image, and the reactions to him confirmed it.

Changing windows, my eyes followed the reception committee as they came to greet him at the next-door house. Shortly afterwards, they called for Debray and took him to the general. No doubt about it. The commander of the Bolivian Armed Forces wanted to talk to the Frenchman. A couple of hours later, they came back with Debray, while the general went off the way he had come. The Frenchman told me nothing about the meeting. He behaved as if nothing had happened and as if I was some idiot who could know about his visits to the bathroom but not about his posh outings. From then on, Debray was not interrogated further, while García kept pressing me for details about my contacts, etc.

One morning, I was told to collect my belongings and the three of us, including Roth now, assembled at the door to the house. We were handcuffed and taken to a clearing where an enormous US army 'banana' helicopter was waiting. We were pushed in through a sliding door in the side, together with a group of Green Berets carrying automatic rifles.

The flying mastodon flew over the jungle. It was impossible to tell in which direction, or how long the journey took, but it was over an hour, in any case. It was all too obvious, however, that wherever we landed in that desert of short flat jungle, we would never ever get out. And that was the idea. We eventually landed in a clearing in the carpet of vegetation. There was a three-sided thatched adobe house with a central patio and a pond; the fourth side was enclosed with barbed wire. It was deep in the jungle.

The living part of the house with wooden windows was at the front, the right-hand side seemed to lodge the guards, and on the left were chicken coops and corrals. A tall, thin middle-aged man in a captain's uniform came out to greet us, followed by a pathetic female figure and a couple of children. The officer in charge of the transfer operation handed over his prisoners, inspected half a dozen soldiers who appeared from nowhere, and ordered them to unload supplies from the helicopter. He said goodbye like someone in a hurry to leave hell, leapt aboard the whistling monster, its blades already whirring, and disappeared into a cloud of dust.

The captain, depressed looking but with courteous manners, a wrinkled face, reddened eyes and Chaplin-style moustache, thought it opportune to inform us that we were all in the same boat, isolated from the outside world by 200 kilometres of jungle. The best thing to do, he said, was relax, keep out of the sun, be on the lookout for snakes, and try to make the best of things. His wife would cook, and the food would be the same for the family, prisoners and guards, providing we did not threaten his family or question his duties as head of this outpost. He then took us to our 'rooms': the chicken coops on the left-hand side, of course, emptied of their former inhabitants. The geese, ducks and hens, having been transferred higgledy-piggledy to the tumble-down shack at the end of the line, were flapping noisily together in the patio round the pond. Soldiers were sweeping the chicken shit off the floor with branches, trying to make room for some recently arrived camp beds, with straw mattresses and blankets. They put one in each room. Debray took the nearest to the house; Roth the one in the middle, and I was in the last one which, judging by the grey feathers, had housed the geese.

The doors, mere symbolic structures to protect the fowl from mountain foxes, let in the sun's rays like shiny metallic sheets. At night, stearic acid candles threw sinister shadows onto the spider's webs. There was no real need for padlocks but they still used planks to bar the doors. It was early June, deep winter, though it made no difference in those latitudes. The next day, the captain invited us to inspect the property after an excellent breakfast served devotedly by his good wife. Away from the house on the left, a couple of hectares had been cleared for maize and vegetables. Staring into the jungle, we could see just how thick and tangled it was, low but impenetrable.

The days went by slowly and peacefully. Chatting in the shade on the patio every morning, a strange friendship formed between Debray, Roth and me, although limited by natural reserve and some taboo topics. Roth was the friend in common, and apex of the trio, and he brought optimism and good humour. One day he said he had a confession to make, and lowering his eyes admitted: 'I'm a member of the army.' We looked at him calmly, as if it was not beyond the realms of possibility, and he went: '. . . the Salvation Army, ha, ha'. He told us of his adventures in New York while he was training for the Peace Corps, when it was fashionable for students to carry knives and whip them out on the slightest

pretext, especially to girls. He was a good sort, and just wanted to
strike it lucky some day as a freelance photographer.

During the month, we received two visits. We were locked up
as a small helicopter landed and, to my surprise the visitors came
to my cell. It was Gabriel García and the Argentine policeman,
not a very high level visit, but exclusively for me. Opening his
briefcase, the Argentine said in a policeman-like voice: 'There
are two Isaac Rutmans in Argentina: one is 75 and lives in Buenos
Aires, and the other, a cripple, is in Rio Gallegos, Patagonia.' He
took out a file of photos, as if they were of underworld villains,
and asked me to identity the fugitive Rutman among the notorious criminals of the Argentine Left. From the police photos, I
honestly could not have even recognized Codovilla (secretary of
the Communist Party) even if I had wanted to. They left me a
carton of cigarettes and a vaporizer. My bronchial infection had
deteriorated in Choreti and I had asked for one. When they had
left and normality returned, Debray said to me cryptically:
'Carlos (he still called me that), lies have short legs!' 'Depends on
the boots the cat wears', I replied.

The second visit was at the beginning of July. The roar above
suggested the marines were landing but in fact it was the enormous 'banana' helicopter. We saw the dust storm briefly before
we were locked up. The visitor was an important figure, significant for the three of us. He was Monseñor Kennedy, Bolivian
army chaplain and US citizen. We were politely invited from our
cells to be introduced to the ecclesiastical dignitary, who professed
interest in our health in the name of the Christian faithful who
had been praying for us and would be pleased to know, via him,
that he had found us alive and well.

We each had our photo taken with the priest, and the committee of Gabriel García and Major Quintanilla took their leave. We
waved them goodbye as a family, as if they were leaving a happy
party. It was clear they were granting us 'among the living' status.

The helicopter returned a couple of days later and we were told
to pack our toothbrushes. There was an emotional goodbye from

the captain and his wife, whom we were abandoning. We looked down on them from the air, waving furiously, in the middle of that great solitude, their children clutching their legs, surrounded by the ubiquitous fowl.

36

On Trial in Camiri: October 1967

Receptions do not always have red carpets. Awaiting us on the Choreti barracks airstrip was a Bolivian army combat unit: trucks, jeeps, officers and couriers shouting orders and scurrying from one side of the helicopter to another, all deployed in organizing a military detail with weapons at the ready, at the door of the machine. We got out to a patently hostile atmosphere as if we were aliens not even to be treated as human beings, because of the mantle of prejudice hanging over us. The key to this animosity was the accusation that we were foreign mercenaries; the guerrillas were portrayed as mainly Cuban, Peruvian and Argentine. The army played up its fatalities as an attack on the national honour of a people whose humblest of sons, mere conscripts, were being killed without anything to 'justify' the massacre.

We were dragged handcuffed to one of the trucks and dumped in the back like parcels. There was a bench on each side and we were distributed along them with soldiers in between. I was at the back of the truck on the right, next to the officer in charge, who cocked a .45 pistol and leant the barrel on my left cheek, forcing me to look at him. It was a very disagreeable sight: his face oozed sadism and a line of saliva appeared to dribble from his obscene mouth. Major Echeverría, commander of Fourth Army Division's intelligence section, proved to be a total psychopath.

The truck drove off down what seemed to be a river-bed but was, in fact, the road to Camiri. The summer rains had caused the rivers to overflow and flood the roads in town, so that every crossroads was ploughed up and little channels of stones made our journey torture, and for me dangerous, because the gun barrel dug into my cheekbones and banged against my lower molar which had been aching for days. The threat of my head being blown off when we hit a pothole – ultimate odontological solution – hung over me until we stopped. We had arrived at Fourth Division headquarters, on the corner of Camiri's main square, where on a Sunday night four months earlier, we had listened to the music of the military band.

I was dragged off the truck and put in a small room. Later, when the situation calmed a little, I discovered what had been happening hierarchically within Fourth Division. Colonel Rocha, whom we had heard on the radio while we were still at Base Camp, had been replaced as commanding officer by Colonel Reque Terán. All the middle-rank officers were new, and there to wash away the humiliation suffered and avenge the dead.

One morning, they took me from my room to an interior patio, which was like a garden. Roth and Debray were already there, each standing with a guard. On the other side of the lawn, behind some ropes like a boxing ring, was a crowd of journalists and photographers. We were introduced to them like some strange species. No questions were allowed and the ceremony finished with no contact except visual, and the popping of camera flashes. A photographer, who identified himself as the correspondent of the Buenos Aires magazine *Gente*, asked if he could approach me to measure the luminosity on his light metre. Given permission, he jumped the rope, came up to me and, putting his apparatus purposefully to my chest, whispered: 'Your wife is in La Paz.' 'Thank you', I replied. At the end of the session, another journalist came up and managed to say a few words to me. It was Carlos María Gutiérrez, from the Uruguayan magazine *Marcha*. He said, as if we knew each other: 'Don't worry, Ciro, I'm going to Cuba to see about publishing Che's "Congo Diaries" and I'll stop them trying to frame you.' I never heard from him again, and Che's Congo book was not published for another thirty years. The army spokespersons announced to the press that, since we had been arrested under the Fourth Division's jurisdiction, we would be tried in a military tribunal right here in Camiri.

A couple of days later, I was told I would be receiving a visit of two half-hour sessions on consecutive days. The major withdrew, giving way to my wife Ana María. A soldier stood by the blank wall facing the bed, and a sergeant posted himself at the door. Ana María and I hugged each other in an interminable embrace that lasted the entire thirty minutes.

The emotion of seeing each other paralyzed us, but the interior strength of the militancy we both tacitly shared – incredible as it sounds now thirty-two years later – meant we acted more like comrades than a loving couple with two little girls. The lump in my throat reflected my concern for my family but in Ana María's ear I murmured details of my failed mission. I explained the core argument of my statement to the Bolivian authorities (and also, by the way, that she had no knowledge of my activities).

I told her she must urgently inform the Cubans of the dire situation the guerrillas were in – no food, medicine, no radio – and that, in my opinion, they could not survive six months in that state. Given that I was describing what I had seen in April, the prediction was terrifyingly exact. I said: 'Remember these words and repeat them to me tomorrow: go to La Paz, find Dr Rea . . . and give him the instructions Che had given me.' I can't remember the exact words but in essence it was to warn the urban network's Rodolfo (Saldaña) or Renán Montero to find a safer place for the money, and get the Cubans to send any available volunteers to the area between the Cochabamba–Santa Cruz road and the guerrillas' zone of action, and somehow miraculously try to regain contact with them. Our time was up and they took her out.

The following day we had another half-hour visit. Ana María and I went over the instructions. She had remembered them correctly. She also brought the news that Debray's mother had arrived in La Paz and apparently declared that I was a CIA agent while her young son was a renowned philosopher with an inquiring mind. This slanderous remark had not helped Ana María get permission to travel to Camiri, but it was finally granted by General Torres who told her she had the misfortune of being married to 'the most dangerous' of the prisoners. This was intriguing. What did he really know and what was guesswork? Or was he just playing executioner?

When they first landed in La Paz, Ana María and Ricardo Rojo, with whom she travelled from Buenos Aires, had contacted a prestigious Bolivian socialist intellectual, Sergio Almaraz Paz, leader of the opposition PIR (Party of the Revolutionary Left) and founder of the *Grupo Octubre*. The contact was made through another Argentine, Gregorio Selser, a historian who worked with the group in La Paz. Almaraz offered Ana María moral support in the hostile environment created by the police, and practical support in negotiating the arbitrary obstacles the army was putting in the way of anyone associated with their Argentine prisoner.

The *Grupo Octubre* tried to help Ana María contact the guerrilla's urban network but Dr Rea was no longer in Bolivia, and without him it was impossible to use the passwords, valid only for him, to reach Rodolfo and Renán. Not only had Dr Rea gone into exile in Chile, but Cuban Intelligence had recalled their man Renán Montero (aka Moleón in Bolivia or Iván when the EGP were training in Havana) from his post in La Paz in March, immediately after the first combat. He was not replaced. I only learned this extraordinary information many years later.

Ana María returned to Argentina and prepared the textual reports to send to Cuba. The EGP leadership in Córdoba asked a *Pasado y Presente* reader without a political/police record – who I knew only as Gordo – to go immediately to Havana. When he reached Havana airport, he was interrogated by Cuban intelligence. They took Ana María's report from him and dispatched him back to Prague on the same plane, without a word of explanation. Havana had decided to side exclusively with the international figure of Debray. They never tried to make contact of any kind with the EGP in Argentina, the grass-roots organization founded by Che.

In La Paz, Almaraz suggested hiring a trusted lawyer, Dr Jaime Mendizábal, to take on my defence. I had always hoped to have an Argentine lawyer but it did not prove viable. From then on, there was a clear intention, and not only inside Bolivia, to isolate my real political 'persona' – to which I contributed initially for reasons of general security – by denying me any contact with the press. Over the next three and a half years, this developed into an elaborate political manoeuvre in which I was not allowed a single interview. Camiri became a focal point for the world's press; journalists of all nationalities converged there, to the joy of local commerce, pensions, hotels and brothels. But, although many journalists – not only Latin Americans – were interested in seeing me, none of them managed to break the *cordon sanitaire* around me. Bolivian Intelligence prohibited it and, worse still, concocted false statements. At the same time, articles appeared presenting me as the counterpart to the main figure Debray: the brilliant European intellectual, 'revolutionary in the revolution', versus the obscure unknown South American.

To understand this more clearly, we would need to know what went on behind the scenes when General Ovando and Debray made their pact at the sugar mill and what happened in government-to-government negotiations. It does not seem quite correct to say De Gaulle and Barrientos; perhaps De Gaulle and the Bolivian Army.

General de Gaulle began by changing the staff in the French Embassy in La Paz, and it was no routine change. From his still quite recent confrontation with the colonialist generals of the French Army – leaders of the OAS in the case of Algeria – he rescued his closest collaborator, Dominique Ponchardier, a colonel in military intelligence. He had appointed him as the ambassador to Bolivia in 1964. A few years earlier, in Vietnam, at the fall of Dien Bien Phu, one woman had come to symbolize the honour of France, discredited by the paratroopers who had liter-ally been killing each other to get on the escape helicopters. She was the last official representative to board the last helicopter after helping the last of the wounded. She was a nurse, Genevieve de Galard-Terraube. Her fame and photo had circled the globe under the nickname of 'the Angel of Dien Bien Phu'. Now she was appointed by De Gaulle as the French Consul in La Paz, with the specific mission to attend to the safety and well-being of the beloved French prisoner. As soon as the '*Consulesa*' got her accreditation, she rushed down to Camiri for the first of a series of visits over the next few months, and periodically during the three years after the sentence.

However, it was not only the French government that showed concern for Debray. The No. 1 enemy of a Bolivian govern-ment at war with 'Cuban' guerrillas, the revolutionary government of Cuba to be precise, hastened to maintain a legal and press presence to support Debray, a personal friend of Fidel. The task fell to an interpreter at the Cuban Ministry of the Interior, a Venezuelan woman called Elizabeth Burgos, with whom Debray had a relationship. They had to obey strict rules that the Bolivians imposed, but then frequently modified. Money seemed to be no object.

Up to this point, everything was more or less what I expected: 'Deny everything, *chico*! We don't know you!' Iván had told me in Havana. At the same time, there was sustained coverage of the famous prisoner by the international press, at its height during the trial but continuing afterwards to a point where ordinary Bolivians started to find it sickening. They didn't see why, as well as bearing the brunt of the fatalities, their own victims, the soldiers, should by contrast be anonymous. And the army used all its resources to maintain that anonymity.

The molar at the very back of your teeth is called a 'wisdom tooth' because it appears when you mature, becoming ready for responsibility, ready to settle down. Its only purpose is to cause you pain. The swelling became so noticeable that they decided to send me a dentist. This could only happen in Bolivia. That idea that the dentist was an honorary army officer did not make me very happy, especially since it was our resident psychopath Major Echeverría who had authorized the treatment. However, the captain who arrived – with soldiers to help install a huge great pedal-manipulated chair in my room – was none other than Dr Zamora, brother of the secretary of the pro-Chinese Communist Party. He was a thin, careful man who was not only very friendly and dissipated my fears immediately but also worked with delicacy and absolute professionalism, without X-rays, breaking the molar to extract it from the gum, and causing me no unnecessary pain or any subsequent complications.

The farce of the military tribunal had now been decided. The first measure was to transfer us from divisional command headquarters to somewhere more user-friendly to facilitate legal access for both the preliminary investigation and the defence. I was told to collect my few belongings and, leaving by the tradesmen's entrance, cross the road to the Officers' Club. Roth and Debray were waiting with their guards at a table on the verandah beside the dining room. We were offered coffee, and while Doña María, the club manager, was serving us, a perfectly orchestrated mob of young 'students' (soldiers in civvies and a few real students) 'broke through' the military police barriers, surged through the dining room and onto the verandah in a furious 'demonstration of repudiation of the foreign criminals', and attacked us.

The scene was set up to demonstrate to the international press both the extent of local hostility and the protection afforded us. The officer in charge, a certain navy captain called Hurtado (a largely symbolic rank in Bolivia), was trying to usher us away quickly through another door. He pulled Debray and Roth with him, but I stayed seated drinking my coffee, waiting for the 'irate crowd'. The attackers did not know what to do with this unexpected about turn of the script and came to a halt. The eventual outcome was that Debray was allowed to hold his first press conference, in which he debated with the 'student' representatives. By then, I had been locked in the room that would be mine for the rest of the year, until after we had been sentenced.

The two rooms allotted to Debray and me looked over the street on one side, and onto the tiled interior patio the size of a tennis court on the other. On its right was a covered verandah leading to the Club dining rooms and on its left an entrance for vehicles. On the opposite side of the patio was the toilet and we would walk over to it a couple of times a day. Debray was in the first room, I got the second. To my great surprise, it already had one occupant: Ciro Algarañaz, the *Casa de Calamina*'s inconvenient neighbour, who in his eagerness to join our 'cocaine business', had fallen between two stools and been arrested by the army on the day of the first battle. Legal proceedings had been brought against the two deserters, one of them called Salustio Choque; Algarañaz and one of his labourers; and us, the two foreigners. Roth, in a separate development, had by now been freed and expelled from Bolivia.

Algañaraz was a poor wretch, who felt superior to the Guaraní labourers he exploited. Engaging in illicit activity, the imaginary cocaine, was normal for his class. He kept to himself, and did not say much, out of respect. His family visited him every day with food and fruit, which he refused to share with me.

The defence lawyers arrived; each under his own steam. Jaime Mendizábal made a good impression on me. He was quite young, with experience defending workers from the Bolivian Labour Union (COB), linked to the Sergio Almaraz Paz *Grupo Octubre*. Our first interview was, however, rather difficult because of the restrictions the army wanted to impose. Jaime threatened to leave Camiri and return to La Paz if he was not allowed to exercise his profession unhindered. They wanted to reduce the interview time to a few minutes and even wanted our meetings to take place in front of officers from the army's intelligence division. Jaime had to waste a couple of days in discussions and only had a few hours left to catch the last plane of the week and get back to La Paz with only a few documents available to him.

Getting funds for Jaime to travel back and forth to La Paz, or lodging in Camiri once the trial started, was difficult. In the end it depended entirely on the good will of the *Grupo Octubre* in La Paz and the solidarity committees mobilized by Ana María in Argentina. The Cubans did not contribute a cent, neither to the defence costs nor to support my abandoned family.

While we were still kidnapped, Debray's mother and the French Embassy had hired a well-known La Paz lawyer, Dr Walter Flores Torrico. But things started to go wrong when the lawyer told the press that his client had interviewed Che in Ñancahuazú. Debray was angry because he had made a pact with the Fourth Division not to make this information public. So, the Frenchman swung from having the most famous lawyer in La Paz to not having one at all, and then taking on his own defence. This was not acceptable to the army and they provided him with an army lawyer, Captain Dr Novillo, who performed his duties adequately.

Meanwhile, Jaime and I were having problems too. He wanted to paint me as a militant figure, if possible a heroic one, which would lend a sparkle to what would be his most important legal role to date, possibly with international resonance. But I stubbornly refused to change the role I had assumed and tried to make him understand. What was the point of taking on the role of imbecile to protect myself and all those behind me, if only a month later I was going to put them all at risk for my own personal glorification? The clandestine Argentine network (albeit inoperative) had been safe so far, and I wanted it to continue that way. Onganía's military dictatorship in Argentina had closed the borders with Bolivia and provided the army with new FAL rifles, a Belgian model manufactured in Argentina. Mendizábal did not like my idea, but his loyalty to his group and to me made him stick to his task, even though he could achieve not much more than providing moral support.

As the tribunal took shape, its members started appearing in the Officers' Club and would come to 'see the prisoners' before sitting down for a few beers courtesy of Doña María. This custom extended to all high-ranking Fourth Division officers given that they lunched, dined and drank in the Club. One way or another, we got to know them all. One evening before dinner, Captain Hurtado fetched me from my cell and took me to the dining room to meet the tribunal's prosecutor, Colonel Remberto Iriarte. He was an educated man who prided himself on his fluent French and English, acting as spokesperson for the foreign press.

Needless to say he was not inviting me for dinner, but for 'a little chat'. We stood together in one corner of the lounge. He began with a nationalist preamble about the brotherhood of Andean nations, their common history, and their continual humiliation by arrogant Europeans. The Frenchman, he said, was an overbearing example of this, making statements attacking the army on every possible occasion. On top of the row with his lawyer, his arrogance had upset the Fourth Division commander, Colonel Reque Terán, who in a fit of pique, had made for Debray a convict's suit of green striped ticking with huge numbers on the back and chest, which the psychopath Echeverría had forced him to wear. They shaved his head and exhibited him to the world's press as the 'French mercenary and war criminal', unleashing an international scandal and irate protests from the French Embassy and the *Consulesa*, as well as prominent intellectuals, from Cortázar to Sartre, García Márquez to Bertrand Russell.

The prosecutor let it be known that they were studying the possibility of reintroducing the death penalty, and that the tribunal would ask for the maximum sentence; that my situation was as serious as the Frenchman's without having the support he enjoyed. To prove it, he showed me – without letting go of the paper – a telegram from the president of Argentina which said 'the government of the Argentine Military Junta which I preside, will not raise any objection to the decision taken by the Camiri military tribunal, and accepts the sentence it deems necessary, whatever it may be', signed: 'General Juan Carlos Onganía, President of the Republic'.

The prosecutor went on: given that the armed forces took a more tolerant view towards me as an Argentine, the government of General Barrientos and the Bolivian army, through him, offered me the chance to receive a milder sentence if I told the tribunal that Debray had borne arms like any other guerrilla and taken part in the battles. I replied that I could not say that, because we had been together the whole time and nowhere near the guerrilla's military operations, and did not even know what was happening in the vanguard columns. It would be a false accusation, against my principles, and besides which, it would contradict my own earlier statements. 'Think about it', he said, bringing to an end our 'little chat'.

A few weeks later, shortly before the trial began, the manoeuvre to take me from my cell quietly at night was repeated. This time Captain Hurtado was accompanied by a sergeant with a submachine gun; they took me to a little room on the other side of the patio. There, waiting alone in the dark, was General Alfredo Ovando, exclusive clandestine visitor to prisoners of varying degrees of fame. He told Hurtado to wait outside, and the sergeant to cover him with the submachine gun from the door. A sixty-watt bulb hanging from the ceiling was the only light in this smelly room with peeling walls.

Ovando was tall and thin. He was wearing a uniform shirt, and his general's stars gleamed on his shoulders. He talked in a low voice and, without any preamble, he said: 'I give you my word as a man and as commander of the armed forces that, when the trial is over, you can leave Camiri for the country of your choice, with your wife and daughters, provided you state during the trial that Debray bore arms and took part in the battles. Only that.'

For a second time, I refused the offer point blank. 'I can't do that, general, because it isn't true and it would be a contemptible thing to do.' 'Think of your little girls', he added. 'I *am* thinking of them', I answered. He called the captain and told him to take me back to my cell.

It is useless to speculate about why the Army High Command wanted to accuse the Frenchman – either through proof or false statements – of having borne arms in combat. On the basis of things I remember or have read subsequently, I can suggest reasons but have no proof. To exchange him for technical and military equipment? Was it the only justification for a harsh sentence? Was the harsh sentence needed to negotiate a way out of non-negotiable positions? Did the French government not want to negotiate because they were convinced there would be a legally acceptable result? Did they have to increase the value added of the merchandise to be redeemed? In any case, their quarrel was not with me, according to another officer who used to try and chat, mostly in good faith and non-aggressively. The officers would begin arriving in the late afternoon, before dinner. They would sit at a table on the verandah beside Debray's door, and depending how many the round was for, ordered a 'metre' or 'half metre' of Paceña beer. Bottles were ordered by the square metre and that determined the duration of the 'session'.

Lieutenant Colonel Libera Cortez was a guy you could talk to. He was the officer commanding the patrol reconnoitring the Ñancahuazú river, after the oil workers had seen Marcos's men but before the first ambush. He was one of the old guard from the Nationalist Revolutionary Movement (MNR). Depending on their degree of inebriation, the officers said theirs was a revolutionary struggle too, so they could not help but feel a certain admiration for Che and his guerrillas. In this war of propaganda and celebrities, he said, 'you're less arrogant, you've scored a point, earned our respect'.

The hoo-ha surrounding the trial meant the officers shared the dangers of war with the spotlight of fame: that is, being invited to the Marietta restaurant by *Life* magazine or *Paris Match*. Camiri had become a sought-after posting. The General Staff school benefited from the local war praxis, and its students settled down there. One of its graduates, Captain, then Major, Juan García Mesa, became the new commander of the intelligence section, replacing Echeverría. They were like chalk and cheese. García Mesa had a big wide smile of perfect teeth which got him nicknamed 'Crocodile'. He was determined to show signs of 'good faith' and prison conditions certainly improved on his watch. He was always trying to debate his vision of Latin American history with Debray, supposedly as part of the school's curriculum.

I left the Club on two occasions but they were not related to interrogations or press interviews. I was suddenly put in a jeep – Tania's jeep, in fact, now in army service – and trundled off to Choreti barracks. There, I was taken to a corner of the parade ground to identify corpses brought in from the jungle by helicopter. Anyone who has ever seen a corpse after a couple of days in the tropics will understand how impossible that is. The corpses, like animals carried away by the river, swell up in the positions in which they die: features, posture, any personal traits, disappear. Their skin is the colour of earth, clothes in tatters stuck to it, stiff, unrecognizable organic matter. Their mouths open in dull sounds like distant echoes, their eyes half closed, their gazes lost in infinity, and an appalling smell. I had heard rumours that Joaquín's group, split off from the main column, had been massacred. But the only corpse I thought I recognized was Negro, the Peruvian doctor who had stayed to look after them. He was on his back on the ground a little way from the others, a hand on his chest, as if he was sleeping in the sun, his face serene. I did not see Tania among the bodies, they were all men. But the number of dead, eight altogether, suggested it really was them, and they had been murdered.

Che noted in his diary, on 4 September: 'The radio brings news of a death at a new clash in Vado del Yeso, near where the group of ten men was wiped out, which makes the news about Joaquín look like a trick; but on the other hand, they gave a physical description of Negro, the Peruvian doctor, killed in Palmarito and his body was taken to Camiri; Pelado assisted with the identification. This seems to be a real death; the others could be fictitious or members of the *resaca*. In any case, there is a strange tone to the reports that are now focusing on the areas Masicurí and Camiri.'

The trial kept being postponed from week to week, and we were now in September. Mendizábal told me he had to go through endless red tape to get travel permits, and any other legal or family authorization would be refused. He had continual problems accessing documents that were crucial to his preliminary investigation, and got them only for a few days at the last minute. He said Debray's lawyer, Dr Novillo, gave him more help than the members of the tribunal whose job it was supposed to be.

The prosecution centred on two main points: Debray and myself were accused of being mercenaries and combatants, responsible for thirty to forty deaths to date, plus the wounded, and charges of theft. They would be asking for the maximum sentence, but it was still not known whether President Barrientos's request to restore the death penalty had been granted. The panorama was sombre and uncertain. The defence consisted of denying our participation in any military action whatsoever: in this the Frenchman's statements coincided with mine. However, in an event of such magnitude, once military action was known to have started, only authorized journalists could be considered neutral. That had been Roth's defence before he was released. It was harder to plead innocence when we were already there, and had arrived clandestinely. The explanation I had concocted began to sound like the only plausible one. And I knew it, having spent many sleepless nights, devoured by mosquitoes, trying to come up with an alternative.

Finally Mendizábal arrived to announce that the trial was beginning. He thought our appearance would play an important role; looking like 'gentlemen' rather than dangerous criminals was more likely to win them over. So he took my measurements to get a suit made up for me in La Paz. I was not happy about it. I did not want to be smartened up. But he said he had discussed it with Novillo, and he in turn with Debray, and had decided to change the outlaw look for a more acceptable one. When he came back for the trial, he brought a grey pinstriped suit which was a perfect fit, with an almost new white shirt, tie and shoes, collected by Almaraz's friends in La Paz.

On the morning of the trial, Mendizábal and Novillo waited in the patio to accompany us to the tribunal building. I came out of our room with Algarañaz in his black wedding suit, but Debray caused a delay by registering his rejection to the 'illegal' military tribunal, refusing to participate in it, and centring all attention on himself. In the end, his media show over, and thanks to his lawyer with whom he had been working for the last few days without mentioning that he rejected the trial, Debray appeared at the door to his room in his normal everyday clothes, a navy blue long-sleeved shirt, outside his trousers, unshaven and uncombed, as befitted a proud prisoner, defenceless and alone, confronting the forces of repression. I tried to go back into my room and change, but the soldiers had run out of patience. They made us get in a canvas-covered lorry, waiting at the entrance, surrounded by a mass of photographers, cameramen and more or less spontaneous demonstrators. A French writer knows how to create a good autobiography early in life.

Ana María had arrived in La Paz for the second time, accompanied by a group of prestigious figures: lawyers from the Argentine League for Human Rights, among them Dr Cerruti Costa, a Peronist; Dr Lopez Acotto, from the Socialist Party; and another from the Communist Party whose name I can't remember. However, no matter how much red tape they went through and strings they pulled through local opposition and even government politicians, they were not given permission to travel to Camiri. General Torres put the responsibility for this firmly on to General Ovando's shoulders, and both of them blamed the state of insecurity caused by popular demonstrations against the 'mercenaries'.

Ana María did not get to the opening of the trial, but Ricardo Rojo, forewarned by his first experience, came overland by train to Oruro and then by 'taxi' to Camiri. Mendizábal helped him to get permission to say hello and spend about ten minutes with me. He was not allowed into the courtroom for some technical reason, so we sat outside and chatted under the trees. Ricardo was a great big man, balding, warm and affectionate, and a true son of Buenos Aires. He had a soothing effect on me, exuding love from my Argentine friends. He even extended his feelings of solidarity to Debray who was with us. He greeted him unceremoniously and the Frenchman took to him immediately. He told me later: 'He is the warmest human being I have ever met!' It did not stop Ricardo Rojo being expelled from Camiri.

Finally, the doors of the courtroom opened and we went in. It was a rectangular hall with a raised podium at the end, rather like a church, with all the symbols of the law on display. Facing the podium separated by an aisle, were rows of chairs and benches, lent by the community. A few stairs led up to the podium and on it, beneath a long banner saying 'The sea is our right, regaining it is our duty' and Bolivian flags draped either side like curtains, was a long table covered by a red cloth with another flag over it, and chairs behind for the five judges. To the left was the prosecutor's pulpit; to the right, the table for the court registrar. In front, on the right and perpendicular to the podium, was the table for the defence counsel and at an angle to him, sat the two principal defendants. Behind, in the second row, were the other accused. Local dignitaries and public figures filled the 200 seats on the floor of the hall.

The tribunal members made their solemn entrance, headed by the president of the tribunal, Colonel Guachalla. The latter had been made to look ridiculous a few days earlier when he was asked the million-dollar question by European journalist-philosophers: 'What will the result of the trial be? The death penalty?' Guachalla said he did not know the answer 'because I am not homo sapiens'. From then on, anyone and everyone added fuel to the fire, taking pot shots at the tribunal's honour.

The world's intellectual class mobilized on behalf of its own, and turned morality and ethics on its head, aligning themselves with those on top of the social pile rather than those on the bottom. A German activist interrupted the opening ceremony to read a communiqué questioning the tribunal's legitimacy and demanding the release of the young philosopher, a paradigm of the fight for freedom. All hell broke loose and an exchange of insults, applause, whistling and shouting paralyzed the proceedings and provoked an energetic reaction from the tribunal's president who banged his gavel so hard the wooden top flew off and hit someone in the second row. The session was suspended until the objectors were removed from the hall. Order was restored, but not gravity.

The main charge and other official documents were read out. The prosecutor set out his stall. Evidence, he said, would prove that we had taken part in the criminal events that had thrown a nation into mourning. For our part, through our lawyers, we pleaded innocent to the charges against us. After the order of proceedings for the prosecution and defence was established, the opening session was closed. Our truck left the Officers' Club for the tribunal each morning, Monday to Friday, and although the show went on for a month, its script and especially its finale having been approved to the last detail, the crowd of locals, foreigners and professional onlookers watched every arrival and departure without fail.

The guerrilla war had intensified, producing more fatalities, so there was no cause for satisfaction. Public opinion, however, seemed to have taken a turn to the left, as a reaction to certain repressive measures taken by the army. It had gone from fighting guerrillas to the criminal massacre of striking miners at the Siglo XX mine near Oruro, on the night of San Juan in June. President Barrientos had been seduced by power and moved away from the populism he had once espoused to adopt the 'National Security Doctrine' methods recommended by the US.

There were days of high tension: for example, when the prosecutor presented his witnesses. Yet, like in the theatre, we knew the scenes of emotion and terror were not for real. Both sides lied. Several soldiers, said to be survivors of the ambushes that happened while we were with the guerrillas, related fictitious events, flushed with excitement. One pointed to me and said: 'He was in the river, among the stones, and fired a submachine gun at me.' Another soldier denounced Debray for something similar. None of it was true. One day, the prosecutor called the two officers captured in the first ambush, Major Plata and Captain Silva, who were questioned by Alejandro while I feigned being an armed guard. I had been afraid all hell would break loose, but now I had a feeling it would not happen. If the army was using false witnesses, it was because the real witnesses had not come forward. It was the sort of thing that might happen if two neighbours or work colleagues met by chance in a house of ill repute, a sado-masochistic brothel or a paedophile sect. Both would keep quiet about it, even if they had not explicitly agreed to. They had seen me, armed, assisting a Cuban guerrilla, but I had also seen them behaving in ways unfitting for Bolivian army officers. In the end, neither of them mentioned the fact.

Major Plata made a very measured statement, only verging on the emotional when he talked of the death of soldiers, mere boys. A disaster befalling them out of nowhere, without warning, an unknown enemy: chaos, wailing, shouting, the size of the tragedy, after the lethal strike. However, in reply to the prosecutor's question about some of the prisoners present, he said he had not seen us, either then, or later. Captain Silva, always the more nervous of the two, exaggerated the gun battle, which in fact had been little more than a few volleys, in an attempt to illustrate the danger he had been in. Yet, looking me straight in the eye, he too denied having seen us. As witnesses, they accentuated the dark, evil side of the action, which 'obliged' the army to promise to wipe out the guerrillas.

That left the survivors of the second battle. The little soldier I captured might have had something to say. But the actual witnesses were all false too, obviously so as they recited texts from memory. I think that panic-stricken little boy waited till he got home to his community in Oruro or Sucre to relate what had happened to him. If he even came out alive, that is.

The prosecutor had to prove all the crimes, not only those committed in battle. The guerrillas were accused of stealing from farmers. This was an important detail, because respect for the property and families of the local inhabitants was crucial to encouraging farmers to support the guerrillas, and the government needed, therefore, to undermine this support by discrediting the ethics of the guerrillas in the eyes of the public. To this end, the prosecutor called a peasant farmer from near the village of Gutiérrez, where we had made our first unsuccessful attempt to escape.

It is useful at this point to look at the social composition of the scant population in this area, using the excellent analysis of the subject by Humberto Vázquez Viaña in his book *A Guerrilla for Che*. The original inhabitants were Guaranís (Chiriguanos), who had settled in the Chaco region long before the Spaniards arrived. The MNR's agrarian reform in 1952 had given the Guaranís ownership of land that was de facto theirs, but the dominant social class was made up of mestizos or Quechuas who came to the region with the idea of farming cash crops, whereas the Guaranís economic life revolved around subsistence farming. They were not interested in expanding or modifying their habitat, but were used to changing habitats according to their moods or the climate. They were also historically famous as the indomitable warriors who had stopped the advance of the Inca empire; defeating them in a famous battle at the fortress of Samaipata (a town the guerrillas took on 6 July). They knew the area like the backs of their hands – two children made a mockery of the army cordon by leading Roth to the guerrillas – and were the true owners of the land.

The witness, however, owned the house where the guerrillas had camped and bought a pig that took us all night to barbecue and eat. He was an ambitious mestizo. A Guaraní would have said we paid him for the pig – as we did in actual fact – but this farmer was moulded by capitalist society. He thought the state would pay him for any damage, so he swore the guerrilla had stolen a hundred pigs, the fruit of years of work, as well as destroying his corrals and fences and threatening the women in his family. The room fell silent, overwhelmed by the weight of the prosecutor's argument and the witness's lies. I passed a piece of paper to Mendizábal on which I had written hurriedly: 'Ask him how many trucks you need to transport a hundred pigs!' Mendizábal understood the irony and took the sting out of the charge, which was left with non-existent pigs scattering in all directions.

37

The Death of Che Guevara: 9 October 1967

Through seeing my lawyer every day and the officers at their libations in Doña María's Club, we gleaned much more information than before, and we knew that military actions were not going in our favour. What is more, the officers were euphoric, a bad sign for us in the short term. They would often exaggerate victory or talk of it in a loud voice on purpose, knowing we were listening, but their upbeat mood was enough of an indication. It is hard to simulate such expectations and it was not all show. Things were not going well for the guerrillas. On top of the catastrophe of the rearguard column being wiped out, there was talk of the vanguard being ambushed, with the death of Coco Peredo and other guerrillas.

There was something in the air; you could feel it in the court-room. With judges whispering among themselves and aides-de-camp going to and fro, the prosecutor was losing his audience. According to Mendizábal, Barrientos thought it was all over, and Ovando considered the defeat of the invaders imminent. On the other hand, it could have been a ruse to counteract the political crisis Bolivia had been thrown into since the massacre of the miners in June.

One Tuesday morning, however, excitement turned to jubilation. The judges were in a pow-wow with the prosecutor on the podium, when he suddenly turned round and declared he was in a position to confirm that the famous Che Guevara had been captured and had died from his wounds in La Higuera.

When I had stood before the pile of corpses weeks earlier, I had been gripped by a sense of tragedy way beyond my own personal feelings. Even so, this news hit me like a bullet, targeting my emotions even more profoundly than that macabre spectacle in Choreti. We were on our feet, I don't know why; perhaps the prosecutor had asked for it, to inform the prisoners. A deep silence descended on the room, broken only by the clicks of the cameras shooting in our faces, and a timid buzz of satisfaction that grew as it circulated round the hall. The spectator part of me got the upper hand and, turning my head full circle, I looked at the images around me. The officers on the tribunal were embracing. Debray put his hand to his forehead, in a gesture of despair, and kept it there. The reporters crowded round us, behind the benches. In the windows, cameras held above heads were filming and taking photos. Time seemed to stand still, until the tribunal broke up for the day.

The following morning, Debray asked for the floor and said he wanted to withdraw his defence. From now on, he wanted to be considered equally responsible for the revolutionary project for which those brave fighters had died. He sincerely wished he could 'meet the same fate as my *compañeros*'.

Che's death also meant the capture of his belongings, among them his diary. Reading it would make the show trial practically irrelevant. Yet I was comforted by Che's words. He had said: 'I have to be careful what I write, I could be ambushed one day and my backpack lost . . .' In fact, despite his desire to meticulously chronicle everyday events, he refrained from making any reference to things that could compromise me in any way. Not a single word describing our old project, or the new one under his leadership. Nor did he write things like my telling him about Rubio's death, which I know affected him deeply. And not only that; he made it look as if Inti told him part of the story, when Inti was up on the hill, in the sentry post, and not down by the river where I was. In short, he did not make matters worse for me, nor mention the work I was to do in Argentina. To me, those words, said in the calm of a conversation at camp, show that Che did not say or write anything in vain.

The tribunal made good use of the publicity, and some paragraphs mentioning Debray were quickly sent from the Army High Command in La Paz. But actually the trial came to a rapid close since there was nothing left to discuss. There was just time for the accused to speak. Debray read a manuscript resounding with emotion that he had penned alone in his cell. It was his best moment. With the full military tribunal listening religiously, he gave an interpretation of American history and current revolutionary events as a continuation of it. The courtroom applauded, so did some army officers.

As for me, my lawyer and I had another disagreement. He wanted me to write an historic speech, reclaiming the essence of Che as an Argentine. But I said if I did that, I would have to start telling the truth, and that meant throwing lots of people to the lions. We did not know what the Frenchman was going to say but that was not why Mendizábal was so insistent. For him, history remembers the grand gestures, the famous phrases, not serious intentions or mediocre reality. I did not give a toss for that argument. So I wrote five lines, in which I disclaimed any responsibility, insisting I had come to Bolivia because I was invited to a completely different kind of event. It took me half a minute to read it out but even then I was very nervous about the public's reactions. The tribunal devoted a whole day to 'sitting behind closed doors' (a military/legal euphemism) and when they came back to the courtroom for the last time, it seemed the fiesta was continuing.

The members of the military tribunal were dressed to kill, and even the military police had new uniforms with a lick of paint for the PM on their helmets. Still greater numbers of international press and specially invited guests packed the doorways, and the courtroom, its windows open to combat the heat, was full to bursting. On the podium, the stars of the show played out the final scene, but the cameras were focusing on the extras on the benches.

The tribunal's president, Guachalla, banged his gavel for silence. Another member read the tribunal's verdict, which found us guilty on all counts. Guachalla then pronounced the expected sentence for the foreign mercenaries, Régis Debray and Ciro Bustos: thirty years – a life sentence – in a military prison. The other defendants were freed immediately, either because they had deserted opportunely or had collaborated, or for lack of evidence.

The journalists fought to get near us, while a kind of general enthusiasm enveloped us rather than those who had been freed. One way or another, we had won.

Part Five

Prison in Camiri

38

A Thirty-year Sentence

Thirty years begin alone. Algarañaz packed his things and departed emotionally, leaving the room for my personal use. Like anyone renting an apartment, I did a spring clean. I stuck a photo of Ana María and the girls on the wall, made myself a reading corner under the window where Algarañaz's bed had been, and tried to mend the huge holes in the mosquito netting covering the windows. I rearranged the furniture. It consisted of a box with a primus on which to make coffee, another which served as a library with a few books, and a table and chair from the Club.

The scenery outside the window was neither attractive nor very active. The routine of the Officers' Club carried on as usual, and it was only on weekends that we heard voices, and drunks having arguments. Through the bars on the window, we could spy a slice of life on a corner of the square. Two houses further up to the right was Camiri's only cinema, with matinées and evening shows on Saturdays and Sundays. That's when youngsters would march up and down and, passing our windows, shouted their messages: 'Régis, my love!' or 'Goodbye, Peladito'. And the most daring among them walloped the shutters.

It is strange how seductive criminals are. From then on the rhythm of the day and its eventual altercations depended on what Régis Debray and his team did. The multitude of foreign journalists who had come so far to see him did not want to leave without an interview, so there were press conferences every day. Only with him, mark you. My thirty-year sentence did not merit a single article. Reporting on Debray became staple fodder for European publications for the next three years, on anniversaries, at New Year, on national days, etc. What with processions of journalists, help from the embassy, the *Consulesa* visiting on average once a month, and his wife every two months, Debray had in no way been abandoned. With the approval of the former president of the tribunal, brand new General Guachalla (all the officers involved had been promoted), and Fourth Division commander, General Reque Terán, authorization had been given for Debray to marry Elizabeth Burgos. He asked me to be his witness at the wedding, but the Civil Registry office refused because I had no legal document in my real name. I don't remember who the eventual witness was but the wedding, presided over by the registrar at seven in the evening in the Officers' Club lounge, was a proper social event. With the help of the embassy, the mother of the groom brought cases of Moët Chandon and Chivas Regal, which the tribunal members plus the Fourth Division top brass finished off like magic.

I was invited although I did not have the proper clothes (I had returned the suit), so Debray and I were like a couple of post-moderns in shirt sleeves, among the be-starred generals and be-spangled ladies of the court. The happy couple withdrew early, around nine, and so did I, since there was no dancing. The honeymoon was spent in the Frenchman's cell, transformed into a fairytale bedchamber for a week.

Rumours circulated that we would be transferred to a more serious military prison, and names of terrible places were bandied about: Viacha, high up in the Altiplano; Coroico, in the tropical rainforest. Debray played his cards in favour of the Panóptico prison in La Paz, a sinister place if ever there was one, controlled by a series of mafias. But it had the advantage of a separate political section (given the volatile nature of Bolivian institutions, the inmates went back and forth), safe from pathological prisoners but exposed to ideologues. Debray was so keen on it that the army got suspicious and, thankfully, the idea did not prosper.

Debray saw himself running an international office, connected by telephone, with diplomatic links and a diary choc-a-block with personal interviews. The alternative, he said, was confinement, human and political degradation.

I thought differently. Our relative isolation made us a special case, and since we survived – thanks to General de Gaulle, not to Debray – as products to be used in some future trade-off, we needed to be kept in good condition. They would not leave us to rot in some god-forsaken garrison, yet being on the crest of the wave did not improve our chances. There were too many offended army officers about.

Although the decision had been made, we did not know what it was, and in any case our lives went on with a semblance of routine. Our mail was controlled, but at least there was some. Ana María hoped to get some money at Christmas and New Year art fairs by selling paintings donated by well-known artists (Alonso, Viola, Deira), organized by Ignacio Colombres of the Argentine Artists Association. I was to have no visits this year, but on Christmas Eve, Doña Maria acted as go-between for a series of anonymous transfers.

I was lying on my bed reading when I heard scraping on the metal mesh window giving onto the patio and a voice saying: 'Don Ciro, Don Ciro!' I then saw Doña Maria destroying my repairs to the netting by trying to push in a bottle of champagne and a couple of packets tied with a string. 'Some ladies asked me to give you these, Señor Ciro', and then 'Don't tell anyone, I don't want to get involved.' There was roast turkey with potatoes, rice with mayonnaise, spicy sauces, jams. The champagne was cold, but sweet unfortunately. Only in Bolivia!

In mid-January, Ana María came for a second visit, the first after the sentence. She installed herself in the Marietta: this hotel restaurant-cum-'three-star' headquarters of international organizations had added private bathrooms and showers to its rooms. After discussions with the divisional commander, she was given a permit for two visits a year, allowing her to see me two hours per day during a stay of two weeks or sometimes a bit more, according to the time and money she could afford. On that first occasion, to compensate for Debray's wedding, they gave her a couple of nocturnal visits.

Her personal situation in Argentina, alone with two traumatized little girls under a military dictatorship, had got worse, and she had had to go and live with her parents in a small apartment in Buenos Aires. My girls, about two and three then, drew pictures as all children do and sent them to me. Their works of art almost always involved a strange person-object with four rolling legs and knobs under a rectangle with squiggles on it: it was the television, where they saw the father they had lost. Ana María brought books, carefully selected because of the cost. Some were donated, others were sent by friends: curiously my most intellectual friends, like Oscar del Barco, sent the worst type, like cowboy novels I had never read in my life, because they thought I would only want to read comics. Only once was a book confiscated: *A Plan for Escape* by Bioy Casares, which had nothing to do with prisoners escaping.

In February, Elizabeth Burgos came again. She crossed the patio accompanied by the sergeant in charge of the keys, who retired to wait patiently with a beer in the dining room. I watched from my window only because something was happening outside, but without paying much attention. Five or ten minutes later, the sergeant had to abandon his beer and answer Debray's call. I then saw Elizabeth walk quickly and angrily out of the Club.

According to the sergeant, Debray had refused the time stipulated for the visit, which was short in fact, only half an hour. He told Elizabeth to go back to La Paz on the plane she had come on, one that arrived twice a week in the late afternoon and left the following day. It was yet another episode in the tug of war between omnipotent forces to which I was a mere spectator. However, a few days later, Elizabeth complained in the *Diario de La Paz* (as far as I remember because my newspaper clippings were burned in the fire in San Rafael, Mendoza) that: 'Ciro Bustos' wife lives in Camiri and they share his room like a normal couple, while I only get thirty minutes.'

Thirty years are nothing, it all depends how they are spent. Having a political enemy next door can bring acrimonious confrontations but also some benefit. A religious fanatic of an enemy can be a daily penance. But a revolutionary Pope, enemy of the human race, is Dante's inferno, requiring infinite intelligence and patience to deal with. Debray and I were scheduled to have thirty years of it, although fortunately, in practice, we only did 10 per cent.

To cap it all, to the rumours of our transfer were added rumours about something mysterious being built in the grounds of Fourth Division headquarters just across the road. Some said it was an impregnable fortress, others talked of a cage like in a zoo. And that's what it turned out to be: a cage.

39

Lunchtime in the Cage

Lunch was the strategic objective of our morning. Mornings spent waiting for it went by slowly, ponderously, altered only by the daily rituals of barracks life: changing of the guard, insulting chore dodgers, square bashing and new profanities. But that all went on outside the cage, on the other side of the walls and mesh netting. Inside the cage, the only turmoil was inside our own minds. Our attention was divided between the small pleasures of freshly made coffee, news on the radio, or the magical power of music, transporting us through the bars of the peephole in the door and wafting us away on the vibrant air of the morning light.

But mornings could be busy too, when the sudden clatter of the cage's chains and locks clearly announced a 'visit'. It might be another lesson in political zoology. A recently-posted major or colonel, accompanied by his wife, keen to see the international fauna, the jewel in the Fourth Division's crown and envy of the entire army. They would open the three doors, and we would have to come out to stand in the patio of the cage like monkeys. We could see the officer and his wife, and sometimes their children, looking at us excitedly, and we had to listen to their stupid questions.

Or it might be some sergeant rushing in all of a sweat to inform us of the new rule, going into effect immediately, prohibiting electric light after ten at night. Tragic news indeed, because the night had to be attacked with a goodly bout of reading, totally divorced from the outside world, far from the cage, alone with our complex and neurotic thoughts. For a few hours we escaped the pettiness of our reality, rediscovered our inner selves, connected with our consciousness. But night has its dangers too. Doctors say it is when our organism lowers its defences, neglects its psycho-physical alliances, and surrenders to death.

What's more, the inhabitants of the night come out. Cockroaches reigned supreme. They were huge, some about five centimetres long, a sort of rusty red colour, appearing from God knows where, and advancing along the supports holding up the tiled roofs until they all but covered them. And they didn't just lie there quietly. They bustled and jostled with almost inaudible crackling noises. Many lost their footing and fell onto the unsuspecting reader, like a fleeting fag end. The rain of falling cockroaches was so bad I managed to beg a mosquito net off the sergeant. Mosquitoes were on hand too, a source of permanent harassment. If my pyrethrum and *palo santo* spiral ran out, I was stuffed. They arrived with the *El Mundo* radio news at around nine and battle was waged all night: not conducive to enjoying reading and music. There were some nice bugs, almost good company; but others were invisible, clandestine, and attacked the few books and clothes we had.

The fiercest creatures were a kind of termite, invisible to boot. Once inside a book, they did not wait to demolish it entirely, as any self-respecting termite would do, but spurred on by a peculiar traveller's instinct, continued without pausing through all the adjacent books, no matter how thick the book, how good the paper, or how famous the author. When they reached the end of the shelf, they began tunnelling homewards, until someone picked up a book and found the insides eaten by the subterranean censor.

The night stimulated feelings. I wanted to live it to the full, make it last longer, delay consciousness. Night also heightened perception of the good and bad around me, as well as the things I longed for; the suppressed desire made me sweat profusely,

running off in rivulets, soaking the mattress. Despite the spotlights on the four corners of the cage that kept the patio
permanently lit, I sensed the dawn approaching with a mixture of
relief and resignation. There was still time for a period of quieter
sleep, free of demons.

Between seven and eight in the morning, the chains jangled,
the door screeched, and guards came into the patio to undo our
padlocks and open our cell doors. We had half an hour for our
ablutions. We shuffled out like lingering ghosts, piss-pots in
hand, and took turns to use the facilities while we discussed the
radio news. Back in our cubicles, we returned to the long morning wait for lunch.

With the inauguration of our brand new quarters, we lost our
access to the food in the Officer's Club, our former home. The
foot soldier's daily fare, *lagua* as it was called, was a soup of maize
flour with noodles and bits of fatty meat or *charqui* floating in it.
To a petty bourgeois stomach, unaccustomed to the rigours of
permanent hunger, it acted like a laxative. With thirty years
stretching before us, the *Consulesa* arranged for Debray's food to
be brought from the Marietta, and Ana María made the same
arrangement for me, paying for it on her six-monthly visits. But
León was not part of the deal. He got the *lagua*.

The food contract with the Italian owner of the Marietta
brought our relationship with the restaurant full circle, marking a
year since that first dinner on its open-air terrace. The restaurant
had had an unexpected boom since then, as Camiri became a
centre of international journalism. On the pretext of attending to
gastronomic specifications, the Italian came to our cage and we
discussed our refined culinary palates with him personally. We
ended up with three alternative dishes: roast chicken with potatoes and mixed salad, pasta with meat stew, and steak with onions
or fried eggs plus chips and salad. No arrangement was made for
wine. We had to wait two years for this shortcoming to be recti-
fied and, left to our own devices, we bribed the guards. Some
situations were really comical: 'Soldier!' we called through the

wire mesh. 'Yes, señor', he answered, standing to attention. 'When you go off duty, buy me a bottle of wine!' I said, more as an order than a request. 'No, señor, I can't!' he replied, uneasily. 'What do you mean, you can't? And while you're there, have a few snacks on me.' He ended up agreeing. An hour later, he was back with a bottle hidden in his clothes. It was about then that León's luck changed.

León was a great guy, a fantastic human being, a disciplined militant whom the Communist Party had put in charge of the *Casa de Calamina*. He had left his wife and children in the Beni but they were abandoned by the Communist Party when it broke with the guerrillas, and he stayed on as a putative farmer. He ended up as guerrilla-cum-cook. Che appreciated him, writing in his diary on 27 September: 'León had a lot of promise.' Sadly, that was the day after the vanguard column was caught in an ambush and he became separated from the group. According to León, he abandoned his backpack but not his gun – not a sign that he intended to desert – and scrambled up to the pre-established emergency point. Nobody else made it up there. He waited until it was clear he had to leave the area. On his way, he came across the house of an oil worker who promised to take him out by tractor, but only if he left his gun which was too noticeable. He lent him clothes to change into but, instead of keeping his word, took him straight to an army post where he turned him in.

During the first year of the cage's life, León shared his cell with Paco for a few months. But their personalities were totally incompatible. Paco suffered from bouts of unbearable depression and was finally moved to a room in the military police headquarters over the road. So León ended up as the only inhabitant of the best room, the new one. But the wider space only increased his sense of isolation, lying alone on his bed, in an empty universe. Not even the thought of lunch helped him pass the hours. When Ana María came, she brought me non-perishables like sugar, coffee, cigarettes and toiletries, and within the realms of the possible remembered León. He urgently needed pulses and cereals, a few tins and cooking oil or fat, to make delicious dishes from his native Beni.

There was a military coup in Bolivia in October 1969, when the army openly seized power and General Ovando became president, and the coup coincided with the 'wine' period, our third year in the cage, when conditions improved. The doors of our cells stayed open until seven in the evening, illegal deals with the guards were much easier, communication between us was freer, and much easier with the outside world as well. I thought chess would be an excellent pastime so I carved a set of figures from a broom handle and drew squares on some cardboard, with the idea of copying games I had seen in magazines and improving my rudimentary knowledge. León was enthusiastic too so we decided to go one better. Our 'suppliers' got us good bits of wood without knots in, and we asked for other materials like sandpaper, saws to cut wood, black shoe polish, cardboard and shaving knives, with which we made instruments to carve with. I designed a chess set inspired by Niemeyer's cathedral in Brasilia which was beautiful and modern and would not be too hard to carve. We set to work.

The first thing I had to do was teach León to work in something so far from his normal work: he was a farmhand, a gaucho. To him, wood was cut with machetes or axes. I drew a proper scale model, with the exact measurements, and numbered the stages he would have to follow. Since we had no workbenches or clamps, we had to carve, polish and file all the figures while they were still on the long broom handle, leaving a good margin between them, before sawing them apart. The fine details, like the horses heads, the queen's crown, the king's cross, the tops of the castles and bishops, were the last steps and the most difficult for him, but he learned and he did pretty well in the end. The black pieces were dyed with shoe polish, while the white ones were left as polished wood. I made the chess boards.

One afternoon, an officer saw us playing in the patio. He liked the chess pieces and wanted to buy them. León sold him his set.

He showed off his purchase to his fellow officers and there followed a wave of orders, that increased with time. León rose to the challenge and virtually ended up with a workshop producing unique quality artisanal chess sets for the local market. I don't remember the price but it rose as the finished product improved, and ended up being a good source of income for León, allowing him to change his diet, his clothes, his spirits and his humour. Although I laboured from dawn to dusk too, all the income went to him. His detailed descriptions and day by day reconstructions of what had happened, every event, every anecdote, drama or amusing situation, were payment enough for me.

Although I aimed originally to write only what I saw with my own eyes, I think it is valid to include what I heard with my own ears too. So I am repeating one of León's stories, probably the only time he told it, as we worked on our handicrafts. One day, while the guerrillas were in one of their temporary camps, with the army on their tails, he went down to get water and found an M2 left beside the stream. Returning to his job in the kitchen, he told Che, who sent someone, maybe Pombo, to find out who it belonged to. He returned with the rifle which turned out to belong to Che himself. The punishment had already been established so Che, who allowed no privileges for anybody, least of all for himself, did kitchen skivvy duties for a week. León told me it was harder for him, the cook, than for the helper, because how could he say: 'Ramón, wash the pans'? He tried indirect methods like: 'The pans need washing . . .' or 'I need water . . .' and the chief went off with the jerry can to get it. 'We're low on wood . . .' and Che went looking for dry sticks for him. There was nothing León could do, or he would have been punished for toadying, something Che could not stand. All Che's appreciation of León was wiped out by a sentence in his diary on 3 October. It said: 'Here ends the story of two heroic guerrillas', one of whom was León.

Sometimes at the weekend, León ordered meat to barbecue: spare ribs, steak, etc., and a carafe of wine. We had real feasts, and even the Frenchman joined in, although being a refined gourmet prevented him from enjoying criollo-style barbecued spare ribs.

The local bourgeoisie and the upper echelons of the army used to pay me to draw portraits of their children and even their wives. In the worse case, they brought old photographs of dead family members, fathers or grandfathers immortalized in inscrutable poses, made worse by horrendous retouching or stylized backgrounds that the actual descendents wanted to make more human and bring up to date. Dogs, cats and horses were likewise my noble models. I sketched officers' wives, Reque Terán's daughters, García Mesa's white horse, all enhanced to make them more beautiful, except for the horse. A local lady brought her three children to my cell, one after another, and finally sat herself. She gave me photos of the drawings that I still have.

One morning, a nurse came to examine me for my bronchial infection. My blood pressure, which was usually boringly normal, took a leap skywards. She was a spectacular woman, tall and strong, and very beautiful. She wore a long skirt buttoned at the front with disconcerting slits up the sides revealing sculptured legs, and an abundantly filled white linen blouse. While she fulfilled her duties with the pressure metre, the thermometer, and tiny syringes, I made various attempts at verbal rapprochement, which was the only thing I could aspire to anyway. She told me not to play with fire. She was General Barrientos's local girlfriend. As well as having been being president, he was a pilot and used to take advantage of his professional skills to make frequent visits to distant garrisons, piloting planes and helicopters himself, trips during which, accidentally on purpose, he attended to his extensive and well-endowed harem. Barrientos was 'El Macho' par excellence.

The woman's reticent replies awakened my interest, and I made sharper, more provocative comments, finally inquiring tenaciously: 'Is he as macho as he's painted? What technique does he prefer?' She intimated that he was without doubt very macho, but not great on subtlety: that he arrived like the master taking possession of his property and left deep in discussion with his advisers. 'What a waste!' I suggested wickedly. 'He should stick to planes; a woman is not a machine, but something much more exquisite, that takes to the air only when she is finely tuned.' And I set out in detail, sitting on the other side of the table from her, what button by button, step by step, kiss by kiss, in all minutiae, a person of such rank should do. 'Would you do that?' she asked, as she gathered up her things, her neck and face covered in blushes.

When the door closed behind her and I was alone, enveloped in the lingering fragrance of her perfumed talc, a state of vague unease came over me. Would I end up in one of those terrible punishment garrisons in the middle of the jungle? More than playing with fire, I had started a blaze. But no. It did not happen. Instead, to my surprise, she came back the following week with a weird and wonderful present: a very beautiful angora cat, with one golden eye, the other a blueish grey. It was her favourite pet. She brought it in her perfumed arms and gave it to me like a warm purring offering. I called her Pocha.

Pocha had absolutely no problem changing owner and domicile and, after a quick inspection of my cell, decided to stay. She lived with us for several weeks and provided continual entertainment, locked in continual battle with the patio mice until there wasn't one to be seen. Then one night tragedy struck; she got stuck in the drain under my cell. Despite my pleas, not even the most indulgent guard was going to dig up the cell floor to save her. You could say she died in my place.

Pocha's disappearance meant regressing to the everyday boredom of the cage, to its petty power relationships, time at a standstill, and life in the fourth dimension. In the outside world there were radical changes in society, political and military catastrophes, and historical advances by mankind, like setting foot on the moon; but our world was a watertight compartment, which had minimum impact, nationally, locally, even on the barracks.

The radio was our umbilical cord. News and music reaching us over its magical airwaves was our sustenance. Initially, I had a small radio that received local stations and, with great difficulty, *Radio El Mundo* from Buenos Aires. Ana María brought me a better one with several short waves so I could listen to national and municipal stations from Buenos Aires with continuous classical music programmes. What a privilege to be able to enjoy a symphony. León inherited my small one, and the sounds often overlapped, with Mahler acquiring unusual rhythms. If there was especially important news at night, I banged on León's wall and held the radio against it so he could hear it more clearly. In the final months, the radio became even more important.

The communications room of the Fourth Division's headquarters was a few metres on the other side of the wall. Throughout the day we could hear the communications officer's efforts to make himself understood, or repeat inconsequential messages to do with the division's internal functioning and even of a more personal nature, to other divisions or regiments round the country. Sometimes climatic conditions hindered reception and voices rose until they were howling. Better results would probably have been achieved by going up onto the roof and doing away with the Hertzian waves altogether. Distant voices, heard through whistling and crackling, as if the communication was coming from a First World War battlefield, asked a troop truck to reply, inquired after last month's payments, or requested a medical pass. A couple of months before our release, the conversations began to concern us and became menacing. A kind of internal opinion poll was being held over the airwaves. There was no doubt that rumours of our release were getting the officer class worked up. The paradox began emerging, like a photograph from the developing tray.

Stuck in the cage, with neither voice nor vote, we were audio witnesses to a tide of contradictory opinions, from clashes between divisional commanders and officers of the High Command. They ranged from benevolent plans for deportation to demands for the firing squad. Sounds, not only voices, dominated our lives. The rattle of the chain on the door opening for lunch could be festive, like a pianola, or funereal, reminiscent of the gallows.

Relations between the Frenchman and myself depended on his mood swings, and the news that arrived officially, via the embassy and Elizabeth, or unofficially, through journalists coming to interview him. Every now and again, we heard the chain on the door jangle and, peeping through the hole in our cell door, would see them come to fetch Debray. He would go out with his best hang-dog look: unshaven, shirt outside his trousers, in sandals, but without quite managing a convincing Monte Cristo. When they came back, you only had to look at him to imagine what kind of mood he was in. He could spend days inside his cell, only coming out for minimum exercise; or he could have sudden bouts of cordiality and seek me out to pace up and down the patio discussing the latest world news, like the 10 million tonne Cuban sugar harvest, the Seven Day War, the moon landing, or, changing the subject, wanting urgent information about Borges, about where in Buenos Aires was the corner of Maipú Street where the writer lived, and how far it was from the National Library. 'I must go and see him as soon as I get out of here', he told me.

Literature was a bridge that could have united Debray and I, but it was a bridge he crossed unilaterally. Over the course of her visits, the *Consulesa* had brought him many important books and he built up a large library arranged in boxes stacked as shelves along the wall separating our cells. It included philosophical publications, including *Tel Quel*, and new unopened books that, after selecting certain ones, he sent back. He told me proudly that he had got his 'prison writings' out by putting single written sheets between the non-guillotined pages of the books he sent back. Yet he never lent me a single one of the numerous books in Spanish that Elizabeth brought, although he could borrow any he found interesting in my small collection.

However, he left his masterpiece of sado-egoism to the end of our last year as prisoners, after Elizabeth's last visit. He had read

The City and the Dogs and *The Green House* by Mario Vargas Llosa that Ana María had brought from our bookshelf at home for me to re-read. The Peruvian's entrance onto the stage of literature in Spanish was a huge event; he was then without a doubt the greatest novelist in Latin America, capturing its turbulent history and the creative genius of its peoples. (He was an enthusiastic admirer of the Cuban Revolution in those days.) Debray and I had also discussed the whole gamut of Caribbean, Central and South American writers, those of the 'boom' and their precursors. On that particular day, he came into the patio, where León was preparing a barbecue, waving a packet of papers in his hand. 'Look what I've got', he said very excitedly, and showed me the proofs of a Peruvian edition of Vargas Llosa's latest book *Conversations in the Cathedral*. It had already been published in Buenos Aires and I had read amazing reviews in magazines from there. The writer himself had sent them from Lima via Elizabeth. Always short of things to read, especially as it had been ages since Ana María's last visit, I was thoroughly delighted and naturally asked him to lend it to me as soon as he could. His reply was memorable: 'I'll lend it to you later, for Christmas . . . let's say Christmas of 1995.' This was September or October of 1970. Ana María brought the book to Chile after our release and I read it there, but thinking back to that unkind retort, he must have already known we would be leaving soon, before Christmas.

The way he behaved for the three years we shared that space, knowing his back was being watched by Castro and De Gaulle, two of the greatest living heroes of the twentieth century, caused me no end of problems. No sooner had we arrived in the cage, in March 1968, than he set up his lines of communication, again through the *Consulesa*, so that his isolation was no more than a relatively fruitful inconvenience, like a writer shut away up a Swiss mountain with his books, papers, pipe and cognac. He planned a method of dialectical cut and thrust with the local centre of power, well coordinated with international support and regular visits from carefully chosen people. Straight off, he proposed a hunger strike to protest our conditions, and wanted to involve Paco and León, the two Bolivian survivors. They had not been tried or sentenced, so they were merely hostages of the army. They had absolutely no protection and knew that they would be the ones paying for any broken plates. I did not agree either, because a hunger strike influences the general public not the oppressors. Without adequate press coverage putting pressure on the state, it achieves nothing. And even so, if the state is represented by an 'Iron Lady', as happened in the UK with the Irish prisoners, dozens of people can die and the powers that be don't lift a finger. We could not even tell the Italian to stop sending us food. The guards would have calmly eaten our lunch, without anyone in Camiri even knowing about it. But he had already decided and I could not refuse without having the whole world on my back. At least I got it restricted to the two of us who were serving sentences, leaving the Bolivians out of it.

The strike went on for ten days and was lifted without any gains except that the *Consulesa* got them to promise to discuss the matter of a transfer again. We went back to our lunch routine, but the anecdote was registered in the Frenchman's laboured autobiography.

Debray subsequently asked if he could hire my lawyer, Jaime Mendizábal, so he could deal with the legal matters related to the negotiations about a possible transfer. I did not control Jaime's time or workload, so I told Debray to ask him himself via the *Consulesa*. Jaime agreed and returned to Camiri. He reassured me that he was still my lawyer even though he would deal with some matters for Debray at the same time. He thought the transfer to prison in La Paz was only useful if we had good political support. If not, the Panóptico was a terrible place compared to the exclusivity of the cage. Working with Debray would also open up a source of income that Jaime had never had with me; the Almaraz group were paying his costs out of solidarity. Cuba and France would be picking up his bill from now on.

Cuba was financing two or three monthly visits by his wife, a brand new 'lieutenant' in the Cuban security services. She arrived laden down with top drawer revolutionary presents: quality cigars in silver tubes; mature Bacardí rum; books, reports . . . During this last year, Elizabeth would stay no more than ten minutes alone with him before coming out and sitting on the wall to get some air. 'I can't stand it', she would say; I don't know if she meant being cooped up in the cell. We used to chat a bit, as if we were not connected in any way, as if dropping the odd slanderous comment was an occupational hazard.

Cuban responsibility for this, like the presents, came from the top. The Cubans who knew me, had worked with me, and knew I had kept silent, held their tongues too, murmuring only on the odd occasion, here and there, their solidarity and understanding. Among them was the Cuban intelligence officer I met in Copenhagen twenty years later. He had received the letter I sent to Furry when he became minister of the interior, and he told me: 'Furry read it in my presence and said "I knew Pelado would write something like this. It is heartfelt, but solid."'

Sitting on the wall under the wire mesh, Elizabeth talked about people we both knew, all of them members of Barbaroja Piñeiro's intelligence apparatus currently re-writing history. She told me who was doing what, recent promotions or postings, what country or continent they were in, as if she felt completely at ease with me, one of the gang, on holiday. But she did not bring so much as a greeting from anyone, no word of encouragement or reproach. Nothing. Not even a matchstick.

Some very important and relevant things had happened during our first year in prison. In January 1968, three Cuban survivors of Che's guerrilla group made it out to Chile, with the help of some of Inti's old contacts in the Communist Party. Six guerrillas had escaped the dragnet, but one of the three Bolivians, Ñato, was badly wounded and begged his *compañeros* not to leave him alive in the hands of the army. Inti and Dario stayed in Bolivia while the Cubans were welcomed to Chile by the left-wing senator and presidential candidate, Salvador Allende. Also in the first few months of 1968, Che's diary, and the hands with which he wrote it and held it on his knees, were suddenly taken to Cuba by an unexpected messenger. He was an old acquaintance of mine, a Marxist and former leader of the MNR: Victor Zanier, friend of Amarú Oropeza, my Bolivian potter friend in Buenos Aires.

The operation was organized by Antonio Arguedas, minister of the interior in President Barrientos's government, an ex-Communist and self-confessed CIA agent during the previous six years. On orders from the CIA, his last order as it turned out, he phoned his ex-fellow traveller Zanier, a former assistant to Hernán Siles Suazo, political leader of the 1952 MNR revolution, and arranged to meet him on a certain corner in La Paz, where Arguedas himself picked him up in an official government car. (I learned this from Zanier thirty years later.) With no more than a laconic greeting after all those years, he handed him a package saying: 'You'll know what to do with this', and dropped him off at the next corner. In it, Zanier found photocopies of Che's diary and a jar of formaldehyde with two white hands floating in it.

Not knowing exactly 'what to do with this', he began by leaving it in the safe house of a friend. Then he organized a trip to Chile, where he contacted the journalist Hernán Uribe of *Punto Final*, the weekly journal of the MIR (Movement of the Revolutionary Left), a left-wing group with links to Cuba. The MIR helped him continue his journey to the island with another of its journalists, Mario Díaz, and deliver the microfilmed diary to the Cuban leadership, and – some time afterwards – Che's hands.

The laurels went to the CIA agent, Antonio Arguedas, who had previously been unmasked as the 'photocopy thief' by the Bolivian Army High Command. They had asked to borrow three pages of the Ministry's only copy; pages which were missing from the edition published in Cuba. Now without the backing of his former boss, Barrientos, who also had links to the CIA, Arguedas had to go on an international pilgrimage with his CIA minders, to try and explain the psychological motives behind his strange conversion from being the head of anti-guerrilla repression to sympathizer of the Revolution.

The global Left, however, was united in its devotion and saw only what the central committee wanted it to see, not what was obvious. And it saw in this agent of imperialism a solitary hero who risked his life and his lucrative lifestyle as a spy for love of the Revolution. Arguedas lived in Cuba for a time (like Ramón Mercader, Trotsky's killer), was showered with honours, received the honorary title of '*compañero*', attended 26th of July ceremonies in the Plaza de la Revolución in the government box, and returned to Bolivia two *coups d'état* later. He was killed in a bomb explosion in La Paz in the 1990s.

But the question is: Why did the CIA tell its agent to give Che's diary to the Cubans? My answer, after much reflecting alone in the darkness of my cell, has the logic of the simple: the diary had to be edited by a source that was above reproach since the masses of avid international readers needed to be satisfied it was authentic. There had to be no doubt about a single comma in the book, which would have been impossible had it been edited by anyone but the Cubans, and in particular if it had been done by the Americans. For the US, the diary represented the incontrovertible confirmation of the failure of a particular line of action, as told by its principal prophet and exponent. But the diary had a different, imperishable, value: the value of honesty itself as the identity of a revolutionary.

The following year, Inti, the Bolivian guerrilla leader, reappeared to proclaim: 'Let's go back to the mountains.' But it was not long before he was found in La Paz and killed by Colonel Quintanilla's secret police. The Peredos' youngest brother, Chato, led another guerrilla attempt in the 1970s in Teoponte, in the Yungas, with a group of Catholic students who, as usual, proved more idealistic than tough practical fighters. Most of them lost their lives to the jungle. The army rescued the survivors.

In April 1969, the helicopter in which President Barrientos was travelling, after attending a ceremony in an indigenous community, got caught in some electricity cables and crashed. Barrientos was killed, and was succeeded by his vice president, Jorge Siles

Salinas, for a short time (presidential terms in Bolivia were never very long). He was succeeded by a woman, Lidia Gueiler, until the liberal-populist faction of the army (the Ovando-Torres line), finally took power again, with General Ovando as president.

Changes on the national political scene were felt only marginally in the cage. Our conditions improved slightly with the arrival of every new Divisional Commander and other officers: longer recreation periods, newspapers and all night light did not turn it into a three star hotel, but things were more relaxed. The plans for our transfer to La Paz did not materialize and I suspect that Mendizábal, our common lawyer, represented Debray legally at higher levels of negotiation. There was no fall in international press interest in the Frenchman, and he had become an illustrious protégé of North American and European intellectuals. Only once, quite unexpectedly, did a visitor ask to speak to both prisoners. A joint interview was arranged. For the first time, both our doors were opened. The officer in charge had instructions to take us into the divisional headquarter's offices. We looked at each other in surprise; we had no idea what to expect.

A tall, round, sweaty Italian was waiting for us in a well-ventilated office, with big windows onto the garden. Our visitor turned out to be one of the world's most important film directors. Fortunately, my passion for cinema meant I recognized him. We Argentines see films from many different international sources, but primarily American, owners of the distribution circuits; French, paladin of our cultural aspirations; and Italian, guardian of our emotional and artistic roots. We also saw Argentine films, and Russian, English, Swedish and German, but Italian maestros were far and away the most familiar and popular: Vittorio de Sica, Roberto Rosellini, Luchino Visconti, Cesare Zabattini, and another more universal genius, influenced by neo-realism, Francesco Rosi. I had seen his classic works of protest: *Salvatore Giuliano*, and *Hands over the City*, which dealt with the relationship between crime and the political system, the criminal and the power of the state.

Rosi had not come to ask us to tell our stories or to get a scoop. It was out of a profound respect for history in which, despite the marginal, secondary nature of our roles, we had a place. Continually mopping his sweaty bald pate, obviously disturbed by the presence of the head of Bolivian intelligence, but in a dignified manner, he told us in Italianate Spanish that he wanted to work on the epic tale of Che in Bolivia, with a view to eventually making a film. He wanted to know what we thought about the idea.

Debray gave me the floor – for a second time – though it would have been logical for him to do it, given his star quality. Taking a deep breath, I began with a few niceties. I don't remember the exact words, of course, but I remember the sentiment. I said what an honour it was to be in the same room as the auteur of *Giuliano*. I said I knew his work and respected it, and for that very reason I thought a certain distance from recent events was needed, because what had happened was much more significant than a just cine- matographic anecdote. And in any case, a complete evaluation would have to include Cuba, the genesis of Che's project in Latin America. Rosi listened attentively, nodding. Debray spoke in the same vein, with more rhetorical precision. The Italian maestro thanked us, I think he was moved and really grateful, and suddenly the meeting was over. I never heard any mention of Rosi's venture again.

My other three visitors, apart from Ana María, met me in that same room for an hour. The first was my brother Avelino who accompanied Ana María when she brought our little girls Paula and Andrea, to help look after them while their mother was with me. The girls are not on my list of visitors because you don't say 'today I met my left arm' or 'I spent time with my legs'. I was worried about the possible effect the cage would have on them, but in the end they came for two days and each spent one night squashed up with me in the camp bed. I don't know who was worst affected, them or me.

Avelino was the brother closest to me in age and political

commitment. He was a doctor in a poor area of San Rafael. He would write his patients' prescriptions and, chiding them, give them money to pay the chemist. I had told Ana María to warn him not to show his emotions in front of the guards. He behaved completely naturally, as if he were mainly concerned with the state of my health, and disbursed snippets of news about the family, my mother, my brothers and sisters, in front of the officer, who even joined in the conversation. Although he had to wait in Camiri for the whole group to return to Argentina, they did not let him visit me again.

My second visit, which I more or less expected, was from one of our lawyers in Córdoba, my friend Horacio Antonio Lonatti. He came on behalf of my old *compañeros* in Salta who had almost all been released by then, except for Héctor and Federico, who were serving longer sentences. It was bound to be a very emotional meeting given Lonatti's exceptionally compassionate nature, the mutual affection we felt for each other, and the difficulty of passing on greetings from each *compañero* under the ridiculous regulations and the censor's watchful eyes and ears. There was no time for full details of all their lives but they sent words of solidarity and encouragement, even though they had had to keep silent during my trial.

The third and last visit was unexpected, although I had intuited something a couple of days earlier. The cinema, now on the opposite side of the road from us, doubled as a loud speaker in the afternoons, with deafening publicity for its own films and a variety of popular entertainment: dances, festivals or bands passing through Camiri. For the past few weeks it had been announcing the forthcoming visit of a 'great Argentine folk quartet' who would be playing on a specially built stage on the football pitch. It was none other than *Los Chalchaleros*, my friends from Salta. They negotiated permission to see me. Only one of them got the permit, and only because it was them. Once again I was taken to the office in command headquarters only to find my dear friend Ernesto Cabeza being very well looked after

by several officers, who were staunch admirers. I had not seen
them for many years, and had avoided their seeing me in Montevideo airport when I was working clandestinely. Accustomed to
international fame, Cabecita was not impressed by the military
fawning, but he was moved by our meeting. 'What a fuck-up,
Che!' he said over and over again, 'what a fuck-up!' He offered
to buy me whatever I needed in the way of clothes, radio, TV,
which we couldn't get in Camiri, and he paid my food bill in the
Marietta where they were staying. We chatted about a range of
unconnected things until our time was up, he said goodbye with
a big hug and went off to a night performance in a nearby town.
We never saw each other again.

General Ovando taking power meant a substantial change in
Bolivia's political scenario. He represented the army's national-
populist sector that wanted to resuscitate the worker-peasant
government of the MNR, of which the officers had nearly all been
supporters. The opposition was the reactionary pro-imperialist
sector to which Barrientos had belonged, and of which General
Banzer was later the heir. Ovando gathered around him a team
comprised of some notorious old lefties and other younger ones
who set out a clearly nationalist programme. In the cage we
quickly detected changes, starting with the new Fourth Division
Commander who, unlike his predecessors, never came to stare at
us in the zoo. Instead, he appointed his aide de camp, a certain
Lieutenant Ortiz, as his personal representative in charge of the
prisoners. He came to see us every day, cordially inquiring about
our complaints and needs.

The cell doors stayed open during the day and sometimes even
until the main door was locked for the night. The priest from the
church next door – Camiri Cathedral, no less – was authorised to
visit weekly but for the sake of political coherence I courteously
refused the first, and last, occasion he came to see me. Debray
accepted, however, and received him on Sundays after Mass.
Meanwhile, the foreign oil companies were nationalized. In
charge of this particular task was the most revolutionary member

of the civico-military government, Marcelo Quiroga Santa Cruz, minister of mines and petroleum. From his parliamentary seat as a young deputy – together with the poet Héctor Broda Leaños, both coming to socialism from the Socialist Falange – he had defended our cause.

Several measures were taken that made us think things would change for us. In the medium term, the Ovando–Debray relationship forged in May/June of 1967 at La Esperanza sugar mill started to function again. A journalist-cum-adviser to General Ovando – Gustavo Sánchez, brother of Major Sánchez, detained by the guerrillas on 10 May 1967 – began visiting the Frenchman in his cell. Halfway through this last year, 1970, Debray was on a good mood day and he told me he was writing an essay on the measures needed to transform a bourgeois army into a popular revolutionary force for President Ovando. To my surprise, he asked me to read it.

It was a work that examined the basis of the Bolivian Army: its origin and its previous attempt at reform during the revolution of 1952. That attempt failed because it did not change the army's mentality and hierarchy by incorporating the masses; it opportunistically and temporarily created workers' militias in the mines instead. An army is born revolutionary, not created after workers' massacres. It is the praxis of historical events that creates class consciousness; the armed wing of the masses that takes power by force. Officers should be trained to defend the interests of the masses, not those of the oppressors. They should be the vanguard, in the forefront of mobilizing task forces for emergencies, reconstruction, education and development. Written with dialectical arguments and expressed in a didactic manner, Debray's essay suggested that the necessary requirement for bringing about this change might not be within the reach of the actual philosophy of the Army High Command, so the first thing to change would be that mentality.

This very interesting essay was handed over on the last visit of Sánchez, Ovando's press secretary, who up until the end of

1970 used to greet me very amiably as he came in and out of the cage. His eyesight must have been as bad as his secret sources of information. Only a few years later, this same Sánchez wrote a book on the capture in Bolivia and extradition to France of the Nazi Klaus Barbie, in which he stated in passing that, at the Camiri trial, I had been given a light sentence of only a few years and released a few months later after collaborating with the army, commanded in those days by . . . the very same General Ovando whom they were helping with the above mentioned work.

This type of double game got the Frenchman into trouble because in his visible battles with the local military authorities on behalf of the press, Debray sometimes lost the plot. This happened to him with Oriana Fallaci, the Italian journalist who 'interviewed history'. She arrived in Camiri to interview the young rebel philosopher for an article, and following the established practice with the Frenchman, the army gave her permission. Debray left the cage as usual, immersed in his lucubrations, and came back a couple of hours later with a certain air of triumph. A few days later, the interview came out in an Italian magazine announcing it had been syndicated worldwide, including in the Argentine magazine *Siete Dias*. In the interview, the Frenchman attacked the Bolivian army in extremely aggressive language, inconvenient for the negotiations taking place at that juncture, and coinciding with the *Consulesa*'s good news concerning the army's intentions.

Debray lost his temper and, desperate to show that his words had been distorted, blamed Fallaci for the inflammatory passages claiming she had misinterpreted what he had said. I remember him asking me if I knew the address of *Siete Dias* in Buenos Aires. He copied the address from a back issue I happened to have, and fired off a reply to be published with the article. The fiery Italian replied with an implacable letter reminding Debray that she had faithfully transcribed what she could hear on her tape recorder and that she found the erratic nature of his opinions contemptible. She finished with a scathing flourish: 'One day, I'll meet you coming out of the Paris Opéra, dressed in your black velvet suit, and I'll give you the slap you deserve.'

40

Night Flight to Iquique: December 1970

Lieutenant Ortiz was a young Military School graduate, immaculately turned out, more like a professor than a soldier. His treatment of the prisoners was the best we could possibly have hoped for. He came early, between seven and eight in the morning when the sergeant opened the cells, but did not interrupt our favourite activity if by chance we happened to be asleep – not an easy matter because the noise of the locks was more efficient than any atomic alarm clock and woke us no matter how deeply we were sleeping. Before Ortiz came, we used to start dressing at the first sound of metal so that we weren't naked when they came in. But at least it was normal noise. Our neighbour's bell ringing for Mass was more annoying.

The lieutenant would come back at midday, like someone who had dropped into his club to read the papers. He kept us abreast of the news, and asked us if we needed anything. He brought things for León and took away requests for others; letters, books and communiqués all passed through his hands with no trouble. In short, he was prepared to do everything we wanted, except let us go. In this new liberal climate, we managed to get details of the latest military coup, an attempt by military hardliners under Banzer to oust Ovando from power. Although it was resisted by the workers La Paz and Cochabamba, it would have succeeded – they had already got President Ovando to resign – had it not been for the head of the army, General Juan José Torres, who decided to take power himself, with the support of the masses. So, victorious anti-guerrilla generals, proclaimed anti-communists, succeeded each other using pro-socialist language, talking about a 'revolution' of the people for the people. I even remember Torres saying on the radio: 'Beloved people, my own beloved people . . .', something that augured tragedies to come.

I used to read late into the night if I had new books, and if I hadn't I would re-read old ones. One of the books Ana María brought me was *Operación Masacre* by Rodolfo Walsh. It had made a huge impact on me when it first appeared a few years earlier, as it used a previously unknown technique for revealing the unspoken truth. It was a menacing foretaste of the role the Argentine military was to play in our future history, and marked the start of my disaffection with fiction – except for thrillers – and my growing taste for faction like that of Truman Capote. At any rate, it would not have passed the censor had it not been for Lieutenant Ortiz. After Ana María's visit I did a strange thing; I read the same book three times. I began as soon as she left, finished three or four hours later, then re-read it into the small hours. At that point I started thumbing back through certain passages and ended up reading bits of it again until morning. Not every book had the same effect. We usually savoured our reading, like dessert, leaving the best until last.

At dusk on 21 December, the sound of a DC3's engines announced an unscheduled aircraft, unusual given how difficult it was to land in Camiri, set as it is in a valley between the mountains, in the days when a pilot's eyes were his landing instruments. But the state oil company often flouted the rules when they used their own runway further out of town. It was a hot, soporific night, and the same old Christmas profferings and predictions on the radio had made sleep even more enviable.

I heard the sound of the chain before the door was unlocked and knew the hands were unfamiliar, not our usual sergeant. It was still dark so I supposed it was the middle of the night and I had been woken up more by the surreptitious movement than by the sound. Sweating profusely, I began to get dressed. Either there were problems with the padlock or it seemed to take longer because of the urgency. By this time, I was beside the door. I could tell various people had come into the patio. I opened the curtain and realised the patio spotlights had been turned off. To my right, I heard a voice whispering to Debray and my immediate thought was that the Frenchman was leaving Camiri. But Debray seemed to be resisting, demanding authorization from his consulate. The whispering got louder. Suddenly, as if by magic, a face appeared at my peep-hole as Lieutenant Ortiz struggled with the lock and called: 'Ciro, it's me. Get ready, you're leaving, you're free!' 'At this time of night?' I said sceptically. 'Trust me. Pack a few things, the minimum', he said.

After the heated arguments we had heard over the Fourth Division's radio, it would have been easy to be sceptical, but my reaction was to trust the obviously delighted expression on the lieutenant's face.

I started packing a few clothes, cigarettes, family photographs, and my radio – my link to the outside world. My books went into a hessian bag we used for shopping. And, despite the stifling heat, on top of the little pile waiting beside the door went Che's jacket. The discussion was still going on next door and on one of the lieutenant's trips back and forth between our cells, I asked him if I could say goodbye to León. Despite having received orders to the contrary, he put his fingers to his lips and opened León's door. León was standing fully dressed in the middle of his cell, under the light, as if waiting. We hugged each other, visibly moved. The lieutenant told him to stay inside, that he would be back. I found the sense of urgency, of illegality, worrying. The Frenchman finally came out, led by a tall, strong, unfamiliar man wearing a bomber jacket who urged him to follow. He greeted me, demanded total silence and told us to walk in single file behind him. Outside the door to the cage, a couple of men with machine guns fell in behind us and we walked by flashlight to the Fourth Division commander's office, alongside what had been our visiting room.

The office was large but dimly lit. Behind the desk was its current incumbent who stood facing us for a brief ceremony. On one side were Debray and me, to our left Lieutenant Ortiz and a civilian in charge who turned out to be Major Torrelio, and behind them armed guards. The commander, half dressed in military uniform and half in civvies, as if he had been dragged out of bed, introduced himself as 'Commander of the Fourth Army Division in Camiri'. He informed us that 'the Armed Forces, in the name of the Bolivian people whom it serves, have commuted the sentence of life imprisonment, are releasing you, and deporting you from the country. Major Torrelio, here, is in charge of the operation and all that remains for me to do is congratulate you and wish you a good journey.' Hand outstretched, the commander stepped towards Debray who had not spoken a word during the whole proceedings. Debray bowed in some sort of acknowledgement but then seemed to back away without offering his hand. This did not seem to bother the commander who without flinching turned to me with the same gesture. I shook his hand. I said I was happy to meet him now without a wire mesh between us, and thanked him for the decent treatment we had received under his command. Turning to Major Torrelio, the commander said: 'Major, the ex-prisoners are in your charge. Carry on!'

The head of the commando unit outlined what we were to do. He made it clear that this was a high-risk operation, that some people opposed this course of action, so we had to be careful. 'We'll go out into the street one by one, turn to the left, and walk separately about five metres apart, without stopping or looking back. When we get to the corner, turn left again. A jeep will be waiting with its doors open, get in as fast as you can. Walk normally in total silence. Let's go!'

All of us except the divisional commander set off after Lieutenant Ortiz through the dimly lit garden. With a couple of men ahead of us, we went out into the street. We turned left as we had been told and walked along an uneven pavement. I could see no one on the corner opposite the Officers' Club where a military policeman usually stood. There were no guards anywhere. We passed the windows of our former residence; the boards that used to cover them were gone.

In my mind, I said my fond farewells to a town I hardly knew. The street was dark, lonely and silent. The cinema stood out, a bulky mass among the flat, semi-colonial architecture on the block. With the windows and doors shut, it seemed impossible it could have made so much noise. I imagined I heard the din of the latest box-office hit: *Breaking Waves*, naturally re-named *Breaking Balls*.

On the corner I saw Tania's jeep, recognizable by its clear grey metal bodywork, now the property of command headquarters. Lieutenant Ortiz put my sack of books and both our bags on the floor of the back seat. He sat in the driver's seat with us behind him. Men armed to the teeth piled in on top of us. Major Torrelio, squeezed between the driver and another soldier, ordered: 'If you see anything suspicious, shoot first and ask questions later!'

The overloaded jeep set off towards Choreti. When the asphalt ended, we took a road to the right, and disappeared into total darkness, pierced only by the jeep's headlights. The road was quite bad but widened out into a curve as we approached a ravine which I did not recognize. The bridge was blocked by a small truck. The major called a halt and his commandos climbed out of the back. They were ordered to move the truck. 'Throw it in the water if you have to', shouted the major. In the headlights we saw them surround the truck while the occupants were trying to fix it. They pushed it off the bridge and sent it crashing down the hillside. The jeep continued, picking up the commandos as it passed them on the bridge. I made the only comment of the journey. 'Great place for an ambush.'

The stages of the operation gradually became clear, starting with something Lieutenant Ortiz had said before leaving the cage, the major's orders when we reached the airfield, and what he subsequently told us. The commandos had arrived in civilian clothes in a DC3 supposedly belonging to the state oil company

YPFB. The flight was obviously unofficial. The commando unit was transferred secretly to Camiri in a YPFB truck, and its office in La Villa was also lent as an operations base. (The YPFB president was a general.) The commandos mixed with the locals in the late afternoon. They ate, then checked out the 'activities' of the local garrison's officers who, after their usual dinner in the Officers' Club, found their way to places of 'entertainment'. At a previously arranged time, Major Torrelio arrived at the Fourth Division commander's house with his orders from the president and the army. He was to be represented in the operation by his aide Lieutenant Ortiz, who every evening took the keys of the cage from the sergeant who locked up. That night Ortiz withdrew the guard. The headquarters of the military police, on the corner of the square opposite Fourth Division headquarters, was likewise taken over, to neutralise any possible opposition.

We arrived at the airstrip, a simple ribbon road of steamrollered gravel in the middle of open ground, with a little emergency hut on one side and a windsock on a mast opposite where the aircraft was standing. We got out, and as we were retrieving our bags Major Torrelio brought us up to date with the mission and the men who had been left behind to tie up loose ends. He said we were awaiting orders from Camiri but in the meantime the area had to be secured until the aircraft could take off in the dawn light. He posted guards at each corner of the airfield and made us get in the plane. The lieutenant said his goodbyes. It was a friendly farewell.

The plane was a troop transport that had not been modified since the Second World War. Inside the fuselage, under the windows, were metal benches moulded into the form of seats running from end to end on both sides of an aisle. We climbed the sloping central aisle nearly up to the cockpit and sat on either side. The aircraft was like an empty tin of sardines, no question of air hostesses. One of the pilots, who had come out of the hut when the jeep arrived and had helped us board, now offered us blankets and cushions, reminding us we would have quite a few hours to wait and it would be cold. 'Try and get some sleep', he said

When we were alone, Debray spoke for the first time since leaving the cage. 'What do you think will happen now?' he asked. 'The order is to deport us, so I'm sure that's what they'll do', I replied. 'Where do you think they'll take us?' he pressed. 'The only possible country in this [the DC3] is Chile. I don't suppose they'll hand us over to Onganía or Stroessner . . .' 'Where in Chile do you think?' 'Iquique or Antofagasta', I said. 'Iquique is nearer.'

Debray wrapped himself in the blanket. I did the same. We did not speak again. The runway in the narrow valley was surrounded by peaks which emerged covered in mist and vegetation as the day dawned. Piloting an aircraft there from memory could only be done by Bolivian pilots who, with their skill and knowledge of flying between the mountains and going up to land in La Paz, were capable of everything.

Unlike in the pampas, the mountains delay the arrival of the morning light. At about half past five, surrounded by this magnificent landscape, Major Torrelio came rushing out of the hut, followed by the two pilots. They got straight into the aircraft while Torrelio gathered his men around the plane for a final talk. He was the last to board. When the door was shut, he came along the aisle to the cockpit, greeting us like kids on a school trip. 'Good morning. Good morning', he said and, banging the inner door with the palm of this hand, shouted to the pilots 'Off we go!' He was no longing wearing a gun, but in uniform showing his rank. We seemed to be the only three passengers on board. Outside, doubling as ground crew, the commandos dragged a generator to the aircraft's fuselage, and soon each of the engines began to cough, splutter and utter expletives, like anyone would at that time of the morning. The plane taxied to the end of the runway where, motors humming in unison, it began to vibrate in a last final effort. Fortunately, instead of exploding, the huge machine set off at speed, calming itself and our emotions with a wonderfully smooth take-off.

Avoiding the nearest peaks, dipping from side to side, we flew over houses that gradually turned into the low square settlement of Camiri. If you did not know exactly where you were, it would be hard to tell from the air. The only point of reference would be the plaza and the church. So, if that square of trees was the plaza, then that would be where . . . but we flew over leaving behind any chance of locating anything. But something did seem to be moving down there, perhaps clothes on a washing line?

During the flight over the mountainous desert and the majestic apparition of the Pacific Ocean, Major Torrelio and Debray struck up a conversation. The major tried to keep it cordial, but the Frenchman turned it into a diatribe, attacking the Bolivian Army, to which this officer – risking his own freedom by taking us to ours – belonged. The Frenchman refused to acknowledge that the Bolivian generals deserved any credit for this plan, apart from as marginal subordinates within a political arena where it had been conceived on a level of 'human dignity and international power', and not by lackeys. The arrogance of the first world, wiping out the most minimal and formal ethical obligation, was staggering to this representative of a humble South American country, who had taken the trouble to explain how the operation to save us was planned and had conceded the indifference of the majority of Bolivians to this solution to a situation created neither by the people nor the army. But nothing would curb the Frenchman's furious, uncontrolled rant. It seemed as if Major Torrelio might eventually, and justifiably, lose his patience. But he did not. His kept his cool.

At the airport in Chile, groups of people were waiting expectantly. Others were running around, trying to get on to the runway; they were members of the press corps who had been tipped off about the arrival of the Bolivian aircraft and its cargo, and local authorities and representatives of the socialist president Salvador Allende, who barely three months earlier, in September 1970, had won the elections as the candidate for Popular Unity, a coalition of parties from social democratic to the extreme left.

We did in fact land in Iquique, a beautiful port city, practically the most northern point of Chile, spread out before the
great ocean and cooled by a light sea breeze, with a whiff of
shellfish and seaweed, and lulled by a background chorus of
seagulls hovering over the beaches and landing on the rooftops.
A century earlier, we would have landed in Antofagasta. Now,
the aircraft taxied alongside the main airport building, amid
roars and whistles, to finally come to rest in front of the crowd.
I suddenly stepped out of the looking glass, back into real life.
All attention was focused on Debray, of course, who was
quickly surrounded by elegant young men with beards who
would not allow journalists anywhere near him. They greeted
him like a fully accredited ambassador and led him to a waiting
car, which swept away with a convoy of vehicles in its wake. I,
on other hand, was to be driven to the airport building by the
police. But while I was still on the runway, a French journalist
welcomed me in perfect Spanish. It was Philippe Gustin, director of Agence France Presse (AFP) and correspondent in
Santiago. He said he had tried more than once to write an article about me in Camiri but could never get authorization. Now
I was in Iquique, a free man, he would like to write an article,
either today or tomorrow.

In Immigration I was asked to identify myself. I had asked Ana
María to smuggle some documents into jail for me so I would
have them if I needed them. I had left the Mendoza identity card
Cholo had once got for me with Manuel in Buenos Aires, when I
changed my identity on my way to Bolivia. Ana María had
brought me my driver's licence and it was that I now showed to
the police. The Chileans did not want to accept the document but
I had nothing else. Someone reminded them that I had just been a
prisoner, not a tourist. A committee of local officials had been
appointed to look after me and I remained in their care until all
the customs formalities were finished.

The real surprise was waiting for me when I left the office. It
was the 'Englishman' George Roth, our former *compañero*. He

explained that neither the international nor the Santiago press had had the details of our escape; or rather they had not been informed in time and were misinformed afterwards. The news was managed at presidential level, naturally, and by the French Embassy who had passed it on to their own press agency for obvious reasons. Roth should have got a prize for determination because he had always assumed that the news would come out via the French. In fact Philippe Gustin, who had interviewed him in Camiri when he was released, had given it to him. Apart from Gustin and himself, the only journalists at the airport were the local press and radio reporters who had been alerted by Bolivian radio.

It was a very pleasant reunion; I had found a familiar face and Roth was visibly moved. He had already realized there was a plan afoot to stitch me up. He was staying at the hotel where as it happened I was also being taken, so he more or less took charge of me. Being released after nearly four years is no easy experience. Your self-defence mechanism has been lowered and things happen at a dizzying pace, faster than your ability to crank up your sluggish psyche. However high your expectations, you still have to face the unknown. The mayor of Iquique was to honour us with a banquet. Roth went to buy me some clothes while I had my first proper bath in years, with perfumed soap and steaming hot water. My room was modest, but to me it seemed exotically luxurious. All I wanted to do was sleep but they came at midday to take me to lunch, by the sea, in the open air.

Long tables had been laid for about a hundred guests on the promenade, looking towards an infinite horizon. Debray was at the head of the centre table, I was on his left and the mayor, a young Socialist, was to his right facing me. The atmosphere was very friendly, and the meal washed down with some excellent Maipo wine. Debray was already behaving like a star, due not only to his upper-class roots but also his superior education. He soon withdrew from the table, escorted to a private meeting by members of the MIR (Revolutionary Left Movement).

Back at the hotel, I found an indignant Roth listening to the radio. The ball had started rolling. The newspaper account of Debray, 'the free man', included the side bar story that, from his document, the airport police had identified the other ex-prisoner as a member of the Argentine Federal police. Roth rang them to insist on a correction, explaining that the document was my driver's licence, issued by the police like everyone else's. But it was not that easy to correct; whether the radio corrected it or not, it would no longer be news. The AFP interview eventually denounced this stunt and cleared things up, but only belatedly.

Next morning, the Chilean and international press focused on the manner of our escape, and journalists in Camiri, fooled by the secrecy of the mission, reported what they could. One apparent witness was the parish priest whose church was next to the cage. In an early re-writing of the story, the flabby old Italian told how he had watched the proud departure of the hero whose confidante he had been. Debray had left bright-eyed, head held high, firm step, applauded as he passed, whereas the other prisoner, pale and dishevelled, needed help to walk . . . Did he bear an eternal grudge because I refused his visits? He had wanted to help me unburden my conscience of its wicked communist thoughts; ideas that harmed the Lord's children and had brought me here. I replied that of all mankind's vicious inventions, religion was the most perverse, because it subjected us to the idea that suffering in this life guaranteed joy in another. Perhaps I offended him. Amazingly, no one noticed the contradiction between the secrecy of the operation and the priest's views, no doubt illuminated by Divine Providence.

Driven to the airport again by the Chilean intelligence services, we took off for Santiago in a magnificent ten-seater twin-engined police plane. We were the only passengers travelling, as if in a luxury Ferrari or on a flying carpet, down the Pacific coast, with the Andes to our left silhouetted in bluish-violet against the sun. At the police airport in Santiago, a committee was waiting to formally receive the Frenchman on behalf of the president. A car whisked him out of my sight forever, without a backwards look or goodbye on his part. Plainclothes policemen drove me straight to their Central Criminal Investigation Unit where, after a very long softening up period in the corridor, I was subjected to a prolonged interrogation by the unit's deputy head.

In the process of setting up the victorious Popular Unity government, power was distributed by quotas to the parties in the coalition. Hence, the balance of power gave the Communist Party second place in a body dominated by the Socialist Party. The other parties made up the cast appropriately. The deputy head of the Investigation Unit was a communist obsessed with Peronism, an evil beast of a neighbour from the not too distant past, and he concentrated his whole interrogation – illegal by the way – on trying to link me to Peronist revolutionary groups he called terrorists. Two or three hours later when he had exhausted the subject, he announced I could go. I still did not have a valid document so I had to have my fingerprints taken again for them to issue me with one. I retrieved my bags, was escorted to the exit, and left on the pavement with not so much as a 'Good Afternoon!'

I did not have a cent. I sat on a row of stones round a flowerbed in front of Teatinos Street police station, not knowing what to do or where to go. I finished cleaning the ink off my fingers with the toilet paper kindly provided for me. Naturally, my fond memories of Chile do not include policemen.

I was forced to reflect on the circumstances that led me from a military cage in Camiri to a socialist pavement in Santiago, a smooth transition which nonetheless left me with no way home, nowhere to sleep, and on the point of collapse from exhaustion. Just then a taxi stopped at the corner, about thirty metres away, and two little girls came skipping towards me, shouting excitedly; they were my daughters, followed by Ana María and our lawyer friend Gustavo Roca, effing and blinding at whoever had given them such misleading information about where and when I would arrive. On arriving from Buenos Aires, they had asked for official confirmation of my whereabouts and were sent to Pudahuel, Santiago's international airport. No one knew anything. They took taxis to two other airports but found no sign of us until someone gave them an unofficial tip-off. Following the trail, they learned that I was in the hands of the police.

Gustavo worked his network of lefties in the government. The Interior Ministry got a grip on this embarrassing situation through its deputy minister, the communist Daniel Vergara. We were put up in the Conquistador Hotel, a few paces from the Moneda Palace, where we spent a sleepless night. Then the media circus began. In the morning, the whole reception area of the hotel was filled with camera crews and reporters, a bit at random because the star of this particular show, Debray, had disappeared, protected by official silence. It was impossible to evade the harassment by saying I was tired, so I agreed to speak to some of them: a local paper, a Bolivian, an Italian, a Swede and an Argentine. Through the Bolivian, Mario Rueda Peña, I took the opportunity of thanking the Bolivian people for their warmth and protection, saying that it was their generosity of spirit that contributed most to our safety and subsequent departure. I had to stick to a bland performance to avoid any indiscreet questions about my political past – which strictly speaking did not exist – or reveal any ideological commitments or militancy, national or international.

A Swedish journalist, who said he was from a Stockholm TV channel, showed not only rigorous professionalism but personal respect over and above the current fashionable political story: the guerrillas and the fate of their emblematic leader, Che. Jan Sandqvist began by cordoning off a part of the lounge from other journalists and interested bystanders. He, with a couple of cameramen, Ana María, the girls and I, sat in leather armchairs going through a process of catharsis about the commitments, decisions taken, and moral values blurred by four long years. The crowd fell silent and heard the whole conversation on microphone extensions.

Debray meanwhile was skating on thin ice with some of the press, having lost the control he exercised from Camiri. Philippe Gustin, who had covered Debray's prison stay for AFP, was dubbed a 'capitalist' for publishing an article under his own by-line, drawing attention to the fact that two prisoners had been released, not just a Frenchman; that both had been judged by the same court in Camiri and given the same thirty-year sentence; and that both had been released after negotiations with the Gaullist government. Joseph Lambroschini, the new French Ambassador in La Paz, had distanced himself from the first declarations Debray made after his release, when he complained of being alone and abandoned in prison. He described him as a spoilt brat who seemed unaware of the care, attention and constant visits provided by the French Embassy and consulate, benefits not extended to other prisoners.

On the second day in our luxurious residence, 23 December, we managed to shake off the press hounding us and go for a walk round the city. If you ask a prisoner what he yearns for he would almost certainly reply 'Go for a walk'. What a prisoner misses most is being able to cross the street, look in a shop window, retrace his steps, walk in the sun or the rain whenever he feels like it. In the Plaza de Armas, diagonally across from the cathedral under some arches in the old town, was a restaurant which matched our limited budget. Gustavo Roca had some official business after lunch and we arranged to meet there. We sat down at a round table, and were being served by a pleasant waitress, when suddenly the most beautiful, unexpected thing happened. The people eating at the tables next to us began to clap, and gradually people stood up at each table and applauded. I don't think they were applauding anyone in particular, just freedom and our reunion. As if reflecting his clients' wishes, the headwaiter came over and offered us a free meal. The TV was on a loop showing the release of the prisoners in Camiri and I (with my family and friends) was the only one available to congratulate. Gustavo said Daniel Vergara, the deputy interior minister, was expecting us.

We went straight to La Moneda, the presidential palace. Vergara, a thin man with a face as sharp as a knife, improvised a welcome speech in his office with real warmth. He apologized for the circumstances of my arrival and promised to make our stay in Chile a truly fraternal homecoming from now on. On Christmas Eve our hotel room was filled with presents and balloons for the girls from the local and international press and from the Office of the President.

I did my interview with the Argentine journalist Miguel Bonasso, a young reporter on *Semana Gráfica*, over lunch in an open-air restaurant on the Alameda. He fitted in quite naturally at our family table and made a fuss of the girls. Keeping certain delicate areas from public knowledge, I told him the story, especially the Bolivian part, which was controversial and being re-written as we spoke. I told him about the Jewish friend whose features I had used to draw the non-existent person I denounced as my contact in Buenos Aires. As I was saying 'Isaquito was a sailor and a socialist, but most of all a wonderful human being,' Bonasso sat up in his seat and muttered: 'Isaquito? . . . You don't mean Isaac Shusterman by any chance?' 'Yes', I said, 'that's him'. He turned out to be a mutual friend, very much liked by both of us. Not long afterwards, Bonasso sent me the published article; he had hardly changed a word of our conversation.

Oscar del Barco, Kichi Kiczkowsky, and other members and friends of the *Pasado y Presente* group from Córdoba, arrived on a lightning visit in a whirlwind of emotions. None of them had had any problems. No search warrants had been issued for anyone in the EGP, and no one had been harassed on my account, even though political developments in Argentina had meant reorganizing cadres and militants. I was still the same old *compañero*. Gustavo Roca went back to Córdoba with them. My brother Avelino arrived at about the same time and we decided to cut short the show in Santiago and spend time at the coast.

Philippe Gustin offered us a cabin by the sea, probably belonging to the Foreign Press Club. Even more surprisingly, and something for which I am eternally in his debt, when we came back he invited to stay us for as long as we liked in his house in Las Condes, an extremely posh area of Santiago. And so it was. We lived in the guest wing of his modern house as if we were with relatives. Moreover, Philippe gave me the keys to his Mini Cooper so we could go round looking for a more permanent solution. This came about via the Popular Unity's Plastic Artists Association, which was controlled by the Communists. They offered me room in a building reserved for sculptors and painters, near the Mapocho, where Balmes, Gracia Barrios and Mesa had their studios.

Curiously, or maybe not, the Communist Party, notoriously opposed to the Cuban line on the armed struggle, decided to take us under its wing, all in the name of Art. A prominent member of the intellectual Left, Miguel Rojas Mix (now an internationally renowned art critic and academic), invited us to stay in his house, a grand villa in a residential neighbourhood a few blocks from the Plaza Nuñoa. We had a bright room on the upper floor for our own private use in a most welcoming atmosphere, complete with wall to wall books, and absolute respect for our political ideology. We had long informative chats and spent some wonderful days there until in February we moved to his house on Isla Negra, where Pablo Neruda lived and where most of the party's sculptors, singers and artists had summer houses.

This solidarity even continued for a few days after we returned to Santiago, until another crypto-communist, an old Argentine friend from Mendoza called Domingo Politti, a photographer for the Communist Party newspaper *Puro Chile*, lent us an apartment for their reporters' use in the popular area of Quinta Normal, the opposite end of the scale to Las Condes. Politti ran the photographers' pool at Quimantú, a publishing project of the Popular Unity government after it acquired the printing works of Zig-Zag, Chile's most famous publishing house. He also found me work in the future Documentation Department. We soon rented a larger apartment on the twelfth floor of a building in

Cienfuegos Street where, before breakfast on the morning Ana
María's mother arrived to visit her grandchildren, we were hit by
a two-minute earthquake. We could not get to the children's
bedroom where they were clinging to each other on one of the
beds screaming. It brought us down to earth; all resentment and
illusions were jettisoned.

The shining light of the Bolivian adventure, which cost its
volunteer heroes and innocent victims so dear, slowly lost its bril-
liance, but concentric circles kept travelling outwards from it,
lighting a powder keg that encompassed the whole continent and
eventually unleashed the greatest wave of repression and killing
since the Conquista, from Guatemala to Tierra del Fuego. It has
affected me, to a greater or lesser degree, ever since.

On her last visit to Camiri, Ana María had brought me a questionnaire from *Punto Final*, the weekly publication of the MIR in
Chile, which had come to her via a journalist friend, Juan García
Elorrio, editor of *Cristianismo y Revolución* in Buenos Aires.
Manuel Cabieses, the editor of *Punto Final*, had suggested I reply
to the questionnaire and he promised to publish it. So there in the
cage, I combined my artisanal work with literature and, although
it did not come easily to me and was limited by my situation, I
was writing my version of what had happened when I was overtaken by events. But the draft travelled with me to Chile among
my books and personal belongings. Once on Isla Negra, Ana
María typed a clean copy on Rojas Mix's typewriter and when we
returned to Santiago we went to the *Punto Final* office to deliver
it to Cabieses personally.

A few weeks later I was 'summoned' to the editor's office and
he returned the 'manuscript'. Cabieses said I should correct the
underlined paragraphs for unexplained reasons to do with impar-
tiality and historical coherence. The text was censured and
covered by notes in the margin in the tiny handwriting I knew to
be Régis Debray's. I had not lived beside him for over four years
without recognizing his handwriting. I had even read the original
of the work he wrote for General Ovando in his small, even and

interfering hand which seemed to write more in the margins and over original lines than in the main text itself, like a second inquisitorial, critical mind. Publication of the questionnaire was apparently subject to the approval of the Savonarola of the Revolution, the only witness, indicating with his hidden finger the true orthodoxy. I made changes, in any case: not because they were right; but because it was important my version of events was known, even though important things had to be hidden. I kept the original censured version but unfortunately it was burned in San Rafael, Mendoza, when the local inquisition condemned my modest belongings to a pre-emptive bonfire, but I still have photocopies of what was published in *Punto Final*.

Then a Bolivian journalist appeared who, although I did not know him personally, was an important piece of the jigsaw. Antonio Peredo Leigue, elder brother of the guerrillas Inti and Coco Peredo, arrived from Bolivia. To my amazement, he had interviewed my *compañero* and friend León in the Beni, where they were both from. When León learned Antonio was going to Santiago and would try to see me, he asked him to take a letter. Antonio brought the letter, which also perished in the aforementioned fire, but what I remember most about it was León's euphoria, his real joy, at my release – and his own when Lieutenant Ortiz returned to open the padlock and take him to the Fourth Division commander's office. There his friend Camba and the other Bolivian prisoners, Eusebio, Paco, Chingolo and Salustio were all waiting to be released together.

León went back to his plot of land, eager to see his wife again, only to find her hitched to a man who had helped her when she found herself alone with her children, abandoned by the hand of God, or rather the Communist Party. In the letter, he said that in the early morning after we left, he stood outside in the patio, looking up at the stars, until he heard the rumbling of the plane's engines. Then he took the sheet off his bed and began waving it in the air, in the hope I might see it and know he was saying goodbye.

Part Six

Exile

41

Chile in the Time of Allende: 1970–1973

Exile means leaving your native land. What you lose are not your possessions, or external trappings. You lose what is under your feet: the land, the landscape that nourishes you. That is why the drama of exile affects everybody, no matter what your social conditions. These days, forced migration driven by poverty and hunger – caused by the developed centre to the detriment of the periphery – might seem beneficial for those who manage to reach the shores of the first world. And for their children it is true, relatively speaking. But when you see an African walking along frozen Scandinavian streets, you understand that they have really lost everything.

When you leave your country voluntarily, driven by a sense of adventure, you carry your land with you, on the soles of your shoes, and you can retrace your steps whenever you wish. The idea of exile used to mean fleeing for political reasons, not emigrating, which was a supposedly temporary measure until you could return with the means to support your family. Political asylum was always a respected institution in Latin America because continual social upheavals made it essential: today my turn, tomorrow yours. But whether imposed by political activity or driven by hunger, the streets of exile have never been paved with gold. That idea is reserved for the beneficiaries of diplomatic accords, corrupt politicians deposed from power, emptying the public coffers, the top dogs, those who can; because in reality, the poor could never go into exile.

I'm not really sure when my exile began. Maybe when I left Argentina? When I left Cuba? Algeria? Bolivia? or Chile? Argentina for the last time, I think, although each time I left a country I loved, parts of me were wrenched away and I was never entirely whole afterwards. I live with the remains, grafted onto a biological structure that resists. But like a graft on a pear tree, the result is neither one fruit nor another.

My political exile, though, began in Chile. The Quimantú publishing house, which organized my documents, accepted me as a fully fledged member, and I found friends there. One great revolutionary fallacy is that you have *compañeros*, not friends. Yet without friends, you can do nothing, not revolution, not art, not even love; because a friend is the piece of wood floating on the storm of passion that you cling on to, to lift your head and breathe. You can have *compañeros* whom you respect, but not someone you go beyond the limits of the mission with, or confide your dreams in. Friendship is something else.

And then Fidel arrived in Santiago. The visit of the champion of the armed struggle to the reformist parliamentarian caused a huge rumpus in South America because it threatened to extend Cuban influence into virgin territory. The Chilean president, Salvador Allende, could mobilize the support of the masses whenever necessary, sometimes with a bit of persuasion. But the presence of the mythical Cuban leader showed that the Revolution crossed national borders and had common roots lying fallow, struggling to grow, coming together to follow in its footsteps.

Multitudes gathered for Fidel, shouting themselves hoarse wherever he went on his long tour, and probably sealed the fate of the Popular Unity government. Nothing would ever be the same in Chile. The Cuban apparatus moved to Chile wholesale, and many Cubans I knew were working in the wings. Yet not one of them contacted me. It was remarkable. Not because of me as a person but because, in their eagerness to reconstruct events (including purely random and superficial things), the Cubans sought out and interviewed survivors, their own and others, members of groups of all kinds, soldiers, neighbours, improbable accidental witnesses, deserters (the so-called '*resaca*'), and even chickens pecking around the area. All and sundry, except for me; the only survivor of Che's original project.

That was the active and visible face of the order to ignore me. Yet there was always a hidden hand doling out favours. Among the spin-offs of Fidel's visit was an exhibition by the Cuban National Publishing House to promote Cuban books. The former soldier in charge of the exhibition made an official visit to Quimantú and we met. I asked if I could buy some of the books on show and he replied: '*Compañero*, you can have any book you want, they're all yours. All of them! Come and get them when the exhibition is over.' So I did. I recovered the books I had abandoned in Holguín, although, of course, they would ultimately end up in a blaze of glory. Borges would say exile is the books you lose when you leave them behind. He's right.

The masses in Chile went through a period of heightened politicization under the Popular Unity government that contrasted with the Cuba I knew. In Cuba the Revolution exercised power with the support of the people, but in Chile the masses kept up a constant pressure on the government, mobilized by the grass roots of the different parties in the Popular Unity coalition and the revolutionary Left, sometimes exceeding their mandate and pushing the government further to the left. Society was becoming visibly polarized and while the Left shouted slogans, the Right plotted its return with the help of their neighbours in the north. In this frenzied atmosphere, it was impossible not to get involved, and I was no exception. Quimantú had, as did every Chilean workplace, a grass-roots organization, the FTR (Revolutionary Workers Front), set up by the MIR (Revolutionary Left Movement), and I was invited to join them. I went to its founding meeting and joined, together with Pancho Nelson López de Oliveira, a young Brazilian journalist with whom I had begun choosing photos to be bought from the Zig-Zag archive to create our Documentation Department under the expert guidance of

María Teresa Moraes, another Brazilian from Rio. Pancho and I were completely absorbed in the FTR and managed some notable achievements.

The MIR offered to let me join directly 'as a cadre', and I happily accepted on condition that my political situation, which was being affected by noises off, was clarified publicly. We were in the middle of discussions when we were overtaken by events.

A significant political shift had taken place in Argentina. The military dictatorship of General Onganía was supplanted in March 1971 by a sector of the army headed by General Lanusse that was more open to negotiation. It aimed to attract public support by calling free elections, after tough concessions to Peronism. These included the return of Perón and allowing the Peronist party – *Justicialismo* – to participate in the elections, but only if they put up a candidate other than Perón himself. The political crisis had exploded and the waters of the confrontation between armed leaders were to sweep the Argentine people into the most tragic period of its history. Numerous organizations preached the armed struggle as the people's way of regaining power and recuperating living standards that had been eroded in one of the richest and most developed countries in the Americas.

The thousands of potential combatants that Che had envisaged took up arms on Perón's behalf, offering their lives and the lives of others, in the largest clandestine mobilization in the Americas. Workers and students were mainly recruited by the ERP (Marxist), Montoneros (Peronist), FAL (ex-Communists), FAR (Peronist), FAP (Peronist). The armed groups became known internationally in August 1972 when some of their members broke out of prison in Rawson, capital of the Patagonian province of Chubút. The leaders managed to hijack a plane and fly to Chile, while soldiers took the rest – eighteen men and women – to the naval base in Trelew and shot them in cold blood.

The ERP (People's Revolutionary Army), the organization with the largest military capacity, contacted me via Dolores

Giménez, one of the members of its political wing the PRT (Workers Revolutionary Party) in exile in Chile. She suggested organizing a meeting with an ERP official in Santiago. They offered me the same as the MIR: to be part of their plans for a guerrilla base in Tucumán, a province in the north of Argentina directly to the south of Salta. My reply to the ERP was the same: everything was conditional on their publicly dispelling all rumours about me. So, things were left up in the air because no one, not even a group as independent as them, wanted to take on positions that were not clear, given Cuba's silence on the subject, although privately they showed solidarity.

Months later, a new meeting took place in Argentina, in San Rafael, with a couple of militants – including another ERP officer – who explained their plan for Tucumán. My reaction was negative. Establishing a rural guerrilla base in that area, without a frontier for a bolt hole, surrounded by highways (the area around Aconquija), seemed to me a trap, a dead end.

The apparent victory of the masses in Argentina, when Perón's candidate Héctor Cámpora became president in May 1973, made us think it was time to go home. Ana María and the girls would go to Buenos Aires first, since I was still involved in what was happening in Chile. I would wait for even more optimistic news from Argentina. I went to the Popular Unity's last huge march which was taken over by the radical Left. Standing in front of the Moneda palace under Allende's balcony, I heard the speech in which he rejected extremist pressure from the grass roots.

Gustavo Roca then wrote urging me to return: 'Come now or you won't be able to fix your legal situation.' The process in Argentina was disintegrating too; the Cámpora people's government lasted a mere two months. Ana María sent a plane ticket and I flew to Buenos Aires on the last day of August 1973, eleven days before Pinochet's fascist coup in Chile. I left my friends in Quimantú, with my Chilean family (the last head of the Documention Department, Lidia Baltra, and her husband Claudio Verdugo) promising to visit us in Mendoza.

A year later, I was returning from a visit to Buenos Aires with Ana María and the girls in my brother Avelino's car. Crossing the San Luís desert at noon, we decided to stop for lunch just off the road under the only *chañars* high enough to protect us from the sun. We followed some car tracks over to the trees. While we were making sandwiches, a little Renault appeared through the heat haze and, following our tracks through the sand, drove towards us blowing the horn. It was Lidia and Claudio. Never has a promise been kept with such punctuality.

42

Argentina: 1973–1976

The noble magic of human nature was felt every now and again in Argentina, electrified by the factional war taking place all over the country, as the net closed in around us almost as soon as we arrived in Buenos Aires. We lived with Ana María's parents in the Plaza Once for a while, and in the mornings I used to go down to the baker's on the opposite side of Yrigoyen Street. The baker, a rough but friendly Spaniard standing behind his counter surrounded by different types of wonderful smelling bread, always made the same joke. 'Good morning', I said, 'a kilo of baguette, please.' 'There isn't any!' he barked, as he weighed the bread. We only ever exchanged those brief words, but one day, looking down as he counted the change, he said: 'Señor, you have to leave the city. Bad people are asking after you.'

When I returned to Argentina, I had contacted my former *compañeros* again: those who had been released from jail when Cámpora came to power, and those who had kept safe doing their regular jobs. A meeting was arranged in Córdoba, a sort of general assembly and welcome home for me. In Camiri I had jotted down some thoughts and my doubts about the possibility of rowing against the present current. I had in mind the example of Peru, where a military coup, supported by the people despite the opposition of the traditional political parties, had brought about an apparent process of transformation, pushed to the left by the spontaneous action of the masses, and the unrestricted political and material support of the Cuban Revolution and the

Soviet Union. I meant the government of General Jorge Velasco Alvarado.

The question I asked myself was: do we always have to oppose populist processes generated by forces outside the proletariat or should we accompany them so we have the right to be present when they define themselves ideologically? Should we go on ignoring the fact that the majority of the working class in Argentina is Peronist just because it is not in Lenin's manuals, or should we try to share their experience from within? I thought we should be with the working class, not confronting them.

I arrived at the meeting with a copy of my report freshly typed by Ana María. It was read out aloud, and the consensus was that there was nothing to discuss and the meeting was adjourned. We all thought the same. Any differences were tactical rather than ideological, and the party line was to stand with the people in the struggle for power, not on the outside.

Others had other ideas. When they came out of prison, Bellomo, Carlos Bandoni, Miguel Colina and Henry Lerner joined the 'Masetti Brigade', an organization formed to continue the struggle of the EGP, but primarily in the city. Later, Bellomo joined the ERP where, together with Daniel Hopen, he led a splinter group that proposed working with the Peronist grass roots. It was called ERP 22, in memory of the executions in Trelew on 22 August 1972, when both Marxists and Peronists were among the dead.

However by this time the leadership of the Peronist movement had been taken over by its right-wing, using its hegemonic presence around Perón, in the Justicialist Party and the CGT (General Confederation of Labour). The unions acted like corporatist bodies and were Perón's shock troops, intensified by the direct influence of residual Italian fascists, regrouped in Propaganda 2, the new order of Licio Gelli, whose private secretary and pocket wizard José López Rega was general factotum to Perón. This sinister figure, essence of the darkest of dark forces operating at home and abroad, played a central role in destroying the popular myth of Peronism, separating the wheat from the chaff: the hope of the working class deposited illusorily in the leader; the reactionary and fallacious structure of the party and the leader. Like the Nazis, their solution was the physical elimination of the enemy.

The attack on the grass roots of the labour movement and their most radical leaders was conceived in the bosom of the Peronist Right, allied to the army (the armed wing of economic power) which finished off the task. Symbolically, its first action came in June 1973, during the gigantic reception at Ezeiza airport for the return of Perón. The Triple A (Argentine Anti-Communist Alliance) appeared on the scene under the supervision of López Rega, now minister of social services, with a programme of selective but widespread killings, which included anything that moved on the left of the political spectrum or was seen as cultural, student, union or social activity. As their political calling card, they began sending letters to their victims with a deadline to leave the county before the death squads arrived. Union lawyers were the first targets, sending a clear message that intellectuals and professionals would not be immune. Rodolfo Ortega Peña, a lawyer and journalist, who had given Ana María support and solidarity in Buenos Aires, was the first on the Triple A list to be killed.

Oscar del Barco and I had gone to eat in a taverna near his house in Cerro de Las Rosas, Córdoba, where Aníbal Troilo records provided the background music. It was a simple place, welcoming and cheap, but that night it suddenly filled up with the deputy governor of the province and his court. Atilio López, a former union leader who had run for office on the same ticket as Obregón Cano, was the most progressive governor in the country. The owner of the bar told him we were there and he invited us over to his table for a chat which continued behind closed doors until the early hours. López was assassinated by the Triple A few months later. Curutchet, another labour lawyer friend of Oscar's whom I knew slightly, met the same fate. We went to his funeral at the headquarters of Agustín Tosco's Energy Workers

Union, and the oppressive atmosphere of threats was palpable inside the building and adjacent streets. The baker's warning could not be ignored and we decided to leave Buenos Aires, a city now in the hands of reactionary swine, for my mother's house in San Rafael, a peaceful wine-growing area to the south of Mendoza, far from the fury of the reactionaries. Or so we thought.

One night at three in the morning, Avelino's wife Alicia knocked on our door and said: 'The police want to search the house.' Our dog Top's furious barking and dashing about implied we were surrounded. I quickly got dressed, took some money from Ana María's bag, undid the butterfly screws holding the mosquito mesh to the window, said goodbye without waking the girls and climbed out into the side garden. As my feet touched the ground, I thought Top might be a problem since I felt his nervous body against my legs. But wisely he had stopped barking. I went towards the hen house intending to jump the side wall into the next-door house, which once belonged to my grandparents and where my cousin Gilberto now lived. I walked through the darkness with Top at my side, silent as a shadow. However, there were police cars shining their headlights into the corners of the garden and I realized I could not escape that way without causing a shoot out. The same applied to my Aunt María's house at the other end of the vineyard. So I went back to my window, replaced the mosquito mesh, put the money back in the bag and, sure I would be detained, went out onto the verandah, pretending to be surprised by the upheaval. The police threatened to shoot the furious Top, so Avelino chained him up and began arguing about letting the police into the bedrooms because of my mother's frail state of health. Avelino's prestige as a doctor, whose patients included army officers and relatives of the local police, saved the situation: we were being searched by the San Rafael police, subordinate to the departmental police who were answerable to the provincial governor who was on the Peronist Left.

Then, without any explanation, they made us sign a declaration, got into their jeeps and pick-ups, and headed down the majestic Ballofet Avenue, before the astonished eyes of our neighbours. The objective of the operation was obviously to look for weapons, but we knew they would be back, so we quickly moved to a rented apartment in the centre of the city. They knew where we were and my mother could sleep in peace.

Contacts with doctors and trades people meant I could keep earning money by painting. The representative of an electronic equipment multinational, who I will call Omar the Turk, provided solid financial support through his endless chain of contacts with winegrowers and wine merchants, who passed clients backwards and forwards and kept me in work. He was not involved in anything political. His story is tragic.

While I was busy framing my paintings for an exhibition, with the catalogues printed and the support of the municipality's secretary for culture, the police again raided our house. (A gang had previously come through the building shouting fascist slogans, daubing the walls and frightening my daughters so much that we had to collect them personally from school.) A friend Moisés, who was helping me with the frames, answered the imperious knock on the door, and returned shouting 'A raid!' The small apartment was filled with corpulent policemen in riot gear turning everything upside down, while Paula and Andrea looked through the windows, like in the films, and shot imaginary rounds of machine-gun fire 'ra-ta-ta-ta!' at them. Perhaps the ludicrousness of raiding a home-workshop full of paintings, and facing the comical resistance of nine and ten-year-old girls, made them again beat a retreat without finding anything.

But the next day they detained me in the street, took me to the police station, and typed up a new file on me at the request of the federal police. They were not convinced of my identity. Either I was an idiot or I was hiding something. They cancelled the exhibition, advertised for the following Saturday in the municipal library. The culture secretary, a young man with Montonero inclinations, insisted on hanging the paintings in the town hall itself, changed the date, and organized radio publicity. I was visited by the military intelligence services (SIE) that night and when the culture secretary came to tell me that the exhibition was off, he was visibly panicking: 'They have tons of proof in your file that you are training the ERP in Valle Grande. None of it is true, of course, but it's your exhibition or my life, Ciro. I have to choose.'

The exhibition did not happen, but there was no time to lament. A letter came in the post. The address was typewritten as was the sheet of paper inside. It was from the Triple A, badly written, recommending I make use of the intelligence I obviously had, and realize it was best to leave the country, for the sake of my wife and daughters. They suggested I make lives for them elsewhere and ended by saying there was no room for people like me in Argentina, or something of the sort. I don't have a copy and I sent the original to Dolores, the friend from the ERP who had come home from Chile only to take her children into exile again. In Córdoba they gave me her new address in Sweden.

During those days of gloom, my mother died, peacefully and of old age. We followed the hearse, with all her brothers and sisters, cousins, nephews, nieces and grandchildren, to the cemetery, where I spied the ominous presence of secret service agents among the tombstones. As an emergency measure, the girls went to stay at the farm of Avelino's old friend Don Ramón, while we cleared our apartment and slept in different places. Omar the Turk had some hangars full of televisions and he offered to store my things. I sorted out my books, and the novels went to Don Ramón's farm. I filled a couple of boxes Omar lent me with other quite innocent books and my painting materials. We made a joke about him being able to sell my palettes if his business went broke.

What happened however – it's best to tell it straight – was that after the 1976 coup the army divided San Rafael into zones and searched them with a fine tooth comb. When Omar saw they were getting near his business, he took the boxes to his house; when the searches reached his neighbourhood, he put the boxes in his Fairlane again to take them back to the hangar. The army caught him in a pincer movement with the boxes and everything. He was 'disappeared' for about a year, and was badly tortured. He only survived by a miracle. Carlos Brega, another friend from San Rafael who arrived in Sweden after us, told us of Omar's Calvary. He spent days hanging from a hook, like an animal in a slaughterhouse or freezing plant, while they destroyed his business and stole his house.

One afternoon I was drinking *maté* in the duty room of the San Rafael hospital with my brother and other doctors, when a nervous nurse said a suspicious looking guy was asking for Dr Bustos. It was Alberto Burnichón, an old friend of our group of artists in Mendoza, who always had a bushy beard and tangled hair. He had gone to see the exhibition only to find it closed and the police asking questions. He suggested he could look after the paintings and our other stuff together with the architect Casnatti, so we could leave the area quickly.

He also suggested I talk to local Communist Party leaders to guarantee our clandestinity. Avelino made the contacts and a meeting with the local party secretary, on behalf of the provincial leadership, was held in the maternity ward of another friend's clinic. I asked for a temporary safe house in Buenos Aires while I made arrangements to leave the country. I had become a known target locally and no one would or could help me. He took my request to Mendoza personally. The following day, he gave me a contact for the national leadership in Buenos Aires.

As soon as I arrived in Buenos Aires, I met the contact in an elegant tea room in the Recoleta, as if we were habitués of this extremely posh area. I was surprised at the name of the contact, a member of the Central Committee's political committee. It was Carlos Alonso, but obviously not my friend the painter. I concluded in retrospect that it was a code name to simplify things. They were both painters from Mendoza and, in fact, the same type of tall, handsome, friendly man. An urgent meeting was arranged and I repeated my request for a temporary safe house. A few days later I got the Central Committee's answer. It was negative. According to the alias Alonso, the party needed all its security resources for itself. The situation being as it was, there was no house available for us.

The Central Committee did send a confidential message. Because of the common ties uniting us, they could give me some advice: 'Hang in there, comrade. Don't leave the country, wait a bit.' And then something memorable: 'In two months things are going to change, because the army is taking over and one of our generals will be in government.' This was in January 1976. In March, General Jorge Videla, later guilty of genocide, took power.

Che said urban guerrillas have no rearguard (hinterland), and without it a collective psychosis that separates the rational from the obsession that affects all revolutionary organizations. Those who planned the carnage knew it and watched how people reacted. They began to distance themselves from what was happening on their block and looked the other way. You can't condemn this predictable attitude of self-defence but you have to take it into account. Having no means of escape generates shared resentment, and only the immediate family responds. Frankly speaking, it makes their home a target, the centre of concentric circles of repression.

I sent the Triple A letter to Dolores in Sweden. The Swedish government took immediate action and, in less than forty-eight hours, they sent a telegram to their embassy in Buenos Aires granting visas to the four members of our family. Meanwhile, Ana María and I slept in *alojamientos*, service hotels which rented rooms by the hour for lovers who had no place of their own. According to *Siete Días*, a popular weekly magazine, there were 400 *alojamientos* in Buenos Aires in those days. 'We fuck, therefore we exist.' They didn't ask for documents and you could spend the whole night quite cheaply. We did this until one night, in an *alojamiento* in Bartolomé Mitre Street, across from the railways tracks, the porter insisted on documents because of 'new laws'. We were in bed, looking at ourselves in the ceiling mirror, when I suddenly decided to leave. Before we turned the corner, walking casually, a patrol car was at the door.

Luckily, Gelly Walker, an Argentine friend we had made in Chile through Payo Grondona, a journalist and singer/songwriter who I had worked with in Quimantú, came to our rescue. We had got on very well but there had been no political connection; nonetheless, she gave us the keys to her apartment while we were waiting, and moved to her mother's. At the weekend, we went to Cholo's house and a nephew of his asked to talk to me privately. He said: 'The state of Israel is offering you passports and tickets to Tel Aviv. There's no commitment to stay, so you can carry on to wherever you choose.' I was grateful for the offer, really moved, but our papers for Sweden were almost ready.

The Swedes seemed even keener than I was and added a sum of money to cover our immediate needs. We discussed how to leave. I did not like the idea of travelling like a normal family, and it was anyway impossible since I didn't have a passport. So we agreed I would go first, by myself, to Rio de Janeiro. I set off by bus one afternoon to cross the Argentina-Brazil border at Paso de los Libres, in the province of Corrientes. Once I was out of the country, Ana María would follow with the girls. The trip from Buenos Aires to Rio took fifty-five hours but you could pass through customs with a simple ID card. I put my few clothes in a bag, crowning it with three LPs I was taking as a palliative to nostalgia: Troilo-Grela, the Duo Salteño and Baden Powell, the best in each of their genre. Ana María was bringing the more difficult stuff: our daughters, a few belongings – including a few paintings Burnichón had freighted to Buenos Aires – clothes, and keepsakes.

The bus left from Plaza Once, half a block from her mother's apartment where Ana María was staying with the girls, but I went alone. It was terribly humid so I had a beer in the bar on the corner while I waited. At a neighbouring table sat one of my former contacts in the original Trotskyist group that became the ERP, his nickname was Pelado too. The two baldies looked at each other as if they were strangers and I went to get the bus. For the ten hours to the border, I could think of nothing but that I was leaving my whole life behind for a second time, perhaps forever. Two things suggested what the future would be. My whole family was coming with me and it was time my daughters finally had somewhere to settle down. Besides, the country I was leaving appeared headed for total destruction. Just a few days earlier, the ERP had tried occupying the Arsenal Battalion barracks in an attempt to steal ten tons of weapons, with disastrous results. Someone inside had betrayed them and the army was waiting to finish them off. The wind of initiative had changed definitively.

Three material things had connected me to Che, but only one of them, the Minox, accompanied me into exile. The second is a side story but I want to tell it now. When the EGP group was formed in Havana and we were equipped for departure during the missile crisis in 1962, Che gave us all Rolex watches. Nowadays they are more of a luxury decoration, but back then it was the only watch that worked without wires, or batteries (they didn't exist), just the simple movement of the arm. Such advantages apart, I don't know why in Cuba they came to be a sign of rank, recognition of performance, an award for merit, or some such. The fact was that comandantes, intelligence agents, people on special missions, or mere show-offs, wore Rolexes even when they were in fatigues. Masetti already had the one he got when he was made a captain, and we were given the more discreet Rolex Oyster Quartz made of stainless steel. I also don't know why there were so many of these gems in Cuba, as if the manufacturers made bulk loads especially cheaply for Cubans, knowing they were going to scatter them round the world. Che was famous for being tight with the public purse.

Anyhow, we left with the Rolexes, trying not to be conspicuous. My watch did not leave my wrist until, on one of my trips out of the Salta jungle, Masetti asked me to swap and take his to be cleaned at the Rolex shop in Buenos Aires. This was not as easy as it sounds, since you had to register as the owner of the gem and declare its origin, etc. – information which guaranteed, in case of theft, that the watch would be sequestered if the data did not match. I never got mine back because the guerrillas were wiped out in Salta, and Masetti's watch, now expensively clean, remained in pride of place on my wrist. When they searched me the day I arrived in Camiri, one officer was telling me to hand over my watch just as the other one found the dollars hidden in the jacket. The ensuing commotion distracted him and miraculously I got to keep the watch. The danger passed of losing it in Bolivia, where harvesting Rolexes from dead Cubans was all the rage, and it survived the house searches in San Rafael too.

I finally lost it one stifling January day in Buenos Aires, on the underground. The Plaza de Mayo–Liniers line, all fifteen kilometres of it, was the longest and most crowded line in the system. Getting on it at all was a feat, although what actually got on was an organic mass of people that spread through into the carriages where they regained their individuality. I was standing awkwardly, steadying myself by clinging to the vertical pole by the door. When the train was about to restart after the first stop, a guy who was propping the door open with his body, grabbed my Rolex and a good part of my skin, and fell out onto the platform as the doors closed and the train picked up speed. It is the only time in my life that I have shouted expletives in public, and to everyone's astonishment I got out at the next stop just to be able to kick a wall silly.

43

Sweden, 1976 to the Present

When I arrived in Stockholm and saw the desert of freezing snow, I discovered I had left my third material memory of Che in the house we had fled in San Rafael. It was the jacket he gave me when I left the guerrilla camp. That too I had miraculously saved throughout my odyssey, because each time I had to move in a hurry, day or night while I was a prisoner, it was the first thing I grabbed. When the moment finally came to leave Chile for Argentina, I decided I needed to have my hands free and the jacket stayed with our friends, Claudio and Lidia. They delivered it to me a year later in the middle of the San Luís pampa.

My brother Avelino and his wife Alicia went into exile shortly after us, but they went to Mozambique so did not take the jacket. After several years in charge of health in the north of Mozambique, when democracy returned to Argentina, Avelino had gone back to San Rafael to look after Rosa, our abandoned sister. We met up once in Barcelona for a few days when we rented a house in El Masnou (a place we knew because Alberto Szpunberg lived there) to reunite the family. Avelino brought Ana María's mother and aunt from Argentina and we brought them back to Sweden for a visit. Avelino and I did not see each other again and anyway the jacket had disappeared, probably while he was away.

I have already told the story of the Minox, bought in Rome to photograph tiny secret documents to send to Che. But its end was quite sad. Once when our budget didn't quite stretch to the end of the month, I took the Minox to the pawnbroker; it was at the very least a technological relic imbued with spy stories from film and literature. The guy behind the counter did not even want to look at it. 'We're in the digital age now', he said.

I caught up with various other people in Europe. In Spain I saw Gustavo Roca. He had passed through Malmö earlier but we missed each other. He put me in touch with Henry Lerner who by then was in Madrid. He and his father had disappeared in Córdoba; the Israelis managed to rescue him alive, but not his father. We sought out Héctor Jouvé in a small perfumed lavender producing valley in the French Alps where his paternal family came from. He had a stone house in a medieval building on the main square, where there was an old communal outdoor bath-house with a sloping tiled roof. Héctor said no one came out of it with their skin intact. We stayed for a few days, reminiscing about our experience. We haven't seen each other since he went back to Argentina.

The death squads kidnapped Petiso Bellomo, killed him and dynamited his body on some waste ground. They did the same to my friend Alberto Burnichón. In Paris, we met up with Cholo, Berta and their children, Hugo and Diana, and for several years staying in their house was the most entertaining part of our holidays, until they followed Diana to New York. In Malmö, we were visited by Payo Grondona from East Germany, Humberto Vázquez Viaña, Loro's brother, and Alberto Szpunberg who stayed with us for a few days.

When I arrived in Stockholm, I had to wait a month for Ana María and the girls. They were first taken to a hotel because the Immigration Office had not been able to inform me of their arrival. Like all political refugees in those days, we then went to Moheda, a luxurious 'concentration camp' in Småland where only the metre of snow stopped us moving around freely. The camp aimed to introduce immigrants to the customs and benefits of the Welfare State and, especially, to the morality of the consumer society which we found extraordinary: this much was given, this much we had to buy. We were equipped with clothes for the

North Pole and, when the six months in the camp were over, were given an apartment, furniture, household items, kitchen utensils, student loans, pocket money and bank accounts. The whole mechanism revolved around your ID, a magic number that represented the individual's very existence as a complex human being of some account.

We had wanted to be as close as possible to the Mediterranean. In a country 2,000 kilometres long, the extreme south (the south of the north, as the Swedes say) is still 2,000 kilometres from Barcelona. And that was Malmö, where we ended up.

We were desperate to know about the drama unfolding behind us. People were 'disappearing', but official institutions offered no protection or responded to public outcry. We needed to make two essential purchases: a powerful short-wave radio so we could listen to Argentine stations, and a family car because in a country that functions on wheels, you can't go anywhere on foot.

The first purchase was the first failure. We had chosen a Satellit 2000 with fifty short waves, but on all fifty we could hear nothing but Radio Moscow; it was on every imaginable frequency. It transmitted the repulsive idyll then being constructed between the Communist Parties of the socialist camp and the criminal dictatorship of the Argentine generals. It was unbelievable. Military missions went to and fro between Moscow and Buenos Aires, both ends receiving medals of merit and friendship with the 'sacred' names of the Liberator San Martin or Vladimir Ilyich Lenin. The Argentine Communist Party's 'our general' was in power.

The Soviet news programmes – long and detailed, especially for Latin America – began with an impassioned account of events since the coup in Chile: dramatic invented stories of a resistance that didn't exist, with battle songs incorporated into the world top ten, making the Chilean defeat the best sung and the best seller. Then, the no less tragic news from Bolivia, where the dictator General Banzer – another member of Operation Condor – had put down the miners with brute force. Yet as 30,000 young men and women, mostly workers, students and professionals, were being 'disappeared', murdered, and thrown into the sea by 'our general' in Argentina, Radio Moscow was reporting the excellent juicy trade agreements being signed in Buenos Aires with total impunity.

According to Radio Moscow, the political climate in Cuba and Argentina was sublime. To add insult to injury, Captain Emilio Aragonés, the secretary of the Cuban Communist Party (who had been Fidel's envoy to the Congo, sent to support – or keep an eye on – Che's campaign), was named as Ambassador to Argentina and on his watch lucrative business deals were made between the genocidal dictatorship and the Free Territory of America. During this tragic period, of every ten dollars that entered the country to end up in the pockets of murderers, eight came from the socialist camp, including Cuba.

'*La Lucha Continua*', says the refrain, but what went on was life with its contingent trials and tribulations. We made friends in Malmö's Latin American colony, the most notorious in Sweden in those days, and thirty years on we still have the same ones. Borges says the bad thing about lists is that they only emphasise what is left out, so I will refrain. But I could not have got this far in my memoirs without the support of Jonas and René, my two friends in Malmö: Juan Carlos Peirone and René Borda.

When I first arrived in Malmö, I met a couple of Argentines, Mario and José Luís, who were voluntary migrants. Mario told me solemnly: 'In this country, when you take your first step outside in the morning, you've already committed an offence.' Not totally unfair, I must say, given the fondness for the penal code over the circumstances of the perpetrator of the offence. Both artists, and my first friends, they had connections in the immigrant substratum, which operated in the service sector. So I ended up working as a docker in the port of Malmö, on its last legs in those days. There was nothing nice about this so-called romantic activity. I unloaded dredgers, guided cranes, or cleaned floors, and there I found my brilliant future career.

Things slowly took on other rhythms, but we always lived among South American exiles. Brazilians like José and Gilen and, especially the Bolivian, Argentine and Chilean families who welcomed us fraternally and are still our support. When the time came to express myself publicly, Jaime Padilla, a Bolivian journalist, was the generous vehicle. Finally, between language courses and presumed artistic activities, I also travelled the country from end to end. I learned to ski in the Arctic Circle, hiked manicured trails with refuges ever fifteen kilometres, where your only obligation is to replace the wood you have used. The Lapps in the north have an intrinsic warmth, and still live life for its own sake. There I met their greatest artists, Martin Hurac and Lars Pirak, and enjoyed their friendship, albeit all too briefly, in Jokkmokk.

I was born on a piece of land that was a mixture of garden and industrial park, with sheds, canvas hangars and workshops. It was the headquarters of the National Highway Administration, a department of the Ministry of Public Works, charged with constructing roads the length and breadth of Argentina's vast geography. My father's job entitled him to a house there, and I grew up with my brothers and sisters among gardens and workshops, carpenters and drivers. The technological enclave was in the north-east corner of an agricultural reserve belonging to the province of Mendoza's School of Viticulture. On one side the boundary was a row of hangars and workshops, and on the other a huge wrought iron railing that gave on to Pedro Molina and Belgrano streets. On the other side of Belgrano were the tracks of the San Martín Railway, not far from the station itself where there was an enormous shunting yard. My first childhood memories were of night-time noises. Familiar distant sounds became friendlier as the night advanced, like a cat purring on my pillow: police whistles on their nightly rounds, communicating 'nothing to report', block by block, between themselves; and the noise of trains moving in the station yard.

When we arrived in Malmö it was a typical Swedish city, with a port and commercial life, quite hostile to foreigners. But over the years it has changed into a replica of Beirut, losing the neat homogeneity of its citizens, the shipbuilding industry and even the port itself, but gaining the enthusiasm of the bazaar, multicultural vitality, and universal gastronomy. I live in a house in the northern outskirts that back onto the railway lines near the motorway to Lund. It is a railway shunting zone. During the day I can't see very much, only the motorway and the turnoff to the brand new bridge joining Sweden to Denmark. But at night, when the hubbub of the traffic calms, with my dog Gema sleeping at my feet, I hear the train drivers manoeuvring the night trains, bumping, banging and tooting, amid the screeching of wheels and blowing of whistles, as if I were back in Mendoza.

Epilogue

History as farce: the 'Rashomon effect'

Political and social events all over the world are conditioned by the actions of their principal protagonists, against a background of economic realities that affect the part they play in those events and mobilize sectors of the population in the eventual outcome. The stance that the masses adopt produces changes, and those changes make History. This is easy to say, of course, but the situation is made more complex and hard to define due to the 'Rashomon effect', whereby there are as many versions as there are participants in the reconstruction of an event. This is because historical situations are manipulated or compartmentalized according to how the actors see them.

Interpretations of these events never coincide, since personal viewpoints are only part of the truth, if they are true at all. Whenever people take up their pens, the re-writing of history begins, and their version of the story is told to the detriment of others — for whatever reason, be it ideology, principles or party line. The 'Rashomon effect' means that each writer obeys not only his editor, but also his ego, his own editorial interests, his psychological projection, and his vanity.

The result turns history into a farce, in which the protagonists become caricatures without pity or feelings, people who organize massacres on paper to fit in with the strategic plans of established powers, or play with the destinies of countries, and the lives of people, with impunity. The end justifies the means. That end can be tyranny or democracy; but it can also be revolution or a socialist society – the mythical goal that is the sociological carrot of faith, behind which come the preachers and those they preach to. Even saints can manipulate this coercive weapon – the carrot – because what is important is their inner conviction, the physical certainty of action, the contempt for the role of deviants. It matters little if today's faith is tomorrow's shame. What matters is that faith moves mountains. The evil lies not in the carrot, but in what the theorists can extract from the carrot.

In the twentieth century, theory triumphed over reality. Theoretical discourse often falsified reality through the structured network of political analysts – with their congresses, seminars and interchangeable university chairs – who had found their raison d'être in developed societies through being offered prestigious platforms for their philosophical lucubrations. Even when nothing was true anymore, they continued writing their manuals about the victorious march of socialism and the inexorable fall of crisis-beset capitalism, giving lectures of revolutionary rigour, publishing their crusading tracts (based on the long marches of others who had taken up the struggle), exhorting young people to join a project they themselves no longer believed in, and who paid with their lives for what they saw as the only way (apart from the atom bomb) to build a new society.

When the dust from the collapse of the socialist camp cleared, the prophets of revolutionary theory were still standing there, staring disdainfully at the pile of rubble, one jumping out of a window, another killing his wife, another going over to the enemy camp, denying the Nazi genocide, ignoring genocide itself as if it were a passing accident. The fault, it seemed, was not to have followed to the letter the golden thread of their thoughts, which were as scientific and precise as a theorem. Now nothing stops them describing the globalized world around the former enemy, Capital, as a high-speed train that is the only one running: you have to climb aboard or stay on the track.

There are others, of course, who had been warning for some time that the train of the revolution had been derailed by sectarianism, and left in the 'party' mire; that the law of dialectic was change as a result of contradictions, evolving from one level to the next in a revolutionary spiral, because revolution is only a desperate emergency measure against totalitarian stagnation, not against the nature of things, and what has to be transformed is the way people think.

The trap, to this day, is to accept changes in a line of thought as a sign of evolution. But evolution is like the law of gravity. It only works in one direction. The apple cannot drop to the ground upwards. Political and social evolution, the evolution of ideas, goes from right to left, not from left to right. Human beings have evolved from subjugation to empires and the law of the jungle to coexistence and solidarity; from oligarchic totalitarianism to democracy; from accepting that half the world is prevented from living a decent life to agonizing over it, realizing that their choice is to share the benefits or perish.

Lying is revolutionary

In the particular bit of history I have related here, especially relating to Che's aims during the latter stage of his life, everybody lied. Naturally I did too. I lied to the army, to the CIA, to the court and, hence, to public opinion. I lied deliberately and by omission. But I lied to protect the interests of people on the outside and, incidentally, to save my own life; not for personal glorification, quite the opposite, since it cost me my pride and self-esteem. Because lying is a double-edged sword: you lie to defend yourself, but it also destroys you and your reputation. You make a choice, take personal responsibility, balance how much you have to gain against how much you will lose.

The events in Bolivia in 1967 unleashed an avalanche of newspaper articles, essays, testimonies, novels and biographies. All manner of people speculated on the whys and wherefores of the events, deformed them, concealed them, or turned them into something sacred, mythical and archetypal. It is only natural that people would want to rescue the magic spirit of Greek tragedies, so as to exalt sacrifice, will power, and the role of example or, on the contrary, to reveal the innate perversion of conspiracy and its ghosts. The bad thing about this is that it can mask false political objectives and, even worse, individual, venal or servile interests. The majority of what has been published about these events falls into this category.

For reasons of international politics, rather than intelligence purposes, the Cuban Revolution maintained a prolonged silence about the events in Bolivia except when it came to eulogizing the figure of the Comandante Heroico and his men who had fallen in the struggle against imperialism, as was their wish. Just as the Stalinist road to socialism choked with thorns and carnivorous plants as it approached the abyss, so too did the Cuban Revolution nose-dive through the undergrowth before finally coming to an inevitable halt. At the end of the day, Cuba is an island in all senses of the word and always sought to protect its own achievements and hold to its own principles.

I provide one simple example from a bona fide source, the Colombian writer and friend of Fidel, Gabriel García Márquez, who tells an anecdote about the anniversary of the founding of *Prensa Latina*, the Cuban news agency. Its first director was Masetti, the Argentine journalist who went to the Sierra Maestra to interview the guerrilla leaders. Che had personally invited Masetti to stay in Cuba subsequently, to take the helm of the project to create the Revolution's own media outlet. To commemorate the anniversary, Gabo had suggested that he should write an article about Masetti, with whom he himself had worked directly. He went to Cuba expecting to get access, through his contacts, to the detailed information he needed from the Revolution's archives. To his surprise, he discovered there was none: no data, no clippings, no reference to the journalistic high spot the creation of *Prensa Latina* had been, and least of all, any mention of its director, Masetti, who was considered to have performed the most daring exploit in Latin American journalism.

The covert chicanery surrounding Masetti's bureaucratic 'disappearance' was pre-empted at the time by the news of the physical disappearance of this little known revolutionary hero. But it was exposed by García Márquez, who witnessed the harassment to which Masetti was subjected by the 'official' journalists of the original Cuban Communist Party until they managed to get rid off him.

Together with Masetti, all information about Che's guerrilla project in Argentina also disappeared from the Cuban archives: the formation of the group in Cuba; who was in it; Masetti's role; how they were trained; the support given by the Minister of the Interior Ramiro Valdés, formerly comandante of Che's 'Ciro Redondo' vanguard column; Che's personal independent leadership of the Argentine group from the start; and his intention of taking total command on the ground once the Salta base had been established. Comandante Guevara's independent action was not marginal, but came from a commitment by Fidel Castro, when the Cuban guerrilla war began, to Che's express wish (after victory on the island) to take the armed struggle to his own country, a commitment that Castro himself has recognized.

History would be rewritten. The Revolution's Americas Department – a body subordinate to the reorganized Ministry of the Interior under its minister José Abrantes – was supervised by Fidel Castro but administered by Barbaroja Piñeiro. He handled the relationships with and training of revolutionary groups from all over the continent, and produced a plan to export the armed struggle to Latin America. It was ideologically not very strict as long as the groups were pro-Cuban. Although the plan failed in 99 per cent of the groups that were sent to fight, it successfully mobilized popular support for Cuba and was a pain in the arse for the USSR.

But in Barbaroja's hands, the idea of strategic control lost touch with reality; he started introducing cards that were already marked.

Realizing he could expect nothing from the official Latin American Communist Parties except control of ideological orthodoxy, he began to weave his fabric with different coloured wools.

In the case of Argentina, he visibly favoured flirting with Peronism because in the long run it was a political force capable of regaining power, something that was obviously never going to happen with the Communist Party. This position, which contradicted Che's view and belittled his vision, became clear when our group left Cuba. We were given rubbish documents, received false messages purporting to be from Che, were subject to indefinite delays, and ultimately received equipment in the field that was worse than useless.

Like the cinema special effect in which an actor's face morphs into that of a beast, the political roots of the EGP leadership and the support we received throughout Argentina (the recruitment, political organization, city networks and country-wide links that I knew from experience) changed in Barbaroja's version from grass roots and cadres who had broken away from the Argentine Communist Party to political and economic support from the branch of Peronism around John W. Cooke, Perón's former delegate in Cuba. This was totally untrue. As an organization, the EGP had no relationship with Cooke, and my friendship with him when we met in Havana was purely circumstantial. Che himself never told Cooke about his Argentina project, despite liking El Gordo personally. Che saw a latent danger in Peronism's heterogeneity, which made working communication unsafe, on top of the risks for him personally of having his name associated with it.

My catching a glimpse in the Buenos Aires shopping arcade of our former EGP core member Miguel, supposedly dead at the hands of a firing squad in Algeria, was part of Barbaroja's double political game in respect of Argentina. It led to the subsequent deformation, or rather total disappearance, of the project founded by Che and his group. I got to the bottom of Miguel's story when I returned to Argentina from Chile in 1973. He had visited the

prisoners in jail in Salta (according to Henry, he told him he was
Jewish when he wasn't) on orders from Barbaroja, for whom he
had been working since he was rescued from Algeria. He wanted
to sound them out about the possibility of their publicly supporting Peronist grass-roots groups and perhaps working together in
the future. Given that the EGP contact already existed through
me, it was strange that Piñeiro never mentioned these plans when
I met him on that Havana corner at dawn. On the contrary, he
suggested that I should help send the Communist youth contingent, the future FAL, to Cuba for training. They were
subsequently stuck in Havana at a time when Che's guerrillas in
Bolivia were in urgent need of reinforcements.

For the next thirty years there would be no mention of Che's
group in Argentina – not incidentally and even less through
historical research – until the anniversaries commemorating
Che's death brought it to the fore. Not because people started
talking knowledgably about it but because one of Che's biographers, Jon Lee Anderson, who had lived in Cuba while writing
Che Guevara: A Revolutionary Life, came to Sweden to look for
me. He wanted to write about the Argentine episode, so Che's
entourage in Havana had pointed him in my direction. Che's wife
Aleida told him: 'There's someone somewhere, you should go
and find him.' Orlando Borrego, Che's deputy at the Ministry of
Industry, agreed: 'Yes, there is someone . . .', and Alberto Castellanos, Che's ex-bodyguard and former Salta prisoner, encouraged
him cryptically: 'The person who knows the whole story is
Pelado, you should talk to him.' Anderson went to Argentina,
followed various leads to the survivors (those who had subsequently survived the dictatorship's killing spree), and talked to
Héctor Jouvé aka Cordobés. He said: 'You need to talk to Pelado
about this.' He then travelled to Spain and saw Henry Lerner,
who got my phone number through Martín Espeleta, another
Córdoban living in Uppsala. Henry asked Martín to ask me if he
could give my number to Anderson, as if I were some state secret.
My number is only not in the phone directory by mistake: it used

to be, but when we moved house after fifteen years I accidentally put a cross in the wrong box and it was removed.

Anderson came to Malmö one Monday in the spring of 1995, intending to return to Spain the following day. He called me from the ferry terminal that connects Malmö with Copenhagen and I went to fetch him. He stayed in my house until the Saturday, sleeping on a mattress on the floor, with my dog Gema standing guard at his door. We talked from morning till midnight for a week: I cooked, he talked and asked questions, tape recorder between us. We continued through a long series of letters and faxes because parts of the tapes were inaudible. He sent me a hundred transcribed pages, but ultimately the book did not tell the whole story. One part appeared to be censored, not through any fault of his, but it was as if Cuban confirmation of events published for the first time – Salta, Algeria – was conditional on not talking about other things – Bolivia, Cubans. Anderson agreed under those conditions, I suppose, although it might also have been because of editorial pressures to reduce the almost 400 excess pages. He sent me a postcard from Finland at the launch of the Finnish edition, saying that he wanted to explain the omissions to me personally, and invited me to his house near Malaga on the Costa del Sol, but at the time I was condemned to 'house arrest', not being able to travel for lack of funds.

None of the other biographers contacted me, except Jorge Castañeda, a Mexican 'art critic', who had caught Anderson's contagious enthusiasm and called me from Princeton wanting to do a telephone interview. I refused. He asked somewhat nastily how I could possibly give an extensive interview to an 'American' and not to him, a Latin American, practically a compatriot. I said: 'He came here so I could look him in the eyes.' He said he would send me his CV and in the meantime I could ask Pierre Schori (a member of Sweden's then Social Democratic government) about him and he would call me again. As if I could pick up the phone and ask the cabinet secretary: 'Tell me, Pierre, who is this Mexican guy?'

A few days later an envelope arrived containing a literary
review heralding the imminent appearance of several biographies
of Che, including those of Anderson, Taibo II and Castañeda, all
very serious and impeccable in intent. However, the accompanying letter – and I have it here in front of me – showed Castañeda's
bad faith. By a 'slip of the finger' it starts: 'Ambigo Bustos'. Two
days later he called a second time, but I still refused: I cannot talk
about a crucial period of my life down a piece of wire with a
stranger at the other end. He said he had no option but to be
guided by Debray's version of events which blamed me for
everything. I replied that a good biography investigates the truth;
it does not parrot abusive versions. With his material already at
the printers, Castañeda never called back, although in his book he
insists that he tried to contact me for a whole year: swine of a
feather end up together. When he became Mexican foreign minister, I sent him a letter suggesting he use his influence to get nearer
the truth. I addressed it to 'Señor Minestro', but he must not have
received it.

The weakest of the biographers, Pierre Kalfon, does nothing
but parrot infamies, and does not even bother to stop and check
dates. His sensitivity has also been contaminated by the bad air of
Buenos Aires, where he lived for some years breathing in the
complex atmosphere of the Argentine Left, which was sidelined
by history and devoted itself to selling T-shirts. A letter of mine
to 'Kalfon Quitado' circled the world for nearly a year without
anyone being willing to publish it, until Cholo managed to get it
published by *Diogenes*, a cultural journal in Mendoza.

Another biography, by Paco Taibo II, is much 'cleaner',
although it does have some imprecise and fictitious moments. In
the first Spanish edition, he mentions an anecdote told to him by
Juan Gelman about a certain Lieutenant Laureano who asked
him to take a report to Che who, caught off guard by this poet
that he admired, accepts it saying 'Let's suppose a Lieutenant
Laureano who is sending me this report exists . . .'. In Taibo's
book, the one closest to the Cuban version of events, the hand of

that great weaver of tales Barbaroja Piñeiro emerges. Hence, Cuba organized everything in Bolivia, before and after Salta, as part of its strategic plan for the continent, to give us (the EGP) cover, using the same Communist Party people later mobilized (for Che): the Peredo brothers, Loyola Guzmán, etc. Nothing could be further from the truth. Apart from the schoolteacher in La Paz and Don Benito in the *finca*, only Loro Vázquez Viaña and Rodolfo Saldaña helped us. Even Fidel himself declared 'it was his operation' (Che's, that is), 'which he planned to join at the second stage'. Taibo's version of events is the Cuban official version: it does not include all those who took part and includes some who did not. I make an appearance only in its thirty-fifth edition in Spanish (it was a huge commercial success), six years after Anderson's book had taken the lid off the pot.

But the efforts of the Cubans in the Americas Department to Peronize our experience do not stop there, despite testimonies to the contrary. For over a year, I replied by fax to the questions of a 'historian' who reached me by phone 'on behalf of' my *compañeros* in the EGP. He solemnly swore that it was time to write the truth and pay tribute to those who had died in that utopian adventure. Technology is a chilly but irrefutable witness. I have kept all his faxes, in his handwriting, and all my frank and detailed answers in which I recount the secret history of the EGP. In response to particular questions, I stressed that we worked exclusively with young people disenchanted with the Communist Party and groups that had split off from the party. Che gave express orders that no Peronists were to be accepted. Before the author of the book *The Lost Origins of the Argentine Guerrillas* wiped my name from the list of participants in the Salta operation, he used part of my written statements to describe Masetti's confrontation with the Communist Party, but only up to the point where they began to contradict Barbaroja's version: that moment when the guerrillas were miraculously supported by grass-roots Peronism and financed by Cooke's group, while Masetti had an attack of anti-semitism and began shooting Jews just for being

Jews – a fallacy I had specifically rejected in my dealings with the book's author, Señor Gabriel Roth.

There is another more recent biography by the Argentine writer Pacho O'Donnell, who rang me twice from Buenos Aires. I used the same arguments with him but agreed to answer some concrete questions. I haven't got his book but I don't think he could have said much with so little. Of course, there must be hundreds of biographical essays that I don't know about. I'm sure they all claim to tell the truth but they probably all do the opposite by accepting as valid the strategic manipulations of 'revolutionaries' or the deformations the enemy uses to further its own interests.

Sometimes they commit infantile errors, as in the case of a quite serious and respected Italian, Roberto Massari, who made a fool of himself when, as an example of the moral decline of Che's guerrillas, he wrote that one *compañero* beat another to death with a rifle butt in a quarrel over food. The 'person' in question was actually Lolo, the deer the guerrillas had adopted as a pet, as Che notes in his diary on 30 April: 'Lolo died, a victim of Urbano's impulsiveness when he threw a rifle at its head.' No mention of food.

These tales are all a continuation of the distortion that began in Camiri, encouraged by official Cuban silence, furthered by others who wanted to show off, and those whose tongues loosened as the general line of deception took shape. It made it possible for Comandante Jorge Papito Serguera, our Cuban support in Czechoslovakia and Algeria, to invent in his memoirs the story that he had gone to Argentina on Che's orders to save Masetti, and had then searched for his body for two months with the help of 'two Catholic nuns who travelled round the area', but found no trace of him. At a time when Che summoned me to Havana and told me to carry on with our work, and when he had two first-class Cuban officers like Papi and Furry who knew the region as well as I did, it was unlikely Che would introduce somebody new to the area, an ex-diplomat in combat zones in Africa.

It was even harder to believe that he would use Serguera as an intermediary with Perón, to try and convince the general that it would be a good idea for him to live in Cuba, as he claims. The abundance of fantasies of this kind are no more than politically expedient lies that change the letter and spirit of the slogan: lying (the truth) is revolutionary.

Left-dependency syndrome

The institutionalized lie produced a sequence of secondary effects that disempowered the Argentine intellectual Left, incapable of overcoming the vertical functioning of a party that had conditioned their reflexes and even their respiratory system all their lives. Arguably, they denied and eradicated the significance of the attempt to establish a guerrilla base, planned and led by the only Argentine to have taken part in an exemplary revolutionary triumph, as the Cuba of Fidel and his *barbudos* undoubtedly was. It not only disappeared from the analyses of national politics, but also from the chronologies of social and political events in the last half of the century. The EGP had turned the needle to the magnetic pole of armed action, fighting imperialism and abandoning the electoral discourses and doctrinal adjustments of the Central Committee, yet they were deleted from history as if none of them had ever existed, as if there had been no real people among the dead, the prisoners or the survivors.

The ridiculous eulogies or criticisms ranged from memories of scouts at weekend camp to the agonies of a generation that bathed a transitional period of world history in their blood, providing the pretext for a savage genocide organized by the traditional power elite, and which achieved nothing but their own disappearance. Yet the experience of the EGP is not even acknowledged as having been at the heart of that tremendous mess. On the contrary, it is ignored or mentioned in passing as a crazy petty-bourgeois adventure, born in the cafés of Corrientes Avenue, where the sacrificial lambs gathered with their backpacks and boots and incipient beards, according to the Communist Party's shameful version.

I am not making it up. One night in a Stockholm taxi going out with friends to eat gnocchi, I silenced a refugee from the Argentine Communist Party who was trying to mock the EGP enterprise (apropos of what exactly I don't remember), without knowing me or that I had been there.

In a country with a passion for investigating, analyzing, dissecting, reconstructing and, in the worst case scenario, carrying out autopsies on political events in order to apportion blame, no one, not participants, researchers or writers, took the trouble to examine the sacrifice behind the utopia sought by a group of young idealists united by Che's aura. A collective amnesia (except for *compañeros* and poets) accepted the black hole decreed in Havana for the Salta events as a non-existent or hard to prove phenomenon which it was better to keep quiet about until all the martyrs had been given their last rites.

For thirty years, the official historians of the Left remembered the events as purely marginal, referring only to military errors and executions, and the futility of voluntarism outside the norms of the labour movement (norms always interpreted correctly by the lucid Left). The 'serious' militants and intellectuals of the united Left abandoned their critical faculties and adopted the two faces of the same fallacy. First, that criticism should only be done internally – something that can never be done without finding the critic's bones in the dungeons, so it is not done. Second, that you must not give succour to the enemy by airing internal mistakes. So that, *compañeros*, is that!

It was terrifying to watch the pathetic spectacle of old, honest, fiery communists after the collapse of the socialist camp, and the morphing of the Soviet Union Communist Party secretariat into gangsters taking over the reins of the Russian economy: nothing has happened; it is merely a cybernetic illusion; the cause and the party will be reborn and, opportunely, bring order to the chaos of the capitalist catastrophe.

Until the day my brother Avelino died (just before we were to meet again), he yearned for the unstoppable offensive of the Red Army that once liberated the world from Nazism, and the iron hand that guided our brothers-in-arms to victory (with 25 million dead of their own). For him, the fact that although Cubans live in shared poverty, they can all read in the waiting rooms of free hospitals, was the only tangible victory of the long-suffering human race.

Acknowledgements

To Richard Gott, who said I did not need anyone's help in writing this book.

To the poet Juan Gelman, who on reading the first few chapters dissipated my fears and gave me enormous encouragement, as well as the pleasure of seeing him again after thirty years.

To the writer Tomás Eloy Martínez, who praised those same chapters and supported me by writing an article even though he did not know me.

To Lidia Balta and Claudio Verdugo in Chile, for thirty years of unwavering friendship.

To Eric Gandini and Tarik Saleh, who made the idea of this book possible.

To Isaac Marchevsky, El Cholo, reader-in-chief and friend, who has supported me politically and morally the whole time from New York, analysing the book's progress every step of the way.

To René Borda, my 'cybernetic' friend, a member of my Bolivian family here in Malmö, in charge of my computer, which (as everybody knows) makes everything disappear, including René, at the slightest lapse in concentration.

To Juan Carlos Peirone, Jonás, artist and architect of the largest group of Argentine friends in Lund, 'Córdoban capital'.

To all those who have been loyal friends, whether readers of these pages as they evolved or not. To Magali Calderón and family, Jaime Padilla, Jorge Varas, María Udriot, María Dahl and her family, Nina Olsson-Borda, Beto Carbonari and Graciela Ratti who always offered their warm hospitality. To Diana Mulinari, who printed copies of the original when it was ready; and to La Negra Amanda Peralta, who made pertinent observations when the original manuscript was about to become a book.

To Alberto Szpunberg and the *compañeros*.

To my beloved dog, Gema, who did not see the book completed.